LONGCHENPA'S THREE CYCLES OF NATURAL FREEDOM
Oral translation and commentary

Books by Traleg Kyabgon

The Circle Of The Sun: Heart Essence of Dzogchen, Shogam Publications, 2022, 9780648686385

How To Do Life: A Buddhist Perspective, Shogam Publications, 2021, 978064868347

Actuality Of Being: Dzogchen And Tantric Perspectives, Shogam Publications, 2020, 9780648332176

Vajrayana: An Essential Guide to Practice, Shogam Publications, 2020, 9780648332152

Desire: Why It Matters, Shogam Publications, 2019, 9780648129318.

Luminous Bliss: Self-realization Through Meditation, Shogam Publications, 2019, 9780980502251

Integral Buddhism: Developing All Aspects of One's Personhood, Shogam Publications, 2018, 9780648114802

King Doha: Saraha's Advice to a King, Shogam Publication, 2018, 9780648114864 .

Song of Karmapa: The Aspiration of the Mahamudra of True Meaning by Lord Ranging Dorje, Shogam Publications, 2018, 9780648114864

Moonbeams of Mahamudra: The Classic Meditation Manual, Shogam Publications, 2015, 9780980502237

Karma: What it is, What it isn't, and Why it matters, Shambhala Publications, 2015

Four Dharmas of Gampopa, KTD Publications, 2013

Asanga's Abhidharmasamuccaya, KTD Publications, 2013

The Essence of Buddhism: An Introduction to Its Philosophy and Practice, Shambhala Publications, 2002 & 2014, 9781590307885

Ninth Karmapa Wangchuk Dorje's Ocean Of Certainty, KTD Publications, 2011

Influence of Yogacara on Mahamudra, KTD Publications, 2010

The Practice of Lojong: Cultivating Compassion through Training the Mind, Shambhala Publications, 2007

Photo facing page: Traleg Kyabgon Rinpoche the Ninth

LONGCHENPA'S THREE
CYCLES OF NATURAL FREEDOM
Oral translation and commentary

Traleg Kyabgon

Foreword by Dzigar Kongtrul Rinpoche

SHOGAM
PUBLICATIONS
2023

Shogam Publications Pty Ltd
PO Box 239 Ballarat Central
Victoria, Australia, 3353
www.shogam.org
info@shogam.com

Printed in Australia and the United States of America

Edited by Deidre Collings

Designed by David Bennett

Library Reference
Kyabgon, Traleg, 1955
Longchenpa's Three Cycles of Natural Freedom:
Commentarial Teachings

Printed book ISBN: 978-0-6456653-2-1 (Paperback)
E-book ISBN: 978-0-6456653-3-8

DEDICATION

May we look at the mind that cannot be looked at
See what cannot be seen
And rest uncontrived
For the benefit of all beings

Dedicated in memory of Traleg Rinpoche IX's
nephew, Tenzin
A man of good heart (1977-2023)

Contents

Foreword

The *Three Cycles of Natural Freedom* by the Omniscient Longchenpa, with a translation and commentary by Traleg Kyabgon Rinpoche, is most wonderful to welcome into our lives. Without doubt Longchenpa is one of the greatest enlightened masters born among the Snow Mountains of Tibet. His Three Cycles have the potential to bring us directly to the state of enlightenment, especially with this commentary by Traleg Rinpoche, who himself is a great knowledge-holder of Mahamudra and Dzogchen. I, therefore, personally feel this volume will greatly enhance the understanding of Dharma in the West, particularly of the nature of mind as presented in the great Dzogpa Chenpo tradition. I wish to thank Traleg Khandro for her tireless efforts to make Rinpoche's teachings available, so we may enlighten ourselves.

Dzigar Kongtrul Rinpoche

Biography of the Author
TRALEG KYABGON RINPOCHE IX

Traleg Kyabgon Rinpoche IX (1955-2012) was born in Nangchen in Kham, eastern Tibet. He was recognized by His Holiness XVI Gyalwang Karmapa as the ninth Traleg tulku and enthroned at the age of two as the supreme abbot of Thrangu Monastery. Rinpoche was taken to Rumtek Monastery in Sikkim at the age of four where he was educated with other young tulkus in exile by His Holiness Karmapa for the next five years.

Rinpoche began his studies under the auspices of His Eminence Kyabje Thuksey Rinpoche at Sangngak Choling in Darjeeling. He also studied with a number of other eminent Tibetan teachers during that time and mastered the many Tibetan teachings with the Kagyu and Nyingma traditions in particular, including the *Havajra Tantra*, *Guhyasamaja Tantra*, and the third Karmapa's *Zabmo Nangdon* (*The Profound Inner Meaning*) under Khenpo Noryang (abbot of Sangngak Choling). Rinpoche studied the *Abhidharmakosha*, *Pramanavarttika*, *Bodhisattvacharyavatara*, *Abhidharmasamuccaya*, *Six Treaties of Nagarjuna*, the *Madhyanta-vibhaga*, and the *Mahayanuttaratantra* with Khenpo Sogyal. He also studied with Khenpo Sodar and was trained in tantric ritual practices by Lama Ganga, who had been specifically sent by His Holiness Karmapa for that purpose.

In 1967 Rinpoche moved to the Institute of Higher Tibetan Studies in Sarnath, and studied extensively for the next five years. He studied Buddhist history, Sanskrit, and Hindi, as well as Longchenpa's *Finding Comfort and Ease* (*Ngalso Korsum*), *Seven Treasuries* (*Longchen Dzod Dun*), *Three Cycles of Liberation* (*Rangdrol Korsum*), and *Longchen Nyingthig* with Khenchen Palden Sherab Rinpoche and Khenpo Tsondru.

When Rinpoche had completed these studies at the age of sixteen, he was sent by His Holiness Karmapa to study under the auspices of the Venerable Khenpo Yeshé Chodar at Sanskrit University in Varanasi for three years. Rinpoche was also tutored by khenpos and geshes from all four traditions of Tibetan Buddhism during this time.

Rinpoche was subsequently put in charge of Zangdog Palri Monastery (the glorious copper colored mountain) in Eastern Bhutan and placed under the private tutelage of Dregung Khenpo Ngedon by His Holiness Karmapa to continue his studies of Sutra and Tantra. He ran this monastery for the next three years and began learning English during this time.

From 1977 to 1980, Rinpoche returned to Rumtek in Sikkim to fill the honored position of His Holiness' translator, where he dealt with many English-speaking Western visitors.

Rinpoche moved to Melbourne, Australia in 1980 and commenced studies in comparative religion and philosophy at LaTrobe University. Rinpoche established E-Vam Institute in Melbourne in 1982 and went on to establish further Centers in Australia, America, and New Zealand. For the next 25 years Rinpoche gave weekly teachings, intensive weekend courses, and retreats on classic Kagyu and Nyingma texts. During this time Rinpoche also taught internationally travelling extensively through America, Europe, and South East Asia and was appointed the Spiritual Director of Kamalashila Institute in Germany for five years in the 1980's.

Rinpoche established a retreat center, Maitripa Centre in Healesville, Australia in 1997 where he conducted two public retreats a year. Rinpoche founded E-Vam Buddhist Institute in the U.S in 2000, and Nyima Tashi Buddhist Centre in New Zealand in 2004. In 2010 Rinpoche established a Buddhist college called Shogam Vidhalaya at E-Vam Institute in Australia and instructed students on a weekly basis.

Throughout his life Rinpoche gave extensive teachings on many aspects of Buddhist psychology and philosophy, as well as comparative religion, and Buddhist and Western thought. He was an active writer and has many titles to his name. Titles include: *The Circle Of The Sun, Heart Essence Of Dzogchen*; *Vajrayana, An Essential Guide To Practice*; the best selling *Essence of Buddhism*; *Karma, What It Is, What It Is't, and Why It Matters*; *Moonbeams of Mahamudra, the Classic Meditation Manual*; and many more. Many of Rinpoche's books are translated into a number of different languages including Chinese, French, German, Korean, and Spanish. Rinpoche's writings are thought provoking, challenging, profound, and highly relevant to today's world and its many challenges.

Rinpoche was active in publishing during the last two decades of his life, beginning with his quarterly magazine *Ordinary Mind*, which ran from 1997 to 2003. Further, Rinpoche founded his own publishing arm Shogam Publications in 2008 and released a number of books on Buddhist history, philosophy, and psychology and left instructions for the continuation of this vision. His vision for Shogam and list of titles can be found at www.shogam.com.

Rinpoche's ecumenical approach can be seen in his other activities aimed at bringing buddhadharma to the West. He established the biannual Buddhism and Psychotherapy Conference (1994 - 2003), and Tibet Here and Now Conference (2005), and the annual Buddhist Summer School (1984 to the present).

Traleg Kyabgon Rinpoche IX passed into parinirvana on 24 July 2012, on Chokhor Duchen, the auspicious day of the Buddha's first teaching. Rinpoche stayed in meditation (*thugdam*) for weeks after his passing. A traditional cremation ceremony was conducted at Maitripa Centre and a stupa was erected on the center's grounds in Rinpoche's honor.

It is a privilege to continue Rinpoche's vision and initiatives, and to continue to make the profound teachings of Traleg Kyabgon Rinpoche IX given in the West for over 30 years available through his Centers' activities and Shogam Publications. Rinpoche's Sangha hope that many will benefit.

Acknowledgements

On behalf of Shogam Publications I would like to thank Deidre Collings for her dedication and vision that propelled the development of this important book, for her expertise and countless hours of careful work devoted to preserving and maintaining the pristine and intended meaning of Traleg Kyabgon Rinpoche's translation and commentary of this remarkable series of teachings on this profound Dzogchen text by Longchenpa. We wish to also thank Claire Blaxell for her detailed assistance with editing and proofreading. To Salvatore Celiento for conducting a careful and detailed final proof. David Bennett for the beautiful cover design and book formatting, and the many transcribers who supported the completion of this book.

This book would not have been possible without Traleg Kyabgon Rinpoche's complete devotion to exposing the true meaning and depth of these profound teachings, in such a way that its meaning can be captured by the hearts and minds of Dharma students throughout the world. His erudite use of the English language helps to breaks down any cultural divide that can easily occur when bringing Tibetan Buddhist teachings to the West. Thank you Rinpoche.

Traleg Khandro

Introduction

This text has been edited from an immediate, oral translation given by Traleg Kyabgon Rinpoche during weekly teachings at his center in Melbourne, Australia, over a three-year period from 1997 to 2000. The commentarial sections at the end of each chapter are taken from question time in those classes. There is no commentary to include if, in a given class, there was no time for discussion. These commentaries present a somewhat fragmentary coverage of Longchenpa's teachings because they are responses to particular students rather than a systematic commentary on the three cycles. Even so, the insights they provide will be invaluable to readers.

This is not a rigorously literal translation. It does not attempt to create beautifully crafted sentences that are meant to match the unparalleled poetic heights of Longchenpa's own writing. Traleg Rinpoche has focused on giving a "meaning translation," while still sticking as faithfully as possible to the Tibetan text in the timeframe available. As Rinpoche stated during one question time, the meaning behind Longchenpa's verses is at times so complex and the depths of the Dzogchen terminology so profound, it could take hours to unpack the full meaning of just a few lines in certain parts of the text.

It should not be lost on the reader that this translation was made by a native Tibetan speaker who had a thorough understanding of Western culture and its psychology, as well as a sophisticated grasp of the English language. Traleg Rinpoche (1955–2012) was also a meditation master and lineage-holder within the Karma Kagyu tradition, highly revered in Tibet and the Western world for his profound realization and a teaching style that connected equally with students of all different levels of understanding.

Longchen Rabjampa (1308–1364), a Tibetan scholar-yogi of the Nyingma school, is widely considered the single most important writer on Dzogchen teachings. Revered as an incarnation of Manjushri and a manifestation of the Indian master Vimalamitra, Longchenpa was honored with the title of Kunkhyen, which means "omniscient." In his early life, he was abbot of Samye Monastery, but he later relinquished that position to live more simply in the mountains of Tibet. Most of his mature life was spent in his hermitage at Gangri Tokar, a cave above Shukseb Monastery to the south of Lhasa, where he engaged in either meditation retreat or studying and composing many of his major works.

Each of the *Three Cycles of Natural Freedom* (*rang-grol skor-gsum*) was composed as a root poem, which is a meaning commentary on the instructions of the "mind series" (*sems-sde*) of Dzogchen. The view of the mind series is that all phenomena arise as the display or adornment of ultimate reality.

The cycles follow the same basic structure: pointing-out teachings followed by a short meditation manual for retreat situations. Longchenpa begins his cycles with a presentation of the nature of the mind. He says we start to recognize that our own mind exists in a state of natural freedom when we establish the true view of our authentic state of being. This state is beyond the grasp of our discursive intellect and is completely unaffected by the activities of mind. Longchenpa then describes the meditative approach based on this view and what to expect from its fruition. The second cycle introduces the nature of the mind as inseparable from the timeless spaciousness of ultimate reality. We have gone astray by failing to recognize that our true condition is beyond contrivance and complete in its original state. In the third cycle, Longchenpa points out that all experiences are ultimately the same because they have the same nature, and that nature never changes. It is therefore counterproductive to cultivate or abandon anything. The supplementary text presents the nature of the mind as the creator of all things. Longchenpa calls our natural state "bodhicitta" and says that no one can teach it or show it to us. Our true nature has to reveal itself. Traleg Rinpoche describes the three cycles this way:

The text is titled "natural freedom" because mind is naturally free, and reality is naturally free. Everything is quite perfect in itself. We don't see that perfection because of the influence of our karmic traces and dispositions. Longchenpa's main point is that it is easy to access our natural state through awareness.

These teachings focus on the nature of mind or ultimate reality as opposed to the mind and relative reality. When we are not fixated on things, but instead recognize where we are and what we are experiencing, we are in our natural state. It is nothing mysterious. We can access it when we are not examining or analyzing too much.

This is a practice manual, not a scholarly work. Longchenpa is focusing purely on Dzogchen here; he is talking about our experiences and has some very practical suggestions. This meditation is not about trying to become nonconceptual or to rid ourselves of negative emotions and thoughts; it's about trying to recognize that our thoughts and emotions arise from, and dissipate back into, the natural state.

Thoughts will still arise, but they will be naturally liberated if we don't fixate on them. That is called "self-liberation," and that self-liberation is the natural freedom of the mind. We don't recognize our natural freedom by using antidotes or by paying too much attention to our meditative experiences as being good or bad, we just leave things as they are. Longchenpa is really saying that if we believe passions are one thing and wisdom is something else, we are mistaken. The whole process is not about changing one thing to another; it is about seeing things in a different light. We are trying to transform our own perspective.

It takes many people to produce a book of this nature—from transcribers, to editors, sub-editors, proofreaders, production editors, and those responsible for layout and design. This was all done voluntarily by students of Traleg Rinpoche. Everyone who worked on this book, along with all the students who had the good fortune to be present at these classes, are delighted to offer these remarkable teachings to the wider reading public. The omniscient Longchenpa says he wrote these cycles on natural freedom specifically for future generations, and they have survived for over seven centuries to find their way to us.

We wish to thank our precious teacher, Traleg Kyabgon, the supreme abbot of Thrangu Monastery, who chose to spend his ninth incarnation with students in the West. May his teachings spread far and wide and may his tenth incarnation come back to us and continue to guide us back to our true home.

Melbourne
July, 2023

LONGCHENPA'S THREE
CYCLES OF NATURAL FREEDOM
Oral translation and commentary

PART ONE

Root Text:
Semnyi Rangdrol—Natural Freedom of the Mind

Chapter One

Freedom Through Understanding the Authentic State

I prostrate to Kuntuzangpo.
Our own authentic state, devoid of attributes and descriptions,
and quite unintelligible to the discursive mind.
That natural state of being
has not come into being due to causes and conditions;
it is spontaneously present and inseparable from the heart of our being.
Our authentic state is untarnished by the fixations of mind,
that are propelled by the notion of subject and object.
It is undiluted, unpolluted, and pristine,
and exists in a state of equanimity.
I must pay homage to it.
We see things, hear things, and taste things,
and the mind has thoughts, ideas, and aspirations,
but they all have their origin in our natural state.
They dissipate back into that state, which is non-differentiated,
non-vitiated, non-polluted, and self-existing.
Our natural state of mind is the topic of this text.
So please, listen to this.

Longchenpa starts by saying that he would like to make prostrations to Kuntuzangpo (Samantabhadra), the primordial buddha, who represents our own authenticity (*ngo-bo*). This authentic state of being (*dharmakaya, chos-sku*) is devoid of all forms of attributes and descriptions. As a matter of fact, that natural state (*rang-bzhin*) is beyond the understanding of discursive mind. It is spontaneously present (*anabhaga, lhun-grub*) and not separable from the heart of our own being (*snying-po dang shar-wa*).

The natural state of being (*rang-bzhin gyi gnas*) is not tarnished or polluted by any of the various activities of mind. Mind has the propensity to hang onto this or that and become fixated on things. The innate tendencies that propel mind to do this are related to the notion of subject and object. When that tendency occurs, we begin to cling to the symbolic representation of things, but our own natural state is completely pure. It is devoid of all these peripheral, superficial, and spurious aspects. The true condition (*gnas-lugs*) is untouched, it is free of that, because our authentic state is impartial and does not fall into any kind of extreme. It cannot be described as good or bad, wholesome or unwholesome. It is all-pervasive and encompassing. That state is so extraordinary, so wonderful, so magnificent, that Longchenpa feels he must pay homage to it.

In terms of the mind, we see things, hear things, and taste things and the mind has thoughts, ideas, and aspirations, but all the things that we experience, sensory or otherwise, "have their origin in our natural state" (*cham del-wa*). The mind has these sensory experiences, but they all occur in the context of our own natural state of being. That is where their origin lies. They originate in that state, and they dissipate back into that state as well so we should investigate the origin of all our experiences as being a non-differentiated state. In other words, thoughts have nothing to do with the natural state. The mind itself conjures up everything we see, hear, smell, touch, and taste but it all occurs within the context of our own natural state. That's what cham dal wa means; it's actually a technical term. Our own natural condition (*gnas-lugs*) is the topic of this text, *The Natural Freedom of the Mind*. Longchenpa understands the natural freedom (*rang-grol*) of the nature of mind (*sems-nyid*) to be non-differentiated, non-vitiated, unpolluted, and self-existing. He wants to present this insight to others.

ESTABLISHING THE VIEW

Longchenpa begins by saying that before we can start with the practice, we need to establish the view (*lta-ba*). We have to have a pure view (*lta-ba rnam-dag*). A pure view is not a view that has a position. It doesn't entail adopting a viewpoint, where we examine something from this angle or that angle, from this perspective or that perspective; it is the view of no view. This is a view that encompasses both periphery and center. It is all-encompassing because it transcends the demarcation line between legitimate and illegitimate, valid and invalid. We shouldn't discriminate between things in that way, investing in some things or evaluating them as more worthwhile than others and seeing other things as worthless and regarding them in a derogatory manner. Only the divisive mind says, "This is good and wonderful, that is bad and terrible; this is legitimate and true, that is illegitimate and untrue." We transcend that divisiveness by adopting an openness that does not entail any particular point of view.

How is it possible to adopt such a view? The practitioner must go into the heart of phenomenal experience, both sensory and mental. When we go to the heart of the matter, so to speak, we find that our own natural condition is not subject to change. There is no origin and there is no cessation. We should not exert ourselves too hard. If we look for it with passion in terms of fanaticism, we will not find it; we will not see it by looking harder. How so? Precisely because that which is undifferentiated and spontaneously existing cannot be perceived so readily with our natural faculties. Our natural state of being is not subject to change, it has no origin or cessation, no center or boundary.

We have to comprehend this natural condition by being in it, not by trying to apprehend it or conceptualize about it. In fact, our natural state of being should not even be talked about using traditional Buddhist terms such as emptiness and non-emptiness. We shouldn't even think of it in terms of understanding or not understanding, because engaging in those forms of mental activity only encourages dualistic notions. We must be in our natural state. If you can do that, you will realize that right from the beginning, enlightenment is what you are.

Our authentic state of being is uncorrupted and pure. It didn't come into existence at any given time and no time can be assigned to its extinction. Our authentic state is atemporal. We shouldn't think of it as pure or impure. We may use words like "pure," "uncorrupted," "unpolluted," and so on to describe the authentic state, but it can't really be called "pure." To say it is pure is another form of conceptualization, because to be pure means it is not impure, and that automatically places limitations on the notion of purity. That which is pure cannot be impure, but since the natural state of being is beyond dualistic notions of purity and impurity, we should not think of it as pure as opposed to impure; we should see it as pure from its own side (*rang-bzhin dag-pa'i*), from its own natural condition. It is not pure in terms of normal considerations.

That is what "natural freedom of the mind" means. That freedom is obtained through and from understanding this point. There is nothing to grasp onto as solid or tangible. Our natural condition is not apprehended in that way. In fact, the natural condition is apprehended as nothing, because it is not apprehended by our natural faculties. That is known as Dzogchen.

THE NATURAL STATE IS BEYOND CONDITIONED EXISTENCE

If we really understand that we are in that kind of state, we won't have to think about bondage and liberation. If we can be in our natural state, we will see that our sensory perceptions, what we see, hear, taste, smell, and touch, have no real substantiality. They are like a magical display. For magic to be effective, there must be a magician, a trick that's performed, and various items at hand. It is a conditional thing. We realize that automatically. Instead of thinking that everything we experience during a magical display has an inherent existence of its own, we automatically recognize it as a conditional situation.

We need to realize that all the things that constrict, constrain, and hold us back, all the things that debase us, are in the end no different from our redemptive experiences. We may experience a sense of happiness through efforts orientated toward our salvific goals and feel good about ourselves when we do those things. At other times, we may think we are going in the opposite direction and feel dragged down, constrained, and compelled by our habitual tendencies. However, all of this should be seen as a dream. We can have good dreams and bad dreams. Our samsaric experiences and our redemptive experiences should be viewed in the same way. Our redemptive experiences are like good dreams and our samsaric experiences are like bad dreams, but both are dreams, all the same.

If we find liberation in the natural state of mind, which is what it's all about, then as soon as something arises in the mind, it becomes liberated by itself. As soon as it has arisen in the mind, it dissipates into the natural state of one's own being without disturbance and without leading to further fabrication. What needs to be understood here is that things can only manifest in that fashion because everything is conditional, everything is dependent on causes and conditions. Whatever comes into being and whatever goes out of being is conditioned by interdependence. When it is said we should view everything as a dream, it means just that.

Things are not completely unreal or nonexistent, but they are dreamlike insofar as everything that we experience is contingent on causes and conditions. Dreams have causes and conditions. Illusions have causes and conditions. Whatever we perceive, whether real, actual or illusory, is dependent on causes and conditions. Examples of this are echoes, drawings, and reflections. When you make a noise in a cave and your echo rebounds, it's as if somebody else were answering back, while a drawing or reflection resembles the real person, but these are all conditional things. Everything that exists is no different.

The source of everything we encounter, perceive, or deal with is uncaused, because it has no cause in itself. That is no different from our own authentic state. Since it is uncaused, it cannot cease to exist. Even in terms of the three times (*kalatraya, dus-gsum*) of past, present, and future, the source of everything is not contingent on time, as we know it. In terms of our natural state of being, we cannot talk about having come from a certain place or state of being and we can't entertain thoughts of going toward certain future places or states of being.

Even in terms of the present, we do not remain. We are not subject to space and time, so there is no dwelling place. It's like a dream. We can't say there is a point we have come from, in terms of a place or our being, and we can't say we are headed anywhere. Even in terms of the present, in terms of our natural condition, there is no dwelling place, we are not subject to space and time. A dwelling place is there only on the phenomenal level. In terms of our own authentic state there is no dwelling place. It is like a dream. Things come and go. We experience all kinds of things, but all these things are only happening on the surface; they are not part of our essential characteristics as embodied human beings.

SAMSARA AND NIRVANA COME FROM MIND ITSELF

The individual who is not wise takes everything at face value, which gives rise to tendencies related to the ego. He or she indulges in the misperception of self and others. A person who is endowed with discriminating wisdom (*prajna, shes rab*), on the other hand, recognizes that nothing they perceive is completely real. How so? They understand it is deceptive, dubious. Deception is the order of the day, so to speak, when one is not wise. We begin to see the deceptive nature of our perception when wisdom is present. What we perceive is not true. When we say "it is not true" a certain thing has occurred, this should be judged and assessed in relation to the delusory state of the mind itself. On that level, nothing we experience and apprehend can be judged as true, self-validating, or self-evident.

The very fact we have these experiences indicates that they have their own function. The way that experiences manifest is valuable because certain things are pleasurable, enjoyable, and worthwhile, while other things are disgusting, upsetting, and frightening. Even though, on the ultimate level, nothing that we experience can be pinned down and regarded as superior to anything else, we shouldn't assume it isn't necessary to make any judgments whatsoever about our experiences. We should and do make judgments on the relative level, but these judgments need to be seen in the overall context of how we operate as sentient beings.

We perceive the six realms of existence and the liberating experiences of buddhas. The six realms of existence all represent the samsaric mind and the lack of freedom that's the experience of ordinary sentient beings.[1]

These perceptions reflect the bondage and imprisonment that is experienced by ordinary beings. Human beings are bound by desire, gods are bound by pride, demigods are bound by jealousy, and so on. All these conflicting emotions (*klesha, nyong-mongs*) are present and active in the minds of samsaric beings. In contrast, there are the liberating experiences of buddhas, because buddhas are no longer subject to such things within nirvanic experience. That absence of conflicting emotions is liberating, open, calm, and tranquil.

In the Dzogchen view, we have to say these two seemingly opposed states of samsara and nirvana are not all that different. How so? These two states of being have nothing to do with the coming together of atoms. That has no relevance whatsoever. Instead, we should be paying attention to how all these things appear to the mind. It is only the mind that we need to relate with; the mind determines where we are at, so to speak. It has nothing to do with the collision of atoms or any tangible thing. Being in an enlightened mode of being or in a deluded state is not determined by anything physical. We could say that the state of enlightenment and the state of bondage are like having a good dream or a bad dream. We should see them as equally real.

We should not think, "I shouldn't cling to my state of bondage in samsara, which is infused with ignorance, I must reject it, I don't want any part of it," and cling onto that notion, thinking it is real, or we will propel ourselves into the pursuit of nirvana with enthusiasm and passion, thinking that nirvana is also real. We think there is a state of bondage that we want to escape and a state of liberation that we want to embrace, and regard both as equally real. When we seek enlightenment on the path, we might have to struggle with this whole idea of what is real and not real. Some things might be seen as more real than others but ultimately, when you become awakened, you will realize that everything you entertained as objectively and intrinsically real was nothing but a reflection of your own mind. That is what you realize upon awakening.

That's how a Dzogchen practitioner should understand the relationship between bondage and freedom. We should not see samsara and nirvana as posing some kind of dichotomy, where there is something called "the intrinsic nature of bondage" and something else called "nirvana that possesses freedom." Such a view holds that samsara represents all the undesirable things we want to relinquish, jettison, escape, and free ourselves from, and nirvana represents the opposite of that. It is enlightenment, liberation, freedom, insight, and autonomy. According to Dzogchen, this kind of thinking is the source of ignorance (*avidya, ma-rig-pa*). Ignorance comes from dividing ourselves in that way.

We should not think samsara and nirvana have totally different natures and that both of those natures must somehow be present in ourselves. We need to realize that whatever we are experiencing—whether it is uplifting, comforting, and liberating or whether it fills us with anger, resentment, and despair—comes from the mind itself, so whatever we experience has the same nature as our own authentic state. We cannot find our own nature apart from that. This is a more enlightened way of looking at our situation.

Where can we look for our authentic state apart from what we experience? We should not reject our experiences. Instead, we are trying to see the nature of those experiences, whether good or bad. This is like fire and heat because it's the nature of fire to be hot. It's only the mind that divides things up. We find fire unproblematic when we use it for cooking or heating, but when it goes on a rampage in the environment, we regard it as awesome and terrifying, but heat is present in both situations. That's what we should understand. It's only the mind that sees things in a dualistic fashion. The underlying reality is always the same.

The divisiveness of the mind comes from discrimination. That is the literal translation here. We can see that water and the reflection of the moon in water are the same, yet different. In a similar way, we have to see things differently yet realize everything that we experience is permeated by the same reality. There aren't several realities, there is only one reality, which is present in two modes of perception of the world.

THE NATURAL STATE AND PHENOMENA ARE INSEPARABLE

We come into contact with a particular world, but the world that we perceive through the sensory impressions is not something that exists independently of us. Furthermore, apart from the causes and conditions which are responsible for the perpetuation of its existence, the world we perceive is not separable from our own authentic state. In other words, the way in which the world exists in its ultimate state is untainted, uncontaminated, and naturally pure, just like images in a mirror.

The mind works in such a way that it has a natural tendency to produce and generate various concepts and ideas and then turn those concepts and ideas into some form of objective reality, but we don't realize that we are dealing with our own mental states, in relation to mental fabrication when we think, "This thing exists, that thing does not exist." This is the source of our delusion. When we engage in this sort of mental activity, it leads to a state of complete confusion and we become deluded.

We need to realize that mind constructs things and not become fixated on the phenomena that appear to the mind. We shouldn't fixate on whatever appears to the mind precisely because it is inseparable from the mind itself. It is an image created by the mind itself. It is an image created by mind. For example, we have many images created as artifacts and there are also the images reflected in a mirror. The image and what the image represents have an intimate relationship, a sense of nonduality (*advaya, gnyis-med*). Even though there is no real duality between subject and object, between perceiver and perceived, we are unable to appreciate that fact. On the contrary, we see things in a dualistic fashion.

This failure to appreciate the nonduality of things must be attributed to our well-entrenched traces and dispositions (*vasanas, bag-chags*), which have existed from beginningless time. These have become habituated. For example, there is no difference between the mind and our dreams, but when we are in the midst of a dream, we don't realize that. We take the people we encounter, the scenery, and everything else that occurs in the dream to be real and objective. Our daily experiences of the world are not all that different from our dream experiences, in terms of the state of actuality. They are not separate. That's what we should realize.

To use another example, when a child who has never seen themselves in a mirror before sees their reflection for the first time, they don't recognize the reflected image as themselves. In fact, they think they are seeing someone else. The child has no idea that what they see as "out there" has anything to do with them. However, a parent can train their child to understand that the image in the mirror is no different from the child. In a similar way, we can begin to realize the nature of ultimate reality (*dharmadhatu, gnas-lugs*) by training ourselves to understand the phenomena of cause and effect.

In a similar fashion, we can also begin to realize the nature of reality. First, we have to go through the training in the sutric teachings that emphasize the notion of cause and effect. The causal vehicle (*yana, theg pa*) emphasizes this notion. After following that practice, we should then contemplate our own natural state of the mind. This is called "the essential vehicle." In these teachings concerned with the natural freedom of the mind, which are intimately involved with the essential vehicle, we are making the effort to understand our own mind. This is not a mind that can be identified as this or that, it is not an entity, but while it lacks any identifiable characteristic in itself, the mind has the capacity to manifest in a variety of ways. This occurs because the mind comes into contact with various external causes and conditions and the individual concerned then goes through certain experiences, but as already explained, this is like seeing images in a mirror or seeing the reflections of the sun and moon on the surface of the ocean.

Now what does this mean? Just as images reflected on the surface of the ocean have no real substance, after all they are just reflections, their lack of substance does not hinder them from appearing. Likewise, what we perceive in ordinary circumstances as the various phenomenal appearances (*aloka, snang-ba*) of the objective world are no different. They cannot be separated from the mind itself, just as the reflection of the sun and moon on the surface of the ocean cannot be separated from their origin in the sky.

In that way, the natural state of the mind is the source of both samsara and nirvana, the source of both bondage and freedom. Without mind, there would be no notion of bondage and no concept of freedom. It's only because of mind that we have these concepts. Both bondage and freedom are expressions of the mind itself. Even though the mind is one simple thing, it allows itself to be open to two states of being, to bondage or liberation. These two states of existence can emerge from the one simple state of being.

Just as a mirror has the potential to be obscured by dust, it also has the potential to have that dust removed. When this occurs, the mirror itself hasn't endured any kind of transformation or gone through any change. At one stage, the mirror may be free of dust, and at another stage, it may be covered in dust, but the underlying reality of the mirror's surface has not gone through any change whatsoever. The underlying reality is the same. What manifests on the surface of the mirror is dependent upon causes and conditions.

The mirror is a metaphor for our own conditioned existence and the reality on which that conditioned existence rests. A mirror can reflect various phenomenal entities and variegated sensory presentations, and just as the mirror can accommodate everything that is reflected in it, the mind is capable of accommodating and indulging in diverse sensory presentations. There is change, there is the notion of transformation, there is this whole idea of progression, as a matter of fact, but fundamentally nothing changes.

The changes occur on the surface and there is no change in relation to our own authentic state. Just as the mirror has gathered dust on a superficial level while retaining its translucency, in truth, the authentic condition remains unchanged. The fact that the mirror has gathered dust has nothing to do with the mirror itself. Likewise, the mind itself is also pure. The authentic state is completely open and unobstructed, just like a mirror. The nature of mind is not even corrupted by the concepts of bondage and liberation, samsara and nirvana. These are experiences that we have but our natural condition can never be disturbed by those conceptual indulgences.

IN THE PRESENCE OF KUNTUZANGPO

Fundamentally, each of us remains in pure presence (*thag-nang*) without any notion of the three times. We are always participating in and continue to remain in the presence of Kuntuzangpo (Samantabhadra), which is no different from us. When we can remain in that state, there is no notion of increase or decrease regarding our perception of what is truly real. It is complete. However, from this state of being, which is unwavering, uncorrupted, and unchanging, various experiences of the sensory world can emerge,[2] but what we experience in terms of the sensory world is like a reflection of the moon on water.

Now the Dzogchen meditator would understand that the various forms of experience that are available to us have no real objective reality external to the functioning states of the mind itself. The practitioner would realize that all of these things are experienced on a daily basis. However, the notion that anything we experience is objective, independent, and outside us, as if they were severed from the person having the experiences, is mistaken. The Dzogchen practitioner sees all of this as illusion-like. The basis of the illusion may be real, but what we think about the experience is nothing but an illusion.

In that way, the Dzogchen practitioner doesn't devote too much time to acceptance and rejection, cultivation and non-cultivation, hope and fear. The practitioner should not invest too much time in thinking, "I need to cultivate this, I need to reject that," trying to prevent certain things from arising in the mind. We shouldn't try to manufacture certain states of mind that aren't there or hope for certain things to happen or not happen. The mind is always like that, and we fail to remain in the state of Kuntuzangpo. The mind is in a state of constant agitation through acceptance and rejection, cultivation and non-cultivation, hope and fear. Longchenpa says we should resist doing that. Don't do that, he says.

When we realize that whatever we experience, both good and bad, are manifestations of the mind, that they are manufactured and fabricated by the mind, we are freed. When we know all the things that we experience, good or bad, pleasurable or painful, exciting or boring, have their origin in the mind itself—that is liberation. Then we don't feel so helpless and at the mercy of circumstances and situations outside of our control. We realize it is the mind itself that is contributing to that condition to begin with. We find freedom in recognizing and understanding that the mind fabricates varieties of situations and states of being.

For example, we may dream we are involuntarily on a battlefield, being assailed from all directions, and we have adopted a very frightening posture, but as soon as the dreamer comes to realize that it's just a dream, it is only something our own mind has cooked up, all our fears and anxieties will subside naturally. In the same way, when we have constant contact with the phenomenal world as we do now, we don't need to renounce, reject, or denigrate anything. Instead, what we need to do is realize that mind is responsible for how and in what way we perceive and live in that world. The world itself is not to be judged, the mind is responsible for conditioned existence. We need to cultivate an increased awareness of how and in what way we perceive and inhabit the phenomenal world. We do not have to renounce the world.

We find freedom when we know our own mental state. We will then see that our authentic state, which is part of reality itself, is unconditioned (*asamskrta, rang-bzhin gyi gnas*). That is nirvana. Our authentic state has not come about due to causes and conditions. It is ever-present (*lhan-skyes*). That eternal presence reveals the fact of nirvana. That eternal presence is nirvana. To know that is to know our own authentic state and that is where we find our freedom. That is the nature of the mind. That is our own authentic state. We can only find peace in the state of being where we have returned home. We cannot find peace elsewhere. Returning home and being comfortable there is nirvana, metaphorically speaking. There is no external source that can bring about peace of mind. Peace of mind arises from its own nativity. We cannot find it elsewhere; it is within, it is inherent, it is not foreign.

ASSIMILATING ALL ASPECTS OF ONESELF

Normally, we deal with our mental states as if they were forces in a regiment. We see them as enemies due to paranoia and begin to attack our own regiments out of fear, thinking it's the enemy force. The way we relate to our own mental states is like that. When we realize that our mental states are not the enemy, but our own troops, all our fear and anxiety will disappear and be replaced by happiness. In a similar way, we will begin to relate to our mental states that way. We gain happiness through knowing that all the disturbing states of mind are just our own doing. External causes are not that important. To know that is in itself liberating and will allow you to experience the natural freedom of mind.

Longchenpa says that, here and now, where he stands, due to the blessings of the past lineage masters, experiences that would have been understood as samsaric, he has now been given the opportunity to see as liberating. His experiences are no longer constricting; they allow him to find himself in the domain of dharmakaya (*chos-sku*), his own authentic state. When the misconceptions he encouraged and indulged were removed, that which was constricting became liberating. When he was able to realize that state of being, everything he experiences became natural, because everything he experiences has become self-liberating. He knows this has come about due to great bliss (*mahasukha, bde-chen*).

What is the source of this great bliss? It has no external origin, no external source, it has arisen internally. This great bliss arises naturally when we can change our perspective on things. In that state, we no longer need to think about acceptance and rejection. Whether we are having the disturbing experiences of samsara that we would have previously regarded as totally antagonistic, or states that are more peaceful, comforting, and joyful, both of these conditions are regarded as teachings of the guru. All the things that we experience can be seen as manifestations of the guru.

That doesn't mean they are manifestations of a particular guru. It means the kind of manifestations that we encounter on a daily level are the guru. They are not something extraneous, something independent of what one is. In that way, the teachings of the guru are unceasing because samsaric chatter has become the most profound teaching of all. In that way, everything we experience can lead us to enlightenment. Everything that we experience becomes an unceasing teaching that will assist and aid us to attain realization on the path of enlightenment.

That is how we attain peace, happiness, and an unceasingly relaxed state of being. We don't attain peace from rejecting certain things about ourselves, but from incorporating and assimilating every aspect of ourselves. That is what leads to happiness and well-being. The authentic state is attained through participating in, being involved with, and incorporating, everything that one is. When one is in the dharmadhatu (*chos kyi dbying*), anything and everything can give rise to a state of well-being. However, that state does not condemn us to total passivity where we lack will, initiative, vision, wisdom, or enactment. On the contrary, everything we experience is seen as having its origin in that state of being. The empirical determinants continue to manifest but the way that we perceive and experience them has changed through discovering our own authentic state.

This includes everything that's going on inside and outside the mind, in terms of the physical world. For example, we can look at how this relationship exists between the unconditioned state of being and the conditioned state of being. The unconditioned state is totally open, authentic, uncorrupted, unvitiated, and unpolluted, while the conditioned state of being is susceptible to corrupting influences. However, they are not as different as we might assume. In terms of our being, how we experience things and the methods we use to achieve so-called enlightenment, there must be that balance. There has to be some sense of mediation between the transcendental and the empirical, between the spiritual and physical, and so on. For this reason, even in terms of our own being, we speak about our authentic state of being (*dharmakaya, chos-sku*) and our physically transformed state of being (*rupakaya, gzugs-sku*).[3] We don't separate the things we experience through the senses and our inner states of mind, from the reality of things, which is emptiness.

Even our perceptual and attitudinal ways of relating to things are not something that we can separate in terms of what we experience and what is there. In terms of practice and how we realize this state, again, we can't separate wisdom (*prajna, shes rab*) from compassion (*karuna, snying-rje*). Simply being in a solitary state where we pursue wisdom and cultivate insight is not at all helpful. We need to engage with the world. We need to be in the world and employ both method and wisdom. Not only that, when we engage in meditation, we can't differentiate between meditation (*bhavana, bsgom-pa*) and post-meditation (*prsthalabdha, rjes-thob*). We can't say, "I'm meditating now," but not take advantage of post-meditation situations. That would again be falling into the trap of placing a demarcation line between meditation and nonmeditation, between compassion and wisdom, between experience and reality, between our authentic state of being and our physical presence, and so forth.

The way to draw the most benefit from our practice is to approach it with a sense of non-artifice. The suggestion here is that our meditation should be non-created, with no agent involved; it should come about naturally. It is about naturally flowing into our own authentic state. That is the consequence of realizing your own being.

The five aspects of buddha's being (*kayas, sku*) and the five aspects of primordial wisdom (*jnana, ye-shes*) that are associated with the mind are the consequence of having realized your own being.[4] They are not found elsewhere or to be sought after as treasures in a distant land. They are native to your own land. The nativity of the five kayas and five wisdoms corresponds to your authentic state of being. What is your authentic state if there is no physical or mental manifestation in one form or another? You begin to see yourself in a physically and mentally transformed state. If you cease to differentiate between the object of apprehension and the mind that apprehends it, there remains only the pure presence of awareness (*rig-pa'i rang-rdzogs*). Dzogchen, the great completion, is to be in that continuous state of presence, without falling into either of the two extreme states of being.

INTRINSIC AWARENESS

It is rigpa, our intrinsic awareness, that a Dzogchen practitioner should try to understand and relate to, because it is through and in rigpa that we will have any notion of the real meaning of the paths and stages of the spiritual journey. Without that continuous state of awareness, nothing makes any difference, even the chanting of mantras or remaining in meditative equipoise (*samadhi, ting-nge-'dzin*). All the qualities needed to achieve enlightenment are already present in that state of awareness because to be continuously aware is closer to our authentic state.

This self-presencing awareness (*rang-shar rig-pa*) is completely unbiased and self-arisen. Whether we as sentient beings recognize this self-presence of awareness or not will have no effect whatsoever on the presence of awareness. As ordinary sentient beings, deprived of and lacking in insight or discriminating wisdom, we may apprehend certain things as this or that on the cognitive level, but that perception will not be able to dilute or vitiate this awareness. On the affective and emotional level, our notion of clinging onto things may bind us superficially, in relation to the samsaric state, but we can never be bound on the level of rigpa, of self-presencing awareness.

When we fully understand this primordial state that we have glimpsed, we can begin to understand why things should not be put into categories such as bondage and liberation, depression and exaltation, and so forth. The primordial state is pure in that sense because both states are accommodated, they are not rejected. That is where peace and happiness come from. There is no point, as a matter of fact, in engaging in meditative exercises that encourage us to develop, concretize, and fortify our already established and rigid states of mind. This is true, not only in terms of how we are encouraged to think about certain things, but in terms of what we should say about spiritual matters.

What is the point in a meditation that encourages us to develop the schizophrenic mentality that separates the sensual from the spiritual? Fundamentally speaking, a real practitioner should understand that even the tantric practices of the development (*utpattikrama, bskyed-rim*) and fulfillment or completion (*sampannakrama, rdzogs-rim*) stages are not separate.[5] Even here, we should not become too fixated on the notions of tantric practice and say, "I am now engaged in the deity practice of *kyerim*; and now I am on the stage of *dzogrim*, which is something different." We need to understand that there is no difference between kyerim and dzogrim, fundamentally speaking. They aren't different, but at the same time, a Dzogchen practitioner should understand that just because they are not two, that does not mean they are one. In other words, we shouldn't get too fixated conceptually, thinking about whether they are the same or different, whether they can work together or not and so on, getting bogged down by details.

According to the Dzogchen teachings, what we should understand is that when we practice, there is no end to it, there is no terminal point. At the same time, we may speak about different vehicles (*yana, theg-pa*)— the Hinayana, Mahayana, Vajrayana, and so on—but a real Dzogchen practitioner should not get bogged down by these distinctions. What a practitioner must understand is that all systems, schools, and approaches that relate to our practice come from our own mind. They are like drawings, as if the mind has drawn sketches on an empty canvas. That is what a Dzogchen practitioner must understand.

When we begin to understand everything that we experience is a reflection of ourselves, not something other, and what we experience is just what it is, nothing more and nothing less, there is self-liberation (*rang-grol*). That is self-liberation. The Dzogchen teachings talk about self-liberation, but self-liberation amounts only to that. It is spoken of in that way.

When we can receive blessings (*adhisthana, byin-labs*) from our spiritual masters, even our conditioned existence is apprehended as our authentic state of being. Due to the blessings of the spiritual masters, our very conditioned existence has the capacity to lead to an understanding of our authentic state. This is so because our authentic condition *is* to be in this natural state, and this state is nothing but a sense of well-being. This well-being has come about from within, not from without, not because we happen to be involved with contingent situations or external factors.

In such a state, we don't need to concern ourselves with notions of cultivation and rejection. Everything we experience is the guru. The guru is no longer seen as an individual being; everything that we experience or that appears to the mind manifests itself as our guru. This notion of the guru does not come from rejection and acceptance. In fact, fundamentally speaking, we don't need to receive instructions from gurus; everything we experience has the capacity to teach us something. That in itself is an aid that will lead us toward enlightenment.

The mind begins to have this sense or experience of total and authentic well-being. This sort of well-being is unceasing and reliable, precisely because it is not subject to the various conditions and circumstances in which we find ourselves. This sense of well-being is discovered within oneself first and foremost, and then it radiates outward, so that everything we experience is imbued with the same sense of bliss. This does not just apply to your experiences; it also applies to the things you experience. This is known as "realizing our own authentic state in relation to the dharmakaya." In terms of our experience, it doesn't mean things cease to operate in the real world, in the myriad forms.[6]

We continue to have multifarious, proliferous, unceasing experiences, but these experiences become *rolpa*. Rolpa is a very technical Dzogchen term that means something like "spiritual indulgence." Everything that we experience through the senses becomes a form of spiritual indulgence. We cannot put a stop to the unceasing myriad forms that we experience in conditioned existence, we can't just put a brake on it, but we can see them as rolpa, as some kind of spiritual indulgence. When we approach our practice along these lines, we will understand that the physical aspect of enlightenment and the mental aspect of enlightenment have come together precisely because we have worked on the physical level through the practice of love and compassion, and we have gained some insight into our own mind through meditation and the cultivation of discriminating wisdom.

In that way, we have brought together method (*upaya, thabs*) and discriminating wisdom (*prajna, shes-rab*) to find our ultimate spiritual goal. In fact, in the context of Dzogchen, method and wisdom are realized spontaneously. Normally, the notion of meditation is seen as having relevance to the cultivation of wisdom, and post-meditation as relevant to the cultivation of love and compassion. In the context of Dzogchen, compassion and insight occur naturally, rather than through meditation where we rest in the natural state of mind and gain insight into ourselves, or post-meditation where we engage in activities to benefit others.

Our own state of being is not created. According to the Dzogchen teachings, our total state of being comes from naturally allowing oneself to be what one is without trying to create anything. When you can allow yourself to be what you are, the five aspects of buddha's being are already present, the five aspects being all the qualities that are present in the body and all the qualities that are present in the mind. All the things you require to reach your ultimate goal are already present. Therefore, Dzogchen practitioners don't just have this notion toward their own situation; they maintain that same attitude toward the external world. Dzogchen practitioners don't think of the external world as having some kind of independent existence that is completely and totally independent of their own situation or existence. Mind and the phenomenal world do not exist in a state of division. This division is resolved in the state of rigpa. That is Dzogchen.

Everything becomes complete when the perceiver (the mind) and the perceived (the external world) become conjoined, without fixation (*graha, 'dzin-pa*), and we find total freedom in the state of rigpa. The Buddhist teachings have the concepts of paths (*marga, lam*) and stages (*bhumi, sa*) and when we are engaged in them, we may also make use of mantras and persevere in the pursuit of samadhi. However, if we can pursue our practice in the way just described, which practically involves finding oneself as one is, all the qualities we hope to attain by engaging in these practices are already present. Our own authentic state is imbued with these qualities. In other words, what we are looking for is already there. This state of being is not different from participating in total presence, which is self-manifesting (*rang-mdangs*).

This kind of awareness is primordial awareness. It doesn't favor positive mental states over disturbing mental states. It is totally unbiased. This sort of awareness isn't something we can get. We cannot get it. We have it. We can't get it because it is already there. Our mind may go on a rampage, apprehending this and apprehending that, visually and mentally, followed by clinging onto this and clinging onto that. These things go on but the rigpa, the primordial state of awareness, is not disturbed by all of that. Unaffected by mistaken apprehension and not bound by the inveterate tendency to cling onto things, we understand that everything is simply present as a magical performance.

NATURAL FREEDOM

The Dzogchen practitioner should make the effort to simply be present without aspiring to a meditative equipoise that can be conceptualized, described, or graded. What is the point of that? Longchenpa says, "What is the point of engaging in a type of equipoise where I can attain the second or third levels of shamatha?" There is no point. Even in terms of tantric practice, in terms of kyerim and dzogrim, we should not make those distinctions. Not only are they not different, but even the thought that they aren't different has to be transcended.

In other words, as Buddhist practitioners, we may be very familiar with the paths and stages and so on, but fundamentally, as Dzogchen practitioners, we have to understand that enlightenment is there but to get there is interminable. At the same time, there are no real systems that we can use to grade people's experiences, where we can say, "This person has attained this level of realization and that person has attained something else." All the various systems and approaches that are described in the teachings are a product of the mind, so the teachings should not be mistaken for what is real. The mind being what it is, formulates certain ideas about reality and the way we should attain and understand that reality. In the end, you should understand that these practices are only methods. These methods should be used, but they should lead to self-liberation. Everything that we experience is self-manifesting (*rang-mdangs*) and in that state of self-presence (*rang-shar*) we can find self-liberation (*rang-grol*).

The natural and unconditioned state of the mind is this awareness. This is the kind of awareness that exists in itself, independent of causal conditions. Therefore, self-existing awareness, which is the natural state of mind, is not something that can be identified as this or that through cognitive categories. It's something we have to experience rather than describe. Furthermore, since self-existing awareness is spontaneously present in the natural state of mind through not being contingent on causal conditions, then strictly speaking, we cannot cultivate it because there is nothing that we can bring into being anew. Not only that, in terms of experiencing our own natural condition, we don't resort to methods that would alter our consciousness. Instead, the mind should be left in a relaxed state, where we are not overly concerned with understanding or not understanding the natural state, or with various meditative methods for creating a state of meditative equipoise, because this, in a sense, restricts the natural freedom of mind.

We should just allow ourselves to enter the natural state without any form of fabrication, and without concerning ourselves with too many questions about whether this natural state exists or does not exist, how it relates to ultimate reality, how it relates to our daily experiences and whether it is unitive or differentiated. In other words, we need to be aware of how easily the mind can be overwhelmed by the proliferation of concepts and ideas. As a consequence, we fail to appreciate the significance of what is already there.

We should not even get too fixated on conventional Buddhist concepts, such as the differentiation between relative truth and absolute truth and so on. These concepts are convenient devices meant to lead practitioners to what is real. However, reality does not represent these two truths from its own side. The notion of two truths is employed by conscious beings such as ourselves to get some semblance of understanding in relation to what is real, but we should always keep in mind that our conceptual categories do not represent reality. If we become fixated on the concepts we employ, we can become confused. Excessive attachment to our ideas, to our cherished views, can in fact blind us or inhibit us from being able to see what is there.

Furthermore, becoming too fanatical about applying oneself assiduously to the pursuit of certain goals can make us lose a broader perspective on things. Perpetuating that kind of behavior will not put an end to our samsaric condition. We wander about in the samsaric state because of our karmic inheritance and the karmic mechanism is sustained by our thoughts of good and evil. We profit or suffer depending on the actions that are being performed. This is what the practitioner needs to realize.

Samsara only exists for as long as we have aversion to certain experiences and attachment to others. Knowing that, we should have compassion for people who don't have this understanding. There may be people who have embarked on the spiritual path, but they do not really understand that from the ultimate point of view, samsara has no reality and there are no sentient creatures trapped within it. In terms of the natural condition, everyone is free, everyone enjoys primordial freedom (*ye-grol*). This is something that ordinary sentient beings don't realize. For that reason, we should have compassion toward them. If our own natural condition is free, we can experience a real sense of well-being. Everything we experience can be an expression of that freedom instead of being a source of confusion and various forms of affliction. Everything that we experience can be seen as an expression of that primordial state, which is unconditioned, and which is primordially pure (*ka-dag*).

How does this come about? How do we deal with our experiences in such a way they no longer lead us astray? This comes from being able to let go of viewing everything in a dualistic manner. We do not think that what we experience exists independently of the experiencer, nor do we think of the subject who has the experiences as different from the object of experience. When we can simply have unfabricated experiences without separating subject and object, all our experiences will become expressions of primordial wisdom. Experiences do not cease to manifest at this point. We continue to have experiences of the world, but now the experiences become ornaments of our natural condition. They become exhilarating and uplifting rather than constricting, confusing, and delusory, fundamentally obscuring our natural mental clarity (*gsal-ba*).

Natural freedom means we are not trying to cultivate certain types of experiences, creating states of mind that give rise to specific experiences or using certain methods to contrive, change, or eradicate other experiences. When we become involved with those types of practices, we just increase our hope and fear—hope of having certain experiences and fear of not having certain experiences or of not being able to eradicate, drop, or let go of certain experiences and so on. However, if we can let our experiences be, they will still manifest, but they will "self-liberate the moment they arise" (*shar-grol*), because they are not bound by the ropes of cultivation or rejection. That is the view of Dzogchen.

Our embodiment will then be revealed as the authentic expression of buddha's being. We will realize ultimate reality through the six senses without modifying or blocking out the six sensory impressions. This natural state of mind should be seen as devoid of center or periphery. It is not touched or corrupted by the concepts of either samsara or nirvana. If you realize that, then whatever you experience will go straight to the natural state of self-existing awareness. To attain enlightenment or buddhahood is nothing other than to realize that. This realization is not only beneficial to us; it will benefit others as well. The attainment of buddhahood—the realization of our own natural condition—serves the twin purpose of self and other.

DANGERS OF THE DUALISTIC MIND

Without that, we won't fully understand what's involved in pursuing a spiritual path. We may get involved with meditation practices, but Longchenpa says, "Alas, they practice concentrative methods that lead to a state not all that different from cattle." When certain people practice meditation, they try to block out all thoughts, perceptions, and sensory impressions and remain in a state of complete vacuity. When they enter this trance-like state, they mistakenly think the aim of meditation is about remaining in a state of nonthought and they find confidence in that.

However, entering a state of nonthought is not the aim of proper meditation. There is no merit in a mind that is unconscious, and this will not bring the cycle of samsara to an end. You will not find liberation from the samsaric condition through this method. Furthermore, if we become fixated on these meditative methods, we will not recognize that they are contrived by the mind and when the mind begins to manufacture things and create artificial states, our ability to realize our own natural condition is diminished.

If we are unable to really understand the natural state of mind and its significance, even if we contemplate the differences between relative and absolute truth, we will not be able to understand the middle view. We will inevitably fall into some form of extremism. If we start getting too caught up in these kinds of discussions, we will become lost in conflicting views and ideas without getting any closer to realizing the uncontrived, natural wisdom.

We should therefore practice Dzogchen meditation by trying to remain in our natural state without getting too fixated on certain topics or discussions about the teachings. We should try to remain in the natural state effortlessly and we should think that the conscious mind (*citta, sems*) and primordial wisdom (*jnana, ye-shes*) are like water and its wetness. Wisdom isn't realized by successfully suppressing the workings of the conscious mind. The conscious mind and wisdom are forever inseparable.

The dualistic mind sometimes leads us to value one and denigrate the other, because the dualistic mind always has to differentiate, separate, and see things in a conflictual way. In reality, the conscious mind and wisdom represent the totality of one's being. The subject that experiences and the object that is experienced have never wavered from the natural condition. It is only dualistic mind that divides and slices things up into bits.

If we want to realize the authentic state of buddha's being, we shouldn't look for it. The natural state is not found by looking; it is experienced through realizing that we are already in it. We should refrain from encouraging the dualistic mind by saying, "This is the natural state, but that is not the natural state," and so forth. Whatever arises in the mind is present, but what is present has no enduring substance. That is all we need to realize. Our experiences are not binding. It is thinking that the experiences have some enduring essence that is binding. If we can understand experience in this way, everything that we experience will become naturally freed. This is the *dzogpa chenpo* view of our natural condition.

The nature of ultimate reality is often represented by space in the Buddhist teachings because space is unconditioned and all-pervasive. Space is not something that can be grasped very easily because it can't be described as having certain attributes. Ultimate reality is also beyond description. Since the nature of mind, our own true condition, is inseparable from ultimate reality, the nature of mind is also comparable to space. However, even this analogy should be seen for what it is. The nature of mind is compared to space only to help us gain a better understanding of it. In reality, the nature of mind goes beyond discursive thought (*prapanca, spros-pa*) and beyond conceptual understanding. We cannot entertain thoughts of existence or nonexistence; we must be free of all biases. The mind should be completely free of ideas about what the nature of the mind is.

INTRINSIC PURITY

That state of being, which is beyond description, is the state of completion in itself. In that state, both samsaric and nirvanic experiences are discovered to be intrinsically pure in their nature. When the mind is no longer agitated by various thoughts and ideas and when there is no mental fixation, we attain what is known as "temporary purification."

When our mental disturbances begin to subside, everything becomes pure. We realize intrinsic purity through that. The way temporary purity is achieved comes from the way we relate to our experiences. When we don't hanker after or latch onto whatever experiences have arisen, but instead leave the experiences alone, they will begin to dissolve into the state of great completion as soon as they have made their appearance. Without dwelling anywhere, they begin to dissolve by themselves, into the state of great completion. That is Dzogchen.

This means that our variegated experiences dissipate back into our authentic condition, which is primordially pure. In this primordial state, there is no task to be accomplished and no agent to be involved in it. There is a total state of well-being because of that. Such a state of mind is not directed toward any specific object, but there is a simple presence of intrinsic awareness, which does not get distorted by attachment or by getting involved with apprehending things to be this or that. As a result, there is joy.

Since the practitioner has been able to realize the proper view, which is impartial and non-partisan, they no longer regard any view or practice as superior and others as inferior. Whatever spiritual experience we might have can only bring about enjoyment. Thoughts of hope and fear and attitudes of acceptance and rejection no longer motivate our actions and we are no longer bogged down by anxieties about the fruit of our actions asking, "Would I profit or not from doing this or that?" The mind can be in a perpetual state of relaxation since everything that we experience in life is a manifestation of our authentic state. It is transient and ephemeral, just like an illusion (*maya, gyu-ma*).

Having adopted this attitude, we are no longer subject to conventional responses to our life experiences, be they good or bad, favorable or disturbing. We embrace everything with a sense of lightheartedness because all experiences are a product of the coalescing or coming together of mind and phenomenal presence. We will have all kinds of experience, but as already pointed out, no matter what the experiences are, we have to realize that all experiences arise from and dissipate back into the natural state. Therefore, we should not become fixated on them.

In terms of phenomenal presence, what we perceive to be the objects of experience are manifestations of ultimate reality. We realize that whatever is perceived as this or that on the phenomenal level has no certainty to it, and the mind is not to be seen as a mental substance or entity of any sort. The mind, which is responsible for all our experiences, is fluid and elusive, unfixed and immutable but it is precisely because the mind is not fixed that it has creative potentiality. The mind has no foundation or root, it is rootless, and because of that, it has transformative power. When we begin to understand the mind in this way, we see that the mind is naturally complete in itself. We don't need to do anything to bring it to completion.

This mental or psychic perfection is not something that needs to be completed by gradually eliminating certain undesirable elements and cultivating certain other desirable ones. Whatever is in the mind will find its liberation in the natural state. In that way, we find true comfort in our own authentic state. Otherwise, if we project ourselves into the future and channel our energy in that direction, we will only distort the natural state. If the mind is left alone, and we begin to become more and more aware of what's going on, everything that arises in the mind can be an occasion for spiritual insight or wisdom.

Instead of aiming toward certain things, we need to learn to deal with mental states as they arise in the present. We need to be able to see what mental state is there. When we don't interfere with our natural state by trying to bring about certain altered states of consciousness, but instead allow the mind to be what it is, without contrivance or intervention, the mind will find its natural freedom. We can experience this state because our mind can find its true resting place. This is not something we can comprehend through discursive thoughts. It cannot be adequately conveyed in words.

Being in this authentic state of nowness, which is primordially pure, is the state of buddhahood. Buddhahood is not to be looked for elsewhere, outside the domain of our own true condition. We need to realize that enlightenment and the one who is looking for enlightenment are inseparable. The seeker and what is being sought are one and the same. It is like an illusion and a mirage. A mirage is an illusion, and an illusion is a mirage.

In that way, the meditator should not even be overly concerned about samsara and nirvana. Focusing too much on the differences between these two states may only further encourage the proliferation of dualistic thoughts. Instead, we should try to be in the natural presence of intrinsic awareness, an awareness that is not manufactured, but is spontaneously present. With that awareness, we will see that everything that exists partakes in ultimate reality. In the context of ultimate reality, everything is the same, because everything that exists is in it; everything is equal in the context of ultimate reality.

Your own authentic state of being, which is the same as the nature of mind, has not come into being, because it is uncaused, just like space. There has never been a time when there was no space. Within the sphere of your true condition, whatever you experience in relation to yourself and the external world is pure by nature. The nature of these experiences is no different from your authentic state because the nature of experience is uncaused and has never come into being. That authentic state is called the "dharmakaya" (the authentic state of buddha's being) and describes the openness of being. That state is totally open, nothing is blocked or prevented from arising, so the natural luminosity (*prabhasvara, 'od-gsal*) of mind continues to be ever-present. This corresponds to the sambhogakaya (the communicative aspect of buddha's being). Finally, the experiences that have certain characteristics of being this or that correspond to the nirmanakaya (the manifest aspect of buddha's being).

We need to have a full appreciation of the wholeness of our being in such a way that all aspects of ourselves are understood in relation to these three aspects of the enlightened state of being. If that is understood, there is no need to manufacture or contrive anything. Your mind can be at ease so let the mind rest with ease. However, as ordinary sentient beings, we don't have this understanding. Instead, our minds are governed by dualistic thoughts, and we continue to wander about in the samsaric condition in a dreamlike state. Even when the opportunity is there to cultivate ourselves on the spiritual path, we don't have sufficient insight to practice in an appropriate fashion.

Our practice may even lead to further perpetuation of the samsaric state because meditation can go astray. For example, we may begin to become attached to a state of absorption, where all manner of mental processes cease. If we remain in that state of quietude and become accustomed to being in a thoughtless state, we may fail to realize this state is just an altered state of consciousness. This is known as *arupa-samadhi*, "the formless absorption." It may also happen that we fixate on the various meditative experiences of clarity or emptiness. That only produces the samadhi of form or *rupa-dhatu*. If the practitioner doesn't know how to deal with the mind in terms of its different mental states and sensory impressions, we will just perpetuate the experiences of the desire realm or *kama-dhatu*. In any case, we will fail to transcend the samsaric condition if we practice meditation improperly.

From the perspective of the Dzogchen tradition, any attempt to condition the mind is erroneous, because for as long as we try to condition the mind in any way, samsara cannot be left behind. If we want to liberate ourselves from this state, we must focus our minds on this important point of the unconditioned state of being. Meditation then, should not be practiced in order to bring about specific states of mind. The meditative state should be a state we can enter into casually, in an unhurried fashion.

GENUINE REALIZATION

When this ordinary mind is left alone without interference, in such a way that we don't even think of samsara and nirvana, our mental state is untarnished by attachment to these ideas. Then everything that arises in the mind will become self-liberated from its own side. We don't need to get rid of anything. Everything becomes self-liberated, because everything arises from the state of dharmakaya and dissipates back into the state of dharmakaya. Everything that arises in the mind is imbued with the qualities of clarity and emptiness, which is sambhogakaya. When thoughts and emotions arise and dissipate, becoming naturally and instantaneously liberated on the spot, that is the same as experiencing nirmanakaya. This is so precisely because to attain nirvana is to understand the nature of samsara.

We must pay attention to the mind during meditation and see that it's in a state of continuous transition, and then we gradually need to pay attention to the nature of whatever arises in the mind. The nature of the thoughts and emotions that have arisen in the mind cannot be an object of awareness because the nature of thoughts and emotions is not something we can identify and label. If we practice in this way, the mind will become freer and more flexible, and our mental fixation will start to loosen. This is the secret of the mind that has to be understood.

We have to realize that the nature of mind is something that goes beyond symbolic representation. It can be experienced but not conceptualized about. We can't focus on it, but we can experience it with spontaneous intrinsic awareness. Therefore, we should let the mind operate as it normally does, without interference, because when we realize that the nature of all our experiences is not something we can identify, we realize the nature of mind cannot be grasped. That's why it is like space.

The nature of mind has no center or periphery. It can't be grasped because it's not produced. It is unceasing and can't be brought to an end. It is spontaneously and naturally present. To be able to grasp something, we need to use certain descriptions such as, "Something has such and such characteristics and attributes" or "Something exists or does not exist." None of these conceptual categories are applicable here. We cannot understand the nature of mind by using temporal concepts like past, present, and future, because it doesn't exist in time. It is neither mind nor the physical object but is the nature of both. This can be experienced only with authentic wisdom, and it can never be grasped in conceptual categories. It is indescribable, purely because it is devoid of characteristics. Understanding this is the same as understanding ultimate truth.

The meditator has to be forever vigilant and cautious about their practice. If you simply develop an unwavering state of meditation or gain some understanding of ultimate reality through analytical insight or a familiarity with philosophical reasoning in the textual materials, these avenues will never bring you to a realization of naked and undiluted wisdom. All those methods and approaches are like pointing a finger to space and saying, "Look at that sky!" We may indeed look at the sky, but the sky is not like other objects in the world because there is nothing to look at.

Pointing to space does have some function. In the same way, analytical insight, philosophical reasoning, familiarity with the textual tradition, and instructions from spiritual masters also perform certain functions, but the key thing is to develop undiluted wisdom within oneself. Only that will lead to a realization of ultimate reality. We should have a direct realization through the practice of meditation and through the blessings of the lineage masters. Then realization will be like the sun that gradually begins to illuminate the darkness, whereby we begin to have a direct realization of ourselves as dharmakaya. Ignorance and wisdom will no longer be seen in a dualistic fashion as separate, and external causes and conditions will no longer sway us. If we realize ourselves to be dharmakaya in this way, we will become completely enriched and all the temporal and spiritual boons (*siddhis, dngos-grub*) will be actualized or brought to fruition in this very life.

Not only will such an individual be able to experience this newfound richness within themselves, but they will also be able to wake others from their slumber so that they will start to seek spiritual fulfillment. Those people who are in a state of slumber look for nirvana or spiritual fulfillment elsewhere in order to arouse themselves. This is like failing to recognize the precious jewels we already have in our possession or like mistaking trinkets for something precious. They are looking for something externally without realizing what is inside themselves. If we ignore our true condition and look for nirvana somewhere else, we will fail to attain true enlightenment. Our spontaneously free, natural condition is the most precious thing. The realization that we have this within ourselves already is what dispels illusion. To have that knowledge or recognition is to tap into our own natural resources. It is like a mine of precious stones. This kind of wealth can bring happiness both for oneself and for others.

Once we have realized this, it will not matter what kind of experiences we have in life. Life will present all kinds of situations, but we don't need to be knocked about by them. Life is like being out in a boat on a river, where turbulent waters produce waves that knock us about. Even so, if we are centered within our own authentic state, we will no longer be affected by what happens in the same way as before. We will no longer react to things automatically, because we have become more accommodating with less urge to act impulsively or habitually. Our mind will be put to rest at all times. That is the mind-state of a yogi. The yogi treats everything that they go through in life as the stream of yogic experience. Everything leads to the Dzogchen state. Nothing is excluded from the state of Dzogchen.

When pure awareness is present, there is complete mental clarity. If something arises in the mind in that state, the meditator doesn't waver from their authentic state precisely because they are able to maintain an awareness that is luminous. This awareness is all-pervading and has no center or periphery so there is no duality between conflicting emotions and their antidotes.

That's why there is no need for the meditator to concern themself with thoughts of acceptance or rejection, separation and accumulation, hope and fear. All these concerns have become naturally liberated. However, we still need to separate genuine from proximate meditative experiences. For example, jewels will sparkle when a certain light is cast on them, but the light that causes the jewels to sparkle and the iridescence that the light produces is not the same as the jewels themselves.

In the same way, we need to separate a normal meditative state from a true experience of self-liberation. Otherwise, we could become fixated on the experience of self-liberation itself. These kinds of possibility exist if we fail to differentiate meditative experiences from meditative realizations. If we become accustomed to having certain recurrent meditative experiences, we could mistake this for genuine realization. What is important is meditative realization, because once realization is attained, it is not subject to change. We cannot go through fluctuations.

If the meditator becomes accustomed to genuine realization, all kinds of meditative experiences would arise from that, but we would be able to manage them properly. An analogy that illustrates this point is that meditative realization is like the sky. All kinds of activities associated with the weather take place in the sky due to the coming together or collision of the elements. These climatic conditions are like meditative experiences. Whatever weather conditions are present, the sky is never affected by them, there is no change; it is the same before, during, and after their occurrence. The same is true for meditative realization and meditative experiences.

If you realize your authentic state, you will not be disturbed by positive or negative meditative experiences. On the other hand, if there are many fluctuations in your meditative experiences, this is because you haven't established yourself in meditative realization. You should search for real confidence and certainty in meditative realization because that leads to stability and steadiness and provides an even foundation. The object of meditation should be to rest in that. This is the view we should cultivate.

To know this is to establish the correct view, the true view. This has to be seen with a superior faculty. We need to realize that progress in meditation is not made simply by becoming familiar with the practice of meditation. It relies on having realization in such a way that whatever we experience leads to realization. Whatever we experience during meditation leads to realization so that we do not think of meditation as a process that involves unloading our conflicting emotions. Since that is the case, we don't need to rely on antidotes so there is no need to become familiar with them. If there is no illness, then there is no need for medication. The essence of meditation, in this context, is to establish an unbiased state of mind where the mind does not hanker after or cling to our experiences.

This brings the first chapter of *The Natural Freedom of the Mind* to a conclusion. The content of the first chapter has dealt with the authentic state of the mind, with how developing a proper understanding of the authentic state leads to natural freedom.

TRALEG KYABGON COMMENTARY ON FREEDOM THROUGH UNDERSTANDING THE AUTHENTIC STATE

The full title of this text is *Dzogchen, which Reveals the Natural Freedom of the Mind (dzogpa-chenpo sems-nyid rang-drol)*. Dzogchen is just that. There are three cycles in this topic of natural freedom: the natural freedom of the mind, the natural freedom of ultimate reality, and the natural freedom of equality. This is a practice manual, not a scholarly work. It was written for practitioners to use. Works like *The Trilogy of Finding Comfort and Ease* are for practitioners, but they were also written for learned scholars by drawing on all three yanas. In *The Three Cycles of Natural Freedom*, Longchenpa focuses purely on Dzogchen. In *The Seven Treasures*, Longchenpa goes through all the Buddhist philosophical systems, but he is not doing that here. He is basically talking about our experiences and has some very practical suggestions for that. There isn't much mind-boggling stuff. It is an advanced practice manual though because he is focusing purely on Dzogchen teachings.

ESTABLISHING THE VIEW

According to these teachings, our natural state of being does not cause things to come into existence, it allows things to come into existence. That is why Dzogchen always uses the example of the ocean or space to suggest reality and Longchenpa will do that as we go along. Space allows various weather conditions to come into being. There can be thunder, lightning, turbulence, or there could be perfect weather where the sun is shining and everything is wonderful. Space allows that but space does not cause it. The causes of thunder, lightning, or good weather are the meteorological conditions, but without space, none of that would be possible. In a similar fashion, our natural state of being allows us to become confused and ignorant, as well as awakened and enlightened, but our natural state of being does not cause these things to happen. The samsaric condition is caused by ignorance, not our natural state. The natural state of being allows it to occur.

The Dzogchen teachings also use the example of the ocean. Sometimes the ocean is so still that there is no difference between the ocean and its waves. At other times, due to weather conditions, there are huge turbulent waves, but the depths of the ocean and these waves are still no different. The depth of the ocean does not cause the waves to be turbulent, but it allows the possibility of turbulence or non-turbulence, because you cannot have turbulence or non-turbulence without the ocean's depths. The undifferentiated state of being allows for a variety of things to occur without itself being anything. Even our moral and immoral impulses have their origin in our authentic state, but our authentic state is neither moral nor immoral. It is undifferentiated and all-encompassing. We find our freedom by recognizing that fact.

THE NATURAL STATE

Longchenpa also describes our natural state of being as unconditioned. The tendency to think in terms of past, present, and future is part of existing as an embodied being but only on the phenomenal level. In terms of our authentic state, past, present, and future have no relevance because our authentic state is unconditioned. They do have relevance in terms of our day-to-day experiences, but Longchenpa says we should regard all of those experiences as dreams. However, dreams can be good, and dreams can be bad so we shouldn't simply regard everything as dreams and then forget about it. He is simply saying that just as dreams occur in a particular context, our experiences can only occur in relation to different things, because nothing can exist by itself. We can't encounter anything that exists by itself; there are always so many different elements involved.

Even when we aspire to enlightenment, there is no real difference between what is happening on the salvific soteriological level and what is happening within the samsaric situation. We may do different things in our pursuit of enlightenment, such as prayers, mantras, and meditation, but all these things are dependent upon causes and conditions. We have to listen to teachings and relate to teachers because nothing can take place in isolation, but our experiences are like dreams, because all our samsaric experiences of rejection, dejection, forlornness, and despair are conditioned. Even the temporary pleasure of finding somebody you think you love, only to be rejected, is conditioned. Things are not completely unreal or nonexistent, but they are dreamlike insofar as everything we experience is contingent upon causes and conditions. When teachers advise you to see that everything is like a dream, they mean "like a dream," they never say it is a dream.

You should also see your body as dreamlike because your body is no more real than your thoughts and emotions. We need to have a body to have experiences. Our body enables us to see, hear, smell, taste, and touch, and everything we know about the world comes from those senses.

Nonetheless, we still see the body as being like a dream. We should even see the external world as being like a dream. We need a mind and a body to practice. We need both. Mind and body cannot be separated so easily while we are in this world. If we lose our body we lose our life, and if we lose our mind, we are in deep trouble as well.

There is a real separation between dreams and reality, but what Buddhists regard as reality doesn't have the same depth and substance that we normally inject into it. In other words, things are not as real as we assume them to be because they are contingent on causes and conditions. Sometimes things work out wonderfully and other times they don't work out so well, all because of causes and conditions. That's why we should always view our experiences as dreamlike, but you shouldn't regard your experience as the same as a dream, or you will be locked up, I'm sure, and then it will be no dream.

SAMSARA AND NIRVANA

We normally think that all these things are happening out there while something else is happening inside our mind, but whatever is happening inside is a reflection of what is happening outside and vice versa. It is like the reflection of the moon in a pond. If you are having a good day and something goes wrong, it might not bother you. If you have had a bad day and something goes wrong, you start thinking it's just one thing after the other and you might come close to believing in some kind of evil spirit, someone out there engineering things to make your life miserable. Longchenpa is saying that this is how our minds work. It is all about our perception of what is going on. Whatever is going on out there is no different from what is going on in your own head. Your perception of the world reflects you and you are reflected in the way the world operates.

We wake up from the dream when we stop worrying about good dreams or bad dreams and recognize that they are both dreams. To wake up literally has to do with not thinking about whether one is having a bad dream or a good dream. A good dream is still a dream. The teachings often use the example of a beggar who is dreaming that he is a king, only to wake up feeling hungry without any food to eat. Longchenpa also says that we should not devalue those experiences because they have a function on the relative level. Without these experiences, we would not have life. We need to have good experiences and bad experiences, but ultimately speaking, none of them have any reality. We have to make that distinction. He is not saying we should have a cavalier attitude toward life thinking, "Nothing matters, it is all a dream, so who gives a hoot?" That is, upon awakening, we realize that all these experiences occur within the parameters of our mental perception. We should think of the states of bondage and freedom, of samsara and nirvana, in that way.

Nirvana is more real than samsara, for sure, but only relatively speaking. According to the Buddhist teachings, there is no measuring instrument that allows us to say, "This is absolutely true and that is absolutely false." The absolute truth is knowing that we have to deal with truth and falsity in this world. We have to do that in both everyday life and on the spiritual level. There is no such thing as the ultimate truth out there, that will one day hit you over the head so that you are rendered senseless, and you will then recover to find that you are the next messiah. Truth and falsity are not like that. They are relative. As Longchenpa is pointing out, we have to make our judgments on the relative level. We have to say, "What I'm doing is more beneficial for me than something else I could be doing," or "That is actually quite harmful so I should avoid doing it," and so on.

You can make these judgments, all the while realizing that it is only a judgment. It doesn't mean that the way you see things is the way they exist or that this should be the case. It is just your way of perceiving it. There is nothing wrong with making those judgments if you see things, make decisions, and carry on with life in that way. You will have more flexibility and may be able to see things a bit more clearly when you are not as rigid, demanding, and opinionated as you otherwise might be. You will recognize that this is just your own perception of the world and as such it is just one way of seeing the world. It is not THE way to see the world. Everyone wants to promote their own view of the world as the way things actually exist. That is what these teachings are saying. This view should not undermine your confidence; it should give you more confidence, because you gain more insight into how you see things and how you relate to them.

THE NATURAL STATE AND PHENOMENA

We don't so much create ourselves by identifying with our idea of ourselves, it is more about fixating and clinging onto our ideas, holding onto our perception of things, holding onto how we see ourselves, how we see other people, and how we see the world. Enlightenment comes from recognizing these things. If enlightenment meant that everything became hazier and more blurred, that could be the cause of enormous mental stress instead of mental peace. In fact, if you recognize these things, your perception may be heightened. The point is that you would not be thinking, "What I see or perceive is real, this is something that inherently exists independent of my psychological makeup, independent of my karmic predispositions, independent of my assumptions, projections, and presuppositions." Longchenpa is saying that we should look into that and see how much influence the mind has on how we perceive the world and how we live in that world. For example, a religious fundamentalist and an atheist would construct the world in very different ways, even though they may be living in the same physical environment. Whatever significance or lack of significance the world has is determined by the human mind.

When Longchenpa says there are two states of being, he is talking about samsara and nirvana. It's like good crops and bad crops that come from the same field or good weather and bad weather that develop in the same sky. Samsara and nirvana have the same source. They arise from and exist in the same state of being; they don't have two separate origins. Just because there is bad weather, you don't go looking for a separate sky. Dzogchen uses the notion of space or sky all the time. Sometimes there is so much activity and turbulence going on, while at other times the sky is clear, but it all takes place in the same context. The natural state of mind allows both states of existence to come about and accommodates them. What this means is that our samsaric tendencies, things that would naturally lead us to become deluded, and our aspirations to enlightenment, which lead to greater wisdom and compassion, should not be regarded as having two different natures. We have only one nature and it can produce two very different ways of being. We should not think there is an animal nature and there is a spiritual nature, where the animal nature is more associated with bodily functions and the spiritual nature is completely independent of that. That is a very dualistic way of thinking. That does not mean they are the same, but the natural state of mind is all-encompassing, so it has to accommodate everything about us.

THE ESSENCE VEHICLE

The essence vehicle is the same as the resultant vehicle, but Dzogchen sometimes refers to itself specifically as the essence vehicle. Dzogchen teachers would say there is a difference insofar as the tantric teachings, which basically represent the resultant vehicle, still have a notion of gradualism. You gradually purify yourself by visualizing various deities, reciting mantras, and engaging in various forms of ritual practices. The essence vehicle, the Dzogchen teachings, emphasizes entering directly into your own natural state. We go into our essential state of being, without becoming too engrossed in the tantric practice of rituals and so on. "Essence" basically refers to our own natural state of mind. The Nyingma school groups the causal and resultant vehicles into nine yanas, the last of which is maha-ati or Dzogchen. The causal and resultant vehicles correspond to the sutric and tantric teachings. Only the ninth vehicle, the teachings of Dzogchen, corresponds to the essence vehicle.

INSEPARABILITY

We need to allow our thoughts to come and go, without judgment or rejection, without thinking, "That was a bad thought, I'm a nice person, why am I thinking things like that?" It is not the thoughts that bind us, as Longchenpa keeps emphasizing; it is the way that we relate to our thoughts that binds us. Thoughts themselves don't have the capacity to do that. The way we relate to our thoughts and make them so entrenched, encrusted, solidified, and concrete is what binds us. They begin to form very rigid belief systems, prejudices, presuppositions, and biases, which comes from feeding certain thoughts all the time, so they become more and more concretized. They become very solid and rigid, and we become immune to change. We become inflexible. Longchenpa is saying that we should always be wary of those tendencies and remain open to our thoughts and emotions. The fact we have them is not the problem, even though we may feel it is; the problem is that we believe certain thoughts and emotions correspond to reality. That correspondence does not happen.

You may be tempted to block or get rid of your thoughts, but Longchenpa is saying that you should not do that. It doesn't matter what thoughts we have; any kind of thoughts is okay, as long as we realize the enormous influence that they have on how we perceive situations and people, and our relationships with people. We have to realize the power of thoughts. We also have to see that thoughts are manufactured and created by the mind itself and that mind is you. Instead of seeing thoughts as free-floating entities that operate on their own accord, independently of you, you realize that thoughts are manufactured by the mind and the mind is no different from you. You are the mind.

We normally try to get rid of our habituated thoughts by taking some kind of positive action saying, "I don't like to think like this, that is not me, it's not helpful to me so I want to get rid of the thinking pattern that I have been indulging in for so long." The Mahamudra and Dzogchen teachings are saying that there is nothing wrong with thinking in a particular way. We may not like certain thoughts, and they may be recurring, but the best way to overcome them is by paying attention to them and noticing them, not by trying to push them away. That is the main thing. It is also important to know that the thoughts are you, instead of thinking, "I'm the victim of what occurs in my mind, I'm being overwhelmed by an upsurge of thoughts and emotions that are outside of my control."

You have to realize these things are happening because of you, because of your own mind and you begin to take charge, instead of being this hapless and helpless creature that thinks, "I can't do anything, I can't help it, I don't want to feel this way, but I do. I don't want to think certain thoughts, but I do." You basically just say to yourself, "It is not a big deal. That's not the problem. To think that I shouldn't have these thoughts and emotions is the problem." You know everything you experience is engineered, manufactured, and fabricated by the mind.

We have to realize that the mind is the one that fashions our experiences of the world. It is not the world that fashions our experiences. Longchenpa is saying that you have to come to that realization. Hoping for a better outcome is the whole issue. You have to start off by not judging, by not being too harsh on yourself. That is why we have to practice and practice and practice and give our mind a rest. Even when you are practicing you do not think, "What am I getting out of this? Am I doing it in the right way? Am I getting somewhere? Am I benefiting from this better than someone else? So-and-so has been practicing for twenty years but I've only been doing it for a short time." Just practice. That is the only way you will find out, and you will find out. There is no doubt about that if you really practice. I always encourage learning and study as well. People should really read, study, examine, and question, but when you practice, you just practice. That is all. Don't question the practice, just practice. Everything will then become more obvious.

Longchenpa is saying that we should meditate and engage in life with a sense of awareness and without being so extreme. We shouldn't think, "I'm going to completely focus one-pointedly on enlightenment, I've had enough of samsara, it's done nothing but drag me down, I'm disgusted by it, I'm revolted. Now I'm going to be so pure, so fantastic, so wonderful." Even if that were to last, even if you could keep that up, that doesn't mean thinking this way is the way to approach your spiritual practice. You have to focus more on awareness, constantly reminding yourself to be aware of whatever you are involved in. It is the loss of awareness that makes us ignorant and oblivious to things. We shut things off, we shut things out, we refuse to take things in, we belligerently refuse to notice things, even when they are jumping out at you.

These teachings are saying that awareness is something that is actually natural to us, but we can't have real awareness if we are chasing after something. We could even be chasing after complete solitude. There is a romantic notion of enlightenment, where we have all of this mumbo jumbo nonsense about being here now, living life on a purely day-to-day level, rather than making heaps of money and leading a comfortable life, or whatever you may be thinking. Longchenpa is saying that there shouldn't be any tension whatsoever between those two. You can lead a comfortable life without having to reject spirituality if you are making the effort to cultivate awareness. If you are not doing that, then you will become lost. We have to work with what we've got. We can't just have escapism, where instead of watching television, we think we are pursuing some kind of altered state of consciousness, where all kinds of fireworks are happening in the mind.

Some people romanticize the stories of the mahasiddhas, but we have to realize their hagiographies traditionally have three levels of interpretation. We have to use some kind of hermeneutic techniques here. They talk about outer interpretation, inner interpretation, and secret interpretation, so when you hear about a siddha stopping the sun from setting, that is only the external interpretation meant for mass consumption. The internal interpretation would be that through yogic exercises this particular siddha was able to bring the sun and the moon energy, meaning the male and female energy, together and hold it at the heart chakra in the central channel. The secret interpretation would be that they realized the indivisibility of compassion and emptiness. The notion of emptiness is not just a physical thing; the experience of emptiness leads to a real spiritual realization. We have to interpret these experiences on many different levels.

One thing that is made very clear in the mahasiddha teachings is that all of the siddhas were told not to reject what they were doing. There was a lazy person who was told to carry on being lazy. There was a hunter, a handsome rogue, and other such characters. They all did many different things and came from many different backgrounds. Some were from a high Brahmin class, others were from untouchable families, some were very poor, some were very ugly, others were despised or rejected by society. Still others were admired until someone found out what they were up to and then they were driven out of town. The point is, it doesn't matter whether the siddha stories are historically true or not. One thing for certain is that there were many siddhas living in India in those days, and they lived their lives in that way. Whether the eighty-four mahasiddhas are historical figures or not is of less significance than the impact reading their stories has on us as practicing Buddhists. Even many current lamas are regarded as incarnations of Indian mahasiddhas. Sakya Trizin, for example, is said to be the incarnation of the mahasiddha

Virupa. Looking at siddhas as supranormal beings is just one way of relating to them. There are other ways to relate to them in terms of their symbolic function in our lives and what they represent within us. Everything in tantra should be related to on those three levels.

THE FIVE KAYAS

The fifth kaya means the three kayas are embedded in the fourth kaya, the svabhavikakaya, which emphasizes the interrelationship between the three kayas, because they are not separate. The fifth kaya is rigpa because all four kayas have their ground in rigpa. Rigpa is the precondition for the existence of the other kayas. I believe that is what Longchenpa is implying. The Buddhist teachings always talk about five of this or three of that, but a lot of the time they are saying you don't have to take it too seriously. Sometimes they even do it for the sake of matching things up. If there is five of something, then you come up with five of something else. You don't need to get bogged down by that. Nirmanakaya, sambhogakaya, dharmakaya , and svabhavikakaya are all just symbols.

ROLPA

Rolpa basically means indulging in sensory pleasures without getting attached or fixated. You can have nice meals, listen to entrancing music, admire beautiful flowers and buildings, and things like that. You like all of these things, and it is very fresh and you are present. Rolpa is not about having knowledge about some dish. When you go to a restaurant and order something, the last thing you want is the server going off on some long description about the dish. Rolpa is just being present. The mind usually can't stop, as we know. Rolpa is basically seeing, tasting, and feeling without conceptualizing. It is a technical Dzogchen word.

POST-MEDITATION

Post-meditation basically refers to when we are not meditating. Sometimes even when we are meditating, we are not meditating, but that's another point. When we meditate, we are supposed to have a particular approach to what we are experiencing in terms of our thoughts and emotions. When we are not meditating, we may still have those thoughts and emotions, but our approach is slightly different. At work, for example, the same thoughts and emotions come up, but we can't use the meditative approach in the same way. That's why it is called "post-meditation." The difference is that during meditation we are trying to take notice of whatever is present in the mind, but in post-meditation, we may try to be aware of that, but we are not really making the effort to be in a meditative state. We are just being aware and alert, more or less—being alert and being aware of what is going on in your surroundings, how you are responding to people, and how other people are relating to you.

You are learning to be aware when you are sitting, eating, sleeping, walking, and lying down. Those physical movements include everything we do when we are not meditating. What we mean by "meditation and post-meditation experiences" is also contingent on the kind of practices we are doing. For example, if you are doing tantric practice, in post-meditation situations you are told to see the world as a divine mandala and other beings as gods and goddesses. You are trying to cultivate the notion of pure perception. Regardless of the practice, we are trying to understand that it is our own mind that determines how well we get along with other people, what sort of world we are living in, or what we think we will achieve in our life. These things are determined by how we relate to our own mind. That is the main factor.

KARMA

Our karmic inheritance is sustained by good and evil thoughts because without thoughts, there would be no action. Our actions are based on the kind of thoughts we have. Our conditions are not what cause us to create karma. Karma is created because of the thoughts and emotions we have in relation to the situation we are in. There would be no escape from samsara if everything was dependent on external conditions because we can't control external conditions. Two people may be in the same prevailing conditions but the kind of karma each person creates is determined by how they respond to that situation, and their response would depend on the kind of thoughts and emotions they have. If you have compassionate thoughts, you might do something that would help someone. If you have aggressive or violent thoughts, you might harm someone. That is basically what karma is. Having certain thoughts in a habitual way creates your habit and you become predisposed to acting in a particular way or seeing things in a particular way. All that is determined by your karmic inheritance, according to Buddhism.

NATURAL FREEDOM

From the point of view of emptiness, there is no relative and absolute truth. Relative and absolute truth are human concepts for trying to understand how we experience things, but ultimate reality doesn't have two aspects. It is one and the same thing. To see things in a nondualistic way does not mean that you see everything as being one. It just means you don't think of subject and object as having some kind of inherent existence on their own accord. They are not to be understood as identical; they are nondual in the sense of being interdependent. Without the object of experience, there is no subject and there will be no experience and vice versa. The fact that we can see trees, mountains, people, and so on is not what constitutes the samsaric world. What constitutes the samsaric world is our mistaking all of that as real; thinking that there is an external world out there and there is the inner world of sentient beings independent from the world outside.

FIXATION

Our fixation (*dzin-pa*) is the problem. Instead of thinking that enlightenment means to go beyond having all these experiences by transcending our ordinary world, we should understand that the same things are experienced, but they are experienced differently. That's all. In other words, an enlightened person would still see tables as tables and chairs as chairs. If they did not, they would be even more confused than an ordinary person.

Dualism arises as soon as you latch onto whatever it is that you are experiencing. As soon as you begin to concretize and solidify your experiences, the mind starts to become rigid and closed. Nondualism does not mean that your experience, the object of experience, and the mind that has the experience are identical. That is not what it means. We are talking about fixation. Whenever you have a particular thought or emotion, the mind latches onto it and doesn't let go. That comes about from perceiving things in a dualistic way. As these teachings are saying, we have to work with dzin-pa. We have to work with this mind that automatically latches onto things and turns everything into something solid. We should not spend too much time trying to suppress certain emotions.

Our experiences are not the problem; the problem is getting too caught up in judgmentalism about those experiences. Instead of thinking that your problems come from being unable to distinguish or discriminate between certain types of experiences, you should be more aware of the natural tendency of the mind to fixate, to jump on your experience, and not let go. We should learn to become more aware of that tendency. It's not sufficient to discriminate or to evaluate our experiences by saying, "These experiences are bad, these ones are good experiences." This means that if there is depression, then let it be there. If you are happy and joyous, that is fine. As Longchenpa said, the nature of mind is comparable to the sky. Instead of thinking the sun should be shining every day, we know that there can be cloudy days, storms, and lightning, and there can be some clear blue sky as well. Everything is accommodated. As Longchenpa says, everything emerges from our natural state and dissipates back into that natural state. That is how we relate to everything from a nondual point of view.

When Dzogchen talks about putting the mind to rest, that just means the mind is no longer so disturbed and agitated and sensitive to everything. It isn't so easily provoked. Even if you do get provoked, you don't dwell on it. You don't get more and more caught up in the whole thing. If you get temporarily upset, you are able to let go. You are able to leave it alone instead of building on it. I was reading a newsletter of Chagdud Tulku where he says something quite interesting. One of his students asked, "Do you still have attachments?" He replied something like, "Yes, I do have attachments, but I know that things I am attached to have no inherent existence. I also know that the I who has these attachments has no inherent existence. Even the attachment itself, which is caused by my own fixation, has no inherent existence. By knowing those things, I can live with my attachment." In other words, he is able to let go and not latch onto thing so tenaciously. We are not just attached to the things that we love and want; we are also attached to things that we do not want. Fixation can be applied in both situations. Attachment is that mind that grasps onto something, that latches onto it and won't let go. That is the problem and that has to be dealt with. The problem is not that we sometimes feel better than at other times; it's about how we relate to those changing states of mind. That is the key issue here.

TRANSFORMATIVE POWER

The mind is rootless because everything is transforming all the time. Every day, from morning until night and even while we are sleeping, the mind is going through all kinds of transformations, whether we like it or not. One moment we are lustful, another moment we are feeling murderous, another moment we think we are in a deep samadhi. This shows that our mind is rootless; it is not fixed and stable. There is no fixed foundation for the mind to rest on. The mind is dynamic, transformative, and unstable. If we realize the mind is that way, it will lead to a realization of the nature of the mind. It will lead us to our authentic state. It is not the case that we go deeper and deeper into ourselves, peeling away layers and layers of obscurations and defilements, until we finally get to the core of something and reach the essence, which is rock hard. It's not like that. That is why the nature of the mind is compared to the space rather than something else.

Our authentic state, as Longchenpa keeps saying, is not something tangible and real in the normal sense. Our authentic state is a state of total openness where anything and everything is possible. Otherwise, our authentic state would be just like any other thing that we experience. The power of the nature of the mind does not lie in its being something; it lies in its not being anything. It is not an entity of some kind. That is why it is not comparable to a soul or an *atman*. You cannot say that our authentic state or nature of mind is immortal. It is more like space. It is like a blank canvas before you have painted anything on it, an empty field before you have planted anything in it, a bare blackboard, or a white sheet of paper. The nature of the mind has to be understood in that way. If you think of music and silence, then silence is like the nature of the mind.

LUMINOSITY

The sambhogakaya is associated with the experience of luminosity. Spontaneous awareness is also part of the sambhogakaya experience. We don't develop intrinsic awareness; we discover intrinsic awareness through cultivating awareness in our practice. The practice of awareness, when we try to be aware of what is going on in the mind, is called "son luminosity" and realizing the nature of the mind is called "mother luminosity." Son and mother luminosity are not something inaccessible; we have experienced them already. The mother luminosity is the other side of the coemergent ignorance that is talked about in the Mahamudra teachings. Ignorance and mother luminosity are present together, they are co-present. It is not the case that first there was the primordial state of wakefulness and then ignorance came onto the scene and dimmed the primordial state of enlightenment. It's not like that. It's like the sun. As the teachings say, the radiance of the sun is there even when that radiance is being obscured by clouds. If there were this original pristine condition and ignorance appeared for some reason and corrupted it, then when we managed to recover the pristine condition, there would be no guarantee that corruption wouldn't happen again.

When the Mahamudra teachings talk about coemergent wisdom or coemergent ignorance, they are basically saying that there is no priority in terms of wisdom and ignorance because one makes the other one possible. Wisdom without ignorance is not possible and vice versa. The teachings compare it to the sun and darkness. The sun's power to illuminate is only powerful for as long as there is darkness to illuminate. That's what is meant by "coemergent wisdom" or "coemergent ignorance." Ignorance and wisdom have come together. Even the term "coming into being" has to be understood in a metaphorical way. It does not mean that ignorance and wisdom came together at some point; it simply means that they cannot be separated. It does not literally mean they came into being at a particular time, as if there was a time when there was no ignorance and wisdom.

REALIZATION

When Longchenpa says the authentic state is luminous and all-pervading, he is simply saying that when awareness is there, you are the awareness. You are in a state of awareness; it's not about being aware of this or that. The awareness and the person who is aware are actually one and the same thing. We can't describe the nature of the mind or our authentic state because it has no characteristics or attributes, so obviously we cannot understand it through concepts, but that doesn't mean concepts and thoughts won't arise. As Longchenpa says, they will arise, but they will become naturally liberated. We have to realize that. That is part of realization also. Realization is not just about being in this nonconceptual state; it is about realizing that thoughts and concepts arise from this natural state and disperse back into it as well. We have to know that they come and go without having any adverse effect on the natural state. You have to keep reminding yourself that this is the case. To understand that is to have the view. You have to keep trying to understand that, to keep trying to see how your natural state of mind relates to your daily experiences.

So far, Longchenpa has been saying that basically none of it really matters if you understand that your natural state is pure, undiluted, open, unconditioned, and not subject to change. You must have a proper understanding of that. If you have that understanding, then anything and everything can come up and you will not get upset. Your meditative state will not be upset. In this meditation, we are not trying to become nonconceptual or trying to get rid of our negative emotions and thoughts. We are trying to recognize that they arise from and dissipate back into the natural state. They come and go. That is the main point. That is called "self-liberation." Self-liberation is the natural freedom of the mind. We do not recognize that state by using antidotes. We should not pay too much attention to our meditative experiences either, thinking something is a good meditative experience and something else is bad. We just view them as meditative experiences and simply leave it at that. If you pay too much attention to meditative experiences, you will go up and down even more if you have not established yourself in the view that your own authentic state is not subject to fluctuation. That is the foundation, the basis.

Meditative experiences fluctuate by nature, not every day is the same, so if you have some understanding that your own primordial state is not subject to change, you can build stability on that. In other words, we can't have good meditative experiences continuously—it does not work like that—but we can gradually build this underlying stability and strength so that irrespective of what is happening, we are not getting pushed and pulled about.

It is difficult to see ourselves as we are getting distracted, but if we know we have become distracted, we are catching ourselves being distracted on the spot. It is not after the fact. That very moment you find yourself distracted, that is that moment. It is not that first your distraction ceases and then all of a sudden you find yourself aware, as if you had been unconscious for that short period. It's not like that. As soon as you realize you have been distracted, that is the moment of awareness. That is meditation. In other words, to become aware is to become aware of whatever is there, distraction included. However, as Longchenpa keeps on saying, stability has to come from our natural condition. We cannot build it upon the day-to-day functioning of our mind. When you have stability, you don't automatically have to become mentally agitated when thoughts and emotions arise. We can gradually have thoughts and emotions of all kinds without the intensity and without getting overwhelmed by them. You have to practice if you want to find that out.

Chapter Two

Realizing Freedom on the Path

LEARNING TO REST IN THE NATURAL STATE

Dzogchen meditation consists of practicing meditation naturally so that our experiences become self-liberated. The meditative state is not created. Whatever arises in the mind has to be seen as inseparable from the state of Dzogchen. We can rest in our own authentic state in such meditation without thoughts of cultivation or rejection. We will then begin to experience external and internal conditions, and samsaric and nirvanic states, with a sense of evenness. Even our sensory impressions are experienced simply, with a sense of relaxation and without judgment or censoring. We experience things like a child and can rest in our own authentic state without conceptual attachments. This is how we remain in our authentic state, which is unchanging and spontaneously established through not having been caused to come into being.

The key method in this meditation is to let the ordinary mind be without artifice, but at rest in a sense of relaxation. Everything that comes up in the mind should be seen as not separate from one's own authentic state. We should view them as the same as ice on the surface of water. Ice shares the same nature as water. We will begin to see things from a nondualistic point of view, because the dualistic mind only encourages thoughts of artifice.

Meditation should be free from the thought of doing. We have to know that meditation is about not doing; it's about resting in our own natural condition. If we can achieve this, our mind will become very open, flexible, and unperturbed. We should rest our mind like an exhausted, world-weary old man. When you practice meditation in this way, don't pay too much attention to the meditation sessions, worrying about how many sessions you can fit into a day, how long they are, and so forth. Pay more attention to making use of whatever you encounter during meditation as part of meditation. Everything that comes up or that we encounter during meditation provides us with the opportunity to experience self-liberation.

The meditator needs to maintain a far-reaching and expansive sense of awareness, an awareness that spreads out in all directions, rather than an awareness that is unidirectional. Your expansive awareness shouldn't be directed toward one thing or another, but instead should be an awareness that is self-illuminating and all-pervasive. There should be no sense of clinging within that sense of awareness. There is just bare awareness. You do not hold onto anything; you can simply let go. You should let your mind rest, just like a madman.

In Dzogchen meditation, the real asceticism, the real hardship in terms of spiritual practice, comes from practicing this way. Cultivating awareness is the essence of asceticism but it must be an awareness that is unbiased and without prejudice. If you can maintain that sense of awareness, even bad things that happen can occasion a sense of insight into the nature of things. The variety of things that continuously assail your mind can be seen as a magical display emanating from the natural state of awareness. Instead of getting bogged down and feeling disempowered by these unpleasant experiences, you should rest the mind with courage and heroism, just like a lion.

As you persist with the practice, your natural state of awareness will be revealed as none other than wisdom consciousness, which overpowers all forms of delusion and illusion. This experience of intense awareness is the source of all self-liberation. Until you can free yourself from conceptual categories by realizing their nature, you must be vigilant day and night, just like a watchful jackal.

Through becoming acquainted with the various aspects of your mind, you will experience a coalescence of your authentic state of being, your natural awareness, and the awareness that comes from practice. When this occurs, you will have the experience of all-pervasive awareness, which is all-encompassing and without reference. You should rest in that state of awareness with complete openness, just like space.

The experience of awareness leads to the state of nonmeditation, a state free from all forms of conditioning and contrivance. In the state of nonmeditation, there is only the spontaneous or self-produced manifestation of natural awareness, where all the polluting elements of the conflicting emotions have subsided. You should remain in that pristine condition of the mind without movement, just like the ocean.

Even when thoughts and emotions do arise, they should be seen as waves on the ocean. The natural state of the mind can never be disturbed. You should rest with stability in that way, just like a mountain.

When you practice meditation in this way, you must see everything with equanimity (*upeksha, btang-snyoms*), so that meditation becomes effortless and the things that arise in the mind do not upset the equilibrium of your mind. Things come up and they disperse, but they are to be neither encouraged nor shunned. You must rest with the flow of this, just like a river.

Thoughts and concepts are not separate from your own authentic state. With that sense of equanimity, you do not differentiate, categorize, or judge what comes up in the mind. Everything that arises leads to a state of enlightenment because whatever you experience is not different from ultimate reality. In this manner, you should learn to rest in your natural state without any particular focus. Our mind becomes freed when it is not fixated on anything, and our meditation becomes spontaneously established.

MIXING MEDITATION AND POST-MEDITATION

To meditate properly in this tradition, you should not repeatedly try to rest the mind, but instead relax into the meditative state, and practice refining your meditation without yielding to laziness. In order to foster this practice on the path, you should desist from indulging in judgmentalism. Instead, whatever adverse circumstance or situation you find yourself in should be used on the path. This is done by mixing the meditative state with the post-meditative state.

Even in daily life, whatever your surroundings, you should try to use that to your advantage. It doesn't matter if you find yourself in the mountains, at a charnel ground, on an island, or in the marketplace. In any post-meditation situation, your mind should be open and without care, so that it can be let loose to contact the object fully. We may use our bodies to dance and our voices to sing and allow our minds to think all manner of things. We stay in a meditative state in this way so that whatever occurs is liberated on the spot. We should also learn to mix the view with meditation so that we can use everything in external situations to our advantage and benefit. In this way, everything should be used to our own advantage so that nothing gets wasted and everything becomes material to advance on the path.

You should also develop devotion to the lineage masters in order to fully benefit in relation to the middle point between the external and the internal. The cultivation of devotion is necessary. You should also exert yourself in post-meditation situations to accumulate merit and purify the mind. Spend time contemplating your own mortality and view everything as impermanent and subject to change. Everything is shifting and ephemeral, like the sounds produced by a stringed instrument, a mirage, or a reflection of the moon on the water. You should remind yourself of the insubstantial and impermanent nature of everything, because while everything appears, nothing has enduring essence.

In post-meditation situations, you should remain mindful and see everything as illusory, from moment to moment. Everything is hard to catch and elusive, precisely because nothing has enduring essence. You should try to maintain a sense of awareness of this, day and night. This is how we mix the meditative state with post-meditative experiences. If we can accomplish this in the post-meditative state, whatever arises will be self-liberated on the spot. The mind will already have established itself in meditation. There will be bliss and the cessation of conceptual proliferation because nothing that has arisen in the mind can disturb our mental equilibrium.

At the same time, when our mind is in a meditative state, nothing that arises from that state will give rise to disturbances. Becoming familiar with this practice of mixing meditative and post-meditative experiences will lead to the ability to mix awareness and experience even during sleep, because we will learn to recognize our dreams for what they are, and those dreams will lead to the experience of the luminosity of mind. In this way, even the waking state and dreaming state are mixed together and thoughts of samsara and nirvana will subside.

We overcome potential distractions and deviations and avoid getting lost through having the proper view. We overcome all kinds of distractions through meditation. We also overcome all the potential problems associated with adverse circumstances as we continue with the practice, because the meditative experiences that we have gained will save us from confusion. The very nature of disturbing thoughts will be revealed as no different from wisdom if we can realize these things and follow these practices. This wisdom is ever-present; it does not decrease or increase in quantity.

THE FREEDOM OF A YOGI

To realize this is to arrive at the original dwelling place (*gdod ma'i gnas-pa*). To arrive at the original place is to establish oneself in the state of nonmeditation. This is the fruition of Dzogchen. Great bliss, or *mahasukha*, is not something you can acquire from elsewhere outside yourself. The ultimate sense of well-being is attained when you arrive at the original place, where all three aspects of buddha's being are completely present. The energy and the power to accomplish your own and others' needs originate from this place and you accomplish this twofold task without exertion. In this state, awareness is constantly present and unbiased.

Someone who has realized this, someone who has come to the original place in this manner is known as a "yogi." A yogi is someone who has achieved realization in this life. Such a yogi has been able to transmute the energies of earth, water, fire, wind, and consciousness into the energy of luminosity. This luminosity adds even more vivacity to wisdom. This is the merging of ultimate reality and wisdom. To have this experience is called "arriving at the original place." A yogi can benefit others and bring light to those who live in darkness through the physical and mental aspects of enlightenment. To realize this, to have come to this stage, is to unlock the secret of the mind.

There is a sense in which we can talk about progression on the path, but this progression should be understood through the analogy of the moon. From the first to the fifteenth of the month, we observe the waxing moon, which appears to be growing. It appears that way to all sentient creatures. However, in reality, there is no actual physical growth taking place, there is no shrinkage or expansion. In a similar way, all sentient beings possess intrinsic awareness, but it is only through meditation practice and through understanding that we come to recognize that this is the case.

Our ability and skill grow and develop as we gain familiarity and experience, while our mind gradually becomes stable and unwavering through meditation. However, while this is how meditators experience the transition, there is no actual increase or decrease in terms of the reality of their own authentic state. This can be demonstrated by observing the moon. Does the lighter part get bigger because the shadowy part is getting smaller, or does the shadowy part get smaller because the lighter part is getting bigger?

In a similar way, does our meditative understanding increase because of a decrease in our obscurations or do our obscurations decrease because of an increase in our meditative understanding? Even when we have become fully enlightened—where all we need to overcome has been overcome, all we need to understand has been understood, and all we need to accomplish has been accomplished—our authentic state has not undergone any change at all. It is just like the moon, in that way.

Once you become enlightened, nothing that you encounter will have the power to disturb you, because you can see that the defilements have no enduring essence or ultimate reality, there are no five poisons to be got rid of and no levels of unsullied, untainted states to be attained. From the Dzogchen perspective, we have not discovered the real secret if we don't approach the spiritual path in this way. By not being able to unlock the secret of the mind, the meditator will constantly struggle and feel torn. There will always be bad aspects to overcome and good aspects to cultivate in order to overpower the bad ones, but approaching and practicing spirituality in this way will only lead to further frustration and eventually to self-defeat. You will be cheated.

Dzogchen meditation is about understanding that the real method is the method of letting things be so that dualistic conceptions fall away by themselves. Otherwise, we may have very high spiritual views, but in reality, we will not make any real progress in our practice because our lofty ideas will not have been brought into contact with what is happening. For as long as we are subject to subtle dualistic conceptions, then even if we can enjoy a modicum of meditative equilibrium, this will only achieve a temporary state of mental well-being. This approach will never deliver lasting peace. No matter how much we try to do better, we will only be dealing with karmic cause and effect. We won't be able to transcend karma.

In Dzogchen practice, the meditator's view should be expansive and open, their meditation should be focused and contained, and their actions should be free from fixation. If whatever they focus their mind on does not lead to mental disturbances, then that person can be seen as a yogi, because they have found real freedom. The yogi is free precisely because they are not bound by the things or situations that present themselves externally. Such a yogi is also free of inner constraints and mental fixation. In that way, such a yogi can go anywhere without fear and without anxiety. They can scale many mountains and cross many valleys without fear. Even if such a yogi does not go anywhere, but just remains at home in their hometown, they can live their life without hope and fear.

TRANSFORMING ADVERSITY ON THE PATH

If the practitioner enjoys certain conditions and is fortunate enough to have an accumulation of merit from the past, the blessings and compassion of the lineage masters, and possession of the appropriate teachings, they are in a unique situation to develop more speedily on the spiritual path. If we have these things, we won't be hampered in our pursuit of spontaneously arisen intrinsic awareness (*lhun-grub rig-pa*). This intrinsic awareness will just reveal itself to us and we will be able to recognize it without fixation. Recognizing intrinsic awareness in this manner is the same as actualizing the dharmakaya, the authentic aspect of buddha's being.

Having realized dharmakaya, everything that we experience

perceptually and conceptually will be experienced from the perspective of dharmakaya. From that point on, we won't need to do anything about our experiences because those experiences themselves will sharpen our ability to transform everything into spiritual realization. Seeing things in this way and becoming accustomed to this type of practice, we will gradually be able to use all kinds of external circumstances and situations and different inner mental states to further ourselves on the path. Even adverse circumstances and situations can be aids for our progress and will no longer be regarded as obstacles.

When we develop the ability to transform adverse circumstances onto the path, we will experience an abiding sense of well-being. Our minds will also become more acute, and we might even begin to develop psychic powers. During our journey on the path, we can expect to have all kinds of spiritual experiences in relation to our spiritual growth. Eventually, we will no longer need to engage in any kind of formal meditation because we will never be separated from bare awareness (*shes-rkyang*), which has the quality of being simultaneously "empty yet luminous" (*stong-gsal*). We will no longer be afflicted by stupor, drowsiness, mental agitation, and so forth. In fact, we will never be distracted so there can be no question of our being attentive or inattentive.

Since we are always in a meditative state, there can be no distinction between the meditative and post-meditative states. Meditation becomes a continuous state of mind because we are established in the state of awareness and are never separated from it. Our awareness never becomes dimmed because we never fixate on our experiences no matter what they are. Without mental fixation and attachment, awareness cannot be corrupted or tarnished. Multitudinous experiences are equalized in the state of intrinsic awareness. We have finally become completely free of fixation on our inner mental states or our external circumstances. This is the experience of Dzogchen.

Having realized the dharmakaya, we begin to see that our physical body has entered the state of nirvana. If we can keep these thoughts about the ultimate goal in mind, we will not deviate from the path. We will gradually develop unusual capacities to deal with the mind and its experiences. Even dream experiences can be worked with as part of our practice. We will gradually develop the ability to change our dreams and can willfully change a bad dream into a good dream. Instead of our dream experiences being beyond our control, we develop the ability to change our thought patterns while dreaming, which means we can introduce change into our karmic history.

Just as smoke emerges from a fire and a sprout from a seedling, our dream experiences will naturally dissipate when we become aware of them and make them part of our meditation. As soon as we recognize what has arisen is a dream, the dream dissipates, and both the dream and the meditation become self-liberated. Meditation is the antidote in this context. Finally, as the meditator continues to use dream practice, they will be able to remain in their natural state, in meditation, and they will no longer have any dreams. You will stop dreaming. Instead, an unceasing luminosity will be present day and night because all our distorted thought patterns have come to cease.

We can thereby attain the nirvanic state through Dream Yoga. The type of nirvana attained here is not a nirvana of quietude, but a nirvana that comes from realizing the nature of mind. The nature of mind can't be changed, conditioned, or improved; it exists in our authentic state. It is a state that is all-encompassing and unbiased, a state of being unaffected by meditation or the lack of it, a state that is spontaneously present. The purpose of Dzogchen is to realize this state. Everything else will become free from that recognition. We will no longer be thinking in terms of outer and inner, subject and object, perceiver and perceived. Even thoughts about what is to be established as real and what is to be established as unreal become self-liberated.

OUR ORIGINAL DWELLING PLACE

The freedom we attain from this realization is not something we can pinpoint, because freedom goes beyond normal concepts of bondage and liberation. When the meditator understands this, they have acquired all-pervasive wisdom (*kun-khyab ye-shes*) and no longer need to be bogged down with thoughts of acceptance and rejection. Since this state of being is unbiased, it doesn't favor one thing as opposed to another. We discover spontaneous great bliss, which is not manufactured, which is not sought after, but which has naturally arisen.

The kind of freedom that we experience is known as "original freedom," "primordial freedom," or "total freedom." This type of freedom is nonconceptual, therefore it is original. It cannot be identified as this or that. It can't even be defined. This original freedom is not something we discover as a new thing. We recognize it as having been there all along. It is freedom attained through awareness, not through overexertion. This kind of original freedom can be experienced when we realize our own true condition, because it is unoriginated, unceasing, non-abiding, and imperceptible. It cannot be grasped by our conceptual apparatus and cannot be adequately expressed through words and sentences. Being in the state of our own true condition is to have a taste of this original freedom.

This original state (*ye-yin gyi ngang*), which has been pure right from the beginning, provides the basis for the most wondrous self-cognizing awareness (*samma-svasamvitti, so-sor rang-rig*). In that original dwelling place, there's no concept of an experiencing subject or an object to be experienced. This state transcends all duality and is a total state of evenness with no fluctuation. It doesn't relate to concepts of time, so days, months, and years don't apply to it. As this state goes beyond the concepts of time and activity, it doesn't relate to our normal perception of the physical world and is devoid of the concepts of mountains, rivers, sun, moon, stars, and so forth.

The original state also goes beyond our concepts of spiritual practice and experience. For example, the visualization of deities, mandalas, mantra recitations, and other practices are completely transcended. The authentic state also goes beyond our psychophysical constituents (*skandhas, phung-po*) because the original dwelling place has not been created. Sometimes it's referred to as "the spontaneously manifesting divine palace."

If we find this original dwelling place, which transcends all conventional thought forms and conceptual categories, we will realize that everything else arises from this source. We will realize that the true deity is uncreated and our normal thought forms and conceptual processes will be transformed into expressions of wisdom. Even our normal perceptions of the physical world will be changed. Our sensory perceptions will become a form of celebration and an offering to divine existence. The sounds we produce can have the same effect as the recitation of mantras. Conflicting emotions will arise as spontaneous insights. Once we gain this glimpse into our own true condition, this change in our experience will happen spontaneously without our needing to exert ourselves in anything.

We begin to traverse the paths and stages of a bodhisattva automatically when we find the original dwelling place. We won't have to try to hold the middle view. We will experience everything as existing in a state of unity because all binary concepts and dualistic notions are purified in that state. We won't be preoccupied by thoughts of cultivation or abandonment because whatever arises will be seen as part of meditation. Without doing anything special, whatever we need to accomplish will be accomplished naturally. Things do not exist in the way the mind divides them. Even the concepts of positive or negative karma are the product of causes and conditions. They don't exist of their own accord, as an independent, self-existing reality.

Longchenpa says that we must realize that nothing has intrinsic reality. It's all just like the reflection in a mirror. A reflection doesn't have any substantial reality; it simply appears due to causes and conditions. In a similar way, nothing we experience has intrinsic reality, but experiences do make their appearance. If we can realize this, everything will become self-liberated. The discriminating mind is responsible for the perpetual existence of samsara and there would be no positive or negative karma without it. When the continuity of the karmic process is ended, we will find ourselves naturally in a state of nirvana.

AVOIDING OBSTACLES AND DEVIATIONS ON THE PATH

A Dzogchen practitioner should realize that, even in terms of your karmic actions, you have to be free of these concepts. At the beginning, you would have to exert yourself to resist unwholesome or negative impulses to avoid creating bad karma, and you should try to create good karma, but you should make the effort to do so without any fixation.

Gradually, as you begin to advance on the path, you should learn to see the existence of karma as contingent upon the discriminating mind. As that is the case, you will stop entertaining overt thoughts of cultivation and abandonment. You should simply focus on your practice and invest all your energy in that, instead of spending too much time thinking about what is to be accepted, what needs to be rejected and so on, and forgetting to focus your mind on what is present.

You should keep company with realized or advanced beings and rely on their instructions and advice, without devaluing the preliminary practices. You should be open to learning what is necessary and then spend time contemplating what you have learned. You should also spend time in retreat and learn how to be alone. It's important to keep your mind focused on practice without getting distracted, to remind yourself constantly about the fragility of life, and to realize the preciousness of your spiritual practice because having the opportunity to practice is not something you can take for granted. Those of us who have that opportunity are very fortunate. You have to remind yourself of this fact, because if you miss an opportunity of this kind, it may not be found again.

If you spend time reflecting on these things, you will stay on track and erect the banner of the practice lineage. You should always ask yourself, "What will happen to me if I die now? How would I handle it?" You must think along these lines and see practice as something you are doing day and night. If you can do that, you won't be so scared of death because you will no longer be simply dwelling in your body, which is a product of causes and conditions and which, at some point, you have to leave behind. You will have found your own original state. In that original dwelling place, as mentioned earlier, there is no concept of coming and going, no concept of birth and death. To rediscover the authentic state of dharmakaya is to be in a state beyond change.

If you can focus your mind on practice in this way, you will have made this life meaningful. Not only will you be able to make this life meaningful, but you can also attain enlightenment in this very life. You will also have the possibility of becoming enlightened in the bardo or post-mortem state. In this way, if your mind stays focused on the path, then by a twist of fate, the karmic seeds that are a product of samsaric existence, which is impure, give rise to liberation, which is pure. You will find your true condition in that way.

A Dzogchen practitioner must contemplate on these things. Otherwise, it is very easy to become side-tracked, and once you have lost your way, there are many places where you can get caught. As a consequence, it won't be possible to find a path that will encourage you to find your original dwelling place. If you lose your way, this life will be full of hardship and pain, and you will leave this world empty-handed.

You should always try to have a proper view and a consistent meditation practice that is always supported by contemplation on love and compassion, because you cannot be a true Mahayana practitioner without bodhicitta. Even when you are practicing Dzogchen, you can never abandon bodhicitta, because without bodhicitta—without love and compassion for others—then even if you are a very good meditator with a regular meditation practice, your character will be hard. Once you develop a hard character, you will become divorced from spirituality.

If you are attached or become fixated on the object of meditation or the techniques of meditation, then you will have no chance of nondual realization. You would also be mistaken if you thought that contemplation on impermanence, the transient nature of everything, is just very basic. If a meditator does not think about impermanence and their own mortality, it is very easy to be overcome by distractions and lose focus. It is important that your meditation doesn't simply become a habit, something you are doing in a routine way. There has to be some sense of your meditation being a novel experience every time you practice. If your meditation practice becomes mechanical, your mind is left completely open to stupor, drowsiness, or mental agitation, because the mind is not alert in that state.

Furthermore, if you only pursue tranquility meditation (*shamatha, gzhi-gnas*) over and over without practicing insight meditation (*vipashyana, lhag-tong*) at all, or you excessively emphasize tranquility meditation and don't properly establish insight, there is a very real possibility that you will get caught up in intellectualism. If you don't practice insight meditation properly, then as you pursue your Dzogchen practice, you may begin to talk about nonduality, unity, and so on, but instead of being able to transform adverse circumstances and situations and use them as part of your spiritual practice, you can be completely overwhelmed by conflicting emotions.

On the other hand, if you do insight meditation but you don't have a proper experience of tranquility, then again you might think you are doing shamatha, but you may in fact simply be in a subtle form of mental stupor. There is no obvious mental disturbance, and due to a lack of experience in shamatha, you may mistake this for tranquility meditation. Even if your tranquility meditation is good, you should not rest with that, but continue to practice tranquility meditation in conjunction with insight meditation. An equal emphasis should be put on both practices.

Once you have achieved the unsullied realization of what is ultimately real through the practice of Dzogchen meditation, your experiences will no longer deviate from that state of contemplation. Everything you experience will aid your approach to enlightenment. Without even trying, you will experience bliss (*sukha, bde-ba*), mental clarity (*abhinvesa, gsal-ba*), and nonconceptuality (*nirvikalpa, mi rtog-pa*). However, if you haven't fully established a proper understanding of what is ultimately real, you will have no basis for building confidence in your experiences.

If you are unable to make full use of the nowness of awareness, even if you engage in regular meditation, you will get too caught up and entangled in obsessive thoughts about what you believe you should abandon and what you should cultivate. Furthermore, without having developed a proper understanding, the mind will become prone to agitation where you think, "I'm having very few of the experiences that I should be having, while the experiences I don't want are multiplying and raining down like a monsoon shower." You will always allow yourself to get frustrated thinking you have not got what you want, that your hopes are unrealized, and you are afflicted by constant doubt.

When you lose the point in this way, even the way you deal with your body, speech, and mind will become distorted and contrived. We may have some sense of well-being, mental clarity, and nonconceptuality, but these experiences will not be real because they are only temporary and frivolous, and we will not gain any lasting profit from them. This is like a baby holding a precious vase. Sooner or later, the baby will drop the vase and it will smash.

These experiences are very fragile and easily lost, so Dzogchen practitioners should always think about gaining an understanding of their true condition. If you can gain an understanding of your own true nature, you will have an unconditional experience of fearlessness and all the wholesome qualities will flow naturally from that. A proper understanding of your true nature can only be discovered through the practice of Dzogchen meditation, where you are able to rest naturally in your own authentic state. This way of approaching meditation is the best and most precious.

There are other methods of meditation that encourage artificial techniques that control our body, contain our speech, and tighten our mind so that the thought flow is stopped. When we practice meditation in this way, we can experience a sense of temporary awareness and achieve a state of mindfulness where we disassociate from all forms of conscious thought and bodily sensations. It is also possible to attain certain absorptive states through this method, where even sensory functions become nonoperational. For example, we may not be visually aware of anything.

However, in terms of our conflicting emotions, such as desire, anger, jealousy, pride, and so on, we don't realize that the conflicting emotions themselves contain seeds for their own liberation by giving rise to wisdom, and we want to get rid of them. Whenever the mind is free from mental agitation and stupor, there is some sort of awareness. We have this attachment to the idea that they need to be abandoned and we diligently apply the methods of abandonment. We may think that just being able to maintain a sense of mindfulness is the same as seeing into the natural condition because of the continuity of our mental states. Meditators may also become obsessed with the idea of watching the mind. They become fixated on watching their thoughts come and go and counting them and mistakenly think that repeatedly practicing this method will lead to the realization of nondual wisdom. However, from the Dzogchen perspective, if we get fixated on any of these methods that involve applying certain techniques, then no matter how much we practice, we will never be able to free ourselves from fixation on ideas and concepts.

Some meditators understand their thoughts to have dissipated because those thoughts have subsided and new ones have risen, and therefore they have achieved some sense of liberation. This is a mistake. When Dzogchen teachings talk about self-liberation, they do not mean that. Self-liberation does not recognize succession. Meditators are also mistaken if they become attached to the idea of all that is wholesome in order to attain future happiness. Here, also, they have not learned to let go of attachment and fixation. For as long as they are fixated on these ideas, they will not attain real freedom. Their future will be either worse off or it might be slightly better than their present condition, but it will not be free.

It is very rare for meditators to see through these kinds of obstacles, shortcomings, and places where they can become lost. With any kind of fixation on the idea of accumulating merit and wisdom—thinking that is what the authentic state means—the meditator would not be able to greatly profit from these practices. As long as we are fixated on the idea of any type of practice, we may gain some benefit, but we will not find true freedom.

Dzogchen practitioners must pray and say to themselves, "Due to my own misfortune and my own karmic inheritance, I am vulnerable, and open to all kinds of deviation and it is so easy to get stuck with a practice that has a limited view." Meditators should generate compassion for anyone this has happened to and pray, "May myself and others have the opportunity to find a path that is undeviating and excellent and by finding such a path, may we be freed."

When the meditator has found the authentic path, then compassion and ultimate reality, which is emptiness, become conjoined. In that instant, we find total liberation in the state of dharmakaya. We are able to enter that state due to the vipashyana experience of discriminating wisdom (*prajna, shes-rab*). We let the mind rest in a state of equanimity (*upeksa, btang-snyoms*) through shamatha practice. Experiences will then be seen as the spontaneous arising of mental phenomena without psychic determinants; it is uncontrived and unconditioned. When we learn to practice meditation this way, the mind will go through changes, but even when distractions and changes occur, we will be at rest. This is what we have to learn to focus on.

We should not discriminate against the traditional meditation obstacles of stupor and agitation and see them as obstructions to meditation. In fact, disturbing and conflicting emotions should be seen as the creative energy (*rtsal ba*) of the mind itself. The conflicting emotions themselves are creative energies that have to be used, precisely because in themselves they have no sense of groundedness or root. In whichever way they manifest, the conflicting emotions can be an occasion for self-liberation. They can lead us to the realization of our own natural state just as we are. When there is actually nothing happening in our mind during meditation, there are no disturbing thoughts and there are no disturbing emotions, and we are simply at rest, we are resting in the nondual condition. That restful state is not something attained apart from whatever has arisen in the mind. We are resting in the mind as it is.

In that way, Dzogchen meditators do not have to worry about what to cultivate and what to abandon; they just rest in the authentic state of the mind. To rest in that state is to find the original wisdom. We have to learn to become accustomed to that, we have to train in this practice. When we find the original wisdom, everything and anything we experience becomes self-liberated. This type of meditation is superior to all others. This is the essence. This method used in Dzogchen contains the essence of all the traditional methods of meditation as well.

TRALEG KYABGON COMMENTARY ON REALIZING FREEDOM ON THE PATH

LEARNING TO REST

Longchenpa is saying that we must be vigilant about maintaining our awareness. We need to think that being aware is the key. You don't need to worry about whether you are meditating properly or whether you are losing track of your meditation. When you worry about those things, there is no awareness. "Vigilance" doesn't mean constantly asking yourself, "Am I aware or not?" You don't need that kind of internal dialogue taking place, just remind yourself again and again to rest and be aware, rest and be aware, that's all.

This is a bit different from the traditional Mahayana practice of awareness. For example, Shantideva's "Meditation" chapter in the *Bodhicharyavatara* says, "Awareness and mindfulness are like having guards posted at the door to keep the thieves out." The thieves are distractions and so forth. For Longchenpa, the guards and the thieves are no different. You are not creating a conflictual situation where you counter your mindfulness and awareness against your mental distractions, so that every time a distraction arises, you apprehend it with mindfulness or awareness. In Dzogchen, just recognizing what is there is enough. That is resting and that is also awareness at the same time. Recognizing is awareness and that is also part of resting.

This is a more relaxed way of handling the whole thing. Instead of beating down the distractions, just recognizing the distractions are there is in itself liberating and relaxing. You do not have to be overly cautious and think, "If I'm not aware, I will get overwhelmed and then I will lose all my awareness and concentration. My meditation will be destroyed, and it will all have been a waste of time." Instead of thinking like that, you should see every distraction as an occasion, not only to become aware, but to realize your own authentic nature, because these distractions are also expressions of your authentic state; they are not separate. As Longchenpa said, it is like ice that has formed on the surface of water. The ice and the water are no different.

Thoughts, ideas, and concepts are both transcended and incorporated. Overcoming thoughts and concepts does not mean that you don't have thoughts and concepts any more. It means that those thoughts and concepts don't lead to distorted ways of thinking, to delusory and illusory belief systems that inhibit you from understanding your own true condition and the condition of the world. That is basically what we have to see through. We don't have to stop thinking altogether or to stop using concepts. We just need to realize that thoughts and concepts are a product of the mind. They have no kind of independent reality of their own. The cultivation of awareness during practice leads to the realization of a natural state of awareness. That natural state of awareness is already present, but we need to cultivate awareness in meditation to realize it. We can't just realize the natural state of awareness without doing anything.

According to tradition, it is possible to become aware while sleeping as well, but I don't think you have to worry too much about that. If you are aware while you are awake, I am sure sleep will take care of itself. The waking state is different from the sleeping state, but on the other hand, they are interrelated. The teachings say that our dream content is a product of and an elaboration on our waking experiences. Whatever state of mind we are in during the day will have an impact on our sleeping hours. If your mind is more focused and aware and has built up more resistance to agitation, worry, and anxiety, that would flow into your sleeping hours as well. Practices like Dream Yoga are done because there is that relationship. According to the teachings, by extension even our after-death experiences are like that. They are different but not altogether dissimilar. Our dream consciousness, sleep consciousness, and waking consciousness all interact and mutually influence and impact on each other. If we cultivate awareness through the practice of meditation, that will also have an impact on our sleeping states. We may not have to do something extra or separate to handle our dream states.

Courage comes into meditation if some violent or vivid emotions or images come up. You do not respond to that by feeling anxious or thinking, "This might overwhelm me, I'm going to lose my concentration, I'm going to lose my awareness and so on." Instead, you should think, "I can handle this, I can maintain awareness in the face of all these things." As Longchenpa said, courage is also about realizing that these vivid emotions are an expression of our authentic state, not something that we have to eradicate. We should incorporate and accommodate them, not encourage or discard them. We don't make the effort to do either. We need courage in the sense of not looking at the whole thing from a dualistic point of view, where we think, "That is the natural state, that is awareness, and they are good things and whatever arises in the mind to upset that state of equilibrium is bad." We will then project all kinds of menacing qualities and attributes onto that emotion and get fearful and anxious, thinking, "I don't have enough resources to deal with this, I will be overwhelmed and fail to maintain awareness." We need to have the courage not to think like that.

You develop courage in proportion to the lessening of your fear because having courage isn't one thing, while being fearful or uncertain is something else. Your level of courage comes from the degree to which you have been able to deal with the things that make you fearful. You just deal with the whole thing in a more practical and very personal way, rather than thinking that a lack of confidence or the presence of fear means you don't have any courage. It's not like that. Just because there is fear does not mean that you can't have courage at the same time. Having the willingness to work with the fear reduces that fear. You develop a sense of fearlessness through that. It is not the case that if one thing is present the other thing must be absent.

Courage can and usually does emerge from not having courage. If we learn to become more patient, we automatically become less impatient. It is the same with courage. Otherwise, we will always fall short of our idealized image of ourselves. We should aim at being completely fearless and courageous and so on, but in reality, on a daily level, we have to grapple with these things. It is not as simple as just *having* courage. You can't have one without the other. You develop courage from the things that you have to overcome. You develop courage by dealing with them, not by ignoring them, or by trying to deny their existence. That is also a part of looking at the whole thing from a nondual point of view. Instead of thinking that a lack of courage is bad and the presence of courage is good, you realize that one can come out of the other. Courage has no relevance to someone who has never known fear. To act courageously is to know fear, but not to get overwhelmed in spite of the fear. A firefighter who rushes into a burning building might be afraid for their own life, but they rush in in spite of that. The firefighter has acted courageously in that instance. It wouldn't be courage otherwise; it would be foolishness, like teenagers doing daredevil activities.

MEDITATION AND POST-MEDITATION
Longchenpa advises us to develop devotion to the lineage masters in the middle point between external and internal, which means between

meditation and everyday experiences. You don't have to be sitting on a cushion in a formal meditative state to do those things. You may be doing all kinds of things externally, but you are also contemplating something internally. The accumulation of merit and the blessings of the lineage masters are dependent on each other. If you have merit, that will be an advantage. You need the blessings of the lineage masters as well. Even if you were not born with a great deal of merit, you can create merit as part of your Buddhist practice. It is never too late. When you contemplate impermanence and the transiency of life, you can see it when you observe things, you can see it when you are doing things, you can see that when you are engaged with the world. The text says we should think about our own death, and we should look around to see that everything else is subject to change as well. Doing that has many benefits. One of the benefits of thinking about impermanence is it brings us back to the present and to noticing and appreciating the moment, rather than getting too caught up with the past or the future, with what might have been or what could be.

Many Westerners think that when Buddhism says that everything is impermanent or like a dream or a mirage, they are saying that nothing is real so why bother. They take impermanence to mean that ultimately nothing really matters, but that is not the proper understanding if it means that you become cavalier or despondent or pessimistic. In fact, if everything is ephemeral, if everything changes, it means that the only time we can be really effective is in the present. The past is gone, it's not there, because of impermanence. The future has not yet come into existence. Even the present moment is in a state of process. In other words, the present becomes more precious and more urgent when we accustom ourselves to this way of thinking. Knowing that everything is subject to change affects us very deeply and personally. We have to open up to that reality and internalize it into our life.

We also need to mix the view and our meditation so that the view doesn't just remain a view but has an effect on our meditation. We don't want the view to just remain an intellectual thing. For example, in going through this text we are learning about the Dzogchen view, but when we also practice what is described here, that view actually begins to show up in our meditation. Longchenpa also says that meditation and post-meditation should be mixed. If we can do that, we will also learn how to mix our daytime experiences and nighttime experiences. If we can mix meditation with everyday experiences while we are awake, we may be able to do that while we are sleeping and even with our dreams. The basic point is that while our formal meditation is extremely important, and we have to do that consistently, we should try to mix our meditation with post-meditation experiences as well. That is important. Meditation is not something you do for a short period but then doesn't relate to anything when you are not sitting on the cushion. It shouldn't be like that.

We will have all kinds of experiences during meditation, for many different reasons, but if we allow ourselves to be aware, then whatever we are experiencing will fall away by itself. We may be feeling a little bit unclear in the mind for a number of reasons, but that is not what we should be concerned about too much. We don't need to be concerned with what caused it; we just need to become aware of that and that is all. If you do that, you are already mixing meditation with everyday life. That is already meditation practice. You don't have to do anything more than that. If you start looking for the reasons for your experiences, you can come up with so many—you might be tired, you might have eaten too much, it may be an upsurge in ignorance, there are all kinds of possibilities. As the teachings say, we can study and we can look for reasons and causes in order to learn about things, but when we are doing meditation, we don't look for whys and wherefores. We just try to be aware of whatever is there. That is all you need to do. That is the practice. Otherwise, as soon as you start to think about why, you have lost awareness.

INTRINSIC AWARENESS

The word "intrinsic" basically means "unconditioned." Awareness or wisdom is intrinsic in the sense of not being dependent upon causes and conditions. Anything that is dependent upon causes and conditions is subject to change because the cluster of causes and conditions will begin to move. If your awareness were dependent on causes and conditions it would change when the conditions change, but as Longchenpa says, awareness is just like the moon in that it never changes because it isn't a product of causes and conditions and is therefore ever-present. Awareness is intrinsic in the sense that it is existing on its own, and it is internal in the sense that it is associated with our consciousness. We can't say that tables and chairs have intrinsic awareness. In terms of experiencing intrinsic awareness, we shouldn't be worrying too much about whether it is internal or external. Just being present, just being aware, is the key thing. It is lhun-grub or "spontaneously established." How is it spontaneously established? It is spontaneously established because it is not an entity, it is not a substance, not even a mental substance.

THE FREEDOM OF A YOGI

Longchenpa says that a yogi can transmute the energies of earth, water, fire, wind, and consciousness into the energy of luminosity. In this case, the five elements refer to the body. The solidity of the body is the earth element, the fluid in the body is the water, the warmth of the body is fire, the cavities are space, and so on. The five elements are all there. Instead of thinking of these elements as something completely physical and our intrinsic awareness or nature of mind as something different, all the elements are affected when you become enlightened. This is related to the idea of rainbow body. The attainment of enlightenment is not just about getting into a mental state; even the body itself is affected by that. The five elements are transmuted into luminosity, in that sense.

If you have attained enlightenment, a rainbow body manifests when the body shrinks at the time of death, because the five elements have been transmuted. The so-called "gross body" of corporeal reality is not seen as some kind of dense matter but as something that is swarming with energies, to use an example from physics. You begin to see the body in that light rather than seeing it as flesh and blood. There is the concept of a vajra body even in tantra. We have a normal body and then we have our vajra body. This has nothing to do with attaining immortality; it is the opposite, in a sense. It is about having a completely different perception of the body so that we don't see it as flesh, veins, arteries, organs, cells, and microorganisms of all kinds. We see it as something that has the potential to be transformed with a change of perception. In other words, to see the body as flesh and blood is only one way of perceiving it. With greater insight, we may perceive the body quite differently. We perceive the body in a particular way when we use a particular mental framework, but when you transcend that framework, you may perceive the body in a completely new way. That already takes place to a certain degree with the difference in perception between someone who knows nothing about how the body functions compared to a biologist or neurologist. Each of them would see the body very differently.

"The nirvana of quietude" basically means nirvana is seen as a form of extinction. The traditional example is that of a lamp, where there has to be wick and oil and so on. When the oil runs out, the flame goes out. In a similar kind of way, when our karma is exhausted, that is a form of extinction. The idea is that you go into a state of nirvanic quietude, so the traditional concept of nirvana is a state of passivity, which is why nirvana is described as "extinction." That is basically the Hinayana concept of nirvana. According to Mahayana Buddhism, and according to the Dzogchen and Mahamudra teachings also, that is not the type of nirvana we should aim toward. We should try to realize non-abiding nirvana. Non-abiding nirvana means that you are not subject to the world of samsara, but you don't dwell in the quietude of nirvana either. You don't abide in either of those two states. This means that we can attain nirvana while we are still in this world. If you can remain in your own original state and maintain your awareness, that is nirvana.

KARMA

According to the Yogacara school of Mahayana Buddhism, you can be compassionately active without leaving karmic imprints.[7] Traditionally, karma is understood like this: first, you learn to create positive karma and try to reduce negative karma; then you learn to create only positive karma and no negative karma at all, and then finally you create no karma whatsoever. That is the understanding of the Mahayana schools, including Yogacarans, but the Yogacarans say you also have to exhaust all your karma, both positive and negative. You have to go beyond karma altogether to be totally free, because even positive karma is ultimately binding. They traditionally use the example of gold chains because whether you are chained in gold or you are chained in iron, you are still in chains. Good karma is also a form of bondage that chains us to samsara, so you must eventually free yourself from that too.

We can free ourselves from karma, but we don't have to go into a state of deep absorption or beyond the world of space and time altogether to do so. You can be a living conscious being who is interacting with others and living in the world in a compassionate fashion without accumulating any karma whatsoever. In other words, when an enlightened being, who has completely exhausted their karma, acts in the world, they may be doing almost exactly the same thing as others. However, they are not really "doing good deeds," fundamentally speaking, because they are completely free. When the Mahayana teachings talk about "non-abiding nirvana," they use the concept of compassion to explain it. It is compassion that stops the realized being from slipping into oblivion, to express it inadequately, but that is really how nirvana is sometimes understood, as some form of extinction.

Just because you are able to perceive and interact with the world does not mean you have to create karma. What is it that creates karma? Karma is created through two avenues: through our conflicting emotions, and through our conceptual distortions. That is what we have to overcome. You don't have to stop seeing, smelling, and hearing things. As Longchenpa is constantly saying, experiences will arise, but all these experiences become self-liberated in the state of awareness. What creates karma is our fixation on those experiences. He says that experiences themselves can be liberating but our fixation on those experiences binds us to the samsaric condition. It is not the case that we have to stop having this or that experience; we just have to learn to not get fixated on them, to not get caught up, embroiled, and entangled. That is what binds us. Basically, the problem is not being able to let go. That is what creates karma. Karma is basically tied up with these habit-forming thoughts and emotions, so when we become fixated, things become repetitious and that is distorting. It is not liberating.

There are differences between the Yogacara approach and Dzogchen. Some Yogacarans have said things that are more idealistic, such as that everything is created by the mind, but that is not the view presented here.

Some commentators say that Asanga and Vasubandhu, the founders of the Yogacara, were not idealists in the Western sense. They did not say that everything is created by mind and so nothing exists externally because there is no such thing as the material world. It was later commentators who became more and more idealistic who were saying that everything is mental. The basic point of Yogacara is just that the world that we perceive is dependent on our karma. The world we perceive is conditioned by the mind but that does not mean that there is no difference at all between the mind and physical things.

TRANSFORMING ADVERSITY

When Longchenpa talks about developing the ability to change our dreams, he is saying that practically all our normal dreams are part of our karmic experience. They may stop when you purify your karma, but that doesn't necessarily mean you will have no dreams at all. There are many Buddhist hagiographies where realized beings have dreams that are significant, unlike our own dreams, which are not really significant. They may be important to us for some reason or another, but they are not really fundamentally significant. Some of the dreams in the hagiographies are considered to be significant because they predict the future or something like that. So enlightened beings may still have dreams, but those dreams are not a product of delusions and nor are they delusion-producing.

ORIGINAL DWELLING PLACE

When Longchenpa says that even our normal perception of the physical world will be changed and our sensory perceptions will become a form of celebration and an offering to the divine existence, he basically means that most of the disturbances of the mind are normally caused by the senses. The senses help to increase our delusions, but through practice, it is possible to have sensory experiences of the world in such a way that this does not happen. What we see, hear, taste, and so on becomes a liberating experience rather than one that leads to attachment, aversion, or other conflicting emotions. When you see that what you experience is liberating rather than constricting, you make an offering of that to the deities. You find it enjoyable, so you offer it to the deities. You often see a skull containing two eyeballs, a nose, and a tongue in the thangka paintings. That represents the offering of the senses. We are doing the same thing when we offer incense, lamps, offering cakes, music, symbols, and so forth. That is another way to make offerings of the five senses.

The tantric vision is to see reality as a divine mansion. We learn to see everything as sacred, as pure appearance. Whatever we see, hear, smell, taste, and touch all become sacred. We normally don't see the sacredness of things because our mind is so impulsive; there is no real freedom of movement in terms of the senses. What Longchenpa is saying is basically the same as what is said in the tantric teachings. You see beings as deities and hear sound as mantra. To see others as deities is just a way of saying that you see all living beings as sacred. They don't necessarily change their appearance. All tantric visualization practices involve both shamatha and vipashyana. You have to focus on what you are visualizing, which is the shamatha component, and you have to realize that what you have visualized is a product of your own imagination and has no substantial reality, which is the vipashyana aspect.

In Dzogchen, vipashyana is about realizing your true condition, as well as all the things Longchenpa has been talking about—not getting fixated, not following the discriminating mind, not getting too bogged down by your notions of good and bad karma, and so on. That is all part of vipashyana meditation. Even terrible experiences can be transformed through Dzogchen vipashyana. On the apparent level of course, they are terrible, but at the same time, if we realize through vipashyana meditation that, horrible though it may be, the experience is not intrinsically real, we may find freedom from that. If you continue to attach reality to those experiences, you are going to be a victim and you are going to be continually subjected to pain and distress.

To be able to do that is to have wisdom, as Longchenpa says. Where does the wisdom come from? It comes from the pain you have experienced. If you realize that the distress that has been brought to your attention is not something that has intrinsic reality, that does not mean you are saying it is not real at all. What you are saying is that its reality is based on all kinds of causes and conditions. One of the primary reasons for that distress is not just what we think has happened but how the mind is responding to that. It comes from how the mind deals with what you think has happened. This is why a group of people could be in exactly the same terrible situation where everyone would agree that what happened to them wasn't so good, but each person might deal with that situation very differently. One person may get over it quite easily, someone else may not be able to let go for some time, and another person may be so traumatized by it that they can't let go at all. Instead of saying, "What happened to me is such a terrible thing," we should look inwardly and see what state of mind has been caused by what we think has happened. What we think happened is not something that exists out there with some kind of intrinsic reality of its own. Its reality or unreality is dependent upon the person.

The Dzogchen method, as this meditation manual keeps reminding us, is about being with whatever it is that we experience. If it's painful, then it is painful. Just recognize that and let it be there, without elaborating on the experience saying, "I'm experiencing distress because of this and that reason, this cause, that past experience," etcetera. Just see that whatever is there, is there, and take notice of that. Awareness and letting go, that is basically what is involved in this practice. Awareness and letting go. Awareness and letting go. It also involves not thinking, "I am trying to let go of this because next time I am sitting in meditation, I don't want to face it again." That is how the mind operates. That is not letting go; it is doing the opposite. If it comes up again, don't get too alarmed, so be it. Let be. If we can do that, then whatever is disturbing the mind will have less power to disturb us. You have to accommodate whatever you experience; accommodate it and allow yourself to be aware of it and then let go. You have to practice those three things: accommodation, awareness, letting go. They are the fundamentals of the practice.

In vipashyana practice, we use discriminating awareness, but that discriminating awareness is different from what we are calling "the discriminating mind." Of course, it is the same mind, but you are thinking differently, because normally with the discriminating mind, there is no awareness, the mind is just operating on automatic pilot. It is so impulsive, automatically judging everything. Judgmentalism, for example, is being discriminating—you are saying, "This is good, this is bad, I like this, I don't like that, I want this, I don't want that." Our mind is operating like that all the time. With vipashyana, with the use of discriminating awareness, we are looking back at the mind to see how it is doing that, to become aware of how the mind normally functions in that way.

You have to analyze things in the context of vipashyana meditation, so it is possible to slide into pure intellectualization in your practice. Vipashyana should not be like that. Discriminating awareness is called *so-sor rtog-pa'i shes-rab* in Tibetan. *So-sor* means "different," *rtog-pa* means "to understand," and *shes-rab* is "awareness" or "insight." With the use of that, you understand emptiness. With the use of that, you understand the insubstantial nature of things. With the use of that, you understand that things do not have inherent existence. That is how you use discriminating awareness.

Otherwise, you could just go on becoming overly intellectual about the whole thing, being pedantic and overly scholastic. As part of spiritual practice, we need to think and we need to learn about the teachings and so forth, but on the other hand, we shouldn't carry it too far and forget how that is related to our practice and our spiritual aims. Learning is a part of the spiritual practice itself. According to Buddhist teachings, the Madhyamaka works of Nagarjuna and Chandrakirti, the Yogacara work of Asanga, and so on, all of the philosophical discussions in those texts, are part of vipashyana practice.

Through reading Nagarjuna you get some understanding of how things actually are and then it makes sense that things are devoid of inherent existence. Then, because of that understanding, you begin to realize that you can't take things too seriously. You can't become too fixated on things, because if everything is devoid of inherent existence, then everything must be dependent upon everything else and therefore it must be subject to change. Knowing this, we become more open to change and to unexpected things happening because our expectation is different. We know that this is how things are. If we don't understand reality this way, we will not be able to overcome our conflicting emotions. On the other hand, if we do understand that everything is dependent upon causes and conditions, we will be able to overcome our conflicting emotions. We don't think about these things because thinking about emptiness is an interesting thing intellectually; we think about them because we want to bring about change in how we perceive things. Philosophical insight and our concerns about spiritual liberation go together. A sound philosophical understanding is part of the whole process of becoming spiritually liberated.

Chapter Three

Spontaneous Fruition

NATURALLY ARISING WISDOM

In Dzogchen, the fruition (*phala, 'bras-bu*) stage is acquired spontaneously. This fruition experience needs to be understood in two different steps: contemporary and subsequent. In the present situation, having developed the proper view and having engaged in meditation, we begin to acquire the relevant qualities and characteristics of spiritual development. Therefore, even now, in the present context, we are able to let go of our fixation on conflicting emotions, whereby the conflicting emotions begin to dissolve by themselves. When we can let go of our fixation on internal and external conditions, instead of being their victims, we gain power over them.

We achieve this by becoming very attuned and sensitive to everything taking place in our inner and outer experiences. When we are attuned to whatever is occurring, we begin to see things more clearly, hear things more clearly, and engage in physical activities in a more proficient manner. These extraordinary faculties and abilities are developed as a result of increased understanding and naturally arising compassion for others. When we come to this point, there is nothing but awareness (rigpa), and that awareness is not different from wisdom (yeshe). That awareness has become wisdom.

Dzogchen meditators are able to make use of every perceptual experience in their lives as part of the skillful means to further their spiritual progress. Our daily perceptual experiences can be seen as no different from the tantric development and fulfillment or completion stages, where we visualize deities, recite mantras, and so on, because we can relinquish whatever conflicting emotions or perceptual experiences we have at any given moment. When we can let go of these disturbing emotions, insight into the nonsubstantiality of those experiences will arise. That insight is the same as the wisdom of Dzogchen.

The Dzogchen meditator has finally come to the realization that awareness and delusion are coextensive. One exists because of the other. But the Dzogchen meditator has to let go of even that concept. Even the notion that they are coextensive, coexistent, and interdependent is let go. We have found total freedom and are no longer given to stinginess or bouts of aggression, no longer susceptible to laziness, unskillful conduct, feelings of worthlessness, or self-deprecating attitudes. We are free of all those things because they are orientated toward dimming our awareness, not enhancing it.

Our awareness has been able to illuminate the ten directions that had been dimmed by our delusory mental states. As a matter of fact, without even trying, we are more generous, patient, and vigorous. We can conduct ourselves properly, engage in meditation with attentiveness, and give rise to insight. Instead of having to work to attain those qualities, they are realized naturally, automatically, and spontaneously. In addition to the usual six paramitas of generosity, ethical conduct, patience, vigor, concentration, and discriminating wisdom, we also realize the other paramitas described in Mahayana literature: the paramitas of means (*upaya, thabs*), power (*bala, stobs*), aspiration (*pranidhana, smon-lam*), and primordial wisdom (*jnana, ye-shes*).

BODHISATTVA PATHS AND STAGES

We have come to understand this realization of our own natural state through practice and also through the blessings of the lineage masters. It is not something we have managed through our own efforts alone; it's more of a cooperative effort. Our own effort and the blessings of the lineage masters coming together bring joy and happiness into our stream of consciousness, because we realize that no disturbing emotions can leave lasting traces of defilements or vitiation in our stream of consciousness. According to the Dzogchen tradition, when we realize this, we have attained the first bodhisattva stage (*bhumi, sa*), which is called "pure joy"(*pramudita-bhumi, ra-tu dga-ba sa*).

We next realize that the meditative experiences we endure have the qualities of bliss, luminosity, and nonconceptuality and are the portentous illumination of the lights of wisdom. That realization corresponds to the second bodhisattva stage called "immaculateness" (*vimala-bhumi, dri-ma med-pa sa*).

Then we realize that all the experiences we have in our lives can be understood and therefore nothing is an obstruction on our path. That realization corresponds to the third bodhisattva stage known as "greater illumination" (*prabhakari-bhumi, 'od-byed-pa sa*).

Next, we realize that all views of the self are insubstantial, which corresponds to the fourth bodhisattva stage called "brilliant shining" (*arcismati-bhumi, 'od phro ba sa*).

The experiences that we attain are not something that just anyone can have. They are only available to someone who practices Dzogchen. Realizing this corresponds to the fifth bodhisattva stage entitled "difficult to attain" (*sudurjaya-bhumi, shin-tu sbyangs-dka'-ba sa*).

Whatever we experienced through and from meditation is now actualized so that what was once dormant is now manifest. This corresponds to the sixth bodhisattva stage called "actualization" (*abhimukhi-bhumi, mngon-du-gyur sa*).

We gradually leave all the disturbing experiences of the past behind and have gone a long way toward enlightenment. This corresponds to the seventh bodhisattva stage known as "gone far"(*durangama-bhumi, ring-du-song sa*), because the samsaric condition has really been left behind.

We are now more and more able to maintain the meditative state during both meditation and post-meditation, which corresponds to the eighth bodhisattva stage called "non-waveringness" (*acala-bhumi, mi-gyo sa*).

When we can always maintain a meditative state, we have become enlightened and have attained the level of ultimate knowledge, which corresponds to the ninth bodhisattva stage entitled "supreme intellect" or "knowledge" (*sadhumati-bhumi, legs-pa'i blo-gros sa*).

This leads to the tenth bodhisattva stage known as "the cloud of Dharma" (*dharmamegha-bhumi, chos-kyi-sprin sa*), which basically means we are enveloped in a cloud of spiritual qualities. Clouds portend rain when they gather, just as the rain of spiritual benefit can pour down from this gathering of enlightened qualities.

The paths and stages of the bodhisattva can thus be traversed very quickly through Dzogchen practice because we cultivate both wisdom and merit when we see into the true nature of our own condition. When you can really look into your natural state, you will become free. The paths and stages refer to just that. They are about the degrees of our own natural state.

A Dzogchen meditator should let go of thoughts of the three times of past, present, and future, and in fact, not even reflect too much on the three baskets of the teachings, the Vinaya, Sutra, and Abhidharma baskets. They are also present in Dzogchen.[8] You will purify your body, speech, and mind through Dzogchen practice and you will be able to genuinely practice shila, samadhi, and prajna: ethical conduct (*shila, tshul-khrims*), meditative equipoise (*samadhi, ting-nge-'dzin*), and discriminating wisdom (*prajna, shes-rab*). As such, you will know that anything and everything can be liberated. To know that is everything. Nothing is superior to yogic experience.

We may talk about the tantric teachings, but if we employ some kind of hermeneutic imagination, we can see that all the tantras are embodied in the Dzogchen teachings. If we look at the whole thing from a Dzogchen perspective, there are nine yanas and they can all be viewed this way.[9] The first four tantras correspond to the Sravakayana, kriya-yoga corresponds to the Mahayana, becoming familiarized with that is upaya-yoga, practicing that is yoga, and combining wisdom and method is maha-yoga and anu-yoga. Actualizing all of them is ati-yoga or Dzogchen.

Dzogchen practice incorporates everything, including the recitation of mantras and meditations that give rise to wisdom, but all of its practices are orientated toward self-liberation. All the paths and stages that lead to ultimate enlightenment are therefore embodied in this practice and the natural wisdom that comes from having realized our own natural mind is Mahamudra. The condition of being complete (*rdzogs*) is already spontaneously present. We might think it is something we have obtained because of engaging in a long process of practice, but it's not something we have found anew. We discover that it has been there right from the beginning.

This stage is referred to by many terms, like "dharmakaya," "buddha-fields," and so on, but it is really beyond description. This is where the original sphere (*dharmadhatu, chos-kyi dbying*) and the original wisdom (*gdod-ma'i ye-shes*) merge. Nothing remains but one-taste (*ekarasa, ro-gcig*) where the three aspects of buddha's being are actualized. Even the subtlest forms of wisdom now become apparent. This is what "omniscience" means in this particular context. When we rest in that state, we realize that our own natural condition is spontaneously established, uncaused, and unceasing, just like space. The mind can engage in all forms of creative imagination in that state because mind is by nature self-illuminating. The mind can create the various mandalas associated with the five buddha-families and then everything we experience becomes a manifestation of these creative imaginings.[10] Everything we experience will reflect our capacity to express our natural condition through the five wisdoms.

ENLIGHTENED ACTIVITY

One's mind has become completely transformed through Dzogchen practice and one begins to see everything in a different way. One is able to make an impact on whatever is going on in the ten directions and four times. One can act in the sphere of mandala and interact with everything from the point of view of the five buddha-families. One's own presence goes above, below, vertical, and horizontal, so that it is like space itself. One's own presence becomes like an opening or an aperture. Basically, one has the sense of actually reaching out, instead of feeling enclosed, and one begins to make contact with others in such a way that it corresponds to the needs of other individuals. Those individuals begin to get some sense of what existence is all about. Doing that is like enacting within the mandala itself, in tantric language. One is acting like the deities one has visualized, but in real life.

As a Dzogchen practitioner, one has now attained total equanimity whereby there is no center or periphery and one is no longer fixated on the idea of the three times. The only time that one thinks of is eternal time, the time of Kuntuzangpo.[11] In that original time of Kuntuzangpo, there is no increase, decrease, or transition. Nothing of the kind exists. However, everything has arisen from that state, including our own embodiment, which is now the physical embodiment of the buddha. Various buddha-fields are described in the sutras, such as Mirngawa, Rinchen, Pemazig, Lerabtu, and so forth, but the buddha-fields in the sutras are not places that you can go. They are actually referring to the original place of timelessness of Kuntuzangpo. That is where you will find everything you have been looking for, in relation to the Buddhas of the three times, the five buddha-families, and the ten bodhisattva stages.

Dzogchen meditation brings us to where we belong, where we are, and everything is already there to be discovered. Having realized that, we can also go into the dimensions of the sambhogakaya, which is separate from our tangible physical condition. As we begin to traverse the various paths and stages, our mind becomes more resilient, aware, and luminous, so that we begin to see everything in a different way. Everything we experience then is associated with the buddha-fields. From this perspective, even our perception of other beings becomes transformed. Even physical objects, such as artifacts, bridges, medicines, precious jewels, illuminating objects, and all the things that people like and want, are seen as things that were brought about willfully by compassionate minds. Nothing in this world is regarded as meaningless. As long as there are needy people, these things should exist for the enjoyment of everyone, and as long as there are needy people, there should be people who are there to help them. The only time we begin to stop caring is when people are no longer in need of love, care, and compassion.

However, there may come a time when the objects of compassion no longer manifest due to changing cosmological catastrophes. For example, this earth could be destroyed, and then no needy people will be left on this earth. We cannot have the reflections of the moon on water if there is no container for that water.

There is also a sense of evolution, insofar as the centrifugal movement of going out to reach others is operating, but concurrently there is the centripetal movement of withdrawing inward into oneself where one finds peace. In that state, even the energies of the five buddha-families that one has been using will be transmuted back into oneself, because the five buddha-families are just natural expressions of the sambhogakaya. So, there is the centrifugal evolution of going outward and there is the centripetal devolution of withdrawing. The image of the waning moon is used to refer to devolution, where one is going inside into the state of dharmakaya.

First, there is the nirmanakaya, with all the expressions of compassion and so forth. Then there are the energies of the five buddha-families expressed through the sambhogakaya. And finally, there is the dharmakaya of entering into the state of undifferentiatedness. Even the sambhogakaya is dissolved into that dharmakaya state. There is no inner or outer anymore, instead one is in the state of mandala. There is no before or after, no concept of increase or decrease, or change of any kind.

However, from that state, evolution can again take place. The centrifugal movement takes place again because there may be other objects of concern that will bring that individual out from the state of impassivity, the state of contemplation. If there are other beings that one should have concern for, then just as before, one would begin to act in ways that would benefit others.

Lamrim Nyingpo—The Essential Stages of the Path
Longchenpa's auto-commentary on the root text of the Mind Cycle

Chapter Four
Retreat Instructions—Pith Instructions for the Paths and Stages

1. WHAT TO PRACTICE IN THIS LIFE

The Buddha, through his skillful means and compassion, expounded the teachings on many different levels in accordance with the personalities and predispositions of varied individuals. While these teachings have been systematized into different vehicles, they are all directed toward the one goal of enlightenment. There are many different ways to cultivate the enlightened mind, but even here, all the different approaches and methods can be reduced to developing an understanding of the dissatisfactory nature of the samsaric condition. It is usually said in the teachings, "The best way to understand this dissatisfactory nature is to cut off our ties to samsara." But here, we are approaching the teachings from the Dzogchen perspective, which encourages us, the practitioners, to attain liberation in this very life. The whole of this text, *Natural Freedom of the Mind*, is devoted to this.

To practice Dzogchen properly, we have to understand three things. First, we need to have some concept of lineage; then we need to understand how the teachings have been transmitted. Finally, we have to develop some appreciation for the profundity of the teachings.

In terms of the lineage, in brief, the transmission has taken place from the time of the primordial Buddha, Kuntuzangpo (Samantabhadra), the dharmakaya manifestation, the Adi-Buddha in dharmakaya form, who transmits the teachings to the sambhogakaya aspect, represented by Vajrasattva. From there, the sambhogakaya manifestation transmits them to the nirmanakaya representation of enlightenment, represented by

Padmasambhava.[12] Padmasambhava was the first living human recipient of these teachings. Padmasambhava transmitted them to his consort, Yeshe Tsogyal, and Yeshe Tsogyal transmitted them to Shri Singha, who transmitted them to Katub Delek, who gave them to Chojye Melong Osel. Longchenpa himself received them from Chojye Melong Osel. That is the summary of the lineage transmission.

Now to understand the teachings that are being transmitted. Their content is about cultivating the teachings in this life and doing it in such a way that we learn the techniques of self-liberation. We are also taught about the intermediary stage between death and rebirth so that we can have an experience of luminosity in that state. Finally, we learn how to attain enlightenment.

To acquaint ourselves with the practice of self-liberation, as taught in the Dzogchen teachings, we must approach the practice in three stages: ngondro, nyuge, and gyesum—the preliminaries, the main practice, and the final part. These are the beginning, middle, and final stages of practice.

PRELIMINARIES

Guru Yoga

To practice the preliminaries (*sngon 'gro*), we must begin with the practice of Guru Yoga, because we have to make some connection to the lineage itself. To do Guru Yoga, you should sit comfortably on a cushion, take refuge in the Triple Gem,[13] and then generate bodhicitta by contemplating the Four Infinities of love, compassion, joy, and equanimity. Then you should spontaneously visualize a lotus on the crown of your head, upon which rests a sun disk and moon disk with Guru Padmasambhava sitting upon them. Padmasambhava is inseparable from your own lineage master and displays all the necessary qualities of an enlightened being. In this case, Guru Padmasambhava is not clothed, but manifests as a heruka or siddha. His complexion is light blue, and he is holding a bell and a vajra. He is embracing his consort with his left arm and is adorned with bone ornaments. His consort is sitting on his lap, holding a skull cup filled with blood in her left hand and a hooked knife in her right hand. She has her left arm wrapped around Guru Padmasambhava.

You should then visualize all the lineage masters and numberless buddhas, bodhisattvas, dakas, and dakinis surrounding this mandala. While not actually doing prostrations, think, "I am prostrating to this mandala that has appeared." You then make offerings and confess your transgressions, so that all the things you feel regretful about are revealed. Then you rejoice in the enlightened activities of the lineage masters and request the guru to turn the wheel of the Dharma. Finally, you should request Guru Padmasambhava, who is inseparable from your own lineage master, to remain in the world and not pass into nirvana. This is the Seven-Limb Prayer. Other prayers have also been written to accompany this practice. Then you should say:

> With the blessings of Guru Padmasambhava, please purify my physical, verbal, and mental defilements and obscurations, so that my body will be transformed into an enlightened body, my speech will become enlightened speech, my mind will become enlightened mind, and I will attain enlightenment in this very lifetime. Please grant your blessings for that accomplishment.

After saying these things, imagine lights emanating from Guru Padmasambhava to all those present. These lights radiate out and envelop you and all sentient beings. As the lights begin to descend, they gradually purify the physical, verbal, and mental defilements of all sentient beings. Then you should think that everyone's defilements, obscurations, and negativities have been removed and expelled, and all living beings have become one with the nature of Guru Padmasambhava. Their nature and the nature of Guru Padmasambhava have become inseparable. These lights radiate from different centers of Guru Padmasambhava's body. White light radiates from his forehead, red light from his throat, and blue light from his heart. These lights enter into your own body through the crown of your head until they completely fill your body. As your body becomes filled with these lights, think:

> I am having an enlightened experience right now—the experiences of bliss, nonconceptuality, and clarity.

Perform this meditation for some time and then conclude by dedicating the merit for the benefit of all sentient beings. In retreat, you should do this practice intensely for seven days. If you practice intensely like this for a week, you will feel the blessings.

Mandala offering

In the space before you, visualize the *yidam*, your own tutelary deity, as the object of your offering. Hold a mandala disk and start piling rice on that disk and with each handful of rice, you represent the whole physical universe, as well as everything that is precious within it. You should include everything that is desired by humans and gods. Don't just offer things that are desirable materially; imagine you are offering all that is good within yourself, such as your merit and positive qualities. As you offer the mandala, think,

> Everyone who is present in front of me is extremely pleased and joyous because of this offering.

Again, you do the practice of mandala offering day and night for seven days. You will increase the two accumulations of wisdom and merit through this practice, which will create the right mental state for spiritual experiences.

Vajrasattva

You should visualize yourself spontaneously within emptiness as Vajrasattva. You are white in color, with one face and two hands, a vajra in the right hand and a bell in the left, adorned with precious jewelry and sitting cross-legged. Then visualize a lotus in your heart chakra, upon which sits a moon disk. In the center of the disk, you should visualize the seed syllable HUNG. The hundred-syllable mantra of Vajrasattva revolves in a clockwise direction around this HUNG. Light radiates from the mantra and spreads in all directions, purifying the defilements of all sentient beings and yourself. As you visualize the revolution of this hundred-syllable mantra around the HUNG, recite the hundred syllables as many times as you can. You also do this practice for seven days. Vajrasattva has the power to purify all the "hard to remove" defilements.

Contemplating impermanence

Once you have completed the above practices, you should spend time contemplating your own mortality and impermanence as part of the preliminary practices. Contemplate the difficulty of acquiring a human birth and the ease with which it can be lost once it is acquired. Not only can your own life end; everything that exists is subject to dissolution, disintegration, and death. You should think of your own death in this way and about all the people you have been close to who have died, and say to yourself:

> One day, I will also be separated from this body,
> which for now I identify as myself.
> Life is as a bubble that can burst at any time.
> I can't say I won't die today.
> It is certain that we all will die.
> Since our body is based on the harmonious workings
> of the five elements, it is very fragile,
> so each day could be my last.

Do this contemplation on impermanence for a further seven days. Constantly thinking about impermanence will help you to see the urgency of practice. This is the best antidote to complacency and laziness and encourages you to apply yourself vigorously to the spiritual path.

Taking refuge

In the space before you, visualize the buddhas and bodhisattvas of the ten directions and three times, your personal deity, the mandalas of the various deities, the sravakas, and everyone else. In other words, you should visualize everyone who is worthy of giving refuge. You should also visualize the body of teachings in the form of texts, and the community of practitioners, so that Buddha, Dharma, and Sangha are all present in front of you, and say:

> Until I attain enlightenment, I will need assistance,
> So I request you to be my guide.
> I want to take refuge in you.

You should recite the refuge formula while doing this and visualize all the enlightened beings present in front of you, thinking that they are endowed with infinite love and compassion. You should think their compassion for you is just as intense, if not more so, than that of a father and mother toward their child. Then think:

I am feeling their compassion and their love. I am being loved
and accepted by them.

You should generate intense emotion from the heart, so that you feel
it in the very marrow of your bones. At the same time, imagine that all
sentient beings are participating in your refuge practice. As you recite the
refuge formula, imagine that others are doing the same. The refuge
practice should again be done for seven days. The benefit of taking refuge
is that you can clear away the obstacles to practice and the disruptions,
interruptions, and disturbances that distract the mind. This will help to
strengthen your practice and realization.

Bodhicitta

The sixth aspect of the preliminary practice is bodhicitta, cultivating
the enlightened heart. We develop the enlightened heart by
contemplating the suffering experienced by different beings through
different mental states. They experience the suffering associated with heat
and cold, the suffering of being subjected to hard labor, the suffering that
is involved with the aging process, the suffering that is present in the birth
process, the suffering of ill health, the suffering that arises from death and
dying, the suffering experienced in relation to conflict and wars, and the
suffering experienced when good things come to an end or when things
that are cherished and loved suddenly disappear.

In order to develop bodhicitta, you should evoke images in your mind
of the various stages and kinds of suffering that living beings endure.
Remind yourself that there are always living creatures afflicted with
various forms of physical and mental torment. Then remind yourself that
the suffering, pain, and distress that beings are subject to is not unnatural.
These beings are in a great deal of pain, and they crave relief from that
pain. We also need to recognize that being subjected to continued
suffering produces a sense of apathy. With this attitude, you should
contemplate the Four Infinities of love, compassion, joy, and equanimity.
If sentient beings have problems with physical health or physical
deprivation, think:

May those who are sick have their health restored.

May those who don't have enough to eat
and suffer from endemic impoverishment,
have wealth and prosperity.

In that way, you imagine the appropriate causes and conditions coming together to bring sentient beings temporal happiness and you visualize them as free of suffering. The suffering that human beings and other creatures experience is caused by feelings of being near and distant, of excessive attachment and excessive anger, so imagine that sentient beings have found some kind of relief from these physical and mental torments.

What you have visualized so far is that the appropriate circumstances and situations for increasing the volume of happiness in the experience of all sentient beings are present and the causes and conditions that bring suffering, pain, and distress are absent. However, so far you have only dealt with the experiences of temporal happiness. You now have to go further and venture into the domain of spirituality.

Here, you not only wish that sentient beings have more happiness and less suffering, but you also wish they will eventually develop the capacity to attain ultimate happiness, which can only be obtained through and from the achievement of full enlightenment. In other words, your wish is that they become fully realized buddhas. While you are practicing this mind-training exercise, you should also recite the formula of bodhicitta, the contemplations on love, compassion, joy, and equanimity. For example, you could be reciting the following:

Through the blessings of the Great Liberator, his sons and
daughters,
please pay attention to me.
As the Conquerors of the past engaged in the practice of
bodhicitta,
As the Conquerors of the present continue to practice
bodhicitta,
And as the Conquerors of the future will practice
bodhicitta,
I, too, would like to engage in this practice, to benefit
myself and other living beings.

Just as the previous Victorious Ones had to familiarize
themselves with the enlightened teachings,
I, too, wish to receive the teachings and familiarize myself
with them. Through this, may I be able to alleviate the
suffering and pain experienced by myself and other
sentient beings.
May whatever I do as a result be of benefit to all living
beings.

When you engage in this practice, you should not be thinking, "I want
to get rid of my own suffering." Instead, you should think, "I want to take
on the suffering of others and give them whatever pleasure, comfort, and
happiness I have experienced or am currently experiencing." In this way,
your mental attitude has to be completely turned around. Normally, we
selfishly want to hang onto everything that gives us pleasure and do
anything to decrease the level of our own suffering.

You should meditate on bodhicitta for seven days in your retreat
situation, just as in the other preliminary practices. The benefits of doing
this practice are that your whole being, in terms of your body, speech,
and mind, will be transformed, because the way you are putting them to
use has been radically transformed. Instead of being self-centered, you
learn to be other-centered, and you become a true practitioner of the
Mahayana, which emphasizes the value and importance of love and
compassion.

Shamatha and vipashyana meditation

The seventh aspect of the preliminary practice is about realizing
ultimate reality. This part of the practice must be done by seriously
engaging in tranquility or shamatha meditation and insight meditation
and then learning to combine the two, without overemphasizing one or
the other.

Tranquility meditation: To practice tranquility meditation, you first
sit cross-legged and settle yourself in that posture, then mentally learn
how to be present. How does one become present? You become present
by not following past thoughts, not anticipating future thoughts, and
not allowing yourself to get caught up in present thoughts.

You practice shamatha meditation for another seven days. The benefit of doing this is that you will learn to deal with your mental states. You will stop the mind from continually ruling you and producing ever more negative thoughts and emotions. You will thereby gain some control over your mental processes and your level of awareness (*jneya, shes-bzhin*) will naturally increase. This will make it possible for you to be more observant so that you can detect the various levels of thoughts and emotions, as well as your various conscious and subconscious states of mind.

Insight or vipashyana meditation: In the context of insight meditation, you are concerned with paying more attention to your thoughts and emotions and your whole range of mental states. You learn to pay attention to these mental states by not rejecting thoughts and emotions. As thoughts arise, you should analyze them by asking yourself, "What is the process by which this thought has been manufactured?" When you think about any object of attention, ask yourself:

Am I thinking in my head?
Am I thinking in my stomach?
Am I thinking in my toe?
Where does this thought reside?
Does this thought or emotion, that seems to have such a powerful effect on my mind and body, have any material form?
Does it have any color?

As you continue to regularly probe in this way, you will gradually see that what appeared to be so powerful, forceful, and real, is actually insubstantial. It is your lack of familiarity with thoughts and emotions that gives rise to the idea that they are real and powerful, but the more you pay attention and the more observant you become, the more elusive your thoughts and emotions will be. You will see that they are intangible and don't reside anywhere. In that way, thoughts and emotions become more transparent and less dense. To understand that is to have vipashyana insight.

A good meditator should not get attached to that understanding. You must even let go of the understanding that you acquire about the nature of thoughts and emotions. In other words, everything you experience should be allowed to come and go like clouds. This means you don't need to suppress anything, deny anything, or reject anything. Just as clouds do not leave any traces as they dissipate, our thoughts and emotions are without trace. The stronger the imprints we make in our minds, the more consolidated our karmic habits become. Through vipashyana practice, our thoughts and emotions become self-liberated; they dissipate on the spot, as they arise. The benefit of vipashyana practice comes from understanding that nothing you experience can be hung onto or fixated upon because everything you experience is as insubstantial as a cloud. That concludes the preliminary practices.

MAIN PRACTICE

Three aspects of mind

Having engaged in the preliminary practices (*ngondro*) we now turn to the main practice (*nyuge*). Here, the meditator first has to learn to integrate body and mind. This integration takes place by relaxing the mind and relaxing the body. If the body is tense and the mind is in a state of intensity, you cannot find your present state of being, you can't grasp what is present in the mind, but when the body and mind relax, you can catch the moment of being aware.

To arrest that moment, you need to realize that all the things you think about, conceptualize, and project onto external situations and circumstances are a result of the workings of the mind itself. What we understand as being external is not totally extraneous to the workings of the mind. Even the notions of samsara and nirvana, bondage and liberation, are dependent on the mind. You need to recognize that the mind is capable of being incredibly productive and creative in its production of images and experiences, just like the dreams we all experience.

You have to understand what mind is—the mind that is so productive, creative, and versatile in its ability to create images. What is that mind? When you focus on the mind during practice, you will come to realize that it has three aspects, its nature (*ngo-bo*), its essence (*rang-bzhin*), and its characteristic (*thugs rje*).

The mind is empty by nature (*ngo-bo stong-pa*) because it is not something that we can grasp onto or identify as this or that. It is not an entity, not a thing. The nature of mind is elusive because it is empty. We will never find a mind that has the characteristics of being an entity of any kind. Its essence is luminosity (*rang-bzhin gsal-ba*) because while we can't pin the mind down as anything or fully grasp it, mind has the capacity to be cognizant of everything that happens. The characteristic of mind is its responsiveness or creative energy (*thugs-rje kun-khyab*) because anything and everything that we experience in the world emanates from that same mind.

Just like a well-polished mirror, the mind is by nature empty of images. The mirror has the capacity to project light. You can put physical objects of all descriptions in front of it and the mirror will accommodate them all. Whether that is a grotesque thing, like a decapitated pig's head, or uplifting, like a statue of the Buddha, the mirror does not accept or reject. The mind also has that capacity and everything and anything can take place there.

You need to know that the mind operates in this fashion. Mind is elusive because it can't be grasped or pinned down as anything, but it also has the capacity to be aware. Even though you can't get hold of it, mind is still aware, and because it's aware, we have many different types of experiences, but we shouldn't get fixated on any of them as they arise. Mind should therefore be left alone, because the more you identify your experiences and put labels on them, the greater your fixation on those experiences, and your thoughts and concepts will proliferate more and more. The mind will just go on a rampage.

How should you deal with this mind that is so prolific in the production of thoughts, concepts, ideas, beliefs, emotions, and feelings? You deal with it by trying to be in the present. When you become attentive in the present moment during meditation, you will see that the mind produces all kinds of thoughts, emotions, aspirations, dreams, frustrations, and anxieties. That is the very mind you need to work with. There is no alternative. We have to work with whatever comes to mind. The great master (*maha-acharya, loppon-chenpo*), Guru Padmasambhava, gives this advice:

Knowing that our thoughts, concepts, and ideas are no different from our own natural state, we don't need to meditate on dharmadhatu as somewhere else or something different. It is enough to know that the method of realizing the nature of thoughts is the very method that will lead to liberation. Thoughts and concepts embody our own authentic state, so using thoughts and concepts in this manner is the supreme path, because everything we experience internally and through the senses becomes sublime through this approach. We no longer pursue ideas of rejecting or abandoning concepts and thoughts because to think of experiences in life as our enemies means we have lost ourselves.

It is obviously so important to learn to focus the mind on your present mental state. When you focus your mind on the present, you don't try to introduce any changes to it, but instead learn to relax into the mind of the present moment by letting yourself go naturally. No matter what arises in the mind, don't try to exaggerate it, elaborate upon it, disown it, or reject it. When you don't do any of those things, you will be able to relax into the mental state of presence effortlessly and with a sense of ease.

What happens when you are in that moment of total awareness? You will observe all three aspects of the mind. In terms of its nature, you will see that the mind is unidentifiable, because it has no intrinsic identity of its own. In terms of its essence, you will realize that being aware of the present moment is in itself part of mind. When you become aware of all the things that are going on in the mind, you will recognize its characteristic. By recognizing the nature of mind in this way, you will find liberation through recognition (*stong-grol*). Understanding that the mind has the cognitive ability to be aware, you will find liberation through understanding (*shes-grol*). Having understood that mind can produce varieties of thoughts, concepts, ideas, emotions, and feelings, you will find natural freedom (*rang-grol*). You will thereby achieve liberation through all three aspects of the mind.

You should not latch onto anything that arises in the mind but instead generate awareness and learn to be in a meditative state while having these experiences. That is the key. When there is awareness, we will find our own natural completion. This kind of experience does not arise because you are striving for it with a sense of vehemence; it arises naturally when you allow yourself to be in the present. It does not come about through thinking, "I shouldn't have this experience" or "I want that experience," but through allowing your mind to rest in the present moment. When that occurs, there is bliss, clarity, and a reduction in mental activity and that is no different from having wisdom. To have wisdom is to have that.

Self-liberation

Once that awareness is established, it is not contingent on external factors. It does not increase or decrease. It remains stable. The key point is to always be present in the moment. You place your focus on the present mental state. You don't need to do anything else because to be aware of whatever is present in the mind naturally leads to freedom. Just having awareness will allow you to attain natural liberation. It is not the case that you first become aware and then you find liberation; to be aware and to find liberation are one and the same thing. They occur simultaneously.

Don't try to do anything with your mental state in the moment that thoughts and emotions dissipate during meditation. Just dwell in that moment before another thought or emotion arises. When another thought or emotion does arise, don't try to identify it as this or that. Just maintain a simple sense of awareness. In other words, you rest the mind through a sense of relaxation, stabilize the mind through the recognition of distraction, and release the mind by not grasping onto it.

The mind should be seen as a container with a hole in the bottom. If you put things into that container, it will not be able to hold them and whatever you put in will fall out as soon as you pick up the container. In a similar fashion, a mind that is aware does not hold onto anything. As soon as things arise in the mind, it has the capacity to let go, moment by moment, instantaneously. When mind can let go of its thoughts and emotions, we can have the experience of self-liberation. This process of self-liberation occurs when the mind is not focused on any particular direction, and we have become accustomed to that openness.

In brief, whatever arises in the mind has the potential to become liberated. This means that whatever experience you may be having, it is compatible with the proper view and meditation. All your experiences are now self-presencing (*rang-shar*), whereby thoughts of cultivation and rejection are no longer a concern. In that way, your samsaric and nirvanic experiences, and your delusory and liberating thoughts, all manifest as expressions of your own authentic condition.

Meditation will become an unceasing activity. It is not the case that there is no meditation when delusions occur and there is meditation when liberating thoughts occur. It's not like that. You have realized the importance and the role of awareness. When awareness is present, thoughts and emotions are seen to be devoid of substantiality. They are neither delusory nor liberating. One finds freedom through that. This is precisely the way conflicting emotions are transformed into wisdom. This is also how we begin to develop the necessary qualities of an enlightened being. These qualities develop naturally however, without your having to exert yourself or apply yourself with vigorous obsession.

How is this possible? It is possible because the whole gamut of our experiences, from the samsaric mind of delusion to the nirvanic mind of enlightenment, are no different from the nature of the experience. The nature of our experiences is inherent within our authentic condition. In that sense, delusions are self-purifying if we can handle them properly in meditation. For this reason, your present state of the mind, whatever it happens to be, is inseparable from your authentic state. That is how we need to understand it. The great master Guru Padmasambhava gives this advice:

> Mind that is left alone in meditation, without cogitation,
> will find no distinction between meditation and nonmeditation.
> When there is no conflictual mind to be found,
> that should not lead to a conflictual mental state.
>
> If there is distraction in our meditation,
> we can bring the mind back to attention.
> If the distraction persists and we can still pay attention,
> that too should not lead to a conflictual mental state.
>
> In that attentive state of meditation

we can have non-attentiveness.
If we apply the mental state of attentiveness,
that too should not lead to a conflictual mental state.

When there is a proliferation of thoughts and emotions,
we can find moments without thoughts and emotions in that state.
If the proliferation of thoughts and emotions continues,
that too should not lead to a conflictual mental state.

When we try to gather the scattered mind,
we find that even in that state there is a sense of stability.
If we are able to bring the mind back and gather that dispersion,
that too should not lead to a conflictual mental state.

In meditation, we may try to tighten the mind,
but there may still be moments of looseness.
If we succeed in tightening the mind,
that too should not lead to a conflictual mental state.

We may be tempted to transform the mind in meditation,
but we may also remain without contrivances.
If we succeed in changing the mind,
that too should not lead to a conflictual mental state.

Meditation practice is a way to cultivate certain mental powers,
but in that cultivation, we may find moments of total relaxation.
If our effort to cultivate mental powers is rewarded,
that too should not lead to a conflictual mental state.

We may try to prevent certain thoughts from arising during
meditation,
but spontaneous thoughts might still arise.
If we succeed in preventing thoughts from arising,
that too should not lead to a conflictual mental state.

It is said that meditation should bring about a sense of humility,
but even when there is humility, a sense of pride may be present.
If we are able to have humility,
that too should not lead to a conflictual mental state.

It is said we must apply ourselves with vigor,
but moments of laziness may be present.
If we can apply ourselves with vigor,
that should not lead to a conflictual mental state.

Meditation is promoted as a way of settling the mind,
but even while we are settling it, agitation may be present.
If we succeed in settling the mind,
that too should not lead to a conflictual mental state.

You should seize your present state of mind, without trying to change it, whenever you are meditating. Just allow yourself to rest in it and divest yourself of all thoughts about inner mental states or external material conditions. Simply focus your mind on what is already there, without trying to get hold of it or avoid it.

You need to maintain an open mind, one that is not divided and neither rejects nor overly embraces experiences. There are many layers of thoughts and emotions. Some are obvious and coarse, while others are more subtle, elusive, and hidden. You must first learn how to notice the more obtrusive thoughts, without allowing yourself to get overwhelmed or carried away by them. That is how you learn to be in the state of meditation. You can find freedom through that.

The mind is very industrious when it comes to producing thoughts and emotions. If you don't try to either suppress them or prevent them, all of your thoughts and emotions can settle naturally. That is how you avoid falling into the states of absorption associated with the form and formless realms. When you practice in this way, you should not be thinking, "This is the mental state that I must have at any cost." Instead, your mental attitude should be more relaxed, so that shamatha can occur naturally. At the same time, because you are not thinking, "I shouldn't have this thought or that thought, I shouldn't have this emotion or that emotion," everything arises spontaneously and there is awareness present.

The practice of vipashyana is also effortlessly accomplished. Insight meditation gives you the opportunity to deal with experiences while shamatha meditation stabilizes the mind. The union of shamatha and vipashyana is realized through Dzogchen practice because whatever arises in the mind doesn't impact on the mind as much as it did. You just see them as momentary experiences. The mind will then provide the necessary condition to develop insight. When the mind is relaxed, you no longer need to be overly concerned about whether the mind is settled or not settled. Due to this, you can realize samadhi or meditative equipoise. The mind is not so clingy, so whatever arises in the mind will simply arise and dissipate, arise and dissipate. As a result, you attain wisdom.

The fundamental flaw of a meditator comes from mental fixation. You therefore have to learn how to let go of that fixation. If you can achieve that, wisdom will arise from that state of being. As you become more acquainted with the experience of letting go, the meditative experience is given a chance to flourish. Meditation will then give rise to the experience of total completion in our mental potential. This takes place in such a way that you obtain spiritual boons (*siddhi, dngos-grub*). You can obtain that in this very life.

Meditation is not about trying to be like an artisan manufacturing an artifact, because the mind can't be shaped in the way physical objects can be shaped. Instead, the mind should be left alone. We just use awareness to recognize what is occurring in it at any given moment. Whatever arises in the mind should be given the opportunity to exist and then we will see that whatever has arisen in the mind is self-presencing. In other words, what has arisen in the mind has not come about through some willful act. When experiences are seen as self-presencing—not as something we have willfully created and manufactured—you will realize that experiences are already present and nondirectional.

To have that sort of understanding through meditation is to understand the mind properly. You will see that it is, after all, the king of the universe. A sense of well-being and happiness will flow from being attuned to the majestic qualities of mind. The nature of mind is unconditioned and unconditionable. It is free from cause and effect. When we find that original state, we have realized the dharmakaya. The dharmakaya is not to be found anywhere else.

SUMMARY

We now come to the summation part of the text (*gyesum*). *Gye* means "what comes after the actual practice." The summation involves how to foster and develop what you have already practiced. This also has three aspects: learning how to be resilient, learning how to foster your experiences in meditation, and learning how to dispel obstacles.

Learning to be Resilient

You need to pay attention to whatever arises in the mind, the moment it arises, in whatever life circumstance you find yourself. You have learned to do this in meditation, now you must learn to do it during post-meditation situations. You need to know how to carry what you have realized in meditation into your daily life. You observe both your external life circumstances and your inner experience of rigpa during post-meditation. You may have had a variety of spiritual experiences because you are accustomed to meditative states, but none of these should be seen as real, tangible, or self-existing. They should be viewed as dreams, magical performances, mirages, or the reflection of the moon on water. The various forms of creative activity that present themselves as real are not real. In post-meditation, you should therefore remain alert and attentive so that, as soon as something arises in the mind, you are able to notice that it is intrinsically devoid of substance and therefore illusory. You should be able to recognize this reality no matter how powerful the experience. That is how we train the mind to be more resilient.

Learning to foster your experiences in meditation

We will no longer find ourselves thinking, "Whatever I perceive, feel, think, or believe has some kind of intrinsic reality." Instead, as powerful as your dreams may be, you know your dreams are not completely real and our everyday experiences of the world are the same. They do not reveal reality. You can learn to be in your authentic state of being even in post-meditation situations if you approach things in this way. When the mind becomes free from the urge to hang onto, grasp onto, cling onto something and fixate on it, then we can remain in our natural state. We can even remain in our natural state during everyday experiences when we are not meditating. This is how we foster our experiences in meditation practice.

Learning to Dispel Obstacles

A meditator can endure many obstacles, some of which include physical illness, mental illness, and problems caused by excessive forms of conceptualization. Whenever you feel you are subject to some undesirable state, you should think, "What is the reality of this distress? Is it caused by a physical illness or a psychological imbalance?" However, instead of regarding disease and illness as having some kind of intrinsic reality, you should view them as the product of causes and conditions and understand that they have no inherent existence of their own. The same thing applies to mental illness and mental imbalance.

If you can recognize this, you can use physical illness and mental imbalance on the path of spiritual practice. They should not be seen as anathema to your spiritual development. Instead of saying, "I don't want to be ill, I don't want this, I don't want that," you take on whatever is distressing, because when the things we find undesirable and distressing are taken on board, we will have a sense of well-being. You should imagine you are happy because you have accommodated these things. You may not actually be happy, but you imagine that you are, and that may bring you happiness.

When you are physically ill and in pain, you imagine the pain is something you can make use of by thinking, "I can use this experience as part of my practice." Instead of seeing the pain as a distracting factor, you view it as something with the potential to help your growth, and you incorporate it into your meditation. If you suffer from a mental imbalance, you should learn to generate the love and compassion of bodhicitta and use that as part of your meditation. Finally, you have to know that physical and mental illness have no inherent existence and are simply a product of causes and conditions. This is how we learn to overcome obstacles in our lives and put these obstacles to rest.

Further practices

With all of these practices, which are meant to foster and increase your practice, you should never underestimate the importance of having a sense of connection to the lineage. That is where we find our real spiritual strength. You have to pray for inspiration and constantly remind yourself how important it is to recognize the delusory nature of samsara. Samsaric activities in themselves are incapable of producing happiness and well-being. You should practice *ganachakra* pujas and make offerings. In other words, along with trying to develop wisdom through meditation, you should engage in activities that are beneficial for yourself and others. We need to create and accumulate merit just as much as we need to create and accumulate wisdom, so the cultivation of love and compassion is absolutely essential.

It is also profitable to go to charnel grounds and to contemplate death and your own mortality, and also to spend time in isolation on top of a mountain. When you are in isolation, you should visualize your teacher sitting on top of your head, giving you inspiration. Then you can jump up and down, run around, and say all kinds of things, while mentally generating the entire gamut of emotions for both happiness and unhappiness. You should imagine things that you want to experience and also things that you don't want to experience. You generate all of that and jump up and down, run around, scream, and go through all these extreme emotions. What are you doing here? You are treating all your actions and experiences as being capable of producing liberation. You can practice this for many days. Doing so will help you gain enormous ground in your spiritual progress.

TRALEG KYABGON COMMENTARY ON
WHAT TO PRACTICE IN THIS LIFE

PRELIMINARIES

The ngondro order presented here may be different from what you are used to, but there is no real order for the ngondro, as such. This is set out as a retreat manual, so you do it this way when you are doing a retreat. You are not counting in this method, you are not doing 100,000 Vajrasattva mantras or mandala offerings; you are doing these preliminary practices to help with your retreat. For example, if you do a three-month retreat, you spend a few weeks before that retreat doing these preliminaries. Longchenpa has already talked about the Dzogchen teachings in the context of *The Natural Freedom of the Mind*. This section is designed to help practitioners go into retreat. If you want to do a three-month or six-month Dzogchen retreat, you should follow this in a systematic way. You should go through the preliminaries each time you go into retreat, devoting seven days to each one.

MANDALA OFFERING

The main point of mandala offering is to learn to let go, to be able to give and not hang on to things. You are learning to have a sense of generosity. You offer up material things as well as all of your good qualities. Even qualities that you may not realize you possess are to be offered. If you are attached to your music collection or your computer, you offer that. In the practice itself, you have a wish-fulfilling tree, a queen, a general, an elephant, and so on, then you can add anything you desire, whatever you are attached to. It is a mental exercise for being able to let go. Some people might think it is all imaginary and it won't really make much difference, but it will. As we say, even the thought of not having something can really make us crazy. There is so much resistance to even thinking about giving up these things. By thinking about them, we are training our mind. People often say, "I can't imagine life without such and such." What we are attached to is different for everybody; it could be people, places, possessions, qualities, attributes, utilities, or whatever.

In the mandala offering practice, you first construct a universe and then you add in all of the things you can imagine offering. You make offerings during the liturgy and then you think of other things that are personal to you and you give them up too. You start by offering the universe. To offer an elephant or a wish-fulfilling cow may not mean anything to you but what you are offering has to be meaningful. That is why you think of things that you are attached to and you give them up. When you add the piles of rice in the liturgy, you think that they represent the universe itself, with all its galaxies, stars, and so on. Mountains and continents are only symbolic representations of the whole universe. You have heavenly goddesses that each represent a particular sensory object, beauty, scents, beautiful music, and all of that. You think of that as well. Anything you find pleasant to smell, anything you find nice to look at, anything you find nice to hear, anything you find nice to taste, you offer it all up.

VAJRASATTVA

Seed syllables are designed to help you focus your mind. They help you to concentrate. There are hundreds of seed syllables because each deity has a seed syllable. You visualize the syllables as you recite them, so that you are basically coordinating your body, speech, and mind while you are doing it. Your body is in the meditation posture, your speech is engaged in reciting the mantra, and your mind is focusing on the seed syllable while you imagine that all the lineage masters, buddhas, and bodhisattvas are present in front of you. You are coordinating all three in that way while doing the practice.

In Vajrasattva practice, you have to visualize the shape of the seed syllable in Tibetan. You visualize HUNG and then you imagine the one hundred syllables of Vajrasattva revolving around that. I'm sure even the Tibetans don't manage to visualize them all clearly. You can get this done in a computer graphic. People have done this, and it looks fantastic. I'm sure you can use that sort of thing as an aid. There's no reason why not. It is just meant to increase your mental capacity to concentrate and to visualize things.

BODHICITTA

When wishing that beings are free from suffering, we are hoping both that their circumstances change and that they realize the causes of suffering for themselves. For example, the traditional texts talk about people suffering from famine, bad weather, deteriorating soil conditions, as well as bad governments, fear of random arrests under dictatorships, and so on. All of those things contribute to the suffering that beings endure. You have to think about the political, economic, and social conditions that contribute to suffering, as well as the person's own mental attitude. Buddhism says that our mental attitude is the real key but that doesn't mean we can ignore the social, economic, and political structures that are in place. As Longchenpa says, we imagine that poor people have enough to eat, that naked people have clothes, and so on. Many people are starving in this world, so we should not indulge in mindless gluttony, but that doesn't mean we should not eat well and enjoy our food. According to Buddhism, we have to enjoy our food; just eating it is not the point, but even when we are eating, we have to be mindful and aware. When we pay attention to what we are eating, we enjoy it more, while at the same time we are not just eating for the sake of it, mindlessly, and without any consideration for the millions of people who go without food every day. These meditative mental exercises, unlike what many people think, are actually more powerful than trying to do something good. If our mental attitude isn't fixed first, we can try to feed the hungry, clothe the naked, and give shelter to the homeless, but our mind will still be in a mess and whatever we do will reflect that. That is why these exercises are so important. So we have to think in terms of people changing their mental attitudes and about people enjoying better physical circumstances, which involves political, social, and economic conditions, so that people have more freedom, more liberty, and therefore more happiness.

According to Buddhism, the reason we have the four cardinal virtues or Four Infinities in the way that they are listed is because first you have to learn how to give and that comes from love. Then you learn how to alleviate the pain, anguish, and torment of other people through compassion. Then you realize that if you don't have a positive attitude, love and compassion are such strong emotions that they may actually drag you down so that you feel despondent and impotent, because you can't do everything you want to. Then you need to rejuvenate yourself, you have to lift yourself up through joy. When you contemplate on joy, you start to think you can take on everything, but you can't keep on riding so high, so you need equanimity to become more level-headed. Instead of going from one extreme to the other, where you are either lovey-dovey or stifled, where you go from being this big motherly or fatherly figure, this protective person, to going all over the place until you collapse, you need equanimity. To develop properly and freely show love and compassion toward all beings, we need to have all four cardinal virtues as part of bodhicitta practice. We need to have love, compassion, joy, and equanimity and there has to be a balance between them as well.

Many people experience burn-out; just trying to love one person can burn you out. You have no energy left; you are drained. It makes sense to really develop all four and make sure that they balance. We can't measure them though; we can't say you need this much of love and that much of compassion because it's not like following a diet. You will know when you are going too far or when you are letting yourself go. Meditation is there to help you.

VIPASHYANA

The Dzogchen and Mahamudra term for "ultimate reality" is *gnas-lugs*. The Mahayana teachings also make a distinction between *snang-lugs* (the way things appear) and *gnas-lugs* (how things exist). This is similar to the Mahayana distinction between dharma and dharmata, or relative reality (*chos*) and ultimate reality (*chos-nyid*). Ultimate reality is the same as the ultimate truth, because how things exist is ultimate truth and how things appear is relative truth. There is a more intimate relationship between how things appear and how things exist in the Mahamudra and Dzogchen teachings than there is in the Mahayana teachings. That's why they say, "The things that appear to the mind are like clouds and the nature of the mind is like space. Just as we would have no clouds without space, we could have no experiences without the nature of the mind." Clouds are symbolic of relative truth and space is symbolic of ultimate truth.

Normally when we say, "how things appear," we are thinking of how things actually present themselves, but that is not what is meant in Buddhism. Buddhism is talking about how they appear to us, how we apprehend something, how we comprehend, interpret, and make sense of it, how we inject meaning into it, how we conceptualize about it. It is not so simple, according to the Buddhist way of thinking. Actually, we can never say, "That is how things appear," because how things appear is so intimately tied up with how we think they appear to our mind. Things don't just pop out; we have to make sense of them. Is it a tree? Is the car that just cut me off and caused an accident driven by some maniac? We have to make sense of all the things we experience through our senses all the time.

So "how things appear" means "how things appear to me, the individual." That's why things appear so differently to different people. You could be walking down a street with all these cakes and savories in the shop windows and one person will think, "This is bliss, I'm in heaven," while another person thinks, "Yuck, this food is so revolting." We do that with everything. So, it's like that. We have to make sense of everything that is happening in our lives, or we would be living in a very nightmarish kind of world, a world that one philosopher called "a bundle of perceptions." If all you could see was a juxtaposition of shapes and colors and nothing else, you would go mad. Even to see color, that in itself requires a lot of thought, it requires a lot of information to start off with. If we see somebody with red hair, either natural or dyed, or with black hair, or if they are Caucasian or Asian or African, we have to have so much information to make sense of it, and we do it automatically.

Buddhism is not saying we shouldn't do that; we cannot stop doing it, we are human beings, and this is what we do. What Buddhism is saying is that we should not believe in that. This is just how we make sense of the world. It is something that we have to do; even in terms of our survival we have to do this. Let's say you are stuck in the jungle somewhere and you have to survive, you have to learn what to eat and what not to eat. You can't just grab something that looks edible because it may be poisonous, you may die in seconds. You have to discriminate; you have to see what is happening. Doing that is not the problem, but thinking this will reveal something about how things actually exist is the problem. We cannot understand how things exist by thinking that way, so we need to become less fixated on those ideas. You are not getting rid of the discriminating or discursive mind; you are rising above it. You can still use the discriminating mind but in a more discriminating fashion. You use it more wisely, so that you don't get bogged down or entrapped by it. You are not thinking, "What I think, believe, see, interpret, and conceptualize is real, it is the real thing." We are always in dialogue with the world, we shape the world, and the world shapes us. Subject and object, perceiver and perceived, it is a mutual reconstruction, a mutual constitution.

This practice includes both mindfulness and awareness. You must have awareness, being mindful is not enough. Being mindful means that you are present, but even if you are present, you can still be unaware. That is the difference. We have to integrate shamatha and vipashyana. In Dzogchen practice, they are already integrated, you are doing both.

MAIN PRACTICE

Longchenpa said that mind has three aspects: its nature, essence, and characteristic. *Stong-grol* is related to recognizing the nature of the mind, and *shes-grol* is related to understanding the luminous aspect of the mind. If the mind had no capacity to be luminous, we would be doomed to remain in a state of ignorance forever, but the mind does have that capacity. To understand that is shes-grol. *Shes* in this context means "to understand" and *grol* means "liberation." *Rang-grol* is realizing that when thoughts, concepts, ideas, emotions, or feelings arise, they don't have to be seen as enemies. They don't have to be pushed away, discarded or abandoned. When you find liberation through that realization, it is rang-grol. So you find liberation through all three aspects of the mind in that way.

When you find liberation, when you become enlightened, you don't lose your memory. You will still remember. To become enlightened is not self-annihilation or ridding the mind of all of its contents. None of the Buddhist schools see the mind like a house and the thoughts, emotions, concepts, ideas, and feelings like the furniture inside it. You are not trying to empty the house of all the unwanted furniture until you have this empty house, and then you feel good. Some people may think that way. They think that through doing Buddhist practice, they will slowly empty their mind of everything until they find a permanently fixed state of total passivity with no activity. However, as you know, Buddhism talks about passivity with activity. A realized being may in fact be more enriched; their capacity to remember, see, understand, and comprehend would increase. That is a standard Buddhist way of understanding an enlightened being.

The benefit of doing vipashyana meditation is that the mind is no longer so clingy and then wisdom can develop. If we do not cling onto our experiences so much, they have less impact on our mind and we may be less affected and less traumatized. The mind can then become more open, more expansive, and more spacious, as it says in the teachings, and with that comes wisdom. But when the mind is clingy and grasping, it develops a monofocal vision. Whatever you are obsessed with or affected by becomes a preoccupation and there is no room to have expansive vision or to be able to see things clearly. The mind has become so narrow and has such a narrow focus that wisdom is impossible.

You need to be aware and just leave it there. You don't have to think, "Why has this thought come into my mind, this despicable, obscene, or upsetting thought—why has it come up?" Just take notice of it and then let go. In other words, meditation is not about eliminating thoughts; it is about being able to let go of your thoughts and emotions and then gradually let go of your past experiences. We should think of our thoughts and emotions as clouds. Clouds leave no traces, they just come, and they go. They come and they dissipate. We should try to view our mental states in the same way. The fewer impressions they leave behind, the better, because according to the Buddhist teachings, that is what constitutes our karmic inheritance, our karmic history. The stronger the impressions, the more we get bogged down by them and then the more tied up we become in our karmic habitual patterns. The less we cling to our experiences the freer we are and the less karmic impact they will have. We should not even cling to being attentive, to being aware, to having wisdom, and so on. We should just be open to whatever arises without thinking, "I need more insight, I need more wisdom, I don't want all this other stuff which is disruptive and prevents me from realizing my spiritual goals."

DISPELLING OBSTACLES

Longchenpa says we can dispel obstacles like mental illness, but it is very difficult to make generalizations about such things. It depends on the individual. We can't say we have to relate to schizophrenia in this way. You need to know what sort of schizophrenia the person has and then deal with that person as an individual. Even if someone is suffering from extreme psychosis like schizophrenia, there is absolutely no reason why they wouldn't be able to gain some benefit from spiritual practice. There is the possibility that they could benefit from it more than other people, provided they can stay focused and on track with their spiritual practices. Just because someone has an extreme form of mental illness doesn't mean they should be excluded. Their mental illness may be more pronounced, but how do we know we are not worse off? You never know. We so-called "sane people" should also be conscious of our psychotic episodes and acknowledge them by saying, "I too am no different from that person in a way. That person is just going through a more extreme emotional state than me." You will then develop some kind of empathy with and sympathy for that person.

Excessive conceptualization (*vikalpa, rtog-pa*) is another obstacle, and this is something that we all experience. That is the worst disease, for sure. Even with physical or mental illness, the unceasing mental activity that accompanies it is what makes the problem worse, whatever form of illness we have. That is the underlying ailment that we are all subject to and that is what meditation is there to redress. This type of activity just never stops. It doesn't stop when you are aware, it doesn't stop when you are not aware, it doesn't stop when you are awake, it doesn't stop when you are asleep, it doesn't stop when you are relatively sane, it doesn't stop when you are losing it, it doesn't stop when you are healthy, it doesn't stop when you are unhealthy. That is the root cause of all our problems, according to the Buddhist teachings.

Longchenpa is not saying that we should not look for certain cures, even with physical illness. We should do that, but if the mind becomes fixated on health and sees ill-health as the enemy—if it sees health as a self-existing entity and ill-health as another self-existing entity—we create a problem. It is our excessive conceptualization that promotes this idea. The best way to deal with obstacles related to illness is to see that physical illness has no intrinsic reality. It is not self-existing; it is a product of causes and conditions. That doesn't mean that we should not watch our diet, eat properly, exercise, and all of those things, but we should not view ill-health as some kind of intrusion. That is true for sanity and madness as well. You don't have to think, "I'm trying to maintain my sanity so that madness doesn't come and take me over and then I won't know what the hell is going on and I'll lose all control." Health and sanity are a relative condition, they are a relative state, in other words. Many people think this is a very abstract, intellectual way of looking at it, but it is not; this is an experiential thing. If you can look at health like that, you will experience things very differently.

FURTHER PRACTICES

A ganachakra is actually about celebrating the senses. You are stimulating the visual sense with visual displays, the audial sense with music, the nasal sense with incense and other aromatic things, your taste by eating delicious food and drinking the most expensive alcohol you can find. In the old days, ganachakras used to be wilder than they are now, but they have always been about stimulating the senses and saying, "This is all part of meditation." If your perception changes, if your attitude changes, then you don't have to stop admiring beautiful things or stop listening to great music or smelling nice things. Ganachakra is *tsog* in Tibetan. There are many stories of the early Indian mahasiddhas having ganachakras but theirs were very different from ours. Their ganachakra was more informal and more like a party. It was formalized in Tibet but the spirit is still there. The spirit is still there. Normally in the Kagyu and Nyingma traditions, the monks do not drink alcohol, but during ganachakra, they would. Ganachakra is a tantric practice, and as you know, even in India the whole tantric movement was initiated by non-monastic practitioners.

2. WHAT TO PRACTICE IN THE BARDO STATE

If Dzogchen practitioners continue with meditation in the manner described above, they will no longer get bogged down by concerns about this life or the process of death and dying because they will have gone beyond the dualistic notions of subject and object. If Dzogchen meditation is practiced properly, you will realize all your spiritual potential and aspirations in this very life. You should therefore practice this meditation so that you can find liberation in this life. Whatever practice you manage to do in this life will have a bearing on the type of experiences you are subject to during the intermediary or bardo state. The concept of the bardo should not be restricted to the intermediate stage between death and rebirth; your living existence is also a form of bardo. To have life means to have come into being. Anything that has come into being must also end, so we must also die at the end of this life. You should therefore engage in meditation practices while you are in the living bardo state so that you can find the natural freedom of mind.

THE BARDO OF DREAMS

First, there is the bardo of dreams, which occurs while you are sleeping. You are awake, then you go to sleep and start dreaming and then you wake up again. The dream state is another kind of bardo, and you can find liberation in that state. If you do not become fixated on the dream while dreaming—through the practice of Dream Yoga, for example— your dreams can become a source of liberation rather than a cause of mental disturbance.

THE BARDO OF DYING

The same thing applies at the time of death. The five elements of the body begin to dissolve when we are confronted with death. For example, when the earth element dissolves into the water element, the mobility of the body is radically reduced and finally stops altogether. At this point, the earth element has dissolved into the water element, and then the water element dissolves into the fire element. At the advent of this process of dissolution, your saliva and mucus gradually dry up and the fluids in your body disappear. When the fire element dissolves into the air element, the body begins to lose its heat. Finally, the air element dissolves into space, at which point the dying person ceases to breathe due to lack of oxygen.

There is a process of dissolution associated with the functioning of the sensory organs as well. The visual sense dissolves into the audial sense and your capacity to see is lost. The audial sense dissolves into the nasal sense and your capacity to hear disappears. The nasal sense dissolves into the taste or gustation sense and you are deprived of the capacity to smell. When the gustation sense dissolves into the tactile sense, your ability to taste is gone. Finally, the tactile sense also vanishes so that even the faintest of sensations vanishes. Then the consciousness becomes withdrawn so that all forms of thought, ideas, concepts, and emotions cease. This is comparable to becoming unconscious. At that point, all the functions of consciousness have dissolved.

THE BARDO OF DEATH

The eight functions of consciousness (*asta-vijnana, rnam-shes tshogs-brgyad*), which comprise the six sense consciousnesses (*sad-vijnana, rnam-shes tshogs-drug*); the ego-mind (*mano-vijnana, yid kyi rnam-shes*), the function of mind that unifies all our experiences into what we know as our own mind; and the unconscious mental reservoir (*alayavijnana, kun-gzhi rnam-shes*)—all these functions of the mind have temporarily come to a standstill.

SELF-LIBERATION IN THE BARDO

If you can put yourself in a meditative state, into the state of samadhi, then it is possible to find liberation while in the bardo. You can achieve enlightenment during the bardo state by realizing the five Dhyani Buddhas. These five Buddhas represent the enlightened qualities of the five poisons of the samsaric condition. You can attain the state of the five Buddhas as they reside in their respective buddha-fields. During the bardo state, you will see many different colors. Each color is a reflection or manifestation of the quality of a particular buddha-family. Each buddha-family represents a particular wisdom, which is the transformed energy of a specific conflicting emotion.

If you see a dark blue light, that represents Buddha Akshobya or Mitrupa.[14] The wisdom associated with this Buddha is called "mirror-like wisdom." This wisdom is the enlightened aspect of the transformed energy of anger.

If you see a white light, that represents Buddha Vairocana or Nampar Nangdze.[15] The wisdom associated with this Buddha is known as "the wisdom of dharmadhatu," which allows us to realize ultimate reality so that we can see how things exist. This wisdom is the enlightened aspect of the transformed energy of ignorance.

If you see a yellow light, that represents the Buddha Ratnasambhava or Rinchen Jungnay.[16] The wisdom associated with this Buddha is named "the wisdom of equanimity." This wisdom is the enlightened aspect of the transformed emotion of pride.

If you see a red light, this represents Buddha Amitabha or Nawithaya.[17] The wisdom associated with this Buddha is called "the wisdom of discrimination." This wisdom is the enlightened aspect of the transformed energy of desire.

If you see a green light, this represents the Buddha Amoghasiddhi or Donyo Drubpa.[18] The wisdom associated with this Buddha is known as "the wisdom of accomplishment." That wisdom is the enlightened manifestation of the transformed energy of jealousy.

You can see then that the different experiences you may have during the bardo of death, in terms of the colors, forms, and so on, can be associated with a particular quality of our own mind in relation to its enlightened qualities. You are able to make this transformation in the bardo, precisely because while you were still alive, you had the opportunity to practice meditation and to learn how to concentrate and be present. You became accustomed to being aware of what was going on in your mind. You were able to let thoughts and emotions arise while at the same time letting them go, so that they became liberated on the spot. This ability to recognize whatever arises in the mind the moment that it arises will help you to transform the bardo experience into an experience of liberation.

Through having developed that kind of ability, then even when you are alive, it is possible that wisdom will dawn upon you, without your even looking for a flash of insight or even anticipating one. The wisdom will arise naturally and with it will come a sense of well-being and a reduction in your conceptual proliferation. That naturally arising wisdom can occur even while you are meditating. The same thing can happen in the bardo state. The insight and wisdom in the bardo can manifest as clear light ('od-gsal). This clear light and wisdom are inseparable. The bardo experience can lead to self-liberation in this way.

If you can remain aware during the journey through the bardo, then your intrinsic awareness is present. This intrinsic awareness has three characteristics. The first characteristic is that intrinsic awareness is not something you can locate and say, "Intrinsic awareness resides here." The second is that the mind imbued with clear light and wisdom is self-luminous (rang-gsal). The third characteristic is that the mind that is aware does not stop functioning. All kinds of experiences continue to flourish; whatever arises in the mind becomes self-liberated naturally. These three characteristics of the nature of mind are present in the bardo state.

THE BARDO OF BIRTH

Having gone through all of that, we come to the next transition period, which is leaving the bardo state and taking birth. In this particular context, we are referring to an "enlightened rebirth" or nirmanakaya, instead of an ordinary rebirth.

Having taken rebirth in a nirmanakaya form, your life is put to good use in benefiting numerous sentient beings. Having attained a nirmanakaya form, you don't reside in that form; you also enter into higher levels of being, on the sambhogakaya and dharmakaya levels. Being in a state of dharmakaya, without wavering, is to remain in dzogpa chenpo, in the state of Dzogchen.

Those practitioners who were advanced on the path would achieve liberation at the time of death. Those who were unable to achieve liberation at the time of death would have the opportunity to achieve it during their journey through the bardo. Those who were unable to secure liberation in the bardo would need to take rebirth, precisely because they have some unresolved karmic history.

However, before you can take on rebirth, you must assume a more subtle body, known as a "bardo body," a form that you assume because you were not able to remain in the state of luminosity. This bardo body is quite unique. As long as you remain in the bardo, you will be housed in this subtle body and have the mental faculty to remember past events and anticipate future ones. As this bardo body is a subtle body, it is not subject to the same limitations as a normal physical body. Therefore, the bardo body can be anywhere that the mind directs its focus. There are no physical obstructions so nothing can impede the movements of a bardo being.

The experiences a bardo being endures take on a dreamlike quality, but that does not mean the bardo being is free from intense feelings or heightened experiences of happiness or pain and suffering. How long would a bardo being remain in this state? We cannot predict the answer to that. It depends on the individual. Some people will find a rebirth very quickly, while others may remain in the bardo for up to forty-nine days.

Individuals who are condemned to wander about in the bardo state come to the realization that they have died, and this comes as an incredibly painful experience because up to that point, the bardo being has not realized that they are actually in a post-mortem state. If you had been a practitioner during your life, you should make the effort to recall your previous practices and then realize that all these bardo experiences, the objects of experience, and the one who is experiencing them, the subject, are interdependent and none of them has any enduring essence. You will be able to eschew your hold on the dualistic notions of subject and object.

Then you can invite and evoke the blessings of the great masters. By doing this, you can liberate yourself from the bardo. Now, if you succeed in doing this, the bardo realm itself will be seen as the realm of the Buddha and all the myriad forms of bardo phenomena will be understood as having no intrinsic reality. It is said that when this understanding dawns, you attain full enlightenment.

However, if you can only manage to recall your precepts and daily practices and apply those, then at best you will come to realize that nothing you experience in the bardo state is intrinsically real. If that kind of understanding is not developed, but you are able to see that whatever you experience is like a magical display or comparable to your meditative visualization of peaceful and wrathful deities, then that again can bring about authentic insight. If you are not able to achieve that, at the very least, you should be able to make use of your practices during the bardo and you will be able to prevent undesirable forms of rebirth.

When you come closer to the time of birth, you should try to maintain a meditative equipoise as you enter the womb, because all kinds of strong emotions relating to attraction and aversion will arise prior to conception and in the prenatal period. So, it is absolutely essential to maintain a sense of equilibrium and you should think of yourself as a divine being and your future parents as a divine couple rather than ordinary sentient beings. You should think, "May I have a proper birth that will be conducive to my spiritual progress. May I be able to obtain the ultimate goal of enlightenment."

If you can take rebirth in this way, you will have been able to choose your rebirth, in which case you will have the leisure and necessary conditions to flourish. If there is no leisure, you cannot flourish and grow. If you have not acquired the necessary conditions, you will again be hampered and inhibited in your growth. However, if you have managed to control your rebirth in this way, you will obtain leisure and the other necessary conditions and find a proper spiritual guide. By following their instructions, then in that very life, you will be able to become enlightened.

TRALEG KYABGON COMMENTARY ON WHAT TO PRACTICE IN THE BARDO STATE

We shouldn't think of the dissolution of the elements as something that happens slowly. It may be slow, or it may be fast; it depends on the circumstances. If you have been languishing in a hospital with some dreadful disease for a long period, your faculties will gradually start to go. If you were involved in a major car crash or something, your death could happen on impact. You would have no time to think, "The earth element is now dissolving into the water element," and so on. There would still be a process, because even when we say, "dead on impact," the body still cools down gradually and so on. It does not all just happen in an instant. There is some kind of process, but how long it takes is unpredictable. You can't measure it and it would vary from individual to individual. A blind person would have no visual sense to be dissolved into the audial sense, and a deaf person would be similarly restricted. That could be a good thing because the dissolution of that sense would be nothing new for them whereas for the sighted, losing that sense could be disturbing. The element and the sense organs dissolve together. When the dissolution of the elements takes place, the sense organs also start to go. It is really the dissolution of the senses that we are losing, not the dissolution of the sense organs—the dissolution of the sense of sight into the sense of hearing, and so on. The sense organs may dissolve too but only as part of the process of decomposition.

The purpose of being aware of all this is so that we can direct our consciousness. Even when the body itself is dead, there is still a sense where it is not dead because a practitioner is able to remain in the body for a much longer period than a non-practitioner. It's not necessarily about the warmth of the body but rather about the posture of the body. Many of these practitioners pass away in a meditative posture. Some may sit like that for a few hours; others for a couple of days. It's actually not rare.

The bardo body continues after your body has died, but this is not like astral traveling because you are dead. There is some problem in saying there is mind that is totally divorced from any kind of body. Mind and body go together so even in bardo, you have a kind of a body. It may not be a body of flesh and blood, but it is another type of body. In other words, bardo beings can see each other and communicate with each other. It is very difficult to imagine what it would be like to have no physical volume and not be located somewhere, but just have the mind. Where would the thoughts be? The teachings also say that beings in the bardo need sustenance; they are supposed to live on smell. The point is that if there is a mind, you have a kind of body that goes with it. We are talking about another kind of being. Obviously a bardo being is not a human being. That is another thing we have to remember.

When you die, you will not be the person you are now, with the name and nationality you have now; you will be a completely different kind of being, an alien kind of being. Even though Buddhism may talk about bardo states, we do not talk about astral traveling. There could be many different kinds of bodies. If you touch an object, the naked eye may not see anything, but the heat of the body has left some kind of mark there and certain instruments can pick that up. Whenever we think about a body or a living sentient being, we always think about beings that are similar to us, but there is no reason why that should be the case. We are advised to remember our precepts, instructions, and daily practices in the bardo because we have to learn to become more aware in the bardo and not yield to our impulses or allow ourselves to be driven by karmic forces. You try to resist your urges and to become more aware. As Longchenpa also pointed out, we do meditation and practices like Dream Yoga when we are still alive for this reason. The same things happen in our dreams; we yield to all of our natural emotional impulses, just like that. However, it is possible to practice becoming aware while you are dreaming so that you can see you are dreaming and that the dream is not something real. You can do the same thing in bardo state. That is the idea in these teachings. So first, Longchenpa talked about how to practice Dzogchen, and then he talked about how to use that in the bardo.

3. THE GOAL OF SPIRITUAL PRACTICE
THE KAYAS

Whether we are practicing in this life or trying to steer the course of our spiritual journey in the bardo state, our ultimate destination is buddhahood. What is buddhahood? In this context, buddhahood is no different from realizing the natural freedom of the mind itself (*sems nyid rang grol*). The natural freedom of the mind is uncorrupted and incorruptible, unbound, not subject to anything, and intrinsically radiant. That natural freedom of the mind is enlightenment and that's what the unvitiated, authentic state of being means.

That authentic state of being, which is the same as the natural freedom of mind, is the unconditioned state of being that you already find yourself within, even though you have not realized it. Just as we can see the sun, moon, stars, and constellations of the galaxies in space, in a similar way, from and within the state of unconditioned being—the natural freedom of the mind, which is the dharmakaya—arises the sambhogakaya, and from the sambhogakaya arises the nirmanakaya.

When you come to the end of your spiritual journey, when you have become enlightened, all three aspects of enlightenment come to fruition. As a result, you can work spontaneously for the benefit of others. You don't have to exert yourself or try to help them, but you can benefit others effortlessly simply through having realized your own authentic condition. That is what attaining enlightenment means. When you engage in the practice of meditation, the end result of that practice is to attain enlightenment.

Now, the same thing applies to the bardo. You are given the perfect opportunity to realize the nature of mind in the bardo state because you come into contact with the radiancy, the luminous quality of the mind, which is totally free from defilements and other pollutants. That is the same as self-recognition (*rang-shar shes-pa*), knowing oneself. When that occurs, you have truly understood your authentic state of being, which is dharmakaya. The experience of the sambhogakaya and nirmanakaya arises from that recognition.

The sambhogakaya is also realized in the bardo state. For example, we talk about five wisdoms, which correspond to the five conflicting emotions. In the bardo state, these conflicting emotions give rise to the myriad forms of bardo phenomena. When you are able to recognize them for what they are, the five wisdoms arise. When these five wisdoms are realized— wisdom of equanimity, wisdom of ultimate reality, wisdom of all-accomplishment, mirror-like wisdom, and wisdom of discrimination—you have understood the sambhogakaya, and from that arises the bardo body, which is the nirmanakaya form.

With the three kayas, there is an evolutionary process of nirmanakaya arising from sambhogakaya, and sambhogakaya arising from dharmakaya. There is also a process of devolution, where nirmanakaya dissolves into sambhogakaya. For example, when the time comes for an enlightened being to leave the world, their nirmanakaya dissolves into sambhogakaya and sambhogakaya dissolves into dharmakaya, and then the recently deceased enlightened being remains in the state of dharmakaya. Again, when the enlightened being's time to incarnate has come, the evolutionary process is put into effect again. Sambhogakaya arises from dharmakaya and nirmanakaya arises from sambhogakaya, and the work of the enlightened being is revived. There is the evolutionary process and the devolutionary process. That's how enlightened beings come and go.

THE PRESENT MOMENT OF CONSCIOUSNESS

The practitioner of Dzogchen has to understand this. They also need to realize that what you want to attain is already present. The seeds of samsaric and nirvanic experiences are already present in this present moment of consciousness. When we don't recognize our present state of consciousness, we are in a somnambulant state, a half-awake state. Ignorance works in that manner. Ignorance has the same effect that stupor and drowsiness have on our minds. It dims the mind and robs it of its clarity. As a result, we stumble around in a state of ignorance and go through ups and downs during our lives, with occasional experiences of happiness and intermittent experiences of mental torment, suffering, and pain.

We wander about in this way and this process will continue for as long as we fail to recognize our present state of mind. However, if we recognize this very moment of consciousness and become familiar with it through practice, then that is nirvana. Then whatever we experience becomes an expression of the sambhogakaya. The buddha-realm of sambhogakaya is something we can experience, even in our present mental state. It is not something we have to wait for. We can also benefit others in that manner.

We may be dazzled by all kinds of colors and shapes when we sleep, but upon awakening, we realize they were not real; it was all created by the mind. The moment we awaken, our dream will cease. When we become enlightened, a similar thing happens, because when we realize our authentic state, all conceptual proliferations cease and we see that everything is imbued with the same flavor, the flavor of ultimate reality.

You should never underestimate the importance of the present moment of consciousness. The nature of this very moment of consciousness is emptiness. Normally, we don't recognize that, and we become fixated; we cling onto whatever is present in the mind. As a consequence, we lose the present moment and we become lost. Even if we attempt to do some meditation, we may be able to enter some kind of absorptive state where all thought functions cease, but we cannot rise above ignorance that way. We have not understood the present moment of consciousness.

This kind of deviancy comes from not being able to use the mind properly. This very moment of consciousness is radiant and luminous, but we can lose that through improper speech and aggression that has arisen through altered states of consciousness. The mind is empty in its nature; you cannot identify it as this or that. Its essence is luminous and radiant, and its characteristic is the myriad displays of the mind in terms of thoughts, concepts, ideas, emotions, and feelings.

These displays can afford us the opportunity to realize the mind in its present mode, but that can also be missed through improper use of the body associated with the realm of sensuality and the emotions of lust and excessive desire. If we haven't managed to be really present with whatever has arisen in the mind, if we are unable to be with that and be aware of it, then we have missed the opportunity to understand ourselves, to understand our own mind. Enlightenment is to realize our own mind, so if we fail to do that, we can't attain enlightenment.

Instead of attaining enlightenment, even if we have embarked on the spiritual path, we will not be able to free ourselves from the relentless workings of karmic cause and effect. We might enjoy a certain sense of mental quietude if we have wholesome thoughts and emotions, and we will inevitably suffer the consequences if we have unwholesome thoughts and emotions. So even if we have embarked on the spiritual path, we simply cannot escape the workings of karma, if we do not recognize the present state of consciousness.

If you do not attain some form of meditative peace, you will remain a very basic human being with no redeeming features. If you do experience some meditative experience in terms of mental quietude, you will attain some altered states of consciousness or samadhi. Even if your meditative state is not fully established, it will not be something that is foreign to you. You will know what it's like to be in a meditative state. When the mental quietude is fully present, that is still an altered state of consciousness, called "the realm of absorption" or arupa-dhatu. Even if you enjoy these altered states of consciousness and experience a taste of mental quietude, this doesn't mean you have transcended the condition of suffering. Even in that state of quietude, you may have completely failed to be present with whatever is in your mind. In fact, you may have forgotten or ignored it.

In the present moment, all three kayas are present. How so? When you observe your present state of mind, you will see that the nature of any thought or emotion is empty. Its nature is insubstantial, so it is devoid of inherent existence. That is a revelation. To understand that is the revelation of dharmakaya. The essence of the very thought or emotion that is present is radiance or luminosity. That is sambhogakaya. That thought or emotion, whatever has arisen, is the characteristic of the mind. That is no different from nirmanakaya.

REALIZING THE THREE KAYAS

Dzogchen meditation culminates in the realization of the three kayas, the three aspects of buddha's being. Dharmakaya corresponds to the nature of the mind because the authentic aspect of buddha's being is devoid of characteristics, attributes, and all forms of determinations. It is open, just like space. The sambhogakaya or symbolic aspect of buddha's being emerges from this state of openness. This corresponds to the full actualization of our vocal potentiality. The dimension of sambhogakaya, resides or dwells in Akanishtha, or in other words, ultimate reality. The sambhogakaya manifests as images of peaceful and wrathful deities, which are its symbolic manifestations. These peaceful and wrathful deities represent the enlightened energy of the tenth level of a bodhisattva and therefore never cease. As long as there is samsaric existence that needs to be redeemed, the manifestations of sambhogakaya will continue to accomplish the task of redeeming it.

From the sambhogakaya dimension arises the nirmanakaya, which corresponds to the physical aspect of buddha's being, *sprul-sku* in Tibetan, pronounced "tulku," which is the name applied to reincarnate lamas. The nirmanakaya manifestation, the projection of the physical body, is not carried out in a haphazard way, but with a sense of purpose, so that the nirmanakaya can operate in such a way that they are able to be at the right place and the right time in all ten directions.

Having attained enlightenment, you will have the capacity to project yourself in a way that corresponds most appropriately with the needs of others who require help. The nirmanakaya can work for the benefit of others through the skillful use of body, the skillful use of speech, and the skillful use of the mind. This capacity, ability, or gift comes from having realized two different types of wisdom: the wisdom that enables you to apprehend the reality of things and the wisdom that enables you to apprehend the extent of things. The first wisdom means to see things in their proper mode or proper condition. The second wisdom means to apprehend things in terms of the existing empirical objects and state of affairs. Benefiting others in this way is known as "enlightened work."[19] This comes from great compassion (*mahakaruna, thugs-rje chen-po*). This compassion is superior to the normal day-to-day experience of compassion.

As mentioned, there is an evolutionary and devolutionary process going on between these three levels of being. There is the emergence of sambhogakaya from dharmakaya and of nirmanakaya from sambhogakaya, and there is the disappearance of nirmanakaya into sambhogakaya and of sambhogakaya into dharmakaya. When the time comes for the enlightened being who has taken on a physical form, to leave this body, the nirmanakaya dissolves into sambhogakaya and the luminosity aspect or clarity of the mind (*gsal-ba*). That state of being is inseparable from sambhogakaya, which is characterized by the five wisdoms.

The two aspects of wisdom are also present in the state of sambhogakaya: the wisdom that apprehends the extent of things and the wisdom that apprehends the reality of things, how things exist. Having attained enlightenment, you can still apprehend individual things in their uniqueness and diversity. You can apprehend the extent of things as separate and diverse. You can also see that the diversity of phenomenal objects is united in having one nature. To understand how things exist is to understand that everything is imbued with one reality. In that way, you can apprehend unity in diversity and diversity in unity. This is a brief description of the fruition stage of the Dzogchen path.

DEDICATION

Through the blessings and the kindness that I have received through my guru and whatever experiences or realization that I have had, I have written this meditation manual with the thought it might be of some benefit to succeeding generations. It is my wish that those of you who are reading this text may want to escape from the prison of the samsaric condition. If you have that desire, then consulting this manual may be beneficial.

However, if you approach Dzogchen practice with a sense of

ambiguity or two-mindedness, or if your mind is fixated on the idea of cultivating certain mental attributes and renouncing others, it will not be possible to develop nondual wisdom because, according to this path, everything you experience should be seen as a manifestation of the source of wisdom. The word dzogs means "complete," so our natural state, which is where we find ourselves, is completion in itself. That complete state is normally referred to as "dharmakaya." Securing that original dwelling place is the aim of this path.

My friends, finding this original dwelling place is like finding your dream home. The most beautiful, most palatial dwelling place you could find. Normally, in ordinary circumstances, when we have a nice house, we have to fill it with valuable objects. In this case, you should fill that original dwelling place with the accumulation of diverse and varied spiritual experiences. If you succeed in this, you will experience great bliss, which is the fruit of having found your original place. You can realize that in this very life. If you have been able to attain enlightenment, you will be naturally inclined to help others without any deliberation or exertion.

You should therefore constantly reflect on impermanence and your own mortality to give yourself that extra impetus so that you don't waste time pursuing unnecessary things. This life is like clouds moving in the sky. It does not stay in one place, even for a second. Your body is like a bubble on the surface of a pool; it is insubstantial and can burst at any moment. Your life and body are very fragile. It is hard to acquire but easily lost.

There are also many obstacles to pursuing a spiritual path. We often have no opportunity to hear the spiritual teachings and even when we do have that opportunity, to apply them and actually practice them is very, very difficult. There are so many obstacles that need to be surmounted. Thinking in this way, you should try to inject yourself with enthusiasm and engender vigor. Readers of this manual, please remind yourselves of this particular fact. Life is fragile and can be easily destroyed.

May what I have written bring spiritual fruition, like the blossoming of a flower bud, and may all sentient beings be transported to the state of buddhahood.

That concludes the meditation manual known as *The Great Completion that Reveals the Natural Freedom of the Mind* (*rdzogs-pa chen-po sems-nyid rang-grol, mahasandhicitta-tisvamutkinama*).

TRALEG KYABGON COMMENTARY ON THE GOAL OF SPIRITUAL PRACTICE

THE KAYAS

Sambhogakaya refers to the five conflicting emotions, the five wisdoms, and the five lights. In the bardo, you see all kinds of different lights and have very intense feelings. It is said that our emotions and feelings are magnified in the bardo. If we can recognize our lust, desire, anger, jealousy, and so on, and if we can recognize what is going on while we are in the bardo, instead of just reacting on impulse because of these strong emotions, the bardo experience becomes sambhogakaya experience. Even the manifestations of different beings are representations of sambhogakaya experience. Most of the deities that we visualize are representations of sambhogakaya experience.

Luminosity corresponds to sambhogakaya because sambhogakaya experiences come from the radiancy of the mind, and that is associated with the five wisdoms, the five poisons, and so on. That is why practically all the deities belong to buddha-families. The mandala consists of five buddha-families. The mandala is a sort of map of the sambhogakaya experience. All the deities must belong to one or the other of the five buddha-families, and they represent the transformed energy of one or the other of the five poisons.

Sambhogakaya experience can also take place in visions and dreams or in certain uncontrollable urges that all of a sudden manifest as something creative. For no apparent reason you become this great writer or something. In the teachings it is said there could be a practitioner who is barely literate and then out of the blue they become this great author. Someone who was seen as a bit of a simpleton now has all this creativity flowing out of them. So that is another form of sambhogakaya manifestation. I normally translate sambhogakaya as the "symbolic aspect of Buddha's being," because according to Buddhism, we live in the world and communicate with it through body, speech, and mind. Speech is particularly associated with communication, and sambhogakaya corresponds to the speech center. Dharmakaya corresponds to the mind, sambhogakaya to the speech, and nirmanakaya to the body. On the sambhogakaya level, communication does not take place through words and sentences. It can arise in visions, dreams, and sudden upsurges of creative energy.

The nirmanakaya dissolves into sambhogakaya and that dissolves into dharmakaya because what is more gross dissolves into what is more subtle. Buddha Shakyamuni, for example, couldn't keep on living forever. Even for enlightened beings, a time comes when the present incarnation has to be "left behind," for want of a better term. When that happens, the continuity of the enlightened consciousness doesn't come to an end with the physical body. That consciousness enters into the sambhogakaya state. The sambhogakaya state, unlike the dharmakaya, still has characteristics and attributes in terms of five wisdoms and so on. There is that symbolic manifestation of the sambhogakaya dimension of buddha's being. Beyond that is dharmakaya which, as Longchenpa said, is like the space itself. It has no characteristics or attributes. You cannot say dharmakaya is like this or like that, but you can say sambhogakaya is like this or like that. For example, as Longchenpa said, the sambhogakaya is the five wisdoms: the wisdom of ultimate reality, mirror-like wisdom, the wisdom of equanimity, the wisdom of all-accomplishment, and the wisdom of discrimination. They function on the level of sambhogakaya with all the imagery of gods and goddesses, the symbolic, psychic manifestations associated with the sambhogakaya level of being.

The grosser kayas dissolve into the more subtle kayas, but then the reverse process takes place. From the dharmakaya arises sambhogakaya, and from sambhogakaya arises the nirmanakaya again. There is this devolutionary and evolutionary process, like an implosion and an explosion. You do not stay in the dharmakaya state. The sambhogakaya again arises from the dharmakaya, and then the nirmanakaya arises from sambhogakaya. Then, when the enlightened being has done whatever needs to be done and the time has come for them to depart from the world, the nirmanakaya dissolves back into sambhogakaya and sambhogakaya dissolves into the dharmakaya. Longchenpa has been going through the bardo journey and bardo experiences. Even ordinary people like us enter into the dharmakaya state at the time of death. That is called "the bardo of dharmakaya" in the bardo teachings. Gross forms of consciousness are dissolving into more subtle levels of consciousness. Then there is, again, the re-emergence of the conscious evolutionary process taking place subsequent to that.

THE PRESENT MOMENT OF CONSCIOUSNESS

Longchenpa says that liberation and dissipation happen in the same moment. This is like turning the lights on in a dark room. The very moment the light is turned on, the darkness disappears. It happens simultaneously. It is not the case that first there is darkness and then light comes. The dissipation of the darkness occurs at the very moment the light comes on. In the same way, liberation occurs the moment a thought or emotion arises in the mind; it doesn't happen subsequent to the occurrence of that particular conflicting emotion. In the moment that conflicting emotion has arisen, liberation has already occurred. However, this does not happen automatically, otherwise we would all be incredibly advanced beings by now. As Longchenpa says, this process of simultaneous liberation occurs when we don't cling or grasp onto what has arisen. There is no question of something coming before something else. We need to have awareness, but we also need to let go of what we are aware of and not latch onto it. If we grasp onto something, it's no longer possible to be aware, we have already become caught up in the entanglement.

The two wisdoms that arise when you become enlightened come from the five wisdoms. Even though I have not seen this written anywhere, I think it would be safe to say that the wisdom of dharmakaya is the same as the wisdom which enables us to see the nature of things, to see how things exist. The other four wisdoms enable us to see the extent of things, to apprehend the individual, unique characteristics of things. But again, those two wisdoms are not totally different; they overlap. Basically, one wisdom is about seeing the relative, phenomenal aspect and the other is about seeing the absolute aspect. For example, the Mahayana teachings talk about relative and absolute truth. Again, we could safely say—although it has not really been said this way—the wisdom that enables us to apprehend the extent of things allows us to see the relative truth more fully, meaning that we see how it works without being lured by the spectacles of the phenomenal world. The wisdom that enables us to see the nature of things understands absolute truth. One wisdom allows us to see the diversity of the phenomenal world, which is relative truth, and the other wisdom allows us to see the nature of that world, which is absolute truth. It is about seeing unity in diversity and diversity in unity.

PART TWO

Root Text:
Chonyi Rangdrol—Natural Freedom of
Ultimate Reality

Chapter Five

The Natural Freedom of Our Authentic State is Realized through Intrinsic Awareness

I prostrate to Kuntuzangpo.
From the very beginning, in the original luminosity,
the unwavering mind is free from any fixation and is totally spacious.
Within the unsurpassed sphere of reality,
arise the three kayas, which are self-established and totally blissful.
I prostrate to this fundamental ground which defies change.

Although the minds of myself and all sentient beings are already purified,
due to the influence of self-deception,
we wander aimlessly in the temple of solitude.
Those who wish to be liberated from this state,
should embark upon the path of the impeccable chariot.
Herein is the quintessential teaching based on the definitive meaning.

What we have to realize from the Dzogchen point of view, is that before the samsaric state of mind came into existence, there was a state where there was no differentiation between subject and object. There were no disturbances from emotional upheavals and so on because the luminosity of the mind is unoriginated and exists in a state of total spaciousness. This is called *yangs-pa che*, which is a very difficult term to translate. It doesn't simply mean just being spacious; it is more like a field, like spaciousness.

The three kayas (*trikaya, sku-gsum*) are the nirmanakaya, sambhogakaya, and dharmakaya. In Dzogchen, all three kayas are already embodied in our own existence. They are the starting point. We do not start as normal sentient beings who are afflicted with emotions and more or less content with that existence. We start as beings who are embodied with these three modes of existence—the *trikaya* or *sku gsum*—because they are self-established within the mind right from the beginning. No guru has had to give that to us; no one has to introduce that to us. We have always been that way. We have always been established as three kayas, so we have always existed in a blissful way.

The fundamental ground is *gzhi* in Tibetan, even though that term is not included here. The ground is the starting point that does not change. Dzogchen says that a person can realize the three kayas because we already possess them. Since we possess them within ourselves already, we are already a buddha, which is *sangs rgyas* in Tibetan. *Sangs* means "to be purified," "to be someone who has overcome emotional and intellectual difficulties," while *rgyas* means "someone who has flowered or grown." So *sangs rgyas* means someone who is purified and has flourished spiritually. According to Longchenpa and Dzogchen, we are already like that. Even when we feel we are afflicted by emotions or corrupted spiritually, we are already a buddha.

The reason we don't realize that is due to the influence of self-deception. Therefore, we wander aimlessly, as Longchenpa says here, in the temple of solitude. The temple of solitude is the samsaric world because that world is almost like a temple. We are so engrossed with our own egocentricity, our own I-ness or ego, that we forget everything about everything else. We forget about the world, and we forget about all the other people. Then he goes on to say that those who want to get out of this situation should get on the path of the impeccable chariot, which is the path of Dzogchen, the great perfection.

The Buddhist teachings include teachings with an interpretive meaning (*neyartha, drang-don*) and teachings with a definitive meaning (*nitartha, nges-don*). The latter are teachings that cannot be interpreted in this way or that because they contain the essential meaning. For example, sutras that say the Buddha subdued a demon are interpretive teachings because they are allegorical for the obstructions of the mind. Teachings that involve understanding the nature of the mind or the nature of the reality are definitive teachings. Longchenpa says this teaching explains the definitive meaning for how to get out of the state of ignorance, not the interpretive meaning because there are no interpretations of mythology involved.

OUR EXPERIENCES ARE ROOTLESS

My friends, samsara is a bottomless pit, where pain and suffering make us agitated and disturbed. We are in this condition because of fixation on the notion of a self, which has arisen from ignorance. We must practice Dzogchen meditation to gain a proper view of our natural state. Whatever we experience in samsara and nirvana has been rootless from the beginning. It is self-manifesting, without permanence or cessation, and beyond the concepts of coming and going. It is experienced within the context of ultimate reality, which is all-encompassing, like space.

We experience varieties of pain and suffering in the course of our lives, and we become very agitated and disturbed due to that suffering and pain. Why is it that we are in this condition? We are fixated on the notion of an intrinsic self. To think there is an intrinsic self is delusory, a delusion that has arisen from ignorance (*avidya, ma-rig-pa*). We engage in Dzogchen meditation because the antidote to the samsaric condition is to develop a proper view about our natural state.

Whatever experiences we have in our lives, both on the samsaric and nirvanic levels, have been originless right from the beginning. Primordially speaking, whatever we experience has no roots; its manifestation is not grounded in any way. Whether the experiences are good or bad, pleasant or unpleasant, they are all equally rootless.

Whatever arises is self-manifesting. It does not fall into the extremes of permanence or cessation because whatever arises in the mind has no permanence. On the other hand, it does not cease to manifest. Whatever arises in the mind goes beyond the concepts of coming and going. There are no extremes within our mental experiences and our psychological states because in reality everything is nondual. We experience everything in the context of ultimate reality (*dharmata, chos-nyid*), which is all-encompassing, like space.

Now, that does not mean that our experiences could get all mixed up and blurry. Every single experience is unique, and we can't mistake one experience for another. Experiences are variegated and of all different kinds and while each experience is unique in itself, as soon as we have that experience, at the very moment the experience arises in the mind, we begin to realize that its nature is beyond conceptualization.

This even applies to our perception of the external world. We think there is an external world that exists independently of our minds, that there is something out there with an independent existence, but that is not so. Whatever we perceive is dependent on our mind. Nonetheless, when we look at the mind itself, we cannot say everything that we experience is produced by the mind. This is very important actually. What we experience regarding the external world is not the mind and it is also not a product of the mind. What is it then? How do things exist? It is like people with cataracts who see falling hair. They think strands of hair are falling through the air due to certain defects in the eye organ. This is a mistaken perception, but one could be thinking that these hairs really do exist out there. The dualistic way of thinking comes into it, and one begins to think, "That is a hair out there and this is me in here."

This dualistic way of thinking is so entrenched in our experience that we even respond with real emotion in dream. We may dream about elephants—people probably don't dream about elephants these days, maybe a Porsche—or a massive build-up of foot soldiers, and think we are in the middle of a battle between warring parties. We may think, "I am in the midst of this battle where warring parties are about to fight," but it is only a dream. When we dream a scene like this, we are afraid, but why are we afraid? We think that what we are experiencing is something other than ourselves. That kind of experience is dependent on the mind. We may be afraid, but that fear is conditional. It is contingent on the mental state we are in while dreaming.

Now, even if our experiences are illusory, we cannot say they are either internal or external. We can't say the illusory state is only mental or the illusory state is stimulated by something external to our mental state. It goes beyond that. When we begin to realize that the source of our experience is not something we can pin down to either internal causes or external stimulation, we begin to realize whatever we experience is rootless. We realize its nature.

When we have that understanding, all fears dissipate naturally. There will be no dualism about what experiences are internal and what experiences are external. It is the mind that becomes fixated on these concepts, but in reality, there is no duality between internal and external states of affairs. Only the mind divides them, which is totally unskillful. We are uneducated and unskilled in the way that we experience things, and we take everything that we experience as true. We get fixated on whatever we experience, and we hold onto it by thinking, "This is the truth, this is it." That is how the illusion of samsara is created.

People who are skillful and spiritually educated know this is not real. They know that we should not see things in that dualistic fashion, and they do not see things that way. Precisely for that reason, they see samsara as nirvana. They find the liberation of nirvana through realizing the nature of the samsaric condition.

THE INSEPARABILITY OF ULTIMATE
REALITY AND PHENOMENA

Our perception of the phenomenal world is grounded in ultimate reality, which is originless because it has not been brought into being by causes and conditions. We nonetheless experience a multitude of things in the phenomenal world. Even though what we experience is diverse, there is no duality to be found in terms of their nature. The relationship between the perceiver and the perceived is like an image and a reflection of that image. In the same way, the diversity of the phenomenal world cannot be separated from ultimate reality. Just like water and its quality of being moist cannot be separated because moisture is an intrinsic characteristic of water, the relationship between ultimate reality and the diversity of phenomena as available to our perceptions, cannot be separated.

When we look at the variety of perceptual apparitions in the phenomenal world, we can say "such and such" a thing has come into existence, but at the very moment of its coming into being, it also reveals its state of nonorigination. As soon as something arises, that very entity reveals its own nature as originless, for that is its true condition.

Those two aspects of reality—the phenomenal aspect and the ultimate aspect—cannot be separated. We may think of reality in terms of a lack of motion, but it does not stay motionless. While we can say a certain thing has ceased to exist, there is no concept of anything ceasing to exist from the perspective of ultimate reality. For ultimate reality, the concepts of increase and decrease do not apply. The nature of whatever arises in the field of our experience is revealed to be originless, unconditioned, and unproduced.

We may try to impose conceptual categories on the various presentations of mind by labelling, naming, and trying to fit them into our existing conceptual categories so that we can grasp their essence. But whatever we try to grasp will be revealed as devoid of essence precisely because nothing has ever been bound, corrupted, or confined in terms of the natural state of dharmata. Everything that arises is inseparable from the ultimate true condition, which is symbolized by Kuntuzangpo.

We may assume that our diverse experiences are substantial and possess an essence but as a matter of fact they do not. We should refrain from fixating on the diversity of experiences, using concepts and ideas to pick out a certain thing in the world and identify it, saying, "This is this and not something else," and so on. The way we identify things in the world depends upon convention, they are unidentifiable as this or that from their own side. Things themselves do not tell us what they are; in other words, they are unidentifiable. The nature of things is like space, and from that perspective, they don't come prelabeled. There is no doer and there is no deed. Things don't reveal their individuality by saying "I am this" or "I am that" as if they came in packages that were already divided.

STRAYING FROM THE PATH

From the Dzogchen point of view, we should maintain the same kind of attitude toward Buddhist practices, teachings, and traditions, because the Buddhist vehicles of the Hinayana, Mahayana, and Vajrayana exist for the convenience and utility of practitioners. In other words, the yana systems are designed by human beings for the benefit of human beings. They didn't arise by themselves already labeled. Longchenpa says that practitioners should therefore beware of people who get caught up in sectarianism because anyone who is obsessed about or attached to one of these systems can be very dogmatic about their specific approach to the development of view, meditation, and enactment.

There are many different levels and variations within these practices in relation to the view, meditation, and enactment that depend on the tradition or system you are affiliated with. If you become totally caught up in one tradition, thinking that it alone represents reality, you will have missed the point. You will have failed to realize what is most important in your spiritual practice: to realize the nature of the mind. It's very difficult to see the nature of the mind when we are obsessed with a particular tradition and its practices.

If you are not careful, you could become a shravaka or pratyekabuddha practitioner or a Mahayana follower of Yogacara or Madhyamaka, where you try to determine the twofold selflessness of persons and the phenomenal world, the difference between the two, and so on. You can get lost because of the danger of getting caught up in a conceptual web from which you cannot extricate yourself. You could spend a very long time in the samsaric condition without being able to fully achieve emancipation. This applies to the tantric practices as well, to the kriya, charya, and anu-yoga stages, and to the development and fulfillment stage practices.

If you become bogged down in the details of these teachings, techniques, and approaches, instead of using them to emancipate yourself, you will get nowhere near your natural state, because that is totally beyond contrivance. You won't even approximate that state because your mind will have become completely immersed in overactive mentation (*manasikara, yid-la byed-pa*). Instead of using these practices to attain emancipation, you will use them to get even more caught up in a contrived state of being, when you should be learning how to be in a state of noncontrivance.

There are many ways to fool ourselves through practice, even for people who are just doing simple meditation. If you develop a certain view through meditation and action, which leads to a cessation in your thoughts and sensations, you might think this mental state is a sign of advancement on the path. Some people might have an experience where there is no concept of the three times and then think their mind of the present moment is completely free. Other people try to count their breaths or to identify their mental events and then try to rest in that state, but instead get swayed this way and that by the waves of disturbing conceptions.

Even people who engage in tantric practices can go astray. Some yogis do prana yoga, where they learn to manipulate and control their breath and to control their physical dexterity. They may engage in sexual yoga. They may get a glimpse of bliss and luminosity through these practices, but again, they mistakenly assume those glimpses to be the same as having a glimpse into the natural state of their own being. Instead of realizing their natural state, they get overwhelmed by lust and desire. People who don't do those practices can get caught up in another way. They become so obsessed by the cultivation of virtue and the abandonment of non-virtue that they have no time to see their real essence and fail to understand their own natural condition.

Dzogchen practitioners should continually remind themselves of the perils of getting caught up in the conditioned mind. This is the same as illusion because these things are projections of a fertile mind. If we aren't skillful in how we use our practices, we will never find liberation from samsara. We will just remain in the bondage of samsara without ever being able to free ourselves from it. You should think that not being able to appreciate the significance of being in the natural state is like having a precious stone and throwing it away because we fail to recognize its value. We instead go looking for something that has no value because of our misperception and delusion. If we are unable to appreciate the significance of the nature of the mind, and if we abandon it and get too caught up in various methods and techniques, we will be totally oppressed by our confusion. This is like being thrown into the snake pit of hope and fear.

Unless we learn to relax into our natural state, applying too much effort will never lead to emancipation. A mind that overtaxes itself will never find freedom. What needs to be found should be found naturally, not by getting caught up in the notion of a seeker and the act of seeking.

If we want to gain insight into our own condition, we don't need to seek or even examine too much. Just allow whatever arises in the mind to be there, without fixation or contrivance, without trying to identify it as this or that, and without thinking about whether it is a good thing or a bad thing. Then you will recognize it as inseparable from your own natural state. You do not even need to go out of your way to find ultimate reality.

A lot of unnecessary energy can be spent just looking for something we think we should find. If we have the Dzogchen approach to meditation, we won't even have to spend a lot of time practicing the tantric development and fulfillment stages, because with this attitude, all we need to practice will come to us more easily. If that happens, we won't have to exert ourselves to manifest the qualities we need to advance on the path; they will manifest automatically. If those qualities are not present, and we overexert ourselves in a foolish and stubborn way, that would be energy misspent. We need to view the various traditions and systems as contingent on our own needs. They were designed by our mind to help us along and have no intrinsic reality from their own side.

ORIGINAL FREEDOM

The only mandala that ultimately matters is the mandala of Dzogchen, the great completion, which is the same as our true condition. In the natural state of being, everything is perfect by itself. The essential teachings of the different spiritual systems are all complete, as are the view, meditation, enactment, and fruition of enlightening experiences. Even the concepts of samsara and nirvana find their completion in that state.

If we realize that our own true condition is beyond contrivance, we will also realize that emancipation is not something we have to attain, but something we have to reclaim. Right from the beginning, we have been free, we just don't know it. In fact, generally speaking, there is no liberation. "Liberation" just means reclaiming the originally free state of being that we are already within, a state where there is no activity, which is called the "kingly state of dharmakaya" (*chos-sku rgyal-po*).

When you realize you are in this state, you also realize that you do not vanish into a state of passivity. You continue to interact with the world through your physical embodiment, contingent on your dharmakaya state. Enlightened beings do not act in the world in the ordinary sense because nothing is done deliberately. Everything is accomplished spontaneously.

This is the meaning of Dzogchen. Dzogchen means to realize that everything is complete in the original state. There is nothing that needs to be added. Everything that appears is already complete in itself. Everything is equal because everything is the same in the unoriginated state. There is no center or periphery and there are no divisions in the mandala of the natural state. To remain in this natural state without fixation is to understand what is truly real.

If you can remain in that state, without entertaining thoughts of acceptance or rejection, cultivation or abandonment, you have developed the proper view of dzogpa chenpo. This is not a view about this or that, so we can't say the view of Dzogchen is this or that.

You must understand this point. Whatever view you fixate upon is just another potential trap. To have real presence of mind without fixation is to have genuine wisdom. We need to understand that to have the proper view comes from letting go of all forms of fixation.

We don't need to make any extra effort to realize emptiness either. If what we experienced externally and internally was not already insubstantial by nature, contemplating and analyzing emptiness would not make them lose their substance. Things are empty of inherent existence because they are insubstantial by nature, so emptiness is already present and at hand. Why make an enormous effort to realize our spiritual goals when what we are trying to realize is already present before and within us? If you understand this point, you will not need to engage in visualization, ritual practices, chanting, mantra recitation, and so on. Not only that, you won't need to hope you are doing the right thing or be afraid you are doing the wrong thing.

Your spiritual goal is already present within you, so you don't need to exert yourself too much in trying to produce something new. You are not trying to bring into being something that is not already there. It is already there so you don't have to bring it into existence. If what you were trying to bring into existence were not already there, then no matter how much effort you made, it would be like trying to extract gold from coal.

That's why it's so crucial to develop the understanding that nothing that appears has any substantial reality. If you let whatever experience you have spontaneously arise, without interference or contrivance, and without trying to vigorously apply antidotes, you have realized the real essence of the supreme tantric teachings. If you understand this approach to spirituality properly, you won't have to worry about mantras, tantras, or various spiritual systems because you won't be fixated on anything. You can remain in the state of natural freedom and even let go of fixation on view, meditation, and action.

There is no differentiation within the mandala of Dzogchen because everything is complete within itself. All the spiritual systems, view, meditation, and action are complete. Even samsara and nirvana are complete in this state of realization. That kind of freedom is attained effortlessly by not trying to condition the mind. When we are not trying to condition the mind, we can remain in the state of ultimate nonactivity, which corresponds to dharmakaya.

The sambhogakaya aspect is also complete because whatever arises in relation to our mental and physical being as expressions of the three kayas, and as various manifestations of the wisdom-mind, helps us to realize that nothing needs to be accepted or rejected. Everything is seen as pure. Everything is seen through pure perception.

Everything that exists does so in the state of equanimity, in terms of reality. Reality does not discriminate so everything is equal and complete in its own individual way within its sphere. This is how we realize that which is unoriginated, that which has no center or periphery. When we are not even attached to that idea, and no longer thinking in a dualistic fashion in terms of subject and object, we have the true understanding of what is meant by "great completion." We don't have to be too preoccupied with the idea of acceptance and rejection, cultivation and prevention. This understanding is called "the supreme view of all views" within the Buddhist teachings. That is what is meant by dzogpa chenpo.

We realize that with a mind that is not directed monofocally on an object, a mind that is free from and devoid of fixation; in other words, a mind that's not given to excessive conceptual activity. A mind that is directed toward something in a singular fashion—a mind that is not expansive, but instead is directed to things in a very myopic way—will make everything we experience a source of bondage. If the mind becomes freer of its inner inhibitions and constrictions, and more expansive instead, then whatever arises will be experienced by the wisdom-mind itself.

NONDUAL WISDOM

If you can apply this supreme view to the external world, you will experience a sense of well-being and a feeling of ease. The more you try to capture the world through conceptual categories, the more elusive it will become, and you will realize it is impossible to pin anything down and make it concrete. If you go a step further through the use of analysis, you will see that the world as we understand it has no intrinsic nature, and hence, is impossible to fully grasp through conceptual categories.

When you change your focus, when you turn your attention onto the mind that tries to impose some order on the world through conceptual categories, you will become more observant of the mind and its functions. You will then begin to realize the mind is in a state of timelessness. When you are fully attuned to your present state of mind, there is no past, present, or future to be found. Not only that, but the nature of the mind has no origin. It does not dwell anywhere either because it has no locus or abode, nor can it cease to exist. This is all precisely because mind has no definable characteristics. Mind is not a thing, it's not an entity, it has no shape or color. That being the case, it's very difficult to identify it as this or that. Whenever we examine the mind, it becomes elusive; it is very difficult to grasp.

We cannot grasp the mind and say, "Now I've found it," yet the mind is what enables us to have experiences. Without the mind, we cannot have any experiences at all. When we do, we normally think, "I had such and such experience," but when we are attuned to our current mental state, there is no mind to be found separate from what is reflected in it. We can't say, "Here is my mind and there are the experiences my mind has generated," as if they were different.

When we are fully present in our current state of mind, there is no concept of external and internal and there is no concept of perceiver and perceived, of the experiencing subject and its experiences. All these dualistic ways of thinking and experiencing are illusory. We think there is something out there external to the mind, and we think there is a mind enclosed within our body, but there is no such separation.

Instead of thinking of subject and object as two separate entities or substances, a mental and a material one, we should think of the relationship between subject and object as similar to a mirror and its reflection. The objects reflected in a mirror cannot be separated from the mirror. We should also think of them as similar to waves and the ocean because waves cannot be separated from the ocean. In reality, we have to realize the indivisibility of things.

When we understand the view of nondualism properly, we will no longer be subject to dualistic ways of thinking, and we won't need to worry about what things to cultivate and what things to abandon because we will realize that everything is complete. This comprehension of nonduality is the same as seeing everything that exists as complete in itself. This is what maha-ati teaches. That is why it is said that even ordinary sentient beings are intrinsically pure and awake despite their delusions, obscurations, and mental defilements. Everyone is intrinsically pure. Everyone is already a buddha. That is why it is said, "You are intrinsically awakened even while you remain in the samsaric world."

You should learn to develop an appreciation of this teaching on nonduality through the instructions of your guru so that you realize that the appearances of the phenomenal world and the mind are inextricably bound to each other. When you understand this point, no matter what happens during practice, it will be fine for you. It won't matter if the mind is a state of turbulence or at rest. A Dzogchen meditator would not think, "I want equilibrium and quietude. I don't want agitation and mental disturbances." They would understand that whatever arises in the mind is part of mind's adornment. In that way, whether you are at rest or in a state of agitation, there is always stability, and you cannot get overwhelmed. That confidence arises from realizing that the way you are in your own authentic state is complete. It never fluctuates, it is never fickle, it is always steady and not subject to sudden changes.

RESTING IN THE NATURAL STATE

Realizing this authentic state is no different from realizing the primordial buddha, Kuntuzangpo. We need to develop the understanding that our primordial state is not subject to change, and the concept of time does not apply to it. We cannot say that our authentic state is in the process of development, that it only existed in a state of potentiality in the past, then it gradually became manifest, and it will be realized in the future. We cannot say that because what was there before and what will be realized is one and the same thing.

The meditator who has embarked on this path should cultivate a totally unbiased, nonpartisan way of seeing things. You will never be able to see things clearly if you view them in a biased way that takes sides. Liberation will become practically impossible then. On the other hand, if you can expand your vision and broaden your view, liberation will be in sight and the ability to see things in a nondualistic way will come easily.

The way to gain insight into our natural state needs to be properly understood. You don't gain this insight by looking with great deliberation, or through repeated analysis, or through conceptualizing about it or using symbols. You only gain insight into your natural state by resting in it directly.

The key to resting directly in your natural state lies in abandoning fixation. For as long as there is mental fixation, you may want to realize nonduality, but you will fail in your attempts because you are fixating on the concept of nonduality. Even if you want to realize the nature of and the relationship between relative and absolute truth, you will only become fixated on those concepts if fixation is still lingering. Even if you desire the merging of opposites, this won't be real and authentic, but just a conceptual construct. In brief, the danger of becoming entangled in mental fixation is immense. You have been subject to the illusion of dualistic thinking from time immemorial, from beginningless time. This tendency will only persist and may even be reinforced in a more refined way if you embark on the spiritual path without relinquishing fixation.

You have to realize the importance of resting directly in your own natural state and not think that you have to find something that can be identified as this or that. When you do that, all your old habits will resurface, and everything will become distorted. You should maintain intrinsic awareness in relation to whatever arises in the mind. There is no hierarchy in terms of your experiences so you should not value certain things and devalue others. If you do that, you have not been able to let go, and fixation still remains.

It is important in meditation to maintain an awareness that is all-pervasive so that the mind is not monofocally directed toward certain things. We do this by not getting too caught up with the idea of using antidotes and thinking about what should be eliminated, ejected, or expelled and what antidotes we could use to achieve that goal, because we can get fixated on that as well. This is the quintessential teaching of maha-ati.

When you realize that, in reality, everything exists on the same level without any hierarchy, you will see whatever is there for what it is and leave it at that. This will lead to the experience of nondual wisdom. There is no room for conceptual paraphernalia and there is no need for intellectual searching because you are not bound by what you have experienced. Your experiences are not tarnished or corrupted by mental fixation.

Just as space does not discriminate in terms of what is within it, neither does ultimate reality or our authentic state. Letting go of mental fixation and developing nondual wisdom is the way to develop the correct view. To realize that is to have a proper understanding. That is truly remarkable.

When intrinsic awareness is fully realized, you will realize there is no separation between samsara and nirvana either. Having recognized yourself and having understood your own true condition, you are also free of the concepts of bondage and freedom. This is also the quintessential teaching of maha-ati.

Even though we are all dwelling in our natural condition, we do not recognize that. In order to introduce the natural state to those who have not recognized it, we need meditation manuals of this kind. Through such texts, we begin to realize our own pristine, unpolluted, uncorrupted, natural state of mind, which is self-luminous. Since there is no separation between the appearances of the phenomenal world and the mind itself, everything that is experienced is seen as the illusory play of mind. It's only through the realization of intrinsic awareness or rigpa, which is nonpartisan, impartial, and unbiased, that we can come to this understanding.

TRALEG KYABGON COMMENTARY ON THE NATURAL FREEDOM OF OUR AUTHENTIC STATE IS REALIZED THROUGH INTRINSIC AWARENESS

We have to keep in mind that while there is no intrinsic difference between pleasant and unpleasant things, there is a difference in terms of our experience. This difference between how we perceive things and how we experience them is dependent on our perception, which in turn is dependent on aspects of the self, such as character, personality, attitude, and so on. On the relative level, there is a difference, because what is painful is painful and what is pleasant is pleasant, but on another level, what is painful is not intrinsically painful and what is pleasant is not intrinsically pleasurable.

An enlightened person who experiences things in a nondual way would still experience them as pleasant and unpleasant. I'm sure even His Holiness the Dalai Lama would express a preference for certain foods. Just because someone is enlightened doesn't mean they no longer have any preferences; they are just not obsessed about their preferences. We, however, are completely obsessed. We always want things to be a certain way. We want tea in a particular way, we want a cappuccino in a particular way; we will only go to restaurants or cafes where they make cappuccinos the way we like them. We get so obsessed, from little things like a coffee, to big things like how we relate to people or the world. We think there is something intrinsically real about it all.

What we experience in the external world is not mind but nor is it a product of mind. Our experiences are neither purely internal nor purely external. Experience is not solely a projection of our mind; there is something going on outside our mind, which has made us perceive things in a certain way. Those perceptions are not entirely external either, because there is a strong mental component attached to them. Whatever we experience is illusory in that sense because everything we experience is conditioned. Things come from within, and things exert themselves from without, all of which makes our experiences conditioned and illusory.

However, when we talk about illusion, we are not talking about mirages or things that are totally unreal. For Buddhists, illusions are quite real; they have their own reality. It's just not the kind of reality we imagine it to be. "Illusion" means our experiences are conditional because they never go beyond the conditioned state. That doesn't mean that nothing is real. If someone were to punch you on the nose, it would be real enough. There are internal mental states and external physical affairs, and we have certain experiences when they come together. The mind and those external events are totally interdependent. Sometimes we can't even draw a line between the internal and the external. Mind is not locked inside our body but it reaches out to the physical world, and whatever we experience in the physical world also reaches into the mind. Where is the border? There is no customs point. All kinds of things get smuggled in and out.

It doesn't matter how much we try to hang onto something, we can't do it, realistically speaking. Even when we get traumatized or "psychologically damaged" by certain experiences, as people say, even that experience is always slipping away. Everything we experience is slipping away. It is relentless, like the aging process. You get fixated on something and try to hold onto it through repetitive conceptual chatter, but that will not create permanency. Experiences are rootless because they are not grounded in anything. There is no permanency there. Fixation on our trauma is only a perpetuation of what we experienced; it is not the same as what we originally experienced. We are just perpetuating the same old storyline, repeating it over and over. It's a re-enactment of the original event, an attempt to convince ourselves that this is what is real. But is it? All experience is rootless. It is illusion, even though illusion is real enough on the experiential level. It is groundless and rootless. This is why experiences are said to be like illusions and not something we should become too fixated on.

The idea of rootlessness implies that freedom is available all the time. We normally get completely fixated. Every time we experience something, we latch onto it and won't let go. Whether it is pleasant or unpleasant, joyous or painful, we just can't let go and we hang on for dear life. To say that our experiences are rootless is another way of saying that we should not and cannot latch onto things in that way. Some Mahayana teachings use the example of trying to keep a handful of sand in your fist. You may hold the sand tightly, but it will keep slipping through your fingers, and when you open your hand, hardly any sand will remain. Our experiences are also like that.

Our perception is our own perception and that's okay. That is all we need and that is all we have. Perception doesn't have to correspond to the truth. What is the truth anyway? When we become fixated on a certain concept of truth, we can't get on with anybody because they don't agree with our version of things. It is liberating to relinquish the need for something to be "the truth." We do need to regard some things as truer than others, but that is good enough. That is reality anyway. If you want more than that, you become a fundamentalist, a dogmatic, opinionated, and judgmental arbitrator of the true, just, and real. The desire to decide what is real and unreal is a very painful experience.

The nature of everything that arises is inseparable from our true condition. They are inseparable in the same way that water and moisture are inseparable. The appearance of things and impermanence can't be divided. In other words, the diversity of phenomena originates at the relative level because they appear to come into existence and to dissipate. However, whatever is taking place is sustained by that which has no origin. There are many traditional examples of this, such as space and clouds. Clouds arise from space and dissipate back into space. Everything that we experience arises from our natural state in the same way and everything that we experience dissipates back into our natural state, which is originless.

They do so because we cannot separate one from the other. Even our deluded thoughts, ideas, and emotions, which are not identical to our natural state, have the same nature as our natural state. They are, in reality, identical. Buddhists always say everything is impermanent because everything is subject to change or stages of decay. Things come into existence, persist for a while, and then disintegrate. There is obviously a "coming and going," as the Buddhist teachings say. We could also say, "The fact that everything is impermanent is a permanent fact." Everything is permanently impermanent because there is no time when impermanence came into existence. Things are eternally and permanently impermanent. "Originless" means something like that.

Longchenpa talks about being oppressed by hope (re-ba) and fear (dog-pa). While rewa literally means "hope," dogpa means more than "fear"; it includes doubt, indecision, and things of that nature. What are hope and fear? We hope that everything will fall into place without any obstacles, and we fear not succeeding. We therefore get bogged down in all kinds of doubts, "Maybe this won't work," "Maybe I'm not designed for this," "Maybe this isn't what I want to do." All kinds of things like that. This even applies to our hope for enlightenment and our fear of delusion, mental obscuration, and samsara. We hope for nirvana, and we fear samsara.

While it is not so difficult to understand what hope and fear mean, it is difficult to know what to do about them. As far as Longchenpa is concerned, we should not approach our spiritual practices with hope and fear. Hope and fear dominate most religious practices. You hope you will go to heaven, and you fear you may go to hell. You hope God is watching you and you fear the devil has already tempted you. These are real experiences for many people. Longchenpa isn't saying that we shouldn't have hope at all. He is saying that, in terms of our practice, we must learn to be with whatever arises without thinking that it portends something wonderful or indicates something terrible. People often say, "Today my meditation was good, I really enjoyed it, I'm making progress." The next time they meditate, they say, "Today my meditation was terrible, maybe I'm deluding myself about progress." We should basically give up worrying about things like that and just practice. As he says, just practice. Feeling encouraged or discouraged by our practice is simply our own mental projection. You have decided that something was good. If someone else had the same experience, they might not make the same decision.

We should not believe anything we think. We do need to make use of the concepts we have, but the world doesn't present itself with labels attached. That applies to our experiences as well. When we say, "That was a good experience," or "That was a bad experience," we are the ones who are making that judgement. The decision that something is pleasant or unpleasant is contingent on a variety of factors, both internal and external. If you have been feeling happy lately, your meditation will probably seem like a good experience and if you've been having a bad week, your meditation will seem even worse. That is what we have to realize. Our experiences are not the absolute indicators of anything. The basic point with hope and fear is that they take you away from where you are because you are projecting yourself into the future, which radically diminishes your capacity to be fully present in the moment. You are in the future, instead of dealing with what is at hand.

Longchenpa says "everything that exists is complete in itself" because in terms of the nature of things, there is no difference between a kilogram of gold and a pile of rubbish. Only the conceptual categories we impose on the world make them appear that way. From the perspective of the rubbish and the gold, there is no difference. It's the mind that slices up the world, it's the mind that evaluates things, and it's the mind that tries to impose some kind of order. But from the side of the things themselves, everything is equal. In other words, a kilogram of gold has no more reality than a pile of rubbish, and a pile of rubbish has no more reality than a kilogram of gold. We use conceptual categories to order the world and make it more intelligible, but the more we probe and analyze, the more elusive it becomes.

If things were very clear, we wouldn't have philosophers, sociologists, and psychologists. We wouldn't have them arguing with each other either. Everything is equal as it is impermanent. If that were not the case, ultimate reality would have a boundary or limit, but ultimate reality cannot have boundaries. If ultimate reality were present in some things and not others, it would not be all-pervasive, which is what it should be by definition. Impermanence does not discriminate so everything is equal in the eyes of impermanence. No one is spared, nothing is spared, so everything is equally impermanent.

All-pervasive awareness basically means that you are not trying to focus on any one thing, even if that thing is a thought or emotion. You are simply learning to be aware, just be aware, that's all—instead of thinking that you are the agent, awareness is the act, and what you are aware of is the object. As Longchenpa said, what we are aware of and the act of awareness are indivisible, like the reflection and the mirror. The reflection and the mirror are inseparable. If you break the mirror, the reflection disappears. The mirror does not think, "I have to reflect." It is the nature of the mirror to reflect. If we allow our mind to be, then awareness will arise automatically. We don't have to try to manufacture awareness. If we can just let ourselves be, awareness will arise.

When we become aware, we don't have to try to be aware of this or that, to reassure ourselves that we are aware. This approach may seem confusing, but this is more like the advanced practice of Dzogchen. Normally, when we start to meditate, we have to learn to be aware of this and that. We can't simply say, "I'm going to rest in my natural state and just be aware." That is the aim, nonetheless. Your meditation should gradually become like that. We are using habits to break down habits.

Rinchen Nyingpo—The Precious Heart Essence
Longchenpa's auto-commentary on the root text of the
Ultimate Reality Cycle

Chapter Six

Retreat Instructions—
The Pointing Out Instructions of Definitive Meaning
on Self-liberation into Ultimate Reality

THE ESSENTIAL INSTRUCTIONS

With the blessings of the Buddha of Infinite Light and
Guru Padmasambhava, the Lotus Born,
who manifests all the qualities of enlightenment,
I will now describe the essential instructions of this tradition.

There are many vehicles within the Buddhist system and all are
authentic in their respective ways. They all have genuine practices and
there are infinite options available. It is quite difficult to even fathom the
possibilities that these options afford us. However, as followers of
Dzogchen, we have to conclude that the esoteric practices of the
Vajrayana are the preferred and most legitimate way to attain
enlightenment. There are many ways to practice the Vajrayana, but
dzogpa chenpo or maha-ati is the ultimate option, because even though
it is associated with the Vajrayana, it contains the ultimate view and path.
Longchenpa says he will expound on the Dzogchen system by
emphasizing the notion of self-liberation into ultimate reality.

To understand teachings of this nature, we have to get three cardinal
points: the representation of the lineage masters, the mind-to-mind
transmission, and the stamp of authenticity of the transmission.

There are many kinds of lineage masters, but in brief, we have to
understand that the three aspects of our spiritual being—the dharmakaya
(chos-sku), sambhogakaya (longs-sku), and nirmanakaya (sprul-sku)—are

the ultimate lineage. Dharmakaya is our authentic state and is represented by the Buddha of Infinite Light, Amitabha. Sambhogakaya is our communicative aspect and is represented by the Buddha of Infinite Compassion, Avalokiteshvara. Nirmanakaya is our manifest aspect and is represented by Padmasambhava. The interaction between these three aspects of enlightenment is responsible for the continuation of the Dzogchen teachings. In the context of the nirmanakaya, we can also include Guru Rinpoche's consort, Yeshe Tsogyal, Vimalamitra, and so on.

Attaining liberation through the mind-to-mind transmission is taught in relation to the capability of the individual concerned. Some practitioners have the capacity to achieve enlightenment in one lifetime, others have the capacity to achieve enlightenment at the time of death or during the bardo state, and those who fail to do that, at the very least, have the capacity to attain enlightenment in a buddha-field.

In order to attain enlightenment in one lifetime, we have to engage in practice in three different ways. The first involves the preliminary practices (*sngon 'gro*), the second is the actual practice (*nyuge*), and the third deals with post-meditation situations. These are the three components in the teachings of the mind-to-mind transmission.

PRELIMINARIES

1. Guru Yoga

The practice of Guru Yoga involves sitting comfortably on a cushion, reciting the refuge and bodhicitta formulas, and then visualizing yourself as yourself, not as anybody else. You visualize a lotus and moon disk resting on the crown of your head. Upon the moon disk is a white syllable AH. Imagine that this white AH is radiating light in all directions and that your own and others' defilements and obscurations, the causes of suffering, are purified. The defilements of body, speech, and mind have all become purified. Then visualize your own body has been totally transformed. It is no longer the body you had before you started this practice session, but has suddenly become translucent and transparent, like a rainbow, so that it is verging on immaterial. Then you should think:

Now this body has become a receptacle for the essential esoteric teachings of the Vajrayana.

Turn your attention back to the white syllable AH, which is now resting on a lotus and moon disc in your heart center. This white AH transforms into your own root guru, who is not separate from Guru Padmasambhava, seated in your heart center and surrounded by all the lineage masters. Imagine they are all totally naked except for bone ornaments, and that each one is holding a damaru and bell. These lineage masters are making a racket, singing and dancing around your root guru, then at the end of the dancing, clouds of dakinis gather around them. While imagining these events, you should think you are supplicating to your guru, while making offerings and confessing your transgressions. When you complete those confessions, recite the traditional Seven Limb Prayer and then say loudly:

> Guru Rinpoche, precious lama, please purify all the obscurations and defilements I have accumulated through my body, speech, and mind and grant me the power and strength that you have developed through your body, speech, and mind. Help me develop insights that are transcendental and superior to anything I have experienced so far. Please, Guru Rinpoche, I beseech you, do this for me.

You can also find other supplications and prayers to add as you beseech your guru to empower you. You want to feel empowered through these supplications.

After a time, imagine these supplications have worked and your request has been granted. Then visualize light radiating in all directions from the congregation. This light is absorbed into your own body so that light is emanating from everywhere, from both within and without, and you are enveloped in light. You need to develop the conviction that the true spiritual boon (*siddhi, dngos-grub*) has been granted. You should imagine that. Then think that this is the need and wish of all sentient beings, not just yourself. This very focused feeling of devotion is something you should feel in your heart. It must come from your own heart.

When you decide to arise from your meditation on Guru Yoga, you should regard everything in post-meditation as the lama and see everything as a magical display or dream creation. If you practice Guru Yoga in this way, there is no doubt you will receive the necessary blessings to properly realize and make use of the Dzogchen teachings. Extraordinary power can be attained from engaging in these practices on Guru Yoga.

2. Mandala offering

After settling on the meditation cushion as before, pile a mandala disk with nine heaps of rice then wipe it clean, just as you would in conventional mandala practice, while imagining the mandala disk represents the entire universe, and that this universe is totally pure, uncorrupted, and devoid of impurities. It is bejeweled and filled with a multitude of precious stones and other representations of the world's riches. It is also imbued with your own internal qualities, strengths, powers, glory, recognition, and so on. Anything contained in the universe with any worth at all is worthy of being an offering.

Then, visualize your own personal guru in front of you, and the whole host of buddhas and bodhisattvas of the ten directions, not only from this world but from other worlds as well, along with all the continents, sun, moon, wish-fulfilling gems, and goddesses. Then imagine all you can offer, everything that is worthy becomes an offering. Everything you personally value, in other words, should be transformed into your personal offering. This can be done mentally. There may be a limit to what you can offer physically, but there is no real limit to what you can imagine. As far as our minds are concerned, the things that are worthy of transforming into an offering are as infinite as the sky. You can also add other supplications associated with mandala practice to your prayers.

Who are the objects of the offering? The gurus, the lamas, the guides, your own personal deities and the mandalas associated with each of them, the dakinis, guides, and dharmapalas or spiritual protectors. These are the objects of your offering. While visualizing this you should think:

> The mandala I am offering is so beautiful, extensive and hard to
> fathom, that when it is received, may you, the Victorious Ones,
> deliver all of us from our state of bondage.

You can again add any other supplications associated with the mandala practice. If you engage in this practice, it will fulfill your need to cultivate wisdom and merit and will concurrently help you to remove the veils of emotional conflicts and conceptual confusion. This is the reason we engage in the practice of mandala offering.

3. *Vajrasattva*

You begin this practice by visualizing a lotus, sun disk, and moon disk in your heart chakra, on top of which rests the syllable HUNG. This syllable has the capacity to transform you into Vajrasattva. In this case, you visualize Vajrasattva as bluish in color, instead of the traditional white, and adorned with bone ornaments, bracelets, anklets, and so forth. Vajrasattva is holding a vajra in one hand and a bell in the other and is in an embrace with his consort. His consort, Dorje Nyima, is red in color, with her left arm around Vajrasattva's waist and her right arm around his neck. In her right hand she holds a hooked knife and in her left hand a skull cup. Vajrasattva is sitting crossed-legged, while Dorje Nyima sits facing him on his lap with her legs around him. You are in an embrace with this female divinity.

You should visualize a lotus, sun disk, and moon disk in your heart center, one on top of the other. In the center of the moon disk is a blue vajra, marked with the syllable HUNG with the hundred syllable mantra of Vajrasattva revolving around it. You then imagine that an external Vajrasattva appears in front of you and is absorbed into you. This is called the union of the *dam-tshig sems-dpa'* (*samayasattva*) and *ye-shes sems-dpa'* (*jnanasattva*). You visualize yourself as a deity and then invite that wisdom deity and become united with it. At this point, you start reciting the hundred syllable mantra of Vajrasattva and think:

> I am not just doing this practice to gain benefit for myself. I'm doing it so that others can also gain benefit from it.

The practice is effective when you realize that we all need to overcome our illusions, delusions, and confusion. You therefore imagine that all of your delusions, illusions, and confusion are being dissipated through this practice and that this is happening to others who are also subject to the same condition. You imagine that you have become purified and that everyone else in need of purification has also achieved that goal. You should pay total attention to the recitation of this mantra without wavering and then end the recitation by dedicating whatever merit you have been able to accumulate through and from this practice for the benefit of others.

As samsaric beings, we are in a state of bondage, and we are habit-bound. The practice of Vajrasattva will help you overcome deep-seated habitual patterns and the emotional afflictions that plague you. That is why Vajrasattva practice is a necessary prelude to the main practice of Dzogchen.

4. The four Brahmaviharas

The four Brahmaviharas are love, compassion, joy, and equanimity. You begin this practice of learning to cultivate love (*maitri, byams-pa*) by thinking that there are so many sentient beings in this world in need of happiness but who instead only meet with unhappiness and suffering. Love comes from wishing that these beings may come into contact with the things they are deprived of that will give them happiness.

Next is the contemplation on compassion (*karuna, snying-rje*) where you think of all the prevailing conditions that contribute to the increase of suffering rather than its decrease, and of all the beings who are in a great deal of torment and anguish. You think these beings should be free from suffering. They should not be going through these kinds of experiences; they should not be subject to this. You develop compassion by thinking along these lines.

Then comes the contemplation on joy (*mudita, dga'-ba*), which is about realizing that beings can be freed from suffering because it is not endemic; suffering can be removed. You find joy in knowing that suffering can be alleviated, dispensed with, and removed. You should think that people who have been subject to all kinds of atrocities, oppression, and misery can also find joy. Joy gives rise to happiness.

The final practice is the contemplation on equanimity (*upeksha, btang-snyoms*), which involves recognizing that all of our problems in life are caused by the two basic tendencies of attraction and aversion. We are attracted to some things and have aversion to other things, from which we develop the emotional problems of excessive attachment, desire, violence, hatred, and anger. You should think:

> I need to rest in the state of equilibrium, where I'm not
> vulnerable to my instinctual drives and emotional upheavals
> but can maintain a sense of composure. This is where I should
> rest, where I must be.

The mind will then become workable. When the mind is given over
to its natural impulses, it's not workable and cannot be used in a
constructive manner, but by resting in a state of equilibrium, the mind
becomes serviceable. You should use your willpower to make this happen.
You should be determined to experience the fruition of all four of these
positive emotions. This is not a passive way of resigning yourself to a
particular mode of being or a certain mental state; you are willfully trying
to bring the desired emotion into the domain of your mental experience.
Equilibrium is brought into our mental experiences with that kind of
wish.

When you have reflected on love and compassion and contemplated
the needs of yourself and other sentient beings, you should remind
yourself that sentient beings are numberless. Your attention should not
be focused on a select group of people you feel a certain affinity toward
and ignoring others. It should be projected out toward the numberless
sentient beings that need love. There is an inordinate amount of suffering
in the lives of all beings, so your love and compassion should be
boundless. You should not be thinking, "I have to cultivate love and
compassion for now, because it's required of me to secure buddhahood
and attain enlightenment. Later on, when I become a buddha and attain
nirvana, these contemplations on suffering can end." That is not so. You
should generate a timeless love and compassion. Wherever and whoever
you might be, love and compassion should be part of your character. You
cannot contemplate on love and compassion without feeling. This has to
come from your heart. It has to be a really heartfelt experience.

This is how we should meditate on the four Brahmaviharas. We
practice the four Brahmaviharas because the mind has to become
workable. Your mind is unruly, rigid, and rebellious, so it is not workable.
If you start to learn how to love, how to have compassion, how to have

joy, and how to be in a state of equanimity, your mind becomes workable. A natural sense of affinity will arise and compassion will come up automatically without your having to willfully bring it into being.

What are you doing when you engage in these practices? You are learning how to become skillful, as laid down in the Buddhist teachings. By acquainting yourself with skill and means through these practices, your mind will be made workable, and become a receptacle for wisdom.

5. Bodhicitta

You should never lose sight of others or the needs of others when you embark on the spiritual journey because you are practicing for both your own benefit and for the benefit of others. This should never be forgotten. Your ability to help others will increase in direct proportion to your experience of enlightenment so the practice of bodhicitta should come from your heart as a deeply felt experience. You should think:

> I am not just looking for my own liberation or salvation when I'm practicing. I'm also trying to free others from their own state of bondage and introduce freedom to those who don't have it.

There are all kinds of different worlds within this conditioned state of being, not just the world we inhabit. Buddhist cosmology talks about the triple world (*tri-loka, khams-gsum*): the realm of sensuality (*kama-dhatu, 'dod khams*), the realm of form (*rupa-dhatu, gzugs kyi khams*), and the realm of formlessness (*arupa-dhatu, gzugs med pa'i khams*). We are living in the world of sensuality, but beings who dwell in the world systems also experience suffering and dissatisfaction. They are defeated by trauma and rendered powerless by these experiences. All these beings experience suffering, even though they are different from us in nature and dwell in other world systems. The key to bodhichitta practice is to think:

> If only I could swap places with other beings, taking on their suffering and giving them whatever comfort, joy, pleasure, and happiness that I experience in return.

There are also many tiers of existence in the realm of sensuality. These are the hell realm, the hungry ghost realm, the animal realm, the human realm, and the realms of the demigods and the heavenly gods. You have to understand that no matter which level you find yourself on, you are never free from death. Whether you are born in a hell realm or a god realm, you will die, because mortality is a pervasive aspect of our existence. Suffering and death can be found everywhere, not just in the hell, hungry ghost, animal, and human realms. They are also found in the heavenly realm of the gods. This is so because all these beings bring suffering upon themselves. They bring about the suffering of suffering. It is so apparent. If you pay attention, you will see it is not mysterious or elusive but very obvious.

Suffering is also present in the realm of form, which is not related to the world as we know it. Beings in that realm may not experience extreme mood swings and turbulent upsurges of emotion; they become attached to the peace that comes from not having that turbulence. They are in a kind of meditative state, and they become attached to that, but this state is not eternal. When the karmic causes and conditions that transported them into that world are exhausted, their future again becomes uncertain. They cannot rest in comfort thinking it is going to last.

In the realm of formlessness, beings are in a state of semi-consciousness and therefore have no opportunity to act or interact with others. They have no ability or opportunity to practice wholesome deeds so their temporary respite from suffering in this realm will not last. Their old trials and tribulations will resurface and they will be engulfed by them yet again.

The suffering of conditioned existence is all-pervasive and isn't only to be found in this world. It is found in all forms of conditioned existence. Sometimes suffering is obvious but other times it is hidden. You may not be aware of the hidden causes and conditions that might allow for the experience of suffering to resurface. You should always remember the suffering of others and think:

> Whatever good deeds I am able to do are not just for myself but also for the betterment of others. May they alleviate the current problems and suffering experienced by the different beings of

the triple world so that there is no suffering to be found anywhere, not only in this world, but in all three worlds of sensuality, form, and formlessness. Everyone should have peace, happiness, joy, comfort, satisfaction, and contentment.

In that way, whatever we do has a twofold purpose. We are not simply trying to satisfy our own needs but we are also doing something for the betterment of everyone else in our world and beyond our world. When we practice with this attitude, these reflections will assist our spiritual progress; they will not slow it down. We will become buddhas through this change of attitude and these practices. Compassion is so important. We must have compassion, and that compassion must flow into the very stream of our being. It is not enough to have momentary bouts of compassion. The very essence of compassion has to flow into the continuum of our being.

6. Intrinsic awareness

The best way to practice the yoga of intrinsic awareness (*vidya, rig-pa*) is to pay attention to your body, speech, and mind. You should think:

> I should not allow my mind to wander in relation to these three aspects of my being, not even for a moment. That is what I need to do. I will pay unwavering attention to my body, speech, and mind.

You need to think in this manner because there is no way for wisdom to arise if you are not paying attention to those three aspects of your being. The gate of wisdom will not be opened. That is why you have to cultivate intrinsic awareness.

7. Vipashyana

The yoga of insight (*vipashyana, lhag-mthong*) is the practice that gives rise to wisdom. This yoga has three parts: examining the nature of thoughts, examining the nature of the mind, and examining each thought as it arises.

1. Examining the nature of thoughts

As you sit on your cushion, you first need to observe the coming, dwelling, and dissipation of mental states: the onset of thoughts, the persistence of thoughts, and the dissipation of thoughts. All different kinds of thoughts and experiences arise during meditation. There will be a myriad of things. As those thoughts and experiences arise, you should examine them:

> What is the origin of these thoughts and experiences? Where do they come from? Do they arise from the perceived sensory world? Do they come from my psychophysical constituents?

When you are able to catch a particular thought as it arises, you should look at it, not only in terms of the fact it exists there in the present, but at how it transforms at that point. Every thought you catch yourself having is getting transformed. You should look at the origin of this transformation:

> Am I having this thought in relation to something external to me or is it coming from within? Where is it? Does my thought really reside within me? Does it reside in my mind?

Then you should pay attention to where your previous thought has gone:

> Where has it gone? Has my thought left me and gone somewhere else into the world or has it disappeared somewhere in the regions of my mind? Has the thought I just had been absorbed somehow or has it disappeared into the minuscule physical particles of my body?

When you practice this yoga, you will realize that past, present, and future have no intrinsic reality of their own. They are rootless. In that way, you will arrive at the realization of the nature of mind, which is no different from dharmakaya, the authentic aspect of buddha's being. When we approach our practice in this way, that will be naturally realized.

2. Examining the nature of the mind

The second aspect entails looking at whether the mind has shape, form, or color. Different imagery arises in your mind that may appear to have shape, form, and color. First you ask:

Is this blue really blue? Is this yellow really yellow? Do these mental images have real color?

Mental images also appear to have shape and form, so enquire:

Is this mental image long? Is it square? Is it round? Is it three-dimensional?

You should pay close attention to that. This is how you examine your mind. Then you should look into your mind and enquire:

Am I male? Am I female? Are the images in my mind male or female or gender neutral or hermaphrodite? Do these images relate to thoughts of being old or young? Do they relate to birth or death? Do these images actually have the characteristic of the things they represent? What is the relationship between the two?

You thus examine your mental images in relation to what they are, what they represent, and their relationship, whatever the images might be. When you think about it that way, you will realize that the mind is free-floating, hard to pin down, and hard to grasp. It has no shape, form, or color, despite what the internal images might suggest. You realize sambhogakaya, the communicative aspect of buddha's being, through this aspect of vipashyana.

3. Examining each thought as it arises

The third aspect is about identifying what is what. Your thoughts may seem constant when you practice meditation, but they don't really remain the same. Each thought is momentary, each thought is different, and each thought is changing within a continuity of other thoughts. A lot of our thoughts relate to remembrance. Many different kinds of thoughts and memories present themselves. You usually look at each mental state as it arises to see if the thought is harmful and something to be discarded. If you have thoughts related to spiritual practice, you think that is something to be cultivated. This way of developing the proper view, meditation, and conduct is associated with the Mahayana. You may have other thoughts related to tantric practice, such as thoughts about the recitation of mantras, sadhana practice and ritual practice, or thoughts related to the development and fulfillment stages. You need to look at all that and say:

> These are only thoughts. The thoughts themselves may be different, but they are all just thoughts.

Identifying each thought as it arises in relation to the subject matter the thought is dwelling on at any given moment helps you to realize that it is only a thought. Identifying thoughts in this way will lead to the realization of intrinsic awareness. This awareness or rigpa is self-manifesting and inseparable from your own experience. Rigpa is the same as dharmakaya, the authentic state of your own being, and you will establish yourself in that authentic state of being. This is achieved through the third practice of vipashyana.

The benefit of these practices of insight meditation is that you will realize the nature of the mind as being wisdom. That is superior insight. Your realization will radiate like the sun itself and this will flow through the continuity of your being. This is something that will come about anew. That is the reason why the practice of insight meditation is important.

MAIN PRACTICE

As you enter into the main practice, you need to begin with the realization that your experiences of the phenomenal world and conditioned existence—the various states of being and the experiences that arise from them—are the display of your own rigpa, just as dreams are the display of our own mind. How does rigpa exist? It has to be seen from three perspectives: emptiness (*shunyata, stong-pa nyid*), luminosity (*prabhasvara, 'od-gsal*), and the myriad manifestations of phenomena (*niruddha, ma 'gags-pa*).

Rigpa is empty (*stong-pa*) in its own nature. It is emptiness and that corresponds to dharmakaya. However, rigpa is not just mere nothingness. Within emptiness there is clarity (*gsal-ba*), our cognitive capabilities, and that arises from sambhogakaya. We have many different experiences because we have this cognitive capability but how and in what manner we have these experiences arise is dependent upon the prevalent causes and conditions. That responsiveness (*thugs-rje*) arises from nirmanakaya.

A Dzogchen practitioner has to realize that the moment you have any ordinary type of experience or mental cognition, that very same experience is no different from the intention of the Buddha himself. Whatever is present in the mind is the intention of the Buddha. If you understand this present experience properly, it has the potential to liberate you from your current state of bondage. It has the potential to lead you to the state of total freedom. As the great acharya, Guru Padmasambhava, says:

> Rigpa is no different from wisdom. Rigpa has the characteristics of being empty in its nature, yet luminous, and because of that cognitive ability, which is also empty, it has the capacity to produce all kinds of experiences independent of internal and external conditions. We can never be certain about our experiences. We can never be certain about what we are experiencing in the way that we experience it. In meditation, we have to recognize that.
>
> It is this same mind, which we cannot totally rely on, that produces these experiences. If we stop relying on it, whatever experiences we have, even the negative ones, become impotent in their ability to influence our mind. Instead, we become naturally freed. This is comparable to the relationship between waves and the ocean, because however disturbing our thoughts might be, they are not separate from our own authentic state. Thoughts radiate from that authentic state of being. There is no other way to find our authentic state apart from realizing that fact.
>
> Whatever our present mental state, it is radiating our own authentic state, if understood properly. There is no other meditation. As meditators, we often become obsessed with the idea of discarding thoughts, with eliminating them in non-reflection and paying no attention to our present experiences. Those experiences and the various aspects of our being are regarded as enemies to be discarded, conquered, and defeated.

We can fall into this misconception and think this is how we achieve liberation, but that approach will only lead to illusion. It is not genuine, no matter how great or sincere our efforts might be. We cannot achieve the desired goal by approaching meditation in this manner.

The Dzogchen view is that we should approach meditation in a different way. We should not be thinking we should renounce this or denounce that, eliminate this and cultivate that, foster this aspect of ourselves and reject that. Our experiences are always related to virtue and vice. Instead of becoming obsessed with thoughts of rejecting vices and cultivating virtues, we should just let whatever experiences we have in meditation be. We will then be able to relate to any experiences we have in conditioned existence, including physical experiences, and everything that we experience will lead to goodness and bliss.

A real meditator doesn't worry about whether they are meditating or not. When you are meditating, you should not be thinking about whether you are meditating properly or not. The point of meditation is not trying to quantify it. For these reasons, the path of Dzogchen is supreme, superior, and profound.

In this present moment, we are always in one mental state or another; it cannot be otherwise. The present mental state is always about something; you are always having one experience or another. When you meditate properly, you do not tamper with that present mental experience, trying to fashion it one way or another, giving it some kind of shape or form. Instead, you pay attention to what is there. Just let it rest. Let it be. Let that present mental state be.

Your attitude toward your present mental state, whatever that state might be, should be to approach it with a sense of relaxation. There has to be an element of letting go. You should try to be loose, relaxed, and flexible and let go without grasping and without fixation. When you let your mind be in this way, by relaxing and letting go, there is a sense of ease. You should practice easing into that state. This is how you should meditate.

Then, whatever arises in the mind should be recognized, whatever it might be—anger, jealousy, love, attachment, bitterness, despair, despondency—it should all be identified with awareness. There has to be a recognition of whatever has arisen in the mind, but again, you should let your mind rest with that recognition.

That form of recognition should not be used to tighten the mind. It should be used to let the mind rest. Fixation is not present when the recognition is there. You just recognize what is going on without being fixated on what is going on. So you should make sure you do not get fixated on what you have recognized or found yourself to be experiencing, whatever that mental state might be. The mind is simply allowed to rest naturally. Then everything you experience will be self-liberated (*rang-grol*) because there is no attachment. The fixation is not there.

Similarly, when a thought arises in your mind during meditation, you have to recognize that the thought is there and see what it is about. If you can recognize the thought and catch it as it arises—something we are normally unable to do—that thought will liberate by itself as well.

This is the way we have to approach meditation. We have to examine the mind and understand it with all its different aspects. If you practice meditation in this way, you will have an experience of bliss (*bde-ba nyams*), an experience of clarity (*gsal ba'i nyams*), and an experience of nonconceptuality (*mi rtog pa'i nyams*). That is the kind of meditation you will have if you approach it in the way described.

Furthermore, you will be able to bring this approach into everyday life as well because you won't be so compelled to latch onto things, external or internal, and your actions will become easier, more fluid, and more flexible. Since you are no longer obsessed about, attached to, or fixated on things, the goal of enlightenment will also be nondirectional. The fruit of spiritual practice is attained by having a nondirectional approach to enlightenment. In the context of Dzogchen, you should try to realize meditation, action, and fruition in this way. Longchenpa wrote the following section in verse form:

Dharmadhatu is not caused or created by anyone.
If you learn to rest naturally in the state of dharmata,
intrinsic awareness (rig-pa) will reveal itself.
You will have many experiences through meditation,
but they should all be seen as reflections of that primordial state.
Self-liberation will come naturally from not grasping onto them.
Your own primordial condition is Kuntuzangpo,
and this is the context in which we become liberated.
The mind in itself is primordially free from the beginning.
You don't have to liberate yourself with exertion or tolerance.
If you just let ordinary mind rest in its own natural state
everything becomes an experience of self-liberation.

When you approach your meditation in that way, everything you experience becomes an experience of self-liberation because you realize that whatever you experience manifests the three qualities of enlightenment: emptiness (*stong*), luminosity (*gsal*), and awareness (*rig-pa*). At that point, you have already entered into the buddha-field, the blissful land of Dechen (great bliss), where all three aspects of buddha's being—dharmakaya, sambhogakaya, and nirmanakaya—have come to the fore. You will then realize that everything you experience is inseparable from your own authentic state. All experiences manifest from that authentic state of being.

In that way, there is no need to condition your mind in terms of your experiences by thinking, "This kind of mental state is conducive to spiritual practice and realization and that kind is detrimental." You don't need to concern yourself with applying antidotes or remedies to your mental afflictions. You will still experience periods of well-being and happiness along with periods of despair and pain, but you have to see them all as reflections that come from your own natural state, just like images reflected on the surface of a mirror. These experiences are reflected on the mirror of the mind so you don't get too caught up in them. This is how the yogi should train themselves on this path. This is how rigpa or awareness is exercised. This method represents the epitome of all the yanas. It is also the essence of the supreme path of the Vajrayana.

BOOSTING YOUR PRACTICE

Longchenpa now gives a commentary on the points he has made. Whatever you experience, you examine that experience and then let the experience be. When you are on retreat, you should use meditation throughout the day and not be overly concerned with this present life and its modes of thought and emotion. Simply focus on the practice of Dharma with real vigor.

THE SIX SESSIONS OF DAILY PRACTICE

1. At dawn, you should view your mind as space itself. The mind is free, spacious, and open, not constricted, bound, confined, or imprisoned. In order to generate nonconceptual wisdom, you should practice shamatha and vipashyana meditation—sitting meditation and insight meditation—conjoined. They should be brought together. Then you should pay real attention to your body and adopt a proper meditation posture. Your eyes should not be wavering or darting here and there. That's how you should meditate. When you practice this way, you will experience a sense of well-being, mental clarity, and the onslaught of conceptual proliferation and thought processes will abate. In the Dzogchen teachings, that is what samadhi is all about. Your samadhi will arise spontaneously. That is what your attitude should be at dawn when you are meditating.

2. In the morning session, you should not get too disturbed by anything that arises in the mind, whether it is stable or agitated. Without discriminating between agitation and stability, if you are able to take notice of whatever arises with the employment and deployment of rigpa, then whatever arises will be liberated instantaneously. At that very instance, whatever has risen in the mind will become liberated. That is what vipashyana or insight meditation is really about. Having this attitude will allow you to gain insight during meditation.

3. At midday, you should be thinking that everything you experience, all physical and mental phenomena, are just like a dream, like a magical illusion, a mirage, the sound of a guitar, a painting, a portrait. Remind yourself of that fact, without clinging onto anything as intrinsically real.

Furthermore, you should regard all sentient creatures as pure, instead of seeing them as bad, evil, and flawed, and try to respect them and develop impartiality toward them. We should have pure perception, respect, and an impartial attitude toward all sentient creatures. You should particularly develop respect toward your teachers and try to develop even more respect toward people who propound the Dharma. Nothing has intrinsic reality, so if you can see things this way and approach others in this manner, you will benefit from it. Your present material condition will improve and so will your spiritual realizations.

4. In the evening, you should contemplate the shortcomings and defects of samsara, on the one hand, and the benefits of achieving liberation, on the other. You should also contemplate the operation of karmic cause and effect in your life and develop a deep conviction in that. Then contemplate how difficult it is to have a human birth, and finally, you should contemplate your own mortality. The benefit of contemplating these topics is that you will not be distracted from what is really important in life and you will see through all the seductions and temptations of the world. These contemplations will provide you with the motivation and impetus to stay on the path, apply volition, and find the vigor to practice.

5. After midnight, you should again remind yourself that everything is like a dream and that all of your experiences while awake are dependent upon the mind. There is nothing out there that exists independently of mind. You have to arrive at some kind of certainty about that. Of course, your experiences are varied and prolific, but you should think that they are just like dreams. Everything that you experience while you are awake is much like the dreams you have while sleeping. You should practice viewing experience this way because it will lead to the experiences of bliss, luminosity, and nonconceptuality. You should then let the mind rest with these experiences. If you can succeed in doing that, you will have no obstacles, because any obstacle that arises will dissipate by itself. This experience comes from dismantling your fixation on the assumption that everything has some kind of intrinsic reality. Thinking that things have intrinsic reality is a form of illusion that is dismantled through this

realization.

6. When you go to sleep at around 3.00 am, you should be thinking that your mind itself has no origin. It is uncaused and free of all proliferating activities. Whatever you dream about during the night will be a source of bliss. Dreams will reveal your luminous nature and lead to great bliss (*mahasukha, bde-ba chen-po*). You should not discriminate between day and night and must continue meditation and post-meditation throughout. You should be thinking that the nature of the mind is uncaused and let go of whatever arises in the mind, in relation to the conceptual activities (*vikalpa, rnam-thog*) of the mind. When we are not conceptualizing, we might fall asleep and start to dream, but that dream will reveal our true nature. Our dreams will be blissful because we have left our conceptual categories behind.

THE CONTINUITY OF PRACTICE

We have to meditate through the day and night in that way. We always have to practice, whether it is day or night; it doesn't matter. This is how you should conduct your practice over a twenty-four hour period in retreat. We have talked about how you should boost your practice and give it some kind of impetus. That comes from knowing that no matter how much or how long we practice, the main point is to rest in the unoriginated state, knowing that whatever arises in the mind has the potential to liberate us in the instant of arising. That is where we find insight. That is where the experience of insight presents itself. A little of the dexterity of insight meditation comes to the fore.

When we can achieve this, the experiences of bliss, luminosity, and nonconceptuality will arise, and we will meditate in that condition where all obstacles dissipate by themselves. When we can also cultivate this attitude before going to sleep, we will recognize that clinging, grasping, and fixation are the source of all our confusion, and we will begin to dismantle all the rigid ideas we have entertained for so long. No matter how long we meditate, whatever we experience is free of causes and conditions. We should look at whatever we experience as spontaneous manifestation, because when we look at our experience in that fashion, it is freed. To be able to do that is vipashyana or insight meditation.

There are three things involved here: *dang-ba*, *khor-ba*, and *byams-pa*. *Dang-ba* means "upliftedness," *khor-ba* means "getting lost," and *byams-pa* means "love." We have to learn how to uplift ourselves with our practice, then we have to recognize how the mind becomes lost, and finally we learn how to foster the practice.

How to uplift yourself through practice

To uplift yourself through practice, you have to understand that whatever arises has no intrinsic nature and therefore everything can be self-liberated (*rang-grol*) the instant it arises. Furthermore, your experiences are nonabiding, have no endurance, and do not rest, even for a moment. When you meditate, the mind does not remain stable. You think it does, but the mind is moving every moment; it cannot stay or rest or abide.

Watching the mind is like watching something being blown around by a gust of wind. Instead of getting worked up and dismayed by these mental activities, you should learn how to let those experiences be. Just as gusts of wind arise, they also come to an end. That is how you should relate to your experiences. Then you will have the experience of self-liberation. If you can regard everything you experience as a spontaneous manifestation, your experiences will be set free.

If you are unable to practice this properly, you should go out into an open field on a clear day, turn your back to the sun, and gaze into the cloudless sky. Your eyes should be wide open as you look into space, and you should make sure that your mind is not wandering. Just rest your mind in that state. This sense of spaciousness will help your proliferating mental activities settle, and you will experience emptiness, luminosity, and nonconceptuality. These experiences are expressions of wisdom, which also arise from wisdom.

These instructions are necessary for novices who have just embarked on the practice of meditation. Having settled your mind through the practice of shamatha meditation, you have to practice vipashyana. You learn not to get caught up in your conceptual mind through vipashyana practice that is based on shamatha meditation. This also goes both ways. Insight meditation has to be based on shamatha, and shamatha meditation can be based on vipashyana. You must combine these practices and use them as supports for one another. You learn not to get caught up in your conceptual mind by combining shamatha and vipashyana meditation.

Shamatha helps to calm the mind so that you can deal with conceptual proliferation (*vikalpa, rnam-rtog*), and vipashyana leads to insight. Everything you experience becomes incorporated into the practice of shamatha and vipashyana. As you go further with the practice, you should be focusing your mind on the notion of presence (*aloka, snang-ba*), and maintain the view that whatever appears has the potential to liberate you. That is how you uplift yourself.

Recognizing how the mind becomes lost

Now we come to *khor-ba*, how the mind wanders and becomes deviated—how the mind can become lost, in other words. *Khor-ba* means "getting lost" and we can get lost in a variety of ways. If you get disturbed by sensory impressions or inner mental states and your mind doesn't want to stay inside but is always getting distracted and latching onto this or that, you should practice shamatha meditation.

As you continue with your practice, you will begin to have wonderful meditation experiences (*vetana, nyams*). As your mind becomes more translucent, you experience a genuine sense of bliss and then attachment to that experience develops. You take pride in that. However, you should not hanker after those experiences or become bloated with pride and think, "Now I'm really getting somewhere." Instead of conceptualizing about experiences, just remind yourself that conceptual experiences have no intrinsic reality whatsoever. Your experiences are varied. You have a multiplicity of sensory and mental experiences, but you have to think of them all as having the potential to liberate you (*shes-grol*) and not cling to any of them. That is how you purify the mind.

If you develop a strong attachment to this life, you should contemplate on impermanence and your own mortality. If you start to fixate on whether your meditative experiences are high or low, superior or inferior, you should concentrate on dismantling that whole idea. If your major problem is a lack of compassion, you should reflect on the fact that all sentient beings in the six realms have been your mother and father and cultivate love and compassion toward them. If your mind has wandered off because you cannot maintain rigpa, you should remember everything you experience in the phenomenal world is a product of your own mind based on causes and conditions. This point is of supreme importance for novices.

If you have an experience of emptiness, you might conclude that the three times are all empty. "Thinking that all times are empty," is the literal translation. If we think that all times are empty, we start to denigrate karmic causality, which violates certain fundamental moral principles. That is a form of demonic possession. If someone thinks in that fashion, a demon has entered their heart. The antidote for that is to practice real compassion (*karuna, snying-rje*), where you think of others and the welfare of others, instead of simply thinking that everything is empty and therefore nothing matters.

When your experience of compassion arises quite strongly and you direct it toward the six types of living beings described in the Buddhist teachings, you may have the tendency to see them as having real objective existence, independent of your mind. You may think they have some kind of intrinsic reality of their own and develop attachment, partiality, and bias toward them. When that happens, you should be focusing on emptiness because that response means that you have not understood emptiness properly. That is another kind of demonic possession. You should think of all things as being unoriginated and meditate on that point.

We need to learn to deal with agitation (*nyam-pa*), which is also a form of deviation or wandering. *Nyam-pa* is a very technical word, an ancient word as well, and not one that is used commonly. However, your mind can become so agitated and disturbed by sensory impressions and inner mental states that it cannot stay inside. You keep turning your attention outward and become distracted and start latching onto things. When this happens, you should practice shamatha meditation. You can have all kinds of experiences through and from meditation, blissful experiences, lustful experiences, attachment, and all kinds of conceptual activities, but you should regard these as just thought constructs without any ground in themselves. When they arise, if you can have an attitude of nonfixation (*'dzin-med*), they will become liberated.

How to foster the practice

Whatever your difficulty in meditation might be, you should employ the necessary antidote to counteract it. In brief, your meditative experiences should correspond to whatever you are meditating on. When you deviate or go astray from those experiences, you have to resort to antidotes and use skillful means to counter those deviations. Using different methods to counter the relevant situation rather than one method for all situations is the supreme method.

If you continue with this practice day and night, you will realize all the qualities of an Aryan, an exalted being. Such an Aryan being realizes the confluence of emptiness and compassion. They relinquish any fixation on thoughts that things have any reality or absolute truth of their own through this realization. They do not have the slightest fixation on things having intrinsic reality, not even the size of the tip of a hair. By letting go of their hold on samsara, they realize nirvana. If you can do that in this very life, you will realize the dharmadhatu, which is no different from dzogpa chenpo.

TRALEG KYABGON COMMENTARY ON RETREAT INSTRUCTIONS—THE POINTING OUT INSTRUCTION OF DEFINITIVE MEANING ON SELF-LIBERATION INTO ULTIMATE REALITY

TRANSMISSION

Longchenpa mentions the stamp of authenticity of the transmission, but he is already discussing that anyway. He says that all the approaches to enlightenment in the Buddhist teachings are legitimate, pure, and authentic, but the Vajrayana approach is the most authentic and, within the Vajrayana, the Dzogchen approach is the one we should follow and practice. He is not saying that Dzogchen is superior to all the other teachings or that the other teachings are incomplete or inauthentic, only that the Vajrayana path is the most reliable and that within that, Dzogchen is what we are concerned with here. He then mentions how the lineage system works within the Dzogchen tradition, but he doesn't go into the lineage in great detail because that is not what he is concerned with. Calling the dharmakaya, sambhogakaya, and nirmanakaya "the lineage" is quite unusual in many ways. You could say that lineage has a subjective dimension with the teacher-student relationship, but there is also an internal dimension where dharmakaya has an impact on sambhogakaya, and sambhogakaya has an impact on nirmanakaya.

The transmission is the same as the pointing-out instructions. I am doing a kind of pointing-out instruction by teaching this text. The pointing-out instructions are very direct in the Dzogchen tradition, unlike the Zen tradition, where you need to have an audience with your master and a conundrum to solve. The pointing-out instructions are really aimed at breaking down our preconceptions. That is the secret. That is also the whole point of transmission, to break down the preconceived notions that students entertain, "I want to receive this or that teaching," "I want my teacher to be bearded, with a top knot," "I want my teacher to be bald and look like the laughing Buddha."

BUDDHA-FIELDS

Longchenpa then says that we can also attain enlightenment in a buddha-field. There are generally two ways to understand the notion of buddha-fields. Buddha-fields crop up all the time in Buddhist discourses, but they are not necessarily clearly defined. There are many ways we can understand them, but generally two ways are the most common. The first interpretation of a buddha-field is that there are other world systems where things are better than they are here. That world approximates to a heavenly or paradisiacal state, where beings do not suffer, they live longer, enjoy themselves more, and have fewer problems, which gives them more time to grow as spiritual beings. It is still a temporary station and any being fortunate enough to secure that kind of privileged birth does not remain there for very long because that paradise is still subject to space and time and must come to an end. The other interpretation of a buddha-field is as a state of mind. When the mind is content, peaceful, at ease, and without afflictions, we could say we are experiencing a pure land. Even the Pure Land School of Buddhism says the ultimate pure land exists in the minds of human beings.

All the same, it would be difficult to discount the possibility that there may be world systems out there where things are better. Why couldn't that exist, at least as a possibility? Before we reject that possibility by calling it "science fiction," we should reflect on that. Even on this planet, the fortunes of people vary greatly from one continent to the other. When we are talking about intergalactic worlds, we are trying to expand our way of imagining things. Who knows? Places like that might be possible. However, even though such places have a good life, it might not last forever, as the teachings say. It's a temporary respite from all the tedium of life that is so characteristic of living in the world we know.

NGONDRO

There may be slight differences between the ngondro practices in the Nyingma and Kagyu schools, but it is difficult to generalize about them here. There is a very structured way of doing ngondro practice, and there is the more freestyle approach. Both the Nyingma and Kagyu traditions have these two alternatives. The freestyle approach is recommended to people already doing other practices while the structured approach is for people whose main focus is ngondro practice. You can find the freestyle approach of the Kagyu school in Karmapa Wangchuk Dorje's *Ocean of Certainty*. There is no difference between the structured ngondro of the Nyingma and Kagyu, apart from who you visualize when you practice. Even though Guru Padmasambhava plays a very significant role in Kagyu practices, we do not include Guru Padmasambhava or Samantabhadra in our ngondro.

Longchenpa is only presenting the ngondro as an adjunct to Dzogchen practice, so he describes the freestyle version. Wangchuk Dorje's *Ocean of Certainty* and Longchenpa's *Three Cycles of Natural Freedom* are meditation manuals to be used in retreat. You spend a few weeks on the preliminaries in retreat and then go into the other practices. You can also do all the preliminaries every day in one brief session before you do your main practice. There are variations like that. The preliminary practices are basically about bringing us back to reality because it's possible to lose focus with some of the other practices. That is why we are never finished with the preliminaries. We have to practice them for as long as we live, no matter how advanced we think we are on the spiritual path.

Mandala practice is all about extending ourselves and giving. When we give, we open ourselves on an emotional or psychological level as well as in a spiritual way, which is part of the cultivation of wisdom. Buddhism always emphasizes wisdom as knowing "how" rather than knowing "what." Someone might be a very knowledgeable person but still lack an understanding of how to live fully, deal with things properly, interact with others, or understand themselves. You have to broaden the connotation of wisdom to include all of that and not think of it as some kind of propositional or theoretical knowledge. Mandala offering provides us with the knowledge of how to be more open and giving. That in itself is wisdom. You should not think that we only create merit by being generous, patient, and understanding and that we have to accumulate wisdom through some other means. Through performing meritorious practices we have already become a wise person. They are not two different things and do not operate independently of one another in different domains. However, there is something of a scale, with pure action at one end and pure wisdom at the other, and between them, the area that requires both.

The exploration of the nature of mind is also a preliminary practice. This is true for both the Dzogchen and Mahamudra tradition. The real practice of Mahamudra is simply being aware. You are not examining or analyzing; you just sit and do your best to be aware. However, exploring the mind's nature and being aware are complementary practices. When you do Mahamudra or Dzogchen meditation in a retreat situation, you are advised to engage in these preliminaries before trying to be present in awareness. That is important to remember. Longchenpa went through each of the preliminaries and stressed how important they were. Even if you are learning to be naturally present, you still have to engage in the preliminary practices because they are not preliminary practices as we understand them. Longchenpa also makes the point that traditional vipashyana meditation is not the ultimate form of meditation. The best kind of meditation is simply letting your mind rest in natural awareness.

THE TRIPLE-WORLD

The triple-world can be seen as discrete entities and as psychological states. People often think they are different and totally separate worlds, but according to Buddhism, that is not so clear-cut. A human being can actually have the experience of a hell, animal, hungry ghost, demigod, or god realm. Traditional Buddhist literature also says we can experience the triple-world system through meditation. We may begin our practice as a member of the realm of sensuality, have meditative experiences of various concentrative states associated with the realm of form, and then progress to the stages of absorption associated within the formless realm, where we more or less lose consciousness. We should also bear in mind that the world we know is not the only world that exists. Mahayana Buddhism elaborates on many different worlds, including buddha-fields. Early Buddhism always said the world as we know it, is only one of many worlds and the beings who inhabit different realms have different forms and experience things in ways quite unlike our own. They are not human beings, in other words. We should not rule out that possibility just because we have not seen these beings. A failure to see something does not mean it does not exist.

We experience many kinds of beings in this world, but there may also be beings in other worlds totally unlike ourselves. The main idea here is that no matter how good the worlds of other beings get, any temporary relief from suffering will be of no real help to them if they have no spiritual focus since they will eventually be transported back to square one. We may become gods and goddesses and live in paradise, but as the teachings say, when the karmic causes and conditions for such a life run out, we will slip back into the lower realms again. On the other hand, if we have some spiritual focus, it does not matter where we are born. We may be in this world of sensuality, but we can progress without ever slipping backward.

The six realms of existence in the realm of sensuality are a traditional Buddhist way of understanding heaven, hell, and the other stages. All the situations in conditioned existence are impermanent. We don't just go to heaven or hell and stay there forever. We cycle through these realms losing whatever we have temporarily gained along the way. However, any spiritual progress we make will stay with us. That is our only safety or security. Without that, we may sometimes be in heaven, sometimes in hell, and sometimes roaming aimlessly in between. We roam around without any direction because we lack insight.

What makes Buddhism so interesting is that both heaven and hell have many levels and tiers. There are many different kinds of hells: hot hells, cold hells, hells where you get killed every second, hells where you are constantly tortured, hells where you get frozen to death only to be revitalized and frozen to death again, hells where you burn to death only to get reborn and burn to death again. When you have paid your dues through this lengthy process, you may make your way back up to the human realm or even go straight to heaven. These descriptions may sound strange, but everyone gets what they deserve here, unlike some other religious ideas of hell, where all bad people are given the same treatment. The Buddhist hells depend on your level of wrongdoing, so some beings are treated slightly better than others. The same rationale applies to heaven. Even in the world we now share, where we live in certain countries with shared social habits and customs, our experiences are very varied. Why should a hell or a heaven be any different?

DEVELOPING AWARENESS

We should focus our awareness on our thoughts and experiences, and on the ground from which those thoughts and experiences arise. In normal English parlance, awareness has the connotation of "paying attention to something," but the Dzogchen view is that whatever we are aware of has its origin in that awareness. The origin of our distractions, weaknesses, attractions, emotional upheavals, dreams, and aspirations is intrinsic awareness. We can use our awareness to bring that intrinsic awareness to the forefront by paying attention to what arises in the mind. Awareness is not just a mental state. It is part of our mental being. Dzogchen is about learning to bring that mental being to realization. When Longchenpa talks about the dharmakaya, sambhogakaya, and nirmanakaya, or the cognitive ability of luminosity, he is saying they lead to intrinsic awareness. They are the same; there is no difference. It is our nature to be aware, even though we are so often unaware.

When we are not meditating, certain thoughts or attitudes are very virulent, entrenched, and appear as solid and real so that they overwhelm and wear us down. When we really pay attention to our thoughts and emotions in meditation, we can recognize their ephemeral quality and see how impossible they are to pin down. They are always changing; they do not remain the same. You have to examine this lack of consistency in your thoughts. One moment you might be thinking, "I hate that person" and the next moment you think they are wonderful. Or you may think, "I love this person so much... but only if they reciprocate that love... which I don't think they are doing," until that person looks more and more like the person you hate. It is funny when we say it like that, but that is the point of these teachings. We take everything so seriously but when we pay attention to our thoughts, we start to see how the mind operates, and our attachments and fixations begin to lessen. We have a lot more room to breathe. The possibility of being different or experiencing things differently becomes a reality.

Longchenpa is simply saying that we need to accommodate our myriad experiences and learn to deal with them properly. When we can see what we experience as a reflection of our own authentic state, we can enjoy it and that will give rise to an experience of bliss. When we cannot see our experiences in this way, we become completely fixated, opinionated, fearful, paranoid, and enmeshed in our own little world and consequently there is no bliss. When we relax into our experiences and see everything as a reflection of our authentic state, we can enjoy and savor whatever we experience.

MAIN PRACTICE

When Longchenpa says we should look at our experiences as a mirage or a dream, he is not saying our experiences have no reality at all. He is saying our experiences are dream-like. If everything were only a dream, we could not talk about being compassionate or caring because it would not matter. We say our experiences are dream-like or like a magical illusion, in the sense of a magician presenting a performance that seems very real. Our experiences are *like* that kind of magical illusion, but it is never said they *are* a magical illusion. If there were no difference between dream and reality as we know it, we would not have to think about karma, compassion, spiritual practice, spiritual realization, social injustice, political oppression, and so on. But we do have to think about these things because life is not a dream. It is just that we have the tendency, as human beings, to go to the other extreme and regard everything we experience as completely solid and real. Buddhism says we should understand that nothing can remain the same. Samsara is not a safe place. Tomorrow the world economy could crash. We cannot predict these things. However, human beings do not normally think this way; we assume everything is stable, permanent, and reliable. These teachings have very real and practical implications. They are telling us we take refuge in our own illusions. Nonetheless, there is a big difference between illusions and hallucinations.

Seeing experiences as free of visible causes and conditions is the ultimate aim of Dzogchen practice, but we first need to get to the point where we can recognize everything as self-manifesting. We have to recognize that everything is a product of causes and conditions before we can get to the level of seeing everything as self-manifesting. "Spontaneously arising" is a Dzogchen expression for this. "Spontaneously arising" means more than recognizing that causes and conditions have no inherent existence—it means our experiences actually arise spontaneously, just like rainbows.

Both Dzogchen and Mahamudra describe the nature of mind as having three aspects: nature, essence, and responsiveness. When we talk about *rtsal, gdangs,* and *rol-pa,* we are really talking about the last two aspects of mind. The nature of the mind is emptiness, its essence is luminosity, and its responsiveness is unceasing manifestation. In Mahamudra, these unceasing manifestations are called the "characteristic" of the mind. In Dzogchen they are called *thugs-rje,* which means "responsiveness" rather than "compassion," because it refers to the unceasing mental activities associated with mind. When we talk about tsal, dang, and rolpa, we are really talking about the essence and responsiveness aspects. We have to remind ourselves that they are all grounded in the first aspect—the empty nature of mind—because all these experiences come from rigpa itself. Rigpa is no different from our natural state, but rigpa also manifests our experience of things.

Dang literally means "radiance" and refers to seeing everything that arises in the mind as a reflection of our own authentic state. Instead of viewing anger, jealousy, unresolved issues, and despair as terrible things, you try to see them as reflections of your own true nature. They are just like images reflected on the surface of a mirror. A mirror does not judge. A mirror does not say, "The things I reflect are bad." We make those judgements, and we make them all the time. When we are not being too judgmental about our experiences, we have the opportunity to let them rest and they become free. Their hold over us is reduced because we are not taking everything so seriously. Then, whenever we become angry or jealous, we don't get so caught up in the drama. The Buddhist teachings say it is like seeing everything as if you were a spectator at the theatre. You know what is going on, but you do not get drawn into it. We normally take our life too seriously and get all caught up in things. We might often be wrong about what we think has happened and we don't even know it.

Rtsal is luminosity or the creative energy associated with our authentic state and rolpa means being able to enjoy whatever experiences we have. The three aspects are not separate. Dang means that you see everything that arises in the mind as a reflection of your own authentic state, tsal means there is a creative energy associated with your authentic state, and rolpa means that you can enjoy whatever is there by not accepting or rejecting it. When we see that whatever we experience is a reflection of our authentic state, then we can enjoy that and then there is bliss. When we are not doing that, we get so fixated, opinionated, fearful, and paranoid, we get completely caught up in our own little worlds. Then, there is no bliss. When we relax into it, and see that everything is a reflection of our own authentic state, we can enjoy and savor what we experience.

Longchenpa talks about focusing the mind on the notion of "presence." *Snang-ba* is also commonly translated as "appearances" and "phenomenal experiences." In the Dzogchen context, "presence" is a very good translation because our experiences are not meant to be seen as something that appears to us. They are just there. Without conceptualizing it, you simply recognize what is present. Both the Dzogchen and tantric teachings say that if we can achieve that simple recognition of whatever arises, our experiences will be pure presence. Our normal experiences are tainted and have no pure presence. We just cannot let things be. It must be emphasized that Longchenpa is primarily talking about meditation here. However, much of what we experience in meditation can be carried over into everyday life so that our impure perceptions begin to present themselves as pure presence.

Longchenpa is saying that if we have problems with awareness, we should pay more attention to the conditions that are present—what is there physically, mentally, socially, emotionally, politically, and spiritually. To have awareness, you have to be aware of something; you can't just be aware without being aware of something. We have to engage with the causal conditions that surround us. That is how we live. We are always in relationship. We develop awareness by knowing that we are in relationship, no matter what, and whether we like it or not. It is not a choice. We don't decide. It's already there. It's a pregiven situation.

It is our constricted minds that make us feel separate from people. An unconstricted mind is able to reach out to innumerable people. However, compassion doesn't mean we have to be intimate with everyone. It just means we have to care for everyone. We can be compassionate toward people without being intimate with them. When we look at it like that, compassion becomes a real possibility. If we had to be intimate with everybody, compassion would be very difficult. We can be intimate with some people, but we can be compassionate toward many people. The Dalai Lama is not intimate with us, but he has compassion toward all of us. When he says, "I care for all living beings," he really means it. We have to separate compassion and intimacy in that way.

Demonic possession refers to a denser form of conceptual proliferation (*vikalpa, rnam rtog*). Tibetan Buddhism talks about *rakshas* and *yakshas*; which are collectively referred to as *dun* in Tibetan (an equivalent of the Sanskrit word *mara*). If we get too caught up in the idea of absolute reality, ultimate truth, or emptiness, we will suffer from one kind of demonic possession. If we become invested in being a lovey-dovey, teary-eyed, sensitive person, that is another kind of demonic possession. We need to maintain a balance between the absolute and the relative. You can't go off on a tangent saying, "Nothing has any reality, everything is emptiness. If I punch you in the face, it is only emptiness. My face is emptiness, your face is emptiness, so cop this!" If the other person is stronger than you, you will wake up with a sore head. Longchenpa is saying that our social and political institutions, our family life and personal relationships, all do have their own reality, but when we get too caught up with them in terms of our own feelings, we get into trouble.

We can apply antidotes in Dzogchen meditation, but the main point is not to try very hard. We want to rest in the unoriginated state, which is something we can all access. Our primordial state does not remain remote, distant, unapproachable, or unrealizable because of our delusions, illusions, projections, disturbances, despair, obnoxiousness, arrogance, and lust. We can use certain countermeasures against the afflictions we have, but there is no single answer to our afflictions. Emptiness is not a countermeasure to every problem. You may think everything is empty and unoriginated and therefore you don't have to behave in an ethical way. You can just go off on a tangent and mistreat everyone, then tell the police when they come knocking on your door, "I have realized the unoriginated state so let me loose." We have to supplement contemplation on emptiness with a focus on compassion. On the other hand, if we get too bogged down with our feelings and emotions, we can stray to the other extreme, so we need to counterbalance that by contemplating emptiness. Longchenpa is making some very important points here, which are very basic and very profound at the same time. These very advanced teachings of Dzogchen are mixed in here with some of the more fundamental teachings of the Mahayana and they are really important for all of us.

We may think the state of unoriginatedness is less attainable than compassion, but perhaps that is not true. The unoriginated state is emptiness, which is the same as understanding the nature of the mind. Our original state is not created by causes and conditions but our experiences are based on causes and conditions. Buddhahood is the same as the unoriginated state or the nature of mind. Being in the unoriginated state or the natural condition is buddhahood, but that experience can nevertheless still be enlarged, increased, and deepened into something even more profound. If you allow yourself to rest in the natural state every time you meditate, you are having a taste of enlightenment already.

That is what Dzogchen teachings always focus on. The point isn't to try to free ourselves from the causes and conditions that give rise to experience, but rather, to see that our emotions and experiences arise from our unoriginated state. Therefore, they are not to be rejected. When we can relate to them like that, they are self-liberated. At first, our aim is to see that everything is a product of causes and conditions. We will ultimately come to the point of seeing everything as self-manifesting, but to get to that level, we first have to realize that everything is a product of causes and conditions.

Chapter Seven

Birth, Death, and the Intermediate State

If you fail to attain the state of Dzogchen in this lifetime, you have the alternative of attaining it either at the time of death or in the intermediate state (*antarabhava, bar-do*). You need to be able to recognize the death and bardo experiences, so you have to prepare for that recognition while you are still alive. There are three aspects to the bardo teachings. First, you need to prepare for the bardo experience while you are still alive by understanding the three aspects of birth, death, and the intermediate state. Second, you need to learn how to generate an awareness of the actual process of death so that you can clearly recognize your own demise. Third, you need to learn how to bridge the intermediate stage between bondage and liberation.

THE BARDO OF THIS LIFE (*RANG-BZHIN BAR-DO*)

The bardo is not just associated with post-mortem states since even everyday life experiences are considered to be a bardo. This bardo relates to your propensity to cling to signs and signifiers and how you should learn to understand your experiences as signs. This section is about the bardo of dreams, which is experienced in your sleeping moments. Your waking moments were already dealt with in the previous chapter.

The bardo of dreams (rmi-lam gyi bar-do)

You can come to terms with death while you are still alive in the practice of Dream Yoga where you gain knowledge of signs by learning how to deal with your dreams. There are three aspects to this practice. First, you learn to change your dreams while you are dreaming so that you can prevent unpleasant dreams from arising or transform them into pleasant ones. Second, you realize the nature of dreams to be devoid of reality. Third, you recognize that dreams are symbolic expressions of the mind's luminosity.

You recognize dreams while you are dreaming when you know that the phenomenal representations in the dream are devoid of truth. That is also how you can purify your dreams. Once you have learned to prevent disturbing dreams from arising and tried to recognize their nature, you need to go a little further and understand that the luminous nature of mind is revealed through your dreams. Whether your dreams are pleasant or unpleasant, comforting or discomforting, they all dissolve into your own luminous, natural state of mind and if you can experience this, you will be liberated in the bardo state.

Dreams are a proximate bardo experience, because dreaming is as close as you can come to death. This is why the bardo of dreams can provide a proximate understanding of how to liberate yourself in the post-mortem state.

The dying process

You must also think about what actually happens at the time of death. What sort of physical and mental processes are going on? What kind of spiritual states are taking place? According to Buddhist metaphysics, the body is associated with the five elements of earth, water, fire, wind, and space.

The first thing that occurs at the time of death is the earth element dissolving into the water element. At that point, the body becomes heavy and weighed down. You may want to raise yourself from your bed, but you will no longer have the power to get up. Simultaneously, the body's capacity to function properly diminishes, and that affects the faculty of seeing, so you cannot see properly.

Then the water element dissolves into the fire element and your blood circulation and all bodily fluids dry up. At this point, your capacity to hear also disappears. You can still smell but your hearing dissolves into the faculty of smell and you can no longer hear.

Following that, the fire element dissolves into the wind element and the warmth in the body dissolves. You feel cold and any heat in your body becomes centered in the heart. At this point, the faculty of smell dissolves into the faculty of taste, and you can no longer smell.

Next, the wind element dissolves into consciousness. Your breath (*prana*) or motility (*lung*) dissolves into consciousness. At this point, you cease to breathe, and all your sensory apparatuses shut down. Your sense of taste has dissolved into the sense of touch or bodily feeling so your tongue cannot distinguish the types of food you are given because there is no longer any sensation as to whether the food is bitter, sweet, or sour.

Finally, the mind dissolves into space. At this point, the mind no longer has the capacity to cognize, to apprehend things, whether they are gross or subtle. Simultaneously, the sense of feeling dissipates into the nature of things, so there is no longer any sensation whatsoever left in the person. You have to understand that this description is very much part of the Dzogchen teachings. Not many Buddhist schools talk about post-mortem existence in this way.

The deceased person still has two elements, the male and the female elements, which reside within the physiology of the person. These are called bindus. There is a white bindu that represents the male element and a red bindu that represents the female element. These two elements come together at the heart. Longchenpa does not say that the male element resides in the cortex and the female element resides in the abdomen because he is assuming you already know that. At the time of death, the male element descends, and the female element rises, and they meet together at the heart chakra, where they become intermingled and entwined.

The bardos of the post-mortem state consist of three stages. The first corresponds to your own authentic state, which is the dharmakaya. The second consists of various displays of mind, in terms of experiences that are imbued with luminosity, which corresponds to the sambhogakaya. The third is the rebirth experience, where you take on a new form and your ability to liberate yourself is conditioned by your destiny, in relation to the six modes of being, which corresponds to the nirmanakaya. The dharmakaya, sambhogakaya, and nirmanakaya experiences reveal themselves to the deceased in a progressive fashion.

THE BARDO OF THE MOMENT OF DEATH
(*'CHI-KHA'I BAR-DO*)

The deceased, for a moment at least, will have a sense of real spaciousness and an experience of luminosity. The sense of spaciousness dissolves into the luminosity to produce an experience of sheer brilliance. You are in your own natural state at this point. The moment of spiritual realization is right there. The deceased has the experience of wisdom (*ye-shes*) in the form of bliss, clarity, and nonconceptuality.

Then even your concept of ultimate reality dissolves into its own natural state, its own natural place, which is primordial space, actually. You realize that the nature of bondage is no different from the nature of liberation and you become closer and closer to attaining the goal of liberation.

At this point, your experience is comparable to a very attractive person holding a mirror up to their face.[20] When you are in this post-mortem state, you should think of your past experiences and your present bardo experiences. You should think of the practices you did while alive and of the bardo experiences you are now enduring. Recall whatever flashes of insight or luminosity you experienced during those practices and try to bring them into your current experiences of luminosity in the bardo state.

THE BARDO OF DHARMATA (*CHOS-NYID BAR-DO*)

The bardo of dharmata follows immediately after death and is an opportunity to experience the full force of your original wisdom. The dharmata experience, where you come into contact with that primordial wisdom, lasts only for an instant. That instant can be broken down into four different bardo moments.

The first moment

An experience of bliss, luminosity, and nonconceptuality arise instantly from your primordial wisdom at the precise moment of death. In your mind's eye, that experience can be like looking at the moon, where you perceive a bright light that is luminous and clear. This visionary experience may not be very clear for some people. It may be more like seeing the illusion of a mirage or smoke so the experience of this first moment may not be so vivid and sharp.

When you come into contact with your own primordial wisdom, all thoughts and attitudes associated with aggression cease. There are thirty-three mental thoughts and attitudes associated with aggression and they all cease. How can that happen? As Aryadeva says, "To be born into this world is relative truth, death is the ultimate truth." That being the case, at the time of death; you come close to your own natural and authentic state and the relative conflicting emotions dissolve. In this first bardo moment, the mental thoughts and attitudes associated with aggression cease.[21] These are:

> General desire, moderate forms of desire, all forms of desire, mental over-activity, mental movement, the mind gone astray, general suffering, medium forms of suffering, extreme forms of suffering, peace, conceptual activities, general fear, medium forms of fear, extreme forms of fear, general covetousness, medium forms of covetousness, extreme forms of covetousness, the tendency to harbor negative thoughts and attitudes, unwholesome thoughts and attitudes, thirst and hunger, feelings, moderate feelings, extreme feelings, acts of cognition, the basis of cognition, discrimination, shame, affection, moderate affection, extreme forms of affection, intentionality, the need to mentally accumulate, and jealousy. These thirty-three thoughts and mental attitudes associated with aggression dissolve at the first moment after death. Thus, it has been said.

The first moment of the dharmata is the experience of apparent phenomena. When these thoughts and attitudes associated with aggression dissolve into your natural state, aggression reveals itself as mirror-like wisdom.

The second moment

The experience of primordial wisdom now becomes even more refined and sharpened. It may be like the experience of looking at the sun instead of the moon, where instead of seeing whiteness everywhere, you see red. The second moment can also present as different visionary experiences, such as fireflies swarming in space. Up to this point, your bardo experiences are known as "manifest phenomenal experiences." With the onset of this second moment, all thoughts and attitudes associated with desire dissolve into your natural state. The forty desiring thoughts and attitudes are:

> General desire, moderate forms of desire, excessive forms of desire, ecstasy, medium forms of ecstasy, supreme forms of ecstasy, self-love, being attracted to things or people, feelings of wonderment, the desire to laugh, feelings of contentment, the physical need to embrace someone, the need to kiss, the need to suck, the need for stability, the desire to exert oneself, the need to feel that you are someone, the need to engage in various activities, the need for companionship, the need for power, the need for enjoyment, the need for excitement, the need for sexual experiences, the need to abandon oneself in the place of pleasure, the need to beautify oneself, the need to make oneself the most attractive person, the need for a good reputation, the need to be virtuous, the need to be articulate, the need to look for truth, the need for certainty, the need to harbor thoughts that encourage these mental attitudes, the need to give help to others, the need to order others around, the need for power, the need to be totally shameless, the need to deceive others, the need to indulge in our own suffering, the need to indulge in a state of intolerance, and the need to engage in excessive physical and mental activities. These forty thoughts and mental attitudes associated with desire dissolve at the second moment after death. Thus, it has been said.

When the thoughts and attitudes associated with desire dissolve into your natural state of mind, desire reveals itself as the wisdom of discrimination.

The third moment

The third moment is quite different from the previous two and is known as "the experiences of attainment." Having had the experience of bliss, luminosity, and nonconceptuality in the first two moments, you experience the attainment of wisdom in the third moment, because wisdom increases considerably at this point. The sign of the third moment is a wavering flame, as if a lamp had been placed in the wind in the early evening light. This experience is a symbolic expression of contact with your original wisdom state. The thoughts and attitudes associated with ignorance now come to cease. There are seven primary thoughts and attitudes associated with ignorance. These are:

> Passivity, allowing oneself to get distracted, allowing oneself to become fixated, allowing oneself to become deluded, not allowing self-expression, allowing oneself to go into a state of depression, yielding to lethargy, and laziness. These seven thoughts and mental attitudes associated with ignorance dissolve at the third moment after death. Thus, it has been said.

When the thoughts and attitudes associated with ignorance dissolve into your natural state of mind, ignorance reveals itself as the wisdom of dharmadhatu or the wisdom of your own primordial state.

The fourth moment

The experience of the fourth moment is like looking at a cloudless autumn sky pervaded by sunlight. When you come into contact with that wisdom aspect of your authentic condition, all your karmic traces and dispositions are dissolved into your own natural state. You become totally immersed in your primordial condition. At this point, the mental clarity of the mind, which you learned to cultivate during practice, and the experience of coming into contact with your original nature of mind during the post-mortem state, merge together. This is called "the meeting of the son and mother luminosity" (ma-bu 'phrad-pa).

The bardo between death and rebirth

If the deceased has not achieved liberation up to this point in the dharmata, the rigpa that has been residing in the heart chakra, moves to the region of the eye organs and the temporary stability that you were able to enjoy in the previous four moments becomes disrupted. Not necessarily visually, but in terms of your mental experience, you will now experience five different colored lights radiating in all directions. These colors become pervasive and fill the whole of space. At the onset of this display of colors, you start to go through further stages of experience. There are five moments in this bardo.

The whole bardo involves a process of devolution and evolution. So far, we have described the process of devolution and now the evolutionary process has been initiated. Your own authentic state puts you in possession of dharmakaya wisdom, the wisdom of authenticity. The wisdom of authenticity is the expression of the Dhyani Buddha known as Samantabhadra or Vairochana. This creates the ground for all kinds of visionary experiences during the bardo, where you will come into contact with a variety of beings.

You believe these beings to be separate, to be independent of your own condition, but they are in fact associated with the buddha-family of Samantabhadra. If you were a practitioner whilst alive, you will recognize these visionary experiences as they occur and see them for what they are, the projections of your own mind. If you recognize them for what they are, you will be able to liberate yourself. If you understand all the things that you encounter on your journey through the bardo state, you will be able to revert back to remaining in your own natural state. In that way, you can go through the second moment, third moment, fourth moment, fifth moment.

As you proceed through this bardo stage, corresponding to those moments, you will go through various experiences associated with mirror-like wisdom, discriminating wisdom, the wisdom of equanimity, the wisdom of accomplishment, and the wisdom of dharmadhatu. The intimation of the wisdoms that you experience during the bardo with the visionary display you encounter in and through your journey, are the embodiments of the corresponding Buddhas. Ratnasambhava, Akshobya, and Amoghasiddhi. These visionary displays appear precisely because the five wisdoms and their five buddha-families are inherent in your psychological makeup.

You don't have just one or two encounters with this or that entity; you will have numerous, countless numbers of entities appearing to you in the bardo. You have to recognize that they are all projections of your own mind. When you have that recognition, you will realize the projector and the projection are not separate. This is where you find liberation in relation to the sambhogakaya aspect of your being.

Vairochana, the first of these five Dhyani Buddhas and their wisdoms, gives you the opportunity to liberate yourself in the dharmakaya state. If that does not occur, you will experience a second, third, fourth, and fifth moment, corresponding to the rest of the buddha-families and their wisdoms. If you can recognize what is occurring during that period, you will be released into the state of sambhogakaya.

So progressive stages of the bardo are happening here: the bardo of dharmakaya, the bardo of sambhogakaya, and bardo of nirmanakaya. When you recognize what is occurring in your own mind, you will experience a very intense sense of radiancy ('od-gsal). It is not that one has not been liberated by the recognition of these visionary experiences as projections of one's own mind, but the energy of the radiancy generated by wisdom is so amazing that it carries one over into all levels of existence. That is how enlightened beings such as Shakyamuni Buddha have come into this world. This is how nirmanakaya beings come into this world. These beings are able to accomplish things in an instant that would require many years of effort for others.

Now, we have to talk about devolution. Having displayed these characteristics and qualities, the nirmanakaya then dissolves into sambhogakaya, and the sambhogakaya dissolves into the unchanging dharmakaya. Remaining in that state is called "nirvana." This is actual buddhahood.

THE BARDO OF BECOMING (*SRID-PA BAR-DO*)

The reason you are yet again drawn back into the bardo of becoming is because there are unresolved karmic issues that continue to dominate your existence. You were reborn and became entangled with the bardo of becoming precisely because, unlike the kind of deceased person we discussed in the previous sections, you were not able to recognize your experiences for what they were and so they did not lead you to self-realization. You had the same experiences that were discussed above, but you didn't recognize them. Just like people who believe their own dreams when they experience happiness and unhappiness, you took your bardo experiences to be real. In a similar way, you wandered about in the bardo of becoming, which is your own state as you experience it.

Since you were not able to liberate yourself during the bardo and rebirth is now imminent, you should focus solely on taking a wholesome and beneficial rebirth. The only way you can do that is by trying to recollect all the good things you learned in your previous life and the instructions given to you by your teachers.

There are two problems to contend with when you are about to assume a new body. The first problem comes from your past experiences, and the second problem comes from anxiety associated with the potential life you are about to lead. You are totally lost and wander aimlessly about. In that instance then, you should recollect your lama's instructions, and if possible, think of everything as having no inherent existence, as being insubstantial. Even at this stage of the bardo experience, if someone is evolved enough, they will see that everything they encountered during the bardo state was insubstantial and devoid of truth.

Those who are not so advanced should be able to see everything as illusion-like and should try to recollect their own practice of tantra. They should remember how they were able to generate all kinds of images during the visualization of peaceful, wrathful, and semi-wrathful deities and remind themselves that the visionary experiences they have just encountered in the bardo are no different.

Those who fail even to do that, have not many options left, except to take refuge in the Buddha, Dharma, and Sangha: the Buddha as the teacher, the Dharma as the path, and the Sangha as the holy community. They should develop devotion, faith, and so on, and then pray that they may be reborn in a very pleasant environment. Through trying to do this you may also become liberated. Thus, it has been said.[22]

Since there is no choice but to be reborn at this point, you should concentrate on investing and channeling all your energy into preventing entry into what are called "bad wombs." You have to make sure you don't enter what appears to be a very receptive womb but is really an inhospitable one. You should also concentrate on being reborn as a human being, not just any kind of being. Being reborn is easy, but to be reborn as a human being is very difficult and rare. Human life is precious. It is priceless and endowed with seven qualities. You should be thinking,

"I want to be born as a human being."

Then you should think of the womb you are entering as a palace, not a fleshy and bloody place of confinement. Your mother's womb should be seen as a palace and the father's semen and mother's egg should be viewed as the essence of divinity. You should think, "I will become a sentient creature through these seeds." Consciousness is produced from the mixture of these divine seeds and when this occurs, you should think, "I will always devote my life to spiritual development and fulfillment and never allow myself to become separated from that." Then generate a deep conviction that having come into contact with your spiritual practice, you will undoubtedly find liberation.

TRANSFERENCE OF CONSCIOUSNESS

In conjunction with the bardo practices, you can also practice transference of consciousness (*sankranti, 'pho-ba*). The simplest version of this practice is as follows. Visualize the psychophysical energy pathway in the middle of your body, like a straw that is hollow inside. This energy pathway reaches up to the cortex. Inside this psychophysical energy pathway, you should visualize a white seed syllable AH, which symbolizes the unpolluted state, at your heart chakra. You should really believe that this syllable has all the characteristics of being unpolluted. Then, with a real sense of vigor, you should chant AH, AH, AH, AH... with real force up to one hundred times.

As you pick up the momentum of chanting this sound, you push the syllable up through the central energy pathway into the cortex and then out from your crown center. That AH represents your consciousness. Your consciousness is then ejected from your body and transported into Amitabha's Pure Land, the Western paradise called Sukhavati or Dewachen. Then visualize that once your consciousness, which is embodied in the letter AH, reaches Amitabha's Pure Land, it enters into the heart of Amitabha, the Buddha of Infinite Light. Then you should rest in a state of nonconceptuality.

If you do this practice correctly with effort, you will see definite signs within seven days. Your crown will become tender or break into a sore, which is a positive sign. This is definite.

You should really only practice this at the time of death. You should not use it in an unskillful fashion—for example, to commit suicide—but only apply it at the time of your natural death. When all the signs are apparent that death is imminent, you should do this.

This is the most succinct pith instruction involved with the practice of phowa or the transference of consciousness. As Dzogchen practitioners are already skilled in various practice methods, they don't need to engage in elaborate practices. Dzogchen practitioners are fortunate ones because we don't need to elaborate on these topics; simple practices are enough.

DEDICATION

I have expounded on the real essence of the secret teachings
that comes from Guru Padmasambhava, the Lotus Born,
through whose blessings we continue these teachings.
In the Land of Snows, at the mountain peak fortress of Urgyen,
I, who go by the name of Unsullied Luminosity, Drime Ozer,
have committed this to writing.
Through this effort, and through whatever merit I have incurred,
may all beings profit, finding temporary happiness in this life
and eternal happiness now and forever.
Everyone is included in my prayer;
no one is excluded from ultimate reality.
May everyone spontaneously realize
the form and wisdom aspects of the buddhas.

TRALEG KYABGON COMMENTARY ON BIRTH, DEATH, AND THE INTERMEDIATE STATE

DREAM YOGA

Dream Yoga is a process where you can stay in the natural state while going to sleep. A simple practice of Dream Yoga would just be to go to sleep with a sense of awareness, instead of dreading tomorrow, reviewing the past week's events. There are also simple visualizations you can do, such as picturing a lotus flower at your heart center and then visualizing a small, luminous, radiating object resting on the petals of the lotus. You concentrate on that while you fall asleep in a mindful fashion. You will have a more restful sleep as well. If you regularly experience insomnia, this technique will be much better than counting sheep. The idea is to sleep soundly with a sense of awareness, but without entering a deep sleep.

It follows that the dream state is also a very potent situation for attaining full realization, because learning to relate to our dreams can be our training ground. That is where we learn how to deal with death, because falling asleep is a form of death. We have no choice but to sleep. We can go without sleep for five to seven days, but finally we will crash, and we would also be dreaming while we are awake. We also have no choice about the content of our dreams. However, we can change the content of our dreams if we start practicing and that will lead to the ability to change our experiences in the post-mortem state.

We can learn to willfully direct our experiences so that we are no longer at the mercy of whatever arises. First, we learn to prevent nightmares and disturbing dreams and then we learn how to transform those dreams. Finally, we learn to use our dreams to realize the luminous nature of mind. The same process is supposed to occur at the time of death and subsequent to death. There is a real parallel there, according to these teachings. Until we are dead, we will not know for sure, but these teachings are saying that sleep is a form of death, waking up the next day is a form of rebirth, and the experiences taking place between sleeping and waking are a form of bardo.

THE DYING PROCESS

This description of the dying process is very much a part of Dzogchen teachings. Not many Buddhist schools would talk about post-mortem existence the way Longchenpa describes it here. When the gross and subtle states of mind have ceased and there is no feeling or sensation of any kind, even space dissolves into luminosity. Our experience of ultimate truth has dissolved into the natural state and there is nothingness. Then we revive and come back to consciousness, which is when we are on the first leg of the next journey into the bardo. That is when the similarity between dream experiences and bardo experiences comes into effect. The dissolution of the bodily elements is not part of the bardo experience yet.

Longchenpa is talking about the gradual and progressive stages of physical and mental dissolution here. This may happen over a short or long time, depending on the individual and the manner of death. What Longchenpa is describing goes from the grosser levels of our experience of the physical and mental elements to the more subtle ones, which is a form of withdrawal into the self. Our senses cease to function stage by stage, in correspondence with the dissolution of the elements. However, space only dissolves into emptiness for a second or so. Some of the other teachings say that death is more like being knocked on the head so that you see stars and fall unconscious.

In Tibetan Buddhism, we pay more attention to the heart region at death, but the area of the cortex is not ignored either. When we die, we are supposed to eject our consciousness through the cortex. It is said that consciousness could escape through the anus and if that happens, you are in deep trouble. This is mentioned very clearly in the texts. The tantric teachings give some semi-material form to consciousness in that sense, because if consciousness were totally immaterial, how could you say it will leave the body through the cortex, nose, ears, or anus? All the orifices of the body are potential escape routes for consciousness. Thus, it is said. It is also said that the orifices used for the exit of the consciousness have implications for the type of realm you will be born in, but personally, I find that difficult to believe. It makes sense to think that consciousness has some kind of semi-material form and therefore to say that bardo beings encounter certain visionary situations. If consciousness were totally immaterial, how could you see colors, hear sounds, smell aromas, and so forth? Only a being of quasi-material form would have those abilities. The teachings say bardo beings have forms and appear in different ways. Although they are not like us, they do have a kind of very refined form, they have physical needs, and they communicate and interact with one another. They may not be perceptible to us, but they are perceptible to each other.

THE MOMENTS OF DEATH

Longchenpa is saying that at the time of death all the concerns that used to be important to us will no longer matter because we are not that person anymore. He is not talking about giving up bodhicitta; he is describing the process of becoming unconscious. When you become unconscious, you simply become unconscious. At the time of death, all your mental faculties shut down and cease to function and then, according to Buddhism, you are revived. The lists associated with aggression, desire, and ignorance could be seen as a catalogue of the energies of existence. The instant existence ceases, those energies stop, only to be regrouped later, like a plague or an undesirable virus that will inflict more pain on you. Just for a moment, you feel the relief, only to be assailed once again. If we are smart enough, we will be in our natural state at this point, instead of in a state of total oblivion or anesthesia.

You have to be present even after all your mental functioning has ceased. We are only talking about moments here. We are not talking about days or weeks. Even while your mind is inactive, you can nonetheless still be aware and present. That is the important thing. Just being there; just being present. When you are revived, your concern for others will return because we always exist in relation to others. It is a basic necessity for the survival of sentient creatures generally. But when you are dead, all of that becomes irrelevant. When I die, I will not be "John Smith" anymore. There will be a real discontinuity.

Naropa experienced the signs of the moon, sun, and smoke as marks of success in practice, so signs like these are not just related to death. If you do bardo practice, you can have these experiences while you are still alive. When people start to do the three-year retreat and the six yogas of Naropa, they will do bardo practices and may have experiences like the ones described here. Longchenpa mentioned that in the Mind Cycle. He said the bardo is not just something we experience at the time of death or in the post-mortem state but you can prepare for the bardo by doing Dream Yoga, the bardo visualizations, and transference of consciousness practice.

The innate capacity of mind to be luminous is mother luminosity and the clarity we are trying to develop in meditation is son luminosity. Mother luminosity gives birth to son luminosity, and these come together. Sometimes the metaphor of the sun and its rays is used. There has to be a sun for there to be sunshine. In a similar way, for luminosity to take on any kind of "concrete" form, it has to arise from our original state. It is a form of rediscovery, not a matter of bringing something new into existence through practice. In other words, wisdom is not something we create or receive or manufacture anew; it is our original state. The Tibetan word *ye-shes*, which is a translation of the Sanskrit word *jnana*, means exactly that. *Ye* means "primordially," *shes* means "to know." So *yeshe* means "having primordial understanding." Becoming enlightened is about retrieving our original understanding rather than learning something new.

To understand how rigpa is located in the heart chakra, we go back to the notion of son and mother luminosity, which is relative rigpa and absolute rigpa. Tibetan medical texts say that when we die, everything centers on the heart. Even when the brain has stopped functioning, the person may still be alive in some rudimentary fashion. The heart may still be pumping blood and maintaining some kind of life. In this sense, rigpa means "where the life force is still centered." Tibetan medical texts and tantric teachings say that when we die, our sentience or ability to sense things withdraws from the extremities and we gradually lose our sensitivity until the only warmth left is centered in the heart. In Tibetan Buddhism, we determine whether someone is dead or not by whether their heart has stopped functioning. At the time of death, we are in our natural state just for a few seconds because there are no thoughts or sensations—you have no thoughts about past, present, or future, no worries, anxieties, or fears. You not even stunned. You are just there— naked, total and aware. That arises from what is happening in the heart rather than whether your brain is functioning or not.

BARDO BEINGS

Culture has nothing to do with the existence of bardo beings. Bardo beings take form irrespective of their birthplace, race, culture, or traditions. We are born, we grow old, and we die. That is a universal truth.

The death experience would be the same for all of us, but you would bring your own cultural imagery with you when you die. The fact you are in the bardo having hallucinatory images would not change. Whether we are Caucasian, African, Asian, Indian, Tibetan, or Chinese, we all dream. We dream about things that are familiar to us and our culture would no doubt determine what we dream. A person isolated from the modern world such as parts of the Amazon jungle is unlikely to dream about driving a Porsche. There is that cultural specificity to dreams. There is also a universal aspect to dreams that makes them common to all human beings. If you were to go to a remote place and tell people you had a dream, no one would ask, "What is a dream?" They would understand. They would all admit to dreaming.

REBIRTH

In the latter stages of the bardo of becoming, you might experience displays of different colored lights, where the color is an indication of the nature of the coming rebirth. Bardo texts also advise us to go toward the sharper lights, instead of allowing ourselves to be dazzled and put off by them and finding comfort in the dull lights. They say we can get frightened by the sharp, brilliant lights and shy away from them, like a rabbit or kangaroo caught in a spotlight and take comfort in a duller, cozy, smoky kind of atmosphere.

You come back as a nirmanakaya being because you do not find liberation during the previous stages. The previous three bardo stages of dharmakaya, sambhogakaya, and nirmanakaya have the potential to deliver you to full enlightenment, but if that doesn't occur, you have to return in an involuntary way. However, you may still have the ability to decide what kind of rebirth you want to take. You would be regarded as a bodhisattva in that case, because an ordinary being has no choice whatsoever. The bardo experience is normally so terrifying that any womb or option that seems like it might save us from going through that experience again will seem good enough, but you will have no awareness of what kind of future life you are taking. If you have been a practitioner in your life, nothing you have learned will be lost when you pass away. You will be able to rely on what you learned and fall back on it during the bardo experience.

So there are three different types of bardos. Immediately after your death is the bardo of dharmakaya and you can go directly into the natural state of mind during that bardo, if you have the ability. You will then become enlightened just like that. If you don't have that ability, you will experience the sambhogakaya state with its five Dhyani Buddhas and their associated colors and corresponding wisdoms. If you choose not to liberate yourself in that sambhogakaya state for some reason, you may reappear in the world in the nirmanakaya form, as Shakyamuni Buddha did. If you don't have the ability to liberate yourself in that state, you will be forced to take rebirth as a samsaric being. You will then be literally torn apart, in the sense that one half of you is still living in the past and the other half is living for the future and filled with trepidation, fear, and anxiety about that future. Rebirth is inevitable at this point, it's going to happen regardless, so Longchenpa makes some suggestions about how to handle it.

Longchenpa is assuming the reader is already a practitioner. If you are not a practitioner, none of this would make any difference. If you are a practitioner, his advice would speak directly to you without your having to manufacture any interest, just as a sportsperson in a coma might be revived by verbal reminders of their sport. We have to understand it like that. Even when we are dead, things will not be all that different. If we have done some kind of spiritual training, we will have the ability to remind ourselves of that by saying to ourselves, "Don't get lost, wake up." You don't need to take the bardo experience too seriously. You might see all these beings, some beautiful and peaceful and some demonic, ferocious, and grotesque, but they are all in your mind, they are not real. You are learning to remind yourself of that.

In the bardo of becoming, if you are unable to see that life has no inherent existence, then you could at least see things as illusion-like. Longchenpa also says that if your mind is focused, you can choose your own rebirth. You can even choose your own parents. Even if you are drawn to a particular womb, you can choose whether you want to go there or not. You can shut the door to that womb.

PURE LANDS

Longchenpa also says that some people can attain enlightenment in a pure land. While pure lands could be said to be more of a state of mind than a physical reality, it would be difficult to discount the possibility of other world systems that we know nothing about, where things are better than they are in our own world system. Before we reject that possibility as more like science fiction than reality, we should reflect on the fact that even on this planet, the fortunes of people vary greatly from one continent to another. When we are talking about intergalactic worlds and trying to expand our cosmological imagination of things, we cannot say whether places like that exist or not. However, even if there are beings in other worlds who are experiencing a good life, their life will not last forever. It can only be a temporary respite, where beings find some relief from the tedium that is characteristic of living in the world we know.

The notion of pure lands is quite strong in Tibetan Buddhism. When people die, we do Amitabha puja and hope that whoever has died is going to Amitabha's pure land, which is called Sukhavati or "Land of Joy," which is very suggestive of an absence of suffering. The traditional texts say music plays there day and night, the gardens do not need tending, it is always perfect, and when you put your foot down on the grass, the grass bounces back by itself. We recite a particular prayer to Amitabha all the time. It was written by a Tibetan lama, but even he begins the prayer by saying, "I have not seen Sukhavati with my physical eyes, I have only seen it with my mental eyes." While Amitabha's pure land is the most famous and people in the West have the tendency to equate it with the Buddhist concept of a Pure Land, many, many other pure lands form part of Mahayana cosmology, which has the notion of an open, unlimited universe, with vast numbers of living creatures that inhabit any part of the known universe and beyond.

PART THREE

Root Text:
Nyamnyi Rangdrol—Natural Freedom of Equality

Chapter Eight

Our Natural State is Spontaneously Established

I prostrate to you, Kuntuzangpo.
All dharmas have always existed in this world as equal.
Why are they equal?
They all have the potential for enlightenment,
and this has been the case right from the beginning.
This primordial state cannot be described or cognized;
like space itself, it abides nowhere.
It is not perceptible to the naked eye,
but is primordially, aboriginally perfect in itself.
It rests in the state of dzogpa chenpo.
I prostrate to this form of bodhicitta,
our natural state beyond cultivation.

THE ABORIGINAL STATE

Longchenpa starts by saying that the Dzogchen teachings embody the ultimate tantric teachings because they don't rely on causes and conditions and the practitioner need not worry about what has to be cultivated or abandoned. Whatever arises in the mind is always elusive. We cannot grasp it, and we cannot pinpoint it because our primordial state is totally open and nonpartisan. We can't talk about bondage and liberation from its perspective because everything has been free within it from the very beginning, yet this very state of openness is what allows our myriad and unceasing experiences to arise. That is why, when you understand where these unceasing experiences come from, they reveal themselves as expressions of wisdom.

All experiences are ultimately the same because they all have the same nature, and that nature never changes. Our experiences change, but the nature of those experiences remains the same. This is true in terms of the external physical world and the sentient beings contained within that world. Many kinds of beings are housed in the natural world—human beings, animals, hungry ghosts, gods, and so on—but the real Dzogchen practitioner would see these beings as expressions of the three kayas. The three realms—the sensual realm, the realm of form, and the formless realm—should also be seen as an expression of the three kayas. From the Dzogchen point of view, there is no concept of past, present, or future to talk about. There is only one time: the time of primordial perfection.

To realize this state of equality (*mnyam-nyid*) regarding all things, we must first divest ourselves of any thoughts of cultivation and abandonment. We can engage in many different kinds of spiritual practices, some inner (Buddhist) and some outer (non-Buddhist). There is also an infinite variety of spiritual practices in the Dzogchen tradition, which are ordered, according to their degree of importance, within a system of spiritual vehicles known as the "nine yanas." Dzogchen practitioners formulated, practice, and abide by this nine yana system because people have varying degrees of intelligence. Ultimately though, there is no such thing as vehicles of spiritual progress, because our primordial state is just like space itself, so even though the Dzogchen teachings talk about cultivating the nine yanas to procure enlightenment, that is only a conventional presentation.

There is no need to renounce anything either. Why so? There is no one who is coming or going. When no one is coming or going, there is nothing to renounce or cultivate. You discover that you don't have to cultivate some things and abandon others when you realize that everything you experience in life is just a display and all displays have the same origin. Whether our experiences are good or bad, they are grounded in ultimate reality (*dharmadhatu, gnas-lugs*), so when experiences arise, they cannot be grasped onto or pinned down. They have this elusive quality because they arise from a state of groundlessness.

Although we attribute all kinds of moral significance to our experiences, in terms of their causes and effects, and we talk about cultivating bodhicitta as an antidote to aggression, in reality, when we realize our own natural state is a state of luminosity, there is no need to deliberately cultivate compassion or wisdom. Natural wisdom (*rang-byung ye-shes*) is already present.

We usually try to improve ourselves through spiritual practices that use external methods, such as rituals and prayers, or engage in inner mental discipline, and we put a lot of effort into that. However, to be a true Dzogchen practitioner, you should drop all that and just remain in a state of effortless naturalness, because when you can remain in your own natural state, you are already in the state of dharmakaya. Dharmakaya is not found elsewhere. In that state, you are not thinking about the past, present, or future. In fact, you can afford to let your mind wander in an almost careless fashion.

Whenever our mind becomes fixated on something, we think, "I am experiencing this, I am having this experience." Instead of latching onto that, you should let it go or you will never be able to drop the grasper and the grasped, the apprehender and the apprehended. You should just let things flow through without judging, without editing, and without any kind of filter. As soon as something arises, let it rest.

Deluded states of mind don't have to be abandoned, because they have the potential to bring about wisdom. There are five kinds of wisdom that correspond to the five deluded states of mind so whatever arises in the mind has the potential to liberate us. This practice is called dzogpa chenpo, the great completion (maha-ati or mahasandhi), because we don't need to overcome, conquer, or abandon various delusory states of mind. Just letting the mind rest in its own natural state will lead you to liberation.

THE MANDALA OF OUR PRIMORDIAL STATE

Whatever arises from its original state manifests in the present as something spontaneously arisen so you should think of the myriad ordinary objects of the world as perfect in themselves. You should think of the world as a whole, as a mandala—as an uncrafted, unfashioned, spontaneously manifesting, palatial dwelling place. You should also think of your body, feelings, conceptual categories, instinctual tendencies, and consciousness (the five skandhas) as the mandala of the five Dhyani Buddhas—Vairochana, Akshobya, Ratnasambhava, Amitabha, and Amoghasiddhi. The five elements of earth, water, fire, wind, and space should be seen as the female Buddhas, the five consorts of the male Buddhas.[23] Your subjective experience and your objective experience can be liberated in that way.

If you can do that, you won't need to reject some experiences and cultivate others, because there is nothing that needs to be altered. There is no need for those kinds of methods because antidotes are unnecessary. This is called "liberation within the state of equality" because everything remains in a state of one-flavoredness when we are in dzogpa chenpo. You should have confidence in the reality that everything is primordially pure and complete. This has to be understood fully.

The mind itself is rootless, because it's not grounded in anything other than itself and is aboriginally pure and empty.[24] It has not come into being as a product of something or someone. It has manifested by itself. The mind itself, which has spontaneously appeared in this fashion, is referred to as "buddha." When meditators become skilled in resting the mind, they are able to rest in a state of equality in that very mode. A mind in this kind of restfulness has no concern for its origin or its ultimate demise, precisely because the concept of time does not apply here—there is nothing to precede certain events or to succeed other events, so we can't count the number of experiences or mental states we may be going through at any given moment. This mind is unbiased, not given to prejudice, nonselective, and free of any potential to get lost or confused.

When the mind is allowed to rest in the state of equality, according to Dzogchen practice, there are no stages to be traversed because nothing has any intrinsic identity of its own. People who are involved in the purification of the mind and embark on the long journey of spiritual practice through paths (*marga, lam*) and stages (*bhumis, sa*), will ultimately find their efforts are not all that fruitful. Natural wisdom is not amenable to change or corrupting influences; trying to change it is like trying to change the shape of space. The moon reflects on the surface of the ocean just the way it is and no one spends time arguing about whether it is pure or not. Likewise, natural wisdom cannot be talked about in terms of purity or impurity. These are very advanced, secret teachings. They are particularly profound and are the essence of the definitive teachings of Dzogpa chenpo.

Our current experiences, whatever they might be, are an expression of our primordial state and are therefore spontaneously established. This is our aboriginal primal state.[25] Myriad variegated experiences of ordinary daily matters arise from this primordial original state and when the Dzogchen yogi realizes their experiences are coming from that state, everything they experience will be revealed as the great mandala. This mandala is our own state. It has not been created; it has arisen spontaneously. That is the great palace within which we dwell.

EXPERIENCES ORIGINATE IN OUR NATURAL STATE

The openness of dharmakaya is the creator of all things. The nature (*ngo-bo*) of the mind is openness. The essence (*rang-bzhin*) of the mind is gentleness because our primordial aboriginal state is luminous. Its responsiveness (*thugs-rje*) is unceasing. In whatever manner experiences present themselves to our mind, at that very moment, we realize their origin lies in our original, primal condition. When we take notice of our aboriginality and take on board the notion of ultimate reality, which is like space, we will find that not even the tiniest particle can exist outside the realm of our natural state.

No matter how many experiences present themselves to our minds, we should recognize that they originate in the original ground of being, at the very moment they arise. When you can recognize this and integrate it with the notion of ultimate reality, you will discover that not even a single particle can exist outside that realm.

From the state of dharmata (*chos-nyid*) arise varieties of experiences of dharmas (*chos-kun*)—physical and mental phenomena—but all these experiences manifest in a spontaneous fashion. They present themselves just as they are. Deluded sentient beings, the world they inhabit, and the myriad things that arise in relation to that world, are no different from the enlightened state of the buddhas of the three times. The Dzogchen practitioner must realize that everything they experience never deviates from their own aboriginal state of thatness (*tattva, de-nyid*), ultimate reality (*dharmadhatu, gnas-lugs*), and so on. You should not focus your mind on realizing anything other than that.

Our primordial state has never been produced by anyone, so from the beginning, we have not been created. Our very nature is pure. If we are caught up in our adventitious defilements, we will become liberated when we begin to recognize their nature.[26] There is no need to exert ourselves or try hard to learn how to overcome our deluded state, thinking we have to do something. How so? Our primordial state is free from causes and conditions, so exertion is unnecessary.

When we talk about the natural, aboriginal state, we should not form an opinion about it or think it "belongs" to anyone, because that natural state cannot be identified. Whatever opinion we form about our primordial state will just be an opinion. It will only be relevant for that time. In fact, the more we examine our natural primordial state, the more elusive it becomes. We find it does not stay anywhere; it is not located in any one place. It is elusive and empty of substance.

The Dzogchen practitioner should come to understand that their authentic, primitive state is free from any notion of saying, "It exists" or "It does not exist," because to say that it does or doesn't exist is another form of mental fabrication. When we relinquish that fabrication, when we allow ourselves to stop engaging in those thought processes, we find our own dharmakaya. All of our opinions are mental fabrication. When we become free of mental fabrication, that is dharmakaya—that is our aboriginal state.

There is no other way to relinquish the hold of mental fabrication. When we can let that go, then nothing that arises in the mind will disturb us, because when anything and everything manifests, it takes place without fixation. The Dzogchen practitioner knows that no experience is different from any other experience. In fact, all experiences are seen as one, because they have the same nature, which is like space. Where do the varieties of experience come from then? They come from mental formations, from the mind that separates things. Even the different Buddhist schools are created by the mind, so the enlightened mind of Dzogchen embodies the qualities of all the teachings because it is all-pervasive and all-encompassing. Just as space allows for things to come into being and accommodates them, the state of Dzogchen is the primordial source of all things. In that state of dzogpa chenpo, the great completion, the myriad things that appear all manifest as equally perfected in themselves.

Our subjective experiences of pain and pleasure, and our value judgments of something being of high status and therefore valuable or low and therefore valueless, should be seen as essenceless, just like reflections of the moon on water. They appear without any enduring essence and they disappear without leaving any traces on the authentic state of our being. Nothing we experience can manifest outside of or above our self-perfected state of Dzogchen. It transcends our dualistic perceptions, so although what we experience is undeniable, the experiences themselves have no enduring substance so no intrinsic reality can be attached to them.

THE NATURAL (AUTHENTIC) STATE TRANSCENDS CONDITIONED EXISTENCE

Dzogchen practitioners must learn to free themselves from the belief in karmic cause and effect and to stop saying, "Some actions are intrinsically worthwhile and other actions are intrinsically unwholesome." For as long as your mind is attached to the idea of good and bad actions, as if they had some intrinsic reality, you will never be able to encounter that which is genuinely real. The authentic condition, which is the ultimate meaning, is uncreated and primordially pure, so whatever presents itself to the mind is without the duality of perceiver and perceived. Our authentic state cannot be perceived in any other way.

If you are too attached to the idea of cause and effect and you believe everything is dependent on causes and conditions, you should examine your own immediate experiences. Look at how you perceive the world through the five senses and observe how the causal mechanism operates there. Then focus on your own mental reactions to these sensory inputs and observe how they are created. If you examine this closely, you will discover that even sensory impressions are like space, because they have no foundation in themselves.

The authentic state of dharmakaya transcends the conditioned existence of cause and effect because this state is not brought about by causes and conditions and no timeframe can be assigned to its origin. It has spontaneously manifested of its own accord. That being the case, what is the use in striving to achieve something that is already present?

All psychophysical entities (dharmas) are devoid of inherent existence, so their nature is emptiness. Sentient beings wander in cyclic existence due to their ignorance and fixation on things and are consequently subject to experiences of pain, pleasure, suffering, and happiness in myriad forms. What you need to realize is that no matter how intense your samsaric experiences are, all of them are like dreams. They have no intrinsic reality of their own, just as our dream experiences, which seem real while we are dreaming, have no reality of their own.

The Dzogchen practitioner must realize that their own authentic state is not affected by any of this. The authentic state is not a created state; it is rootless, without foundation, and naturally sublime. It is the state of buddhahood and its nature is emptiness. This has to be understood. Even when we try to grasp onto things and make them intelligible through thoughts and concepts, their nature is emptiness. This means that, in their nature, they are neither one nor many—their nature is neither oneness nor a plurality of distinct realities.

Untutored practitioners can become fixated on the truth of certain things, but that becomes the instrument that binds them to the samsaric condition. This problem also arises when we have a strong allegiance to a particular school of thought, where we can get lost in a maze of argument and counterargument with no opportunity to find liberation from such a state. We get caught up in definitions, instead of trying to penetrate the true reality of things, and we begin to think the interpretative teachings are the genuine teachings and the law of karmic cause and effect is the ultimate view. If we see karmic causes and effects as real in themselves, we will not realize the part played in all of this by the mental imputations we project onto the objects of experience. We cannot put an end to the samsaric condition that way.

TRANSCENDING THE NINE YANAS
According to the Dzogchen system, the entirety of the Buddhist

teachings is encapsulated in the nine vehicle (*yana, theg-pa*) system of sutra and tantra. The sutric teachings are known as the "three causal yanas" and refer to the exoteric aspects of the Buddhist teachings. They emphasize renunciation, prevention, and the application of antidotes. These three yanas comprise the hearers (*sravaka-yana*), the solitary realizers (*pratyekabuddha-yana*), and the enlightened warriors (*bodhisattva-yana*). The sravaka trains in renunciation, the pratyekabuddha trains in the prevention of harmful thoughts and deeds, and the bodhisattva trains in insight into emptiness which, as the antidote to all disturbing thoughts and emotions, eradicates the root of delusory states of mind.

However, the Dzogchen view is that we should see the spontaneously arisen wisdom (*lhun-grub ye-shes*) that is present in the mind as already perfect and complete in itself. It doesn't need to be interfered with in any way. We cannot improve on it because it's already perfect in itself. The Dzogchen practitioner doesn't need to think they have to discover the uncontrived, spontaneously arisen natural state of mind by engaging in practice for three countless eons. We don't arrive at the natural state of the ground of being as something that has come into existence anew.

The tantric teachings are the esoteric aspect of the teachings which is called the "fruition yana;" a blanket term for all aspects of the secret mantra system. These yanas are divided into two stages, which comprise "three outer" and "three inner" tantras.

The first of the outer tantras is called kriya or "action" tantra and emphasizes ritual practices. The emphasis in Kriya-tantra is not on realizing the natural state of mind, as is the case in Dzogchen, but on visualizing deities, where you see the deity as a lord and yourself as their servant. This approach still involves the notion of dualism because you regard yourself as separate from the deity. You are not entirely free from the hold of hope and fear either, because you are concerned with abandoning some things and cultivating others. As long as hope and fear remain, you will not find liberation, so this level of tantric practice is incomplete. It is tainted with thoughts of dualism, of one and two.

The next outer tantra is the upa or "application" tantra. Again, even though our natural state is pure in its own intrinsic nature right from the beginning, this practice is still concerned with the visualization of various deities. The relationship between the practitioner and the deity is more intimate here because it's more like the relationship between siblings or friends. However, this tantra is still tainted by traces of dualistic perception, because even though the essence of the deity and our essence are the same, our thoughts are still governed by the perception of things to be cultivated to advance our practice and things to be abandoned to expedite that process. If the tantrika is caught up in dualistic ways of perceiving themselves and their relationship with the deity, they will never gain insight into the essential meaning of the truth.

The last outer tantra is the yoga or "union" tantra and involves five devices that bring about the actualization of awakening.[27] Yoga tantra also involves cultivating four spiritual charismatic powers.[28] Tantrikas are still trying to condition the natural state of mind when they pursue these practices. Our own natural state has never come into being, so it is birthless from the beginning. It is not birthless because of its antiquity. It is birthless precisely because it has never come into being at a given time, so the quintessential meaning of the nature of the mind cannot be perceived through ordinary modes of apprehension. Therefore, even though we may progress through various stages in yoga tantra, we will not even get close to the realization of the authentic, undiluted, uncorrupted, and natural state of our own being.

Then there are the three inner tantras. The first one is called maha-yoga or "great union" tantra. Practitioners of maha-yoga undertake very serious tantric sadhanas, which include the four branches of mantra recitation, familiarization with the sadhana, engagement in the sadhana, and completion of the sadhana. However, from the Dzogchen perspective, there is no need to apply so many techniques to free the mind. Since the nature of the mind is already free and intrinsically pure, we would be trying to do something that was impossible to do, so there would be no point in trying. Again, we shouldn't be too concerned about acceptance or rejection because these are obstacles to the realization of what is truly real.

The second inner tantra is anu-yoga or "supreme union" tantra. Here, tantrikas are trying to realize the indivisibility of the spheres of ultimate reality (*akanistha, 'og-min*) and natural wisdom. Since the essence of everything is the same, what is the point in thinking about cause and effect and attempting to transform or change anything? Just as the nature of space is pure, our own natural state of being is open and all-pervasive, so why concern yourself with the experiences of bliss and emptiness that are accessible in anu-yoga practice?

The third inner tantra is ati-yoga or Dzogchen. In ati-yoga practice, unlike the other tantric systems, there is no need to practice the development (*utpattikrama, bskyed-rim*) and fulfillment (*sampannakrama, rdzogs-rim*) stages of tantra, because the natural state of your own mind is bodhicitta. This natural state has no center or periphery. You have to understand that your lack of freedom, the experience of the state of bondage, has taken place within the expansiveness of your own being.

GOING ASTRAY IN DZOGCHEN

If you don't understand this and instead see the state of expansiveness literally as emptiness or vacuity, you will fail to understand that everything exists in the state of equality and is therefore complete in itself. You need to have a proper view, one that does not fall into extremes, to understand the natural state of the mind. As previously explained, the Dzogchen practitioner needs to practice without exertion and without thoughts of loss or gain. If you continue to entertain these thoughts, then your nondirectional state of mind, which is pure by nature, will become bound and imprisoned. As a consequence, your power to realize the essential point of thusness will be taken away. Practitioners who are in this kind of spiritual dilemma are in the most deplorable position and will suffer the evils of cultivating distorted teachings and practices. This is encouraged by their allegiance to various spiritual disciplines that mainly emphasize developing this or that extreme view.

Since our authentic state is not something that can be lost or gained, such practitioners will never have the opportunity to realize thusness. The unfortunate practitioners who have fallen into these kinds of spiritual deviations will be holding onto the notion of paths and stages as ultimately significant and will attempt to traverse them. In the process, they will suffer the disease of overexertion. Their fixation on the preservation of the spiritual pledges and vows they may have taken in the context of their practice will ultimately do nothing to purify their minds. Instead, these obsessions will become the very instruments that prevent them from achieving liberation. They will become the instruments of bondage.

Spontaneously arisen wisdom, which is a buddha's intent, is not a gift to be received, for the simple reason that the state of enlightenment is as all-pervasive as space itself. Its essence is the same as space. Who is there to travel the path of enlightenment? The true Dzogchen practitioner will realize that the only place to travel to is the boundaryless sphere of ultimate space.

We must see the importance of gaining realization effortlessly, without being perturbed by thoughts of loss and gain. The myriad things of this world have no origin in themselves so there is nothing to obscure the natural purity of the mind. It is only our fixation on proliferating thoughts that gives rise to the delusions of the mind and the problem of going astray. What constitutes going astray? It is about trying to reach a destination when nothing has intrinsic reality. Delusions arise from trying to see into that which cannot be looked at.

Practitioners who engage in the causal or fruition yanas do their best to train in the respective teachings of each tradition, but as long as they have the notion of self-exertion, they will never be free from the dangers of going astray. They will continue to fall under the influence of delusory mental states and won't see the true nature of things. For example, if we are motivated to seek all that is good, then for as long as we are trying to find true goodness, we will not be free from the possibility of going astray if we are deluded about what needs to be realized.

If you feel you need to look for that which is intrinsically good and sublime, then know that you should not. Instead, you must come to a level of certainty about your own intrinsic goodness and see that this mind of ours is primordially, intrinsically pure. The mind may feel the urge to look for its own intrinsic nature, but that which is looked for and that which is looking are the same. It is an illusion to think we can find our intrinsic purity as something separate. That is why mind, which is

226 Longchenpa's Three Cycles of Natural Freedom

intrinsically and primordially pure, should be left alone without contrivances and antidotes.

The Dzogchen practitioner should therefore view the nine yana system as graded, in relation to their spontaneously arisen, unitary consciousness. They must regard it in the same way that they see water and its ripples— as the same yet different. If you can understand that in relation to the yanas, you will have nothing to fear in terms of becoming lost, going astray, or becoming confused and deluded. Ultimately, the natural state of your being is not something that can be seen by looking. It is not something that can be found by seeking because it has always been present right from the beginning. You should remain in that state without feeling the need to eliminate superfluous obstructions.

From the ultimate point of view, there is no concept of wisdom, ignorance, profundity, peace, or subtlety; they are irrelevant, as are the concepts of duality, and the relationship between concepts and things. We simply project our mental conceptions onto things, either by exaggerating their characteristics and attributes or by denigrating those characteristics and attributes. In that state of ultimacy, what is, simply is—in its own nature, in its primordiality; it is spontaneously present, without being contingent on anything other than itself. It is the great thusness. Hence, what is, is spontaneously present. That is why there is no need to exert yourself to discover it.

How can we see anything when there is nothing to be seen? Nothing can be seen, from the ultimate point of view, because the myriad things of this world have no origin in themselves. They are unborn (*anutpada, ma skyes-pa*) by and in their nature. In the state of ultimacy, cause and effect are not operative, and we should see this very clearly. To see it like that is the essential instruction that we have received from previous great masters. The ultimate meaning of reality as such is like space. It has no center or periphery. We should not get too fixated on the causal vehicle or fruition vehicle, or on the practice of the tantric development and fulfillment stages. Instead, we need to try to rediscover our own perfection in the state of natural completion, which is attained through realizing the nature of the mind. This is the supreme authority wherein all the qualities and attributes of enlightenment are spontaneously present and perfected.

Without attachment, and through laying aside hope and fear, we experience the stability of samadhi and realize the essence of the mind is not something to be seen through our mind's eye. We have to forego all conceptual categories and formulations to realize this state. We will never see the true condition of things—how things are, as opposed to how things appear—by engaging in analytical meditation, where we investigate and examine, because the conceptual mind is incapable of comprehending how things truly exist.

Even if you have been fortunate enough to be introduced to various methods and practices, some as hard to find as precious stones, you will not see the true nature of things through these methods alone. If you can just let the mind rest without being afflicted by hope and fear, then that is it: you will see what is there without looking. To think there is something else that needs to be done besides this, or to think some other method is more effective than this, is a form of illusion. To be always two-minded and uncertain will only have a corrosive effect on your ability to secure your goal, because mind becomes confused. All you need to realize is that there are many different things, but they all have the same nature. Keeping that in mind, you should try to realize the nature of your own mind, without interfering with its natural condition.

EVERYTHING HAS THE NATURE
OF ULTIMATE REALITY

The ability to remain in your own natural state is the ability to remain in the buddha-field of the three kayas. There are buddhas who teach and audiences who listen to those discourses, and all the conducive environments and their favorable causes and conditions are also present within that field. When you understand this, you can stop trying to be like an artisan and let the mind rest. Without creating anything, you should let the mind rest naturally. In that state of eternal nowness, there is no past, present, or future, there is no nirvana or samsara. Without leaving anything out, everything is unified into one. You must remain in that state, for this is the essence of enlightenment.

The primordial buddha and the reality of things are presently realized.

This natural state of being is not a product of creation. It is primordially pure and cannot be adequately conveyed to others in words or through the use of other symbolic representations. It cannot be conveyed through these modes of communication, and it cannot be comprehended and understood by merely reading what is written in words and sentences on a piece of paper. This mind is the quintessence of all the spiritual vehicles because in the state of enlightenment, everything has to be gathered into one central point, and when that is realized, everything is understood simultaneously. All the myriad things that exist are inseparable from the sphere of ultimate reality.

When we are in the state of authenticity, the past, present, and future are united as the primordial expression of enlightenment itself. When we dwell in a place that is as vast as space, where mind is not disturbed by discursive thoughts, we remain naturally in a state of equality. In this place, we do not identify anything as this or that, because there is nothing to compare it with and because it cannot be characterized.

Being in this state is truly wondrous! All experiences are seen as the natural display of the mind. Everything is complete in itself and therefore beyond discourse. It cannot be fully articulated through verbal expressions and yet it is spontaneously established of its own accord. When we are in this natural state, there is no hankering after things and no possibility of being swayed this way or that, because to be in this state is to be in the pure buddha-field. The brilliance of the mind that is present in that state, proclaims the victory banner over all forms of regression, because you are in a state that is as expansive as space itself.

In relation to the nature of the mind, whose essential quality is luminosity, even methods such as harnessing the mind or relaxing the mind are not needed. Even the spiritual ornaments that adorn our awakened state—the accumulation of wisdom and the accumulation of merit—are naturally released in a nondual fashion, free from discursiveness. Without looking for the nature of the mind, it appears, yet at the same time, it has no enduring essence.

For these reasons, the Dzogchen meditator must refrain from trying to identify the contents of their experience by saying, "My experience represents this or that." You should let the mind rest naturally because when the mind is left on its own, without interference, it is the state of dharmakaya. Everything that you need to attain enlightenment, will be there, just by having freed yourself from the discursive thoughts of the mind. Your goal will be accomplished naturally.

This royal king of the mind (*kun-byed gyal-po*) is devoid of embellishment, so you should not entertain ideas of acceptance and rejection. The nature of mind is already awakened, so you don't need to think in terms of cause and effect. This self-manifesting nature of the mind has never come into being, yet is spontaneously established in the present. Whatever arises in the mind in this present moment is free from conditioning or contrivance. To understand this is to have the proper view—the correct, nonerroneous view—because to realize the natural state of mind is itself the great completion or dzogpa chenpo.

In terms of dharmata, things are not in a state of movement, and there is no plurality because they all dwell in the same reality. In terms of dharmas, the individual things that exist come and go unceasingly in their variety and diversity, and each is distinct and different from the other. This is how dharmata (ultimate reality) and dharma (empirical reality) reveal themselves. In terms of ultimate reality, we cannot say anything has come into being, because just like space, it is free of empirical determinations. The mind also, in its nature, is free from defilements because wisdom is intrinsic to it. Ultimate reality is all-pervasive—it is not located anywhere but is present everywhere—so we call it the great completion or dzogpa chenpo.

The ground of our natural state of being is not a thing, an entity or a dharma, so there is no need to engage in any activity with a sense of deliberation or deliberateness. In other words, we do not need to cultivate that ground by using various dharmas or things. Just let whatever arises in the mind rest as it arises. To understand that is to understand the most secret pronouncement one can make about the key points of practice.

This natural state of awareness, which we all possess, is not a product of causes and conditions. It is simply present. We can have many different experiences in relation to that awareness, but they are all to be seen as the magical display or creative activity of the mind itself. You shouldn't think about cultivating some things and renouncing others, because your experiences are already liberated in their nature as the creative activity of the mind. That is what is meant by "self-liberation" or rangdrol. Whatever arises has the ability to liberate itself into its primordial source. This is how you develop a firm understanding of what is involved in Dzogchen practice. An understanding as unshakeable as a mountain will develop, and everything you experience will find its way back to the original circle or ultimacy.

TRALEG KYABGON COMMENTARY ON OUR NATURAL STATE IS SPONTANEOUSLY ESTABLISHED

THE ABORIGINAL STATE

When we talk about our aboriginal state, our original dwelling place, our natural state, our authentic state, our primordial state, and so on, it is very important to see that this is not an abstract thing or something inaccessible. The very point that the Dzogchen and Mahamudra teachings are making is how easy it is, through awareness, to access our natural, original, aboriginal state. When we are not fixated, when we recognize where we are and what we are experiencing, we are in our authentic state. It is nothing mysterious, not something we cannot grasp. As Longchenpa says, we can access it when we are not examining or analyzing too much.

We always examine and analyze things, even with our meditation. People say to me, "How do I know I'm doing the right thing? How do I know I'm progressing with my meditation? How do I know I'm not going backward, that I'm advancing on the spiritual path? How do I know?" Longchenpa is saying you should not care about that. Just simply do the practice. If you see yourself in a particular state, then you are in the natural state, there is no difference. When we get all worked up over our spiritual practice, it becomes the same as what happens in our daily life. "Am I better than somebody else? Am I better than my colleagues at work?" We are competing all the time.

We should drop all that and focus on learning. We have to learn.

Longchenpa is one of the most learned Dzogchen masters ever. When we are always learning, always being inquisitive, always wanting to learn more, that is different from being too analytical, too judgmental, too caught up in dividing things into pieces, even our own beliefs. That is seen as very unhelpful. It is similar to the difference between practicing awareness and being self-conscious. When people are trying to be aware of their mental states, they often come to me and say, "I get so self-conscious when I'm meditating, I feel exposed." You do not have to be like that. Awareness is not about being self-conscious. Self-reflection is complementary to awareness, but if you don't apply awareness, self-reflection, and so on properly, you will get all caught up. Sometimes people think that to be aware requires analysis. "What am I experiencing? What is happening? Why am I thinking this instead of something else?"

We have to pay attention, we have to be aware, and we have to learn and broaden our mental horizon by listening to the teachings, reading, and practicing through our experiences. We can do that too. However, always turning your attention on yourself and thinking, "What is happening now? What is going on?" is absolutely unhelpful. That is a waste of time and will not help you on the spiritual path. That will only inhibit you and constrain you from developing the awareness you need to reclaim your aboriginal state.

This text is mainly dealing with the equality of our samsaric condition and our transcendental condition. We are free, yet at the same time we are bound. Even the notion that we are a spiritual person, as opposed to someone who is debased or going astray from a spiritual condition, is immaterial. Longchenpa is addressing people who are so "spiritual" they are in danger of becoming too one-sided. Being overly spiritual in a conventional sense can become a retarding factor in your development.

That is not to say that you should not be a spiritual person. At this stage of your practice, you would have become thoroughly spiritual. Now you have to realize that being a spiritual person no longer means that you have to comply with religious rules and regulations that are both conventional and conditional. As we know, a lot of rules and regulations are governed by our cultural and religious conventions. There is a sense of freedom involved here. Sometimes people feel they are being really spiritual and become so convinced that what they are doing is right, they become intolerant of other approaches. We need to have a balanced attitude, where we can be a spiritual person without having to reject many of the things that are associated with being a human being. There is a danger of becoming attached to spirituality and somehow missing the point. We can always miss the point.

Longchenpa starts this text by saying that experiences can reveal themselves as expressions of wisdom. Our normal life experiences and even our terrible experiences have the potential to wake us up. We can learn from our mistakes and our experiences. When it comes to our spiritual experiences, there is no difference whatsoever between them and our ordinary ones, in terms of their nature. We may have highs and lows and bumpy rides through life's journey and we may have to slay a few dragons along the way, but in terms of their nature there is no difference between these experiences. That is what you should be thinking. You should not be thinking, "I want to feel good; I want to be healthy and fit; I don't want to be sick; I don't want to feel deprived of energy," or "I feel ugly, I'm losing my battle against my impulses and instinctual desires," and so on. Instead, you should think that all of these things are just like reflections in a mirror, as the Dzogchen teachings say. A mirror reflects all kinds of things. A mirror reflects whatever is around it and accommodates everything equally. It doesn't matter what is in front of it.

We are similarly counseled to become more accommodating about the whole gamut of our experiences, instead of thinking about what we want or don't want, what we desire or don't desire, going from this extreme to that like a yo-yo. Real stability of mind comes from being able to say, "I am experiencing this, it's there, but what I'm experiencing is a reflection of my own true nature." Instead of thinking, "I feel love and compassion so I'm closer to realizing buddhahood," and then "I got angry and shouted at somebody and all the practice I've done has dissipated." We should not think like that, because even our negative thoughts and emotions are a reflection of our own natural state. The Dzogchen approach is about accommodating experience. We should not think that to be spiritual means we must have certain wholesome experiences, and that having experiences that we don't approve of or that other people might not like, means that we are going backward or having a relapse. The point is, if we have a different attitude toward the whole thing, there will be no relapse.

THE MANDALA OF OUR PRIMORDIAL STATE

When Longchenpa talks about seeing the world as a mandala, he is not talking about the mandala of a deity, but that we see the world as a sacred space. We see everything as sacred in itself, not because we are visualizing the world of a deity as sacred, but because everything is already perfect in itself. Everything has its own place. It is perfect in that way. Common ordinary objects are spontaneously perfect of their own accord. Even though the Dzogchen teachings continually emphasize that we shouldn't get caught up with applying too much vigor, we nonetheless need to apply some form of gentle effort to learn to be effortless. In a similar way, we first have to make a gentle effort to see ordinary common things as sacred, and then we will be able to see it that way naturally.

Longchenpa says we should see the five skandhas as representative of the male qualities of enlightenment and the five elements as representative of the female qualities of enlightenment. I don't think "which belongs to which" is what really matters; it is about the integration of the two sexes. The Buddhist teachings call the world and the sentient creatures that dwell in that world "the container" and "the contained," because you can't have one without the other. In a similar fashion, the five skandhas and the five elements go together. Even the body itself has the five elements inherent within it. They are inseparable. The real emphasis is on the integration of opposites, which includes our sexual identity. For example, in Buddhist iconography, the five Dhyani Buddhas are portrayed with their consorts.

In terms of our mental activity, according to Dzogchen, all of the skandhas are involved, because our mind functions in a very complex way. It is not just one thing, but many things, which is why we always talk about causes and conditions. Even though the cause for a particular experience is present, we will not have that experience if the conditions are not present. So when the conditions are present, we cannot avoid having the particular experience. For example, if the cause for getting angry at someone is there but the appropriate circumstances and situation are absent, you would not wander around shouting at everybody. It is only when the appropriate circumstances are there that the anger rises. It's the same with things like jealousy, resentment, or bitterness. When the appropriate conditions are absent for you, you might think, "I don't know why people get jealous; they are just stupid." But when the appropriate conditions arise in your own life circumstances, all of a sudden you are the one being jealous. It is only when the causes and conditions are both present that the jealousy becomes manifest.

I'm using negative experiences as examples, but the same applies to positive experiences. You may have a talent for music, but if the appropriate conditions are not present, your musical skill may never develop to its fullest capacity. According to Longchenpa, whatever causes and conditions are present in relation to what we experience as a living, breathing, human being, in the end what we should take notice of is not what we are going through, but our aboriginal authentic state. All the experiences that arise from causes and conditions that we confront on a daily basis have their origin in our aboriginal state. We have to learn to reclaim that and to return to it, because we have left it behind through ignorance, through delusions, misconceptions, misperceptions, and so on.

EXPERIENCES ORIGINATE IN OUR
ABORIGINAL STATE

Longchenpa talks about dharma and dharmata, *chos-kun* and *chos-nyid*, our psychophysical entities and our authentic state. Dharmata is no different from our aboriginal, native, primitive state. In other words, it doesn't matter whether we are sometimes vulnerable to, or get seduced by upsurges of negative emotions; what is important to know is that their origin is aboriginal, primordial, native. What does "native" mean? "Native" means that something is not foreign, so our aboriginal state is our native land. It is where we belong, but we wander in our native land without even realizing it. We feel disconnected from our native land even within our home territory, so to speak—we are adrift in our native land. This means that if we really gain conviction in our aboriginal state, nothing we experience on a daily basis will disturb us in the way it normally does. Hence, the importance of Dzogchen practice, because it is the way back to the place where we belong, a way to reclaim our aboriginality. The word "aboriginal" means that.

Longchenpa says the nature of the mind is openness, its essence is gentleness, and its responsiveness is unceasing. Normally it is said that the nature is emptiness, the essence is luminosity, and the responsiveness is unceasing, but here Longchenpa describes the essence as gentleness. That is because, in terms of our aboriginal state, everything arises spontaneously. He always talks about spontaneity, naturalness, being uncaused, and so on. That has the connotation of gentleness as well. When something is spontaneous, no external force, condition, or circumstance has brought it into being. It has arisen naturally, of its own accord, which suggests a sense of gentleness. Normally, everything we experience is very reliant on external factors, and some violence is done to whatever has come into being because of causes and conditions, whether that be human beings, insects, plants, or natural objects. Even rocks are shaped in a particular way because of the weather, the climate, and so on. That is a form of violence.

When Longchenpa says that relinquishing our thought processes is the same as the dharmakaya, he is talking about excessive speculation. We are prone to thinking, "What is enlightenment? Am I getting enlightened or not?" That is not important. The practice is the most important thing. We should practice while accumulating knowledge, but you can accumulate knowledge without getting too caught up in critical analysis. Even Western logicians admit that logic has its limits. These days that is widely accepted. In the old days, when Western philosophers were known as rationalists, people like Spinoza, Schopenhauer, and so on thought that reason corresponded to reality, that our human capacity to reason about the world reflected the way the world operates. These days no one would accept that.

With regard to Western logic, there are only two forms: formal deductive logic and inductive logic. Formal deductive logic is totally useless in terms of the real world because what is important is not what is true in the world but what is true in terms of the consistency of the argument. The conclusion is already present in the premise, so it doesn't really explain anything about the world. Inductive logic reasons differently about the world in terms of factual states of affairs, so the conclusion is not present in the premise. You cannot logically prove that the sun will rise tomorrow. You can never do that. You cannot logically prove that pigs won't fly. Formal logic is closely related to mathematics, but the world is not as orderly as mathematics so anything and everything can happen. It is arguably impossible to conclusively prove anything. We cannot conclusively prove there is rebirth, nor conclusively prove there is no rebirth. Should we rely so much on logic? Of course, it is very important to think clearly. As spiritual people, we should be grounded, we should be lucid, and we should think clearly, but at the same time, we have to appreciate the limitations of our rational capacity.

Longchenpa describes our aboriginal state as tattva. Tattva means "thatness." It refers to how things are without our mental projections. Sometimes people translate it as "things as they are." Longchenpa uses gnas-lugs, which means "how things are." Lugs means "mode," so modes of existence, how things exist. Snang-lugs means "mode of appearance," so "how things appear." Things may appear to us as substantial, as having some kind of inherent existence, which is snang-lugs, while gnas-lugs means how things exist without our mental projections.

THE NATURAL (AUTHENTIC) STATE TRANSCENDS CONDITIONED EXISTENCE

When Longchenpa says that Dzogchen practitioners must learn to free themselves from the belief in karmic cause and effect, he isn't saying we should dispense with the whole notion of karma altogether, but that we shouldn't see karmic causes and effects as having any kind of ultimate reality, in themselves. We should become less attached to them and instead try to develop more conviction in what is genuinely real, and that goes beyond the dualistic concepts of cause and effect. Our attachment to and fixation on things is what fuels the karmic mechanism. When we are meditating, that is greatly reduced, so we become free.

According to the Dzogchen teachings, what binds us to the samsaric state is our fixation. What frees us from the samsaric state is being able to liberate ourselves from that fixation. Longchenpa is saying that any kind of fixation is limiting and imprisoning. That is true even if we are fixating on the idea that a particular school of Buddhism possesses and conveys the ultimate truth, while other schools do not. We can get caught up in that as well. Ignorance is what prevents us having a free state of mind, and ignorance is perpetuated by fixation. We are always latching onto something or other. If it's not something mundane, we latch onto something spiritual. We even get fixated on our spiritual experiences or insights. The Tibetan term is *zin-pa*, which means holding on to something very tightly, not being able to let go of obsessions and preoccupations. There are all different kinds of fixation, from mild fixation to pathological fixation. Preoccupations, obsessions of all kinds are more extreme manifestations of fixation of the mind.

Even dependent origination has no intrinsic reality. It's not the case that how we see things conventionally is erroneous and now we have to see everything as governed by dependent origination, which is real. We should not get too bogged down with the idea of cause and effect, because even to talk about cause and effect is a way of trying to apprehend things. We shouldn't think that causes and effects have some kind of objective, inherent existence of their own. This is not only the Dzogchen understanding, but even Nagarjuna, the founder of the Madhyamaka school, makes this very clear. This is why the *Mulamadhyamikakarika* has a chapter on causality, where Nagarjuna analyses the relationship between cause and effect. Are cause and effect the same or are they different? What is their relationship? How is the effect related to the cause? How is the cause related to the effect? What do we mean when we say that something caused something else? The more we probe into these things, the more we realize it's not all that easy to describe that relationship, which is why the nature of cause and effect is emptiness. As Nagarjuna says, if cause and effect were the same, there would be no difference between them. On the other hand, if cause and effect were different, how could one thing give rise to another? If that were possible, anything should be able to give rise to anything else. So dependent origination should be seen as a way of understanding things on the relative level. Understanding dependent origination will help us to realize emptiness, but the nature of dependent origination is also emptiness.

Longchenpa is saying we shouldn't get attached to the idea of emptiness either. We shouldn't take it to mean literal emptiness, because everything exists in a state of equality, and everything is complete in itself. This means that thinking something is valuable and something else is not valuable or thinking that something is beautiful and something else is ugly are mental projections. In terms of things in themselves, they are perfect. A piece of stone is perfect in itself, and a piece of gold is perfect in itself. They exist in a state of equality.

TRANSCENDING THE NINE YANAS

Longchenpa says the Dzogchen practitioner has to transcend the sutric and tantric practices of the nine yana system, but that is not true for us yet. We are basically trying to become familiar with these kinds of teachings; we are not ready to practice them. We should still be relying on our tantric practice while we are introducing these practices of Mahamudra and Dzogchen. You shouldn't be thinking that tantric practices are not worthwhile. Longchenpa is presenting very advanced teachings here. Only after becoming familiar with the tantric practices and doing them for some time can you say, "I have to go beyond tantric practice." We do need to do tantric practice. We need to use different techniques and methods, because we are not ready to simply dispense with all techniques and methods.

However, we have to understand that ultimately, tantric practices are not an end in themselves, but a means for working through our layers of defilements and obscurations. Tantric practices are very good at that, because you can use your body, your vocal cords, and your mind. You can imagine things; you can construct and deconstruct all kinds of images in your mind. All of these things can be used as part of your spiritual practice. Even when you visualize Tara or Chenrezig or other deities, you are thinking, but you are thinking in a meditative way. Visualization keeps your mind focused. If you aren't concentrating, you can't visualize so you are using thoughts as part of meditation. The deities you are visualizing are described very vividly in the sadhanas, so you try to follow and visualize that. This is why the visualization practices are built up sequentially. You don't just sit on the cushion and start doing the sadhana, you have to build up the visualization and then you have to destroy it as well.

We are using all these mental faculties as part of our meditation because our minds work like that. We imagine and visualize all the time. Even Dzogchen teachers would say tantric practices are important. In this case, Longchenpa is just talking about Dzogchen, so he is pointing out that other methods have limitations. In other texts, he encourages people to do tantric practice, so we should not see any kind of contradiction there. The main thing is not to get stuck on tantric practice and think that is the goal of your practice. They are just different methods.

Kriya means "action," so action tantra emphasizes rituals. Almost all your attention is given to the physical side of ritual practice. Upa or application tantra puts the emphasis on the mind as well as the body, so it includes visualization practices. Yoga tantra emphasizes contemplation so the emphasis is really on the mind because you are identifying yourself with the tutelary deity, establishing yourself as the god or goddess. Mahayoga is about reciting mantras, doing hundreds of thousands of mantra recitations. You have to do that kind of thing, repeating a particular practice over and over and over in one day. You do not just do it once and leave it; you do it for twenty-four hours straight sometimes. You go into retreat and do a practice over and over, sometimes only sleeping for one or two hours a day. Doing something over and over, even on the mundane level, can have many different psychophysical effects. You can go through all kinds of experiences, both physically and mentally, because of the intensity of the practice. Longchenpa also said that apart from the recitation, you visualize and give rise to proliferation of mental images, then draw them back into yourself so that all the images disappear. The visualizations become more and more complex as you advance and then you draw them all back so that there is nothing left. You also have to do that over and over.

In Dzogchen, the idea of space is extraordinarily important. Akanishtha is *'og min* in Tibetan, which literally translated means "there is nothing that is underneath." It is all-encompassing. Akanishtha, in that sense, means "encompassingness." Our samsaric condition and our nirvanic condition exist in the form of equality and in a state of perfection. Whether we are in a nirvanic or a samsaric condition, we are still in the state of Akanishtha, the state of perfection. There is also a sense of being in perfect beauty. According to Dzogchen, beauty doesn't have to be beautiful as opposed to ugly, as a one-sided thing. It is the beauty that comes from being in a perfect state, just as you are. It is the state of feeling good about the way one is. Instead of thinking "I should be in a nirvanic condition," you are able to be in a state that goes beyond that and just feel totally spacious.

The higher tantras encompass the lower tantras, but the lower tantras do not encompass the higher ones. They are integrated in that sense, but even when you are doing advanced tantric practices, you would still be doing basic ones like Tara or Chenrezig. You wouldn't be thinking that you no longer need to practice them because you are doing more advanced practices like Chakrasamvara or Hevajra. Sometimes we need to project the deity outwards, as we do in Tara and Chenrezig. You look up to Tara and you ask for different things. You petition her and you think that Tara is going to grant your wishes and needs, that she is looking after you. That is a perfectly legitimate form of practice. Sometimes, if we are feeling discouraged, fearful, or uncertain, we do practices of this kind and feel we are being looked after and protected. We believe this deity has the capacity to grant our wishes. That can also have a beneficial effect on us because, as human beings, we need that also. It's all well and good to do sitting meditation but it's also helpful to do sadhana practices and visualizations so we can receive other kinds of benefit. The teachings and the lamas all say that the blessings we receive are real.

GOING ASTRAY IN DZOGCHEN

Longchenpa says that delusions are caused by trying to see into that which cannot be looked at, because the one who looks, and the mind that is being looked into, are the same. For example, people might say, "I'm looking at the sky," but that is quite different from saying, "I'm looking at a painting." Space is not there as an entity when you are looking at the sky. Similarly, when we say, "I'm looking into the mind," it is only a figure of speech because you cannot see the mind, not even with your mind's eye. This is about eliminating our normal expectations.

Whenever we say, "look" or "see" we automatically assume there must be something to look at or something to see. What Longchenpa is saying is we should drop those kinds of expectations. Being and seeing are the same. When you say "looking," you automatically create a separation in terms of what you are looking at and the one who is doing the looking. The mind is trying to look for its own nature and that can only cause more confusion. Being in that natural state is seeing, but there is no seeing in terms of seeing something separate. Normally, when we see something, it is not the same as the one who is looking. There has to be that coalescing of being and experience.

When Longchenpa talks about going astray, it is to warn us that we shouldn't get too fixated on the methods and the teachings. They are just skillful means. We have to use them to attain enlightenment, but we should not become too dogmatic, get caught up in sectarianism and dogmatism, or become fundamentalist about our beliefs. At the same time, we should appreciate their usefulness for progressing on the path. Again, Longchenpa's point is that whenever we become dogmatic about something, we go astray and become deluded. Then we get stuck. He is speaking about the whole nine yana system and he says we shouldn't get fixated on any of it. That includes vows. For example, to take vows is a good thing in itself, but more importantly, taking vows helps you to progress on the path. Nonetheless, the vows have no reality in themselves. That would also be the view of Mahayana Buddhism. The nature of the vows is emptiness, so we can't get hung up on them. This means we have to be alert when we are practicing, and ask ourselves, "Am I getting too obsessed with this practice? Am I carrying on and on about it?" That is the thing—as human beings, we latch onto anything that we find useful or beneficial or comforting. Whatever it might be, we latch onto it, and it becomes "reality." Longchenpa is telling us that we have to be relaxed about it as well, because the essence is the same; it is like water and its ripples. So the nine yanas are like that and we should view them that way. They have the same essence, but different manifestations, and different uses.

EVERYTHING HAS THE NATURE
OF ULTIMATE REALITY

The spiritual ornaments that adorn our enlightened state are our meditative states, our joy, compassion, experience of spiritual ecstasy, and so on. These are the experiences that we have when we overcome certain limitations within ourselves, when we have been able to deal with our negativities, delusions, and obscurations of mind. According to the Buddhist teachings, there are spiritual qualities that correspond to that. For example, instead of hatred, we have love, instead of feeling disempowered, we are empowered, instead of feeling ignorant and confused, we have wisdom and insight, instead of selfishness, being self-absorbed, and egotistical, we are caring and engaged, and so on. They are the qualities that adorn the enlightened state.

When Longchenpa talks about the ability of thoughts and emotions to self-liberate into their primordial source, he is referring specifically to meditation practice. This is a practice manual, so whenever he says things like that, he is speaking about the practice of meditation. We normally say, "Anger is not good, I shouldn't have anger, I must have more love, maybe I should do Lojong practice." Longchenpa is saying as a contrast to that approach, we need to know how to let that immediate experience be and it will settle by itself. Again, we need to stop thinking in terms of acceptance and rejection. For example, you can't literally carry that same frame of mind into your daily life, because you can't do something horrible and then say, "Let me self-release that action into its primordial state." That would be absurd. That is not the approach Longchenpa is suggesting.

However, in post-meditation, we still need to avoid getting caught up in negative states and work at being in a healthier frame of mind if we want to advance on the path. He is saying that when we are practicing on the cushion, to think about things like that will only disturb the mind more. We shouldn't get too fixated on cultivating the mind in post-meditation either, because in the end, there has to be a harmonious relationship between what we call "view," "meditation," and "action." Dzogchen teachers always say we should be positive, but that doesn't mean positive as the opposite of negative. It is positivity that comes from going beyond the constraints of both positivity and negativity. That is the aim, but we still have to make choices that are beneficial, wholesome, conducive, and self-liberating in everyday life. We have to avoid things that drag us down and make us depraved, deranged, corrupted, that push us to the edges of madness. At the same time, when we think like that, we shouldn't be too fixated.

If we don't get too fixated on the things we need to cultivate or abandon, it will help break down the dualistic thoughts that are the source of all our problems. Gradually, once you learn not to get too fixated, your actions will naturally become positive without you having to fight your negative tendencies. It ceases to be a conflictual situation, where you might have the desire to do good, but your inclination is to do evil. Trungpa Rinpoche invented the expression "basic goodness" to distinguish it from our normal concept of goodness. Our normal concept of goodness is something that is opposed to evil, but basic goodness is more than that. It is goodness that goes beyond being good.

Chapter Nine

Resting in the Natural State

VIEW

We must apply great diligence when we learn to form the proper view, but we should not engage in that form of inquiry until we have learnt to rest the mind in its natural state. We learn how to relinquish our fixation on the objects of cognizance by knowing that whatever arises in the mind has the potential to be self-liberated. This potential has both vastness and depth, just like the ocean, so the mind doesn't waver even when you aren't deliberately meditating. That mind is not something that can be articulated fully through words, and it is equally difficult to conceptualize the significance of being aware while in a state of nonmeditation. When you can let go of the dualistic notion of apprehender and apprehended, everything you experience becomes an expression of undiluted, untainted awareness.

This form of meditation is intrinsically pure by nature. When you are in that state, you are no longer concerned about whether you have understood what needs to be understood or failed to understand it. Understanding and not understanding are equalized. You don't think of the meditative state as something that needs to be hung onto, and in fact, would have no desire to do so. Your meditation would be devoid of such unnecessary psychological embellishment. The mind is productive and creative, and it gives rise to thoughts, ideas, concepts, and emotions, but the mind also has the capacity to rest and be calm. The Dzogchen meditator does not distinguish between those two states. They just rest in their own aboriginal nature.

What does the mind normally do? It either wants to project itself outward or it wants to introvert into itself. If you are dealing with either of those states in your meditation, you are not fully engaged in the meditation practice. That form of practice is called "common" or "ordinary" meditation. As a Dzogchen meditator, you have to apply intrinsic awareness to whatever experience you have because everything will be equalized and completed in that awareness. You will realize that nothing you experience has any enduring essence because its nature is unconditioned. In addition, you should refrain from making any distinction between meditation and nonmeditation and see them as equally irrelevant. You know how to rest the mind in its own natural state, so no matter what experience arises in the mind, you can rest into that given moment of experience.

In Tantrism, we talk about the development and fulfillment stage practices, where the development stage relates to the visualization of deities and the fulfillment stage relates to understanding the true nature of phenomena. These tantric practices have the capacity to produce the state of samadhi, an altered state of consciousness, where we experience bliss, luminosity, and nonconceptuality. We may pursue these practices and have these experiences, but as long as they are conditioned by our mental expectations, any insights we gain from them will be corrupted by our psychic tendencies. Instead of leading to liberation, they might only strengthen the very factors that bind us to the samsaric condition.

Why are we lost and wandering in the samsaric condition? Our origination, our coming into being, and the place where we dwell, have a continuous effect on our current situation so we wander around and around in cyclic existence. But as Dzogchen practitioners, we need to understand that from the ultimate point of view, there is no karma, and if there is no karma, there cannot be psychic tendencies. In reality, we cannot grasp those things, so a Dzogchen meditator knows how to be nondualistic.

Dzogchen meditation is not about analyzing and investigating the mind—as we do in traditional vipashyana practice—because everything we experience is beyond conceptualization. When we have that attitude, how can samsara exist? How can mental anguish result from the samsaric condition? Our unconditioned state in itself is without ground so we are birthless. Our true origination cannot be characterized as this or that because it is impossible to convey this reality through linguistic expression.

This primordial, aboriginal condition is not something to be sought. You must realize that you are already in that condition. To be able to remain in that state is the majestic quality of meditation. You no longer get swayed this way and that by accidental or fortuitous experiences, because whatever has arisen in the mind is not swayed. In other words, even while you are experiencing this or that, you are not swayed. You remain unmoved.

Overcoming dualism

We need to have the correct view about the ground because the meaning of our existence has to be found in our own groundedness. There are many ways to present this ground, but fundamentally speaking, it is about nonacceptance and nonrejection. When we stop accepting and rejecting things, awareness is already present. When awareness is present, anything that arises in the mind will automatically settle by itself, because there is no fixation. This state of nonfixation is the dharmakaya. That is how we dwell in the state of our own authentic being.

When we are in this original, aboriginal state, we are enveloped by the ultimate sphere of reality. When we recognize that, we make a temporary entry into that state which is atemporal, so we shouldn't think, "I will become enlightened at a future date and then I'll be endowed with the three aspects of buddha's being." The nirmanakaya, sambhogakaya, and dharmakaya are not something to be attained at a later date. When we enter into that state which is beyond time, we have already found enlightenment. Buddhahood has become actualized.

We no longer need to be bogged down by hope and fear because our own aboriginal state is uncreated and self-presencing. Being in that state is Samantabhadra (Kuntuzangpo) because we cannot condition or influence that state of being. It is beyond corruption and perfect in itself. We have to rest in this natural state, but we don't do that by thinking, "This is the essence of the mind," as if the essence of the mind had some kind of limit or boundary to it. We rest in the natural state by not meditating.

We are not trying to be in the meditative state. We simply flow with the continuum of our experiences, as if we were traveling on a river. When we are so free and flexible and able to ride with the current of our experiences, there won't be the dualistic problem of getting lost or confused. Instead, we will have an exhilarating experience of freedom. We will finally be released into the natural openness of our own being. When we are liberated within this state, we no longer need to concern ourselves with whether we have established ourselves in the practice or not. A true sense of relaxation will arise from that lack of concern. We will have discovered a sense of ease.

We won't be wondering whether certain experiences are true or valid and other experiences are untrue and invalid, because ultimately, these dualistic thoughts have the same origin. Everything is perfect in itself as an expression of Kuntuzangpo. This aboriginal state of ours is devoid of attributes. We cannot characterize it because it has no mass, no shape, no form, and no color. We cannot even talk about it in terms of existence or nonexistence. Instead of thinking about whether it exists or not, learn to ease into that natural state of being by not contriving the process.

The radiance of wisdom

When we rest in that state with ease, that doesn't mean we stop experiencing things. Myriad experiences will still proliferate, but the Dzogchen practitioner will see those very experiences as the light or radiance (*gdangs*) of wisdom. The manifestation of experiences cannot be separated from wisdom any more than waves can be separated from the ocean. Since our natural, aboriginal state is already present, there is nothing we deliberately need to do to attain it. There is no need for that. Everything we experience has an inbuilt tendency for self-liberation without our having to apply extraneous antidotes. This is the Dzogchen view, the correct view we must hold as Dzogchen practitioners.

In that way, you don't renounce anything, but you let rest whatever experiences you have, and they become complete and fulfilled in themselves. You don't think about tightening or loosening the mind because when awareness is there, wisdom is present, and everything is seen with the eye of nondual wisdom. It must be emphasized again that your original state is something to be realized, not something to be secured or obtained through a laborious process. You need to realize you are already in it. It is not to be attained because the mind itself is imbued with luminosity and free of embellishment, defilements, and obscurations. That is what you should be meditating on, as a Dzogchen practitioner.

The essence of our own condition cannot be characterized because it is the state of wisdom itself. It is a state of spontaneity, so there is no need for meditation. We have to be loose and let go without conceptualizing and without being subject to thoughts of hope and fear. Bondage and liberation do not exist in terms of our intrinsic nature. Our superficial perception of things does not relate to our true nature, so they are not grounded or rooted in that nature. When we have that experience, whatever has bound us to samsara will have the ability to liberate us from it.

We shouldn't think that because we have conflicting emotions, we have to then find an antidote to deal with those emotions. There is no duality between the conflicting emotions and the antidotes that we employ and deploy to deal with them. The world in itself isn't defective. It is not imbued with the qualities and attributes that we ourselves project onto it. We realize that mind is the all-creator and we rest in that. This represents our own self-existing awareness.

Resting the mind

Don't try to contrive the mind, but just be spontaneous and do not allow your mind to yield to prejudices and biases. You will then find yourself in a state of nothingness—a state without characteristics and beyond conceptual determinants. While not being fixated on them, you have to know that you are dwelling in your own state of being. That is how you should learn to rest your mind. This is the essence of all the teachings, so you have to listen to this. Your ordinary everyday obsessions and fixations will no longer have the hold over you they once did.

Your natural state cannot be realized when you are fixated on things, but it can be realized when you learn to rest in that natural state. There is no need to try too hard or try to be good. Doing so may only further bind you to the samsaric state. You will get entangled between your natural tendency to want to be free and your thoughts of not wanting to be free, because you think the spiritual life should be a certain way and so on. You are free as you are. You have to learn to rest in that.

The past is gone, so you cannot meditate on the past. The future has not yet come so what is there to meditate upon there? The present has no meditator and no object of meditation. You should know past, present, and future are all equalized in this way. There is nothing to meditate on in any of the three times. If you can approach meditation in this way, your mind will be able to relinquish its obsession with objects of fixation. When the mind is relaxed, whatever you cognize, perceive, and experience can just be left at that, and the power of the mind will be such that you won't even be able to conceptualize about it. Then there will be bliss.

Finding the way to rest in your natural state is what is meant by "realizing equality and completion." When you have arrived at that point, you will not have to think about skillful means and wisdom. They will be realized automatically because they arise from a place that has no origin. They have nothing to do with biases or prejudices and there is no concept of a self that is flourishing or degenerating. It is absolutely free of those. We don't need to stop our normal experiences to arrive at that point and we can embrace any object of experience that may arise.

What is the reason for this? We no longer see an apprehender as a subjective thing, and we do not think about what we should renounce or what techniques we should employ or deploy to better ourselves. Everything has become self-liberated. In fact, we are not even meditating. We are able to let ourselves be in equality and completion.

In that state of being, there is no high or low, no objects that are sacrosanct and none that are abased, because there is no taking sides with something or running away from something else, as part of your practice. When you are in that natural state of being, nothing has to be renounced because you know you are free of hope and fear, and you don't need to conceptualize about the various factors of life. This is called "bodhicitta," the enlightened mind. Everything is lucid, clear, and purified. That is where you should be resting.

You also have to realize that whatever you encounter in life is created by the mind. The nature of that mind is unwavering and has been so right from the beginning. The nature of that mind doesn't discriminate between things and the characteristic of things, between dharma and dharmata. It doesn't discriminate between samsara and nirvana either because everything is experienced with a sense of equanimity. You need to have mindfulness and to stop looking for liberating experiences. Just learn to remain in that state of equality.

Our own authentic state of being is vast, and devoid of such concepts as center and periphery. The mind becomes lucid and self-illuminating when we don't conceptualize about our true state of being. We don't hang onto ideas of what that true state of being is by developing certain ideas or images about it, and we don't try to get rid of ideas or images about it. We need to understand that our natural state is all-pervasive. The natural state is in the form of a sphere of being. It is a way of being that is intrinsically genuine because of its primordial nature. This is so because our natural state of being allows the total perfection of mind to occur and thus allows the light of wisdom to radiate from the depths of our being.

MEDITATION

Misguided views about the mind

Practically everyone who embarks on the Buddhist path wants to transcend dualistic thoughts, but owing to lack of skill in understanding what is required to achieve that goal, many practitioners unwittingly get entangled in conceptual paraphernalia by forming definite ideas about ultimate reality. They fail to have any direct experience of what is truly real and instead get trapped in a proliferation of concepts and ideas about it. For example, we may develop ideas about the hierarchical system of Buddhist practices, saying certain practices are advanced and profound and others are more elementary. In reality, all the different systems and practices in the yanas have the same nature: none of them have any intrinsic or inherent property.

Instead of getting caught up in thoughts about which vehicles are superior and which are inferior, we should devote our time to determining the true meaning of things. While this true meaning cannot be articulated or conveyed through words and sentences, it can be experienced as that which is unborn and pure. It is pure precisely because it is not sullied or vitiated by the conceptual activities of mind. Even though mind, as we know it, is restless and hardly ever at peace, we will discover mind itself to be without turbulence, if we learn to be in our natural state. The mind itself is unwavering. That unwavering state of mind is the mind of the buddhas.

So many misguided practitioners want to do something with their minds. They want to improve and change them, so they think, "If I engage in such and such a practice, I will be able to transform my mind." They hope they will be able to purify their mind by introducing certain methods and using something external to the mind as a way to change and purify it. They think, "I've been wandering aimlessly in the samsaric world due to my deluded mind, but through the diligent and vigorous application of certain methods and techniques, I will be able to transform my mind and attain the final release of nirvana." Practitioners who think in this manner have failed to understand the true meaning of the essence of things. They are ignorant of the power and potency of the mind and the fact that it is already present.

Other practitioners believe that meditating consistently over time will lead to a realization of the state of nonmeditation where their minds will become like space without a trace of the defilements and obscuration that cause them so much mental anguish. However this can be seen as an incorrect view. A true practitioner would understand that to think this way is to lose the true meaning and stop them being able to develop the correct view. Such a meditator has no real confidence in the true power of the mind and relies on techniques and methods to improve their mind. These techniques are imported from outside the mind in the hope that they will gradually be able to attain the state of nonmeditation. That cannot happen. The mind does not become purified by techniques and methods imported from outside.

You can only understand the profound meaning by becoming

acquainted with your own mind. If you understand your mind, it will not matter what meditative experiences you have during meditation. Those experiences may be uplifting or disturbing, but they will never upset the stability of your meditation. To come to this understanding will make you a very skilled and wise person. Dull-witted practitioners will not comprehend this point because they cling to the notion of cause and effect, believing the relationship between cause and effect to be real. Such practitioners do not understand the principle of interdependence, even when it comes to the immaterial nature of the self. These practitioners understand the operations of the mind in the same way that they understand the operation of physical objects. When we sow seeds, after some time we see the shoots and then the seedlings, so there is a connection between the seeds, the shoots, and the seedlings.

Sometimes we begin to think there must be some kind of causal connection even in relation to space, but trying to understand space in terms of cause and effect would be futile. It is the same when it comes to trying to understand the mind. We bring our fixation on cause and effect to our understanding of the nature of the mind, but the nature of the mind has nothing to do with cause and effect. You cannot understand the mind by trying to work out how the causal situation applies to it. In fact, if you conceptualize about it, you may even find contradictions, because the mind is immaterial, the mind is not a thing, not an entity.

What is the point in trying to condition the mind by working out how the causal nexus applies to it? What is the point in that? That is like trying to see what grows in space. Nothing grows in space. There are no flora and fauna there because space is not an entity, not a thing. It is unconditioned. Similarly, we should let ourselves be in our own natural state because that cannot be conditioned either. We can fashion all kinds of things out of gross material substances and objects, such as soil and so on, but our own authentic state is like space. Even if we exert ourselves, trying really hard to understand it by making use of various methods, that will have no impact whatsoever on our natural state of being. Our natural state neither increases nor decreases because it is not contingent on anything outside itself.

The mind as we know it is obviously very active. It can produce all kinds of thoughts, ideas, images, and perceptual and sensory experiences. All these mental states have their origin in our karmic patterns so if we continue to judge, evaluate, and discriminate between our meditative experiences, we will only be perpetuating our habitual patterns. Our mind is predisposed to that. If we are to break out of that habit, if we want to bring our deluded samsaric experiences of the world to an end, we need to approach our practice differently.

Developing confidence in the mind

We must develop unwavering confidence in the mind itself. It doesn't know of before or after. It doesn't know change, and because of that, the mind as it is, in itself, is uncorrupted and unvitiated. It is the state of buddhahood, the state of enlightenment. Therefore, when we meditate, we shouldn't deliberately try to bring about certain meditative experiences, but we should just let the mind be. By letting the mind be, we rest in our own natural state of being.

You shouldn't waste your energy trying to do this or that in order to improve your meditative experiences. No one would think about trying to change space because everybody knows it would be futile. Similarly, when you are meditating, you shouldn't allow yourself to worry about your practice, asking, "Am I making progress with my practice or not?" Instead, you should think that in terms of your natural state of being, it doesn't matter. Do not get anxious and think, "Have I realized anything? Have I attained any kind of realization after all this time?" You should not think of realizing something and not realizing something as totally different states by looking at them in a dualistic fashion.

You should not view your meditative experiences dualistically. That is another habit that meditators have. Instead, just meditate with whatever arises in your mind, good or bad. Anything and everything that comes up in the mind can be meditated with. When you stop trying to do anything with your experiences in meditation and meditate with whatever is there, you are in your authentic state. If you do that, the true essence of luminosity will manifest continuously, irrespective of what is going on in your meditation. Meditating with whatever is there is the key to rest.

When you develop the courage to meditate with whatever is there, you will see that mind itself is in a continuous state of illumination. It is just like the sun and moon. In addition, you will have a real and genuine sense of well-being and happiness. This is why we let go of thoughts of something being superior or inferior to something else and so on. Your mind should not be fixated on anything during meditation. You should not strive to attain any particular definable state of mind. Instead, relax with whatever is there because this will bring about a sense of physical and mental well-being. If we approach meditation in this way, nothing will have the power to bind or hold us hostage to any situation. Everything will have the potential to liberate us.

We must have confidence in the mind that is free from exertion; the mind that is pure, majestic, kingly, and beyond biases. The mind that is not partial to anything is the source of a wisdom that illuminates everything and makes everything clear. There is nothing lacking in the mind. Everything we need to attain self-realization is already there and beyond change. This kind of meditation does not deviate from the proper approach. That is how we should rest the mind.

ACTION

Whatever activities you engage in will manifest as meditation if you follow the instructions given here, and you won't yield to distraction during the various situations and experiences you encounter in daily life, even when not in formal meditation. To attain that level of proficiency is an indication of your mastery over the practice of meditation because you can enter the meditative state spontaneously. You will see that the divisions between view, meditation, and action lack true substance because you have realized nondual wisdom. You will understand everything you experience as the inseparability of the relative manifestation of phenomena and ultimate reality and will now see it like the moon's reflection on water.

Without deliberately steering yourself toward good deeds, every action you perform during the six periods (dawn, morning, midday, afternoon, dusk, and midnight) will become a noble act. Everything you do, including sleep, will be noble. That is the real action in relation to view, meditation, and action. Actions that are spontaneously performed become noble acts without our intending them to be so. Any action performed with discrimination or deliberation—where you think, "This is a noble act and that is ignoble," and you choose the noble act—will not be the pure action of a Dzogchen practitioner.

Nor are the actions of the Dzogchen practitioner disturbed by thoughts of hope and fear. You should not think, "Such and such an act must be avoided at all costs and such and such an act must be performed," with the hope that the act performed will bring reward, or with the fear that performing the act will bring misfortune. These kinds of mental disturbances have to be avoided. As long as there is attachment to the object of desire, whatever that object might be, and a mind that is divided in favoring certain options and trying to avoid others, it will not be a pure action. When a magician performs a magical trick, the audience might fall for the trick because they don't understand the mechanics of it, but the magician is not fooled. The audience may respond to the illusory trick with attachment, but the magician does not react with attachment because they have no fixation. A yogi should perform their actions without attachment, in the same way.

We will come in contact with various things in this world, but nothing we meet can actually be pinned down, defined, or truly identified as this thing or that, in any absolute sense. They are unidentifiable because there is nothing to be identified. Our definitions of things are our own conventions, and they are superimposed onto things by the mind. The things themselves do not have definable characteristics so we can only ever identify them on a provisional level. However, things do appear to us. We do encounter and interact with them, but if we know they have no essence—that they are elusive and cannot be grasped or pinned down—we will develop the ability to let go. When we realize that subject and object are not two in this way, we will experience the self-liberation of Dzogchen.

A Dzogchen practitioner must act on the spot in a very precise manner, in accordance with how things are. If you fall under the influence of dualistic thoughts, saying, "I need to perform this action," that particular act has already been influenced by dualism and you will fail to see the true condition of things. The thought that entered your mind is distorted, with great deliberation, because trying to refrain from negative actions is another form of extreme. It's like the audience's response when they have been duped by the magical display. All kinds of emotions, such as fear or desire, might arise in response to that display and the audience gets caught up in the intrigue.

In a similar way, when your mind is dominated by dualistic thinking, you are not free, and your actions are not free. The nature of the mind is primordially free, so you don't need to be overly concerned about action or nonaction and should not get bogged down with dualistic thoughts about abandonment or cultivation. In fact, trying too hard to "do good" is a form of sickness. You should not torment yourself with such attitudes. Your actions and attitudes should be in tune with how things are—nondifferentiated and not split into two.

The sphere of ultimate reality has the characteristic of equality or evenness and is all-pervasive. Primordial wisdom isn't any different from the nature of the mind, which is Dzogchen. Your actions should therefore be carried out with a sense of ease, in tune with the apprehension of the essential meaning of your spontaneously arisen, authentic condition.

Since everything can reach the level of completion spontaneously, you shouldn't try too hard to do this or that. We do not attain realization through making deliberate choices, but by learning to tune into the natural, authentic state of how things are. You don't need to change anything. Just learn to attune to that which is primordial and has been present right from the beginning.

Why do we need to try to bring something new into existence? All we need to do is rediscover the primordial state of being. You don't need to cultivate something or try to dispel or purify something else. You do not need to do any of that. In other words, you should have a nonbiased, nonprejudicial mind, a mind that does not favor something at the expense of something else, a mind that does not latch onto something or other. For example, if we become overly obsessed with the concepts of samsara and nirvana, we will give rise to hope and fear—the hope of attaining nirvana and the fear of being left in samsara for a very long time.

You should learn to stop being too concerned about concepts of good and bad or cultivation and abandonment, because whether you are engaged in meditation or engaged in activities, all these things have their root in the mind. They are not outside the mind. That being the case, what need is there to think about abandonment and cultivation? What need is there to do ritual practices or confess your past non-meritorious deeds?

You can gain a kind of samadhi by practicing meditative concentration, but if this experience makes you more constricted, it becomes a real form of mental unwellness. This occurs because in the enthusiasm and excitement of attaining this level of meditative concentration, you become fixated on the purity aspect of that mental state and it becomes contaminated. Whatever arises in the mind should be enjoyed, just like a king feasting on the objects of sensory pleasure. A mind free from thoughts of good or bad, acceptance or rejection, is true action. However, even a fragment of conceptual fixation on identifying our mental states or something in the external world and we have already become lost.

Nobody thinks of trapping space or creating something out of space because space is intangible. Our authentic condition is just as expansive and intangible, so we should think of it as comparable to space. From the Dzogchen perspective, what we know about the world through our senses is skillful means and the mind that processes these sensory impressions is superior insight. You will become free of dualistic fixation in that way. The perceiver and perceived are freed into the wide-open expanse that is the natural state of your being. This natural state of being embodies all the qualities we normally try to attain through conventional Buddhist practices, such as the accumulation of wisdom and merit, and the development and fulfillment stages of tantric practice. If you stop being fixated on what appears to the senses, you will be able to enjoy everything, because nothing has the potency to affect you adversely.

The origin of both phenomenal appearances and the mind lies in that which has no beginning. That is dharmakaya itself and its true nature cannot cease. We have all kinds of experiences within that state, and these are made possible because of the cognitive nature of the mind, which is lucid and luminous, but also insubstantial and unidentifiable. That is the aspect of sambhogakaya. We will continue to have myriad experiences, both internally and externally, and each one of them will have the potential to become liberated. That is the expression of nirmanakaya. In that way, all three aspects of buddha's being are present within our own embodiment.

DZOGCHEN AND THE PATHS AND STAGES

Having discussed the role of view, meditation, and action in the context of Dzogchen practice, we will now discuss how the whole spectrum of the traditional Buddhist path is embodied in Dzogchen. If you have followed the instructions properly, you won't try to prevent phenomenal appearances from arising and you won't conceptualize about or elaborate on the experiences themselves. That is how you deal with experiences. Your spiritual experiences are no different.

Once we have embarked on the spiritual path, we can make use of two types of spiritual vehicle: the "causal vehicle" (*hetu-yana, rgyu theg-pa*) and the "fruition vehicle" (*phala-yana, 'bras-bu'i theg-pa*). The causal vehicle refers to the exoteric or sutric teachings and practices and the fruition vehicle refers to the esoteric or tantric teachings and practices. The positive qualities of both these vehicles are already present in the simple practice of Dzogchen meditation. This is so because all the spiritual vehicles that we employ and deploy on the path are related to our natural state of being, which is a treasure chest of meditative experiences. The causal vehicle includes the paths and stages of the bodhisattva, and the fruition vehicle includes the empowerments, yogas, and tantric stages.

The causal vehicle

The causal sutric yana comprises five paths (*panca-marga, lam lnga*) and ten stages (*dasa-bhumi, sa bcu*) of bodhisattva accomplishment. These paths and stages are all simultaneously present in the practice of Dzogchen. Meditators who have realized the true essence of the samsaric condition of bondage and the nirvanic condition of liberation, would have understood dzogpa chenpo, because they have looked into the depths of ultimate reality and seen it as primordially pure. Ultimate reality has not suddenly become pure; it has been so from the very beginning.

Seeing into the ultimate state of being is the same as realizing the first bodhisattva stage, called "pure joy" (*pramudita-bhumi, rab-tu dga'-ba sa*). The second bodhisattva stage is "the state of being unsullied" (*vimala-bhumi, dri-ma med-pa sa*) and is attained when you relinquish your hold on dualism so that your mind is not dominated by the confusion that arises from dualistic ways of thinking. The third bodhisattva stage is known as "greater illumination" (*prabhakari-bhumi, 'od-byed-pa sa*) and is secured because the radiance of your understanding begins to become manifest. The fourth bodhisattva stage is called "brilliant shining" (*arcismati-bhumi, 'od-phro-ba sa*) because it also consists of the radiation and dissipation of that light generated by understanding. The fifth level bodhisattva stage is called "difficult to attain" (*sudurjaya-bhumi, shin-tu-sbyangs dka'-ba sa*) because what you come to realize here is not common knowledge. This stage is also realized in the very moment of sitting in Dzogchen meditation. The sixth bodhisattva stage is called "directly facing" (*abhimukhi-bhumi, mngon du-gyur sa*) because various spiritual qualities that were not there previously now become apparent.

The seventh bodhisattva stage is known as "gone far" (*durangama-bhumi, ring du song sa*) because you have now gone a long way from the familiar territory of the samsaric state. Qualities associated with this stage are also present in the practice of Dzogchen. The eighth bodhisattva stage is "non-waveringness" (*acala-bhumi, mi-gyo sa*) because the bodhisattva now remains in the original state without wavering. The ninth bodhisattva stage is known as "supreme intellect" (*sadhumati-bhumi, legs-pa'i blo-gros sa*), because the bodhisattva finally begins to understand everything that needs to be understood. There are no further mysteries because everything that needs to be explored has been explored. The ultimate and tenth bodhisattva stage is called "the cloud of Dharma" (*dharmamegha-bhumi, chos-kyi sprin sa*) because instead of the usual clouds of ignorance and confusion that shroud the unsullied, pure, and natural state, your wisdom, which is like the sun, is enveloped in the unsullied spiritual qualities of an advanced being.

These ten bodhisattva stages are already present in each moment of your practice in Dzogchen meditation. Even though we may speak about the levels of a bodhisattva as taking place in a progressive fashion, they are in fact all present simultaneously in the practice itself and do not have to be understood in a sequential fashion.

A similar understanding should be brought to the five paths that are outlined in the sutric teachings: the path of accumulation (*sanbhara-marga, tshog lam*), the path of application (*prayoga-marga, sbyor lam*), the path of seeing (*darsana-marga, mthong lam*), the path of meditation (*bhavana-marga, sgom lam*), and the path of no more learning (*ashaiksha-marga, mi-slob lam*). Dzogchen meditators traverse the five paths in the following manner. The paths of accumulation and application are traversed while engaging in activities that are in tune with the Dzogchen understanding of your true being. The path of seeing is attained from developing the nondual wisdom that enables you to see things as they are. The path of meditation is successfully traversed through the growth of your understanding and by becoming familiar with the true nature of things. The path of no more learning is attained as the fruition stage when you establish yourself firmly in the state of enlightenment. Dzogchen meditators must understand that these sutric paths and stages are already simultaneously present in their practice in this way.

The fruition vehicle

The fruition vehicle of Buddhist tantra should be understood along similar lines. The whole point of tantric practices that involve visualization, mantra recitation, chanting, music, and so on is to purify the three gates of body, speech, and mind so that you can establish them as the basis for great wisdom (*maha-jnana, ye-shes chen-po*) to burst forth. Again, all the tantric precepts, practices, and associated attainments and realizations are already embodied in the practice of Dzogchen.

There are many different kinds of tantric practices associated with the four abhishekas or tantric "empowerments": the vase empowerment, the secret empowerment, the wisdom empowerment, and the empowerment of logos.[29] These empowerments authorize you to engage in certain esoteric practices that are not normally available to practitioners.

These esoteric practices invariably consist of two different approaches: the development stage (*utpattikrama, bskyed rim*) and the fulfillment stage (*sampannakrama, rdzogs rim*). The orientation of these two practices is to marry the object of apprehension and the apprehending mind. We unite subject and object by realizing that the myriad forms assumed by the phenomenal world are not so different from the ultimate reality of emptiness. The function of these two stages is to bring those together (*yugananda, zung-'jug*). There are many divisions and subdivisions within the tantras, but they all come down to those two main approaches. In brief, all the spiritual attainments, realizations, and newly realized spiritual qualities of tantra are present in Dzogchen practice, even if you are not directly involved in tantra. Without even trying, all the qualities we would have to go out of our way to cultivate with great diligence, are spontaneously accomplished in Dzogchen practice.

SPONTANEOUSLY MANIFESTING WISDOM

You will not have any spiritual vision at all if you are bogged down with thoughts about doing things, but if you can jettison such thoughts—if you can transcend them or go beyond them—you will acquire the necessary spiritual vision. You will never see what has to be seen by searching and analyzing and you will never accomplish anything by meditating. This is because meditation is not another form of activity. Meditation is about allowing yourself to be in the state of your own being. Only when thoughts of doing, applying diligence, and so forth are dropped, will you go beyond temporary concerns, and the realization will dawn on you that the essence of your own mind is inconvertible. It is already the mind of a buddha.

The question has to be asked, "Does this authentic state of being actually exist?" It exists insofar as it has been the essence of both our state of bondage and of the state of freedom that we are capable of securing. This has been the essence of samsara and nirvana right from the beginning. This state is all-pervasive because it permeates past, present, and future. Time divisions are no barrier because the authentic state of being stretches over all three times. The mind is inseparable from ultimate reality because the mind in itself, as opposed to the mind as it manifests, is not contingent on cause and effect. Mind is not an empirical entity and cannot be seen through normal means because it has no definable characteristics. It is intangible, just like space.

Spontaneously manifesting wisdom is grounded in itself, without wavering, and its nature is translucent, just like a pristine lake. This self-existing wisdom does not apprehend objects through conceptual means because everything is revealed in its true condition. If this innate wisdom was dependent on something other than itself, it would not be self-manifesting. It would be contingent on the objects of apprehension and then be swayed this way and that by the things that present themselves to it—but that is not the case. Self-manifesting awareness is ever-present because it is not contingent on anything other than itself.

It isn't even conditioned by past, present, or future so we can't think about wisdom as having not been there in a remote past, of coming into being at some point, or of gradually diminishing until it disappears. All these perceptions should be seen as reflections mirrored in spontaneously existing awareness. This state of being is unceasing and all three aspects of buddha's being exist in harmonious relationship within it, without the concept of coming together or being separated from each other. The nature of your true condition is emptiness, which corresponds to dharmakaya. Its essence is luminosity, which relates to sambhogakaya, and its unceasing responsiveness is inseparable from the essence of awareness, which is nirmanakaya.

It is possible to recognize objects of thought with the aid of wisdom. These acts of wisdom are known as "creative energy" (*rtsal*). Even though the natural state of our being is unwavering, certain objects of thought present themselves—just like waves in the ocean or reflections in a mirror—and the thought of recognition arises as a result of those causes and conditions. If no objects were present, there would be no thought of recognition. There is that relationship: the presence of an object of thought entails the thought of recognition.

Since the objects of thought are presented to the apprehending mind, some people say they are also spontaneously produced. If we do not recognize the nonduality of what is presented to the apprehending mind (things which are contingent on causes and conditions) and the apprehending mind (whose essence is not dependent on causes and conditions), we will remain fixated on concepts. If we realize that the ground of our being is the source from which everything arises, then even though the objects of thought and their recognition are present, we will apprehend things through the wisdom mind. We have to learn not to discriminate between the nature of the mind (which is unwavering, devoid of perturbation, and with the quality of awareness), and the act of apprehension (which is contingent on the presentation of objects). Many practitioners do not understand this key point and engage in distorted forms of meditative concentration.

Other practitioners are so eager to remain in the state of their own being that they try to block all forms of apprehension, recognition, and physical and mental feelings and sensations. This approach might enable them to attain various rarefied states of absorption (*samapatti, snyoms 'jug*)—which provide access to the form (*rupa-dhatu*) and formless realms (*arupa-dhatu*)—but these states of quietude do not lead to liberation. On the contrary, the habitual use of these practices only leads to mental impressions that become further seeds for perpetuating your stay in cyclic existence.

There are others who believe we should be paying attention to the mental acts themselves. The mistake of the first group is to become introverted and concentrate on inner mental equilibrium and quietude. The mistake of the second group is to become extroverted, by focusing on the external, and thinking anything and everything that arises is an expression of wisdom and awareness. They think everything has the potential to be self-liberated and end up tracing the footsteps of their mental states and acts, but since they have not been able to access the stillness of their own authentic condition, they get lost in the proliferation of mental activity. As a result, they do not leave the boundaries of their normal state of mind, which is the realm of sensual desires (*karma-dhatu*). These meditators fail to understand that their state of being, and its manifestation of wisdom are inseparable and cannot be understood dualistically.

There are still other practitioners who fail to appreciate the provisional nature of the tantric development and fulfillment stages because they fail to understand that these practices rely on manipulating the relationship between cause and effect. They instead expect certain practices to automatically lead to their corresponding results. If we don't understand the provisional nature of tantric ritual and practice, the obsession with it can also obscure our ability to realize the essence of the nature of the mind. The opportunity to attain liberation from the samsaric condition is then taken away.

Nothing that arises in the mind should ever be encouraged or discouraged in Dzogchen practice. It should be paid attention to within the context of our own authentic state of being and then realized through awareness. We are trying to attain a state of mind where we stop thinking about everything dualistically, so we shouldn't look at the authentic state of being and what arises in the mind from a dualistic point of view. Whether the mind is active or stable, we should view it with a sense of equality.

Everything partakes of the same reality

Right from the beginning, your own authentic state has not been separate from Dzogchen, the state of great completion. You do not need to abandon or cultivate anything to realize it, because the mind in itself is the mind of a buddha. The mind in itself has never been a prisoner of conceptual entanglement. If you are able to naturally rest with whatever arises in the mind, without conceptualizing about phenomenal experiences and the mind, you will find freedom in dharmakaya.

Whatever you need in order to secure enlightenment is already present within you. You don't need to import anything from outside to achieve that goal, so you should think, "The phenomenal world may present itself in myriad forms through the six senses, but these myriad forms are understood with just one mind." Instead of trying to analyze the relationship between the mind and the sensory impressions, which we regard as something made by an external world independent of the mind, just let your sensory impressions rest. If you do that, the sensory impressions and the mind will blend into each other. Just as a mirror and the images reflected in it are inseparable, your authentic state of being and spontaneously arisen wisdom are inseparable.

When you understand this inseparability, your mind will not get lost in the external world when it recognizes something through the senses.

Instead, you will realize that the mind itself is reflective—it is like a mirror on which all the sensory presentations are reflected. Furthermore, everything that exists partakes of the same reality. The wisdom that enables us to understand this is also spontaneously arisen. It has not come into being based on causes and conditions, so it cannot be conditioned or susceptible to corruption.

The wisdom mind is not dependent upon causes and conditions in terms of our mental continuum. However, the experiences that we have due to the discursive mind are a product of our karmic traces and dispositions and these are dependent on causes and conditions. For that reason, we continue to wander in samsaric bondage. We have experiences of momentary happiness and intermittent experiences of suffering, pain, and so on for the same reason. Specific causes bring about specific results in the same way that sowing specific seeds on a patch of land gives rise to specific crops. However, the ground of our being is not contrived. Its nature is unsullied and pure, and the concept of cause and effect does not apply to it. Furthermore, the ground of being is like space because it has never come into being, never ceases to exist, does not dwell in any specific location, and is not subject to change through the passage of time. It cannot be adequately expressed or even conceived, yet without having to look for it, it is already present as an expression of reality.

This state of being can't even be understood as something that is defective or that has positive qualities, because to think that way is to think dualistically. This state of being is no different from dharmakaya. It is one and the same. Therefore, we should not attempt to condition it by engaging in methods that try to introduce changes or employ transformative techniques. We don't arrive at this original dwelling place by trying to journey toward it. We cannot restore it by engaging in purificatory practices. We will not find it by looking for it. We simply learn to relax into it naturally.

In your own authentic state, sambhogakaya and nirmanakaya are spontaneously present, without your having to bring them into existence or realize them anew. You should learn to relax into your own authentic condition without exertion, then rest in the nature of the mind—an expansiveness like space. It is primordially pure, not because it has become pure through the removal of adventitious defilements, but because it is pure from the beginning. We therefore don't need to manipulate the cause-and-effect mechanism.

If you want to realize that your own mind is the same as dharmakaya, you should not get fixated on what arises in the mind. If you don't get fixated on or attached to whatever you recognize but can remain in a state of being that is open, all-pervasive, unbiased, and aware, that is Dzogchen. You need to rest there, without thoughts of doing anything even in terms of spiritual practice, because doing something will not aid your ability to grasp what is true. Without grasping, interference, or contrivance, without trying to identify, label, or judge, and without falling into extreme thoughts or actions, you remain in the great expanse of dzogpa chenpo. This way of dwelling in your natural state is not the same as trying to rest in a particular space. If there is a place to rest, it is not Dzogchen. You should simply rest without trying to identify or label anything.

TRALEG KYABGON COMMENTARY ON RESTING IN THE NATURAL STATE

VIEW

Our psychic tendencies are the karmic habits we have that predispose us to certain things. We are different from each other in all kinds of ways and those differences have their source in our karmic inheritance—our genetics are also part of our karmic inheritance—so we have not come into this world innocently. We have dropped into it with a lot of baggage. However, according to the Dzogchen teachings, even our psychic karmic tendencies should be seen as reflections of our state of wakefulness. If we can view them that way, we can liberate ourselves from the confining and conflictual influence of our negative habits. Even the experiences of jealousy, anger, and resentment have an inbuilt capacity to be self-liberated so instead of thinking, "I have to get rid of this, I can't stand it, I'm so jealous, I'm so bad," we need to acknowledge that these negative emotions have the capacity to liberate themselves. This, in itself, is liberating. We will experience bliss and exhilaration if we can do this.

Longchenpa is saying we will have the exhilarating experience of release into the natural openness of our own being when we realize the nature of our mind, but we are normally so fixated on our subjective experiences that we find it difficult to imagine a lack of personal identity. Longchenpa wrote this text because we just don't see it like that. We are completely fixated on our ego-identity. We think of it as ourselves and attach so much significance to it, but Longchenpa says there is a part of us that is not related to our ego history at all. He calls this our "aboriginal state of being." We don't have to ask, "Does it exist or not? How do I know it exists? How do I know it is real?" If you can drop all that and just practice, you will be in it.

You will already have entered into an atemporal state where you are beyond time. When you are in that state, you are not just in the here and now, as opposed to not being in the past or the future, but you are present in terms of the totality of time. The past, present, and future are all embodied and contained in that state of total presence. This text is about equalizing or equality, so here Longchenpa is saying that the three times are equalized, in that the present contains the past and the future. Not only that, when you are present, you have the capacity to step out of temporal concepts. You stop thinking about being in the now. When you can be in the present, you equalize time differences and experience going beyond the concept of time. You will not even think, "I am in the here and now," or anything like that. You are just being present. The Dzogchen and Mahamudra teachings talk about *dus gsum byer med*—where *dus* means "time," gsum means "three,"" and *byer med* means "undifferentiated"; so "the three times are undifferentiated."

While the Dzogchen teachings talk a lot about acceptance and put a lot of emphasis on accepting everything, it is not saying that we should accept everything that we do. When Longchenpa talks about being natural and freeing yourself from habits by not yielding to your natural instincts, even if those habits involve spiritual practice, he is saying you have to relinquish those habits. The interesting thing here is that we have to learn to relinquish so many things, while retaining one element of fixation on the practice. However, even that fixation has to be let go of later on. As we advance, we are always reminded not to be fixated, not to be too judgmental, not to get caught up in things, not to be moralistic. The text has been emphasizing that point. However, you still have to practice. We can't just say, "I'm free," and wander around barefoot in the streets. That will not work. We have to take the practice seriously. Even though Longchenpa talks about nonmeditation, he is not saying we stop meditating. Nonmeditation is about not taking our meditation too seriously. We still have to do it. It is like Nagarjuna talking about "the emptiness of emptiness." First, you have to realize emptiness and then you have to also realize that emptiness is without intrinsic reality, which is basically about not getting fixated on the concept of emptiness.

Longchenpa also talks about not discriminating between things and the characteristics of things. For example, we don't discriminate between the concept of a tree as a thing, and its branches, leaves, type of wood, seeds, and so on as the characteristics of that thing. That is how it is, according to Buddhist philosophy. A glass is a thing, but whether it's made out of crystal, whether it's a champagne glass or a wine glass, and so on, are its characteristics. This even applies to human beings. A human being is the thing, and whether we are old, young, Tibetan, Chinese, Russian, and so on are the characteristics. That is what is meant by *dharma* and *dharmata*, by "things and their characteristics" and the "nature of things." What Longchenpa is saying here is that there is no difference between them. The thing, whatever it is, is no more important than the characteristics it happens to have. Actually, that is very traditional Buddhist philosophy. Nagarjuna also talked about it like that. We may talk about a table, but it is only the characteristics of the table that define it. The point is that normally we think the thing is more important than its characteristics. We think the substance of a thing is more important than the characteristics of the thing. But Buddhism is saying that there is a mutual relationship between the two. You can't have one without the other.

That is actually very profound. We normally don't think like that. We are always looking for the substance or the essence of something. However, there can be no such thing as matter without form, or substance without attributes. That would be nothing. A thing has to have shape and form. Even subatomic particles have shape or form when seen with scientific instruments. You can even see the shape of DNA. You can't see it with the naked eye, but you can see its shape and form through a microscope. Anything that exists has form. The point is that whatever the form, it is indistinguishable from its characteristics. Human beings have this fixation on the abstract. We may talk about humanity, but there is no such thing as humanity. Humanity consists of different kinds of people: young, old, short, tall, black, white, Asian. Our characteristics have just as much to do with how we are defined as the abstract concept of humanity.

MEDITATION

When we meditate, we need to have some kind of goal, but getting hung up on our goals can be a big obstacle because expectations can ruin everything. This is true in life, as well as in practice. What we imagine something to be like in life and what we actually find there may not match and that can be the cause of much anguish. However, we need some idea of what to expect from meditation practice or we will be totally lost. We want to become more realized or enlightened, we want to stop suffering so much, or we want to have a more peaceful life where we are at peace with ourselves and other living beings. To develop a definite idea about what you want is a very idiosyncratic thing, because your idea of enlightenment might be different from someone else. Each person has certain ideas about the experience of enlightenment, which are shaped by their own very idiosyncratic and personal experiences. That is why we should approach our practice with a sense of open-mindedness where we are not thinking we have it all worked out in advance. That way, we will not get so worked up when it doesn't happen that way. If you can be more open, you will deal with what comes up as you go along. Your practice may be more fruitful then.

Longchenpa emphasizes that we need to understand there is no duality between our conflicting emotions and the antidotes we use to deal with those emotions. We might still use antidotes, but we shouldn't get fixated on them and start thinking our emotional conflicts are something to be attacked. We need to stop thinking that the antidote and the emotional conflict are so different. Tantrism talks about homeopathic solutions to things. If you are sick and afflicted with a specific physical ailment, you may be injected with the very virus you are suffering from. For example, the tantric teachings say only an injection of snake venom will cure you of snakebite. Even modern medicine approaches things that way. We should also meditate with that attitude. You should stop trying to combat, exile, or renounce whatever problem you think you have, and start dealing with it in that homeopathic way because the antidote and the problems are the same, in some way.

That is the essence of the tantric teachings and also the Dzogchen and Mahamudra teachings. We should not be trying to kill the disease, but we always get fixated like that, not only on our daily problems but on our physical diseases and our emotional, psychological, and spiritual problems. We should stop thinking like that. You might still need help, but you should not think, "I can conquer this." There is another way to deal with it, another way to handle it, that is much healthier, a different approach that is not so aggressive.

We normally use specific antidotes for certain obstacles in meditation, but when you are doing Dzogchen meditation, you don't use antidotes. There is no conflict between these approaches. We need to do meditation practices that use antidotes, in order to establish ourselves in the practice. That is also why we do tantric visualization practices. We have to do any kind of practice that will help. The point Longchenpa is making here is that if we understand our true condition, then sooner or later we should stop doing those practices. In the meantime, we have to practice different kinds of meditation alongside Dzogchen or Mahamudra meditation until we have some experience of the nature of the mind.

The other meditations are just techniques that help to make the mind more pliable. "To make the mind pliable" is a Buddhist expression. The idea here is that our mind has certain habits that are so well-entrenched that the mind is not at all flexible or elastic. Our minds have become very rigid, so we need to do different types of meditation to soften them up— meditation on loving kindness, meditation that makes use of antidotes, meditation that requires visualization, and so on. Even in tantric practices, as we progress, we realize that Tara is within us, Chenrezig is within us, Yamantaka is within us, Chakrasamvara and Amitabha and all the other deities are within us. To discover, or recover, the innate spiritual qualities we already possess, we may need to engage in these kinds of practices, otherwise, our spiritual qualities will lie dormant, and we have no easy access to them.

When we visualize and recite mantras, the qualities of Amitabha, the qualities of Chenrezig, the qualities of Tara, and so on, become manifest. This is tied up with making use of skillful means. We have to be skillful in terms of the techniques and methods that we use. You can use different techniques, but you should always remember they are only techniques. You should not mistake the technique for the real thing. As it is said in the teachings, "If Buddha had taught only one method to reach enlightenment, his teachings would be very limited, but his teachings are vast and potent. There are numerous methods that many different kinds of people are able to find a method suitable for them."

That doesn't mean we can just reject a particular method or technique because we don't enjoy doing it. There are some practices we may be advised to respond to despite our disinclination, because we can't always rely on our instincts. I'm not saying you should just do a practice because you have an aversion to it, but trying to overcome resistance to a particular practice might be a liberating experience in itself. You may end up liking that practice after a while. We have so many teachings, methods, and techniques, but they all have the same purpose: to break down our ordinary samsaric habits. If we continue to respond to our practices in a habitual way, our ability to break down that habit becomes diminished, so sometimes we have to be counterintuitive and do something that we don't like doing, because that may be an enriching experience.

We also need to have certain conditions to practice meditation in the proper manner. We need to meet people who know about meditation, we need to have the opportunity to practice it ourselves, and then we gradually need to learn to practice properly until we become adept at it. All of those things help. Having access to appropriate literature, hearing teachings on relevant topics, engaging in regular practice, having a fairly conducive environment for practice without too much pressure in your life, and having relatively good health—all kinds of things play a very significant role in how we practice and how we progress. Then, when you are proficient at Dzogchen meditation, you practice it by not taking everything too seriously. We over-exaggerate or underestimate things all the time. We either exaggerate something or we downplay it because we are fixated on our experiences.

An ability to loosen our grip on what we are experiencing is the key. We need to stop taking everything we experience as a life-or-death issue. When something happens to somebody else and that person starts carrying on, we ask, "Why can't they get a grip on reality or on themselves?" but when something happens to us, we don't think that way, which is basically what Longchenpa is talking about. We take everything very personally and internalize it: "This is happening to me." It becomes a very dramatic and overwhelming experience. We shouldn't deny our own experiences, trying to pretend we aren't having this or that experience or trying to suppress it. On the other hand, we shouldn't indulge in our experiences either, by playing them up or adding fuel to the fire. If we leave a fire alone, it will go out, while tampering with it will only fan the flames. That is the line of reasoning Dzogchen uses. If we interfere with our experiences, they only get worse.

ACTION

Longchenpa says that from the ultimate point of view, there is no karma, but he doesn't mean that we have to be free of karma to start seeing it that way. He means that if you start to see it along these lines, you will stop producing karma. Even if you are a karma-producing individual, once you start to practice and see things in this way, you will stop producing karma. We produce karma precisely because of our dualistic thinking so if you stop thinking dualistically, the production of karma will also stop. Even Mahayana teachings say that a buddha doesn't intentionally go out of their way to benefit people. To benefit people comes naturally because it is part of the nature of an enlightened being to benefit others. As the teachings say, "All kinds of living beings prosper because the sun is shining, but the sun isn't thinking it has to radiate warmth; it's the nature of the sun to be that way. In the same way, it is the nature of an enlightened being to benefit others." Enlightened beings benefit others without deliberation and because of that, they are not creating good karma as opposed to bad karma, but they have stopped creating karma altogether.

This means that anything enlightened beings do is wholesome; it is wholesome almost by default. Just as it is unthinkable for the Christian concept of God to do anything evil, because God is the embodiment of all that is good, in some ways, an enlightened being has no choice either. A buddha's wholesome actions are not performed because they want to avoid doing evil; it just comes naturally for a buddha to do that. It is far better for us to perform an act because it comes naturally to us, than to try to do something good because we are afraid of doing something negative. All Buddhist traditions say we have to overcome karma. The difference is that conventional Buddhist teachings instruct that we do it over a long period while Dzogchen says it is possible for anyone if they approach it this way.

All serious practitioners have to think about cutting through the karmic chain and all of the Tibetan Buddhist schools accept that this is achieved by seeing the illusory nature of things. However, the ways they do that are different. Most schools come to that conclusion by meditating on and contemplating emptiness. They try to realize that both good and bad karma have the nature of emptiness and that karmic phenomena are relative phenomena rather than absolute. Good karma doesn't exist in itself, and bad karma doesn't exist in itself. They are both relative and, as such, karma can be overcome by realizing emptiness. The traditional example is that bad karma is like an iron chain, and good karma is like a gold chain, but both chains bind us to samsara. We have to break out of both those kinds of chains.

It is very important for us to think in terms of good and bad karma— wholesome and unwholesome deeds or meritorious and non-meritorious deeds—but we have to keep reminding ourselves in the back of our minds that this is a provisional thing. Karma is something that will help us on the path, but it eventually has to be transcended, so the purpose of spiritual practice is not just to accumulate good karma, merit, and wisdom and reduce negative karma. Nonetheless, it is still extremely important that we take karma seriously and think in terms of wholesome and unwholesome deeds. We have to do it like that because even though karmic phenomena are ultimately unreal, they still have what you might call "functional reality" on the relative level. Karma still works; it is still operating on the relative level.

DZOGCHEN AND THE PATHS AND STAGES

Karma is important when we talk about the paths and stages of spiritual practice. We purify our body, speech, and mind—our three gates of being—by reversing our karmic impulses so that they become the basis for great wisdom. We are confused and enmeshed in the samsaric condition through a lack of skill in how we use our body, speech, and mind, and that creates and accumulates unnecessary negative karma. By reversing our karmic impulses, those same three gates can become the basis for enlightenment. That is why tantra talks about indestructible body, speech, and mind—vajra body, vajra speech, and vajra mind— because they suggest a sense of groundedness or immutability.

All tantric practice is orientated toward the sanctification of body, speech, and mind. We are not just trying to spiritualize our mind; we are spiritualizing our material form as well. That means that we don't become disassociated from our material being when we become spiritual. There is the tendency to think the body is impure and only the mind has the potential to become pure—we just have to wait for the body to become a corpse to be really free. Many spiritual traditions think this way, but Tantrism is not one of them. Just because negative karma can be created through physical means, and we can suffer physical karmic consequences, that doesn't mean the body is intrinsically evil. The body has become an instrument of the confused mind because we don't know how to make skillful use of it. If we know how to use it skillfully, the body becomes divine. That is why a lot of Dzogchen practitioners try to attain rainbow body.

The sutric teachings have different names for the karmic body and the wisdom body. The "karmic body" is *lu*, and when it is transformed through enlightenment, it becomes the "spiritualized body" or *sku*. The mind that has realized wisdom is *ye-shes*. There is no notion of the physical and mental aspects coming together or separating. Something that has never been separate from the beginning cannot come together or get separated. "Coming together" means there are two different things that used to be separate, which means there is the potential for separation again. Even with meditation, it isn't just the mind that can make us more conscious and aware; the body can do that too. The body has its own sense of awareness and intelligence. We need to have confidence in these things.

Confidence is extremely important in tantric practice, where it is called "divine pride" (*lha'i nga rgyal*). When you identify with a deity, you develop confidence that you have the powers, attributes, and qualities of that deity. You do not develop this pride from your own worldly attributes, but through recognizing your spiritual potential, which goes beyond ego. Everyday pride is almost always based on us comparing ourselves to others, but when we have real confidence, we won't bother to make those comparisons because we will be secure within ourselves. Ordinary pride is just ego's way of covering up our shortcomings and trying to make us feel secure. Buddhism advises us not to invest in our self-perception or to build our sense of self-worth on it, because everything we are proud of can potentially be lost. When we invest in things and then lose them, we can become completely defeated and even suicidal, where we don't want to exist any more; we can't face the world. If we have real confidence, we will be secure within ourselves and the loss of something we cherish will not break us.

SPONTANEOUSLY MANIFESTING WISDOM

If you can meditate on the sensory impressions without immediately jumping to conclusions, you will be able to observe your mental reactions. That is called "self-liberation," because you can just leave it at that, without any elaboration on the narrative. Even if you have nothing immediately in your sensory field, you can still be thinking about certain things or objects, so instead of trying to suppress your thoughts or block your sensory impressions, you experience those mental occurrences with awareness. Your experience then becomes self-liberated. According to Buddhism, even sensory impressions are dependent upon thoughts, because we don't actually have direct access to physical objects. We are "looking through a glass darkly." We never actually see a chair or table in their immediacy, but our perceptions are mediated by what is called "meaning generality."

We usually approach meditation as a form of activity where we are trying to manipulate the cause-and-effect mechanism: "If I have this approach to my meditation and I deal with it in this or that fashion, it should lead to the experience or state of mind I want." That is normally what we do, but Longchenpa is saying that as we progress, as we get more deeply involved in Dzogchen meditation, we should gradually drop that idea. According to Dzogchen, we do not give rise to wisdom. Wisdom is innate, not acquired, so we do not gain wisdom; we discover that it is already there. In other words, our practice does not give birth to wisdom, and we don't acquire wisdom through practice either. Practice simply allows us to peel away the obscurations and defilements that cover and conceal our innate wisdom.

Longchenpa talks about two different aspects of wisdom. Wisdom in itself is innate and full, with nothing to be added or subtracted. Practice does not make that wisdom grow, and lack of practice does not diminish it. On the other hand, when we do practice, we begin to see things more clearly, to have more insights, and so on. So there are these two aspects. Practice leads to the realization of primordial wisdom. If the only thing we needed was innate wisdom, then everybody would realize it. But that is not the case. Certain conducive conditions have to be present for our innate wisdom to arise. Longchenpa is constantly talking about having the right attitude and approaching practice in the correct manner. Not approaching practice properly distances you from the realization of your innate wisdom. For example, ice has the potential to melt, but certain conditions still have to be fulfilled to melt it. To use a Mahayana example, the *Uttaratantra* says, "You can't extract oil from coal, but you can extract it from mustard seeds. Nevertheless, certain conditions have to be fulfilled to extract that oil from the mustard seeds." Nothing will happen if you just pick up some mustard seeds and wait, even though the oil is already present in the seeds.

The main point of Dzogchen practice is to let go of all techniques and rest in the natural state where all our mental and physical phenomena can reach a level of equality and completion. This means that because ultimate reality is all-pervasive—because everything is imbued with it—nothing exists outside of it. Everything finds its full expression in and through ultimate reality. Even our neuroses, confusion, and conflicting emotions find their true expression in and through ultimate reality. If we understand that, we can find freedom even through delusion and we can develop wisdom. Delusions are completed when we realize that. Our delusory states have the same nature as our mental states that are conducive to enlightenment. When we stop conceptualizing about the objects of thought, those objects can be apprehended through wisdom, and they will be seen as the creative energy of the mind. We can have mental activities going on without becoming lost in conceptual activity. If we remain open and aware, without falling under the influence of conceptual categories and judgments, we can recognize things and then let them go. We will then see everything as the creative display of mind.

Chapter Ten
Spontaneous Fruits of Enlightenment

We approach completion of the spiritual journey, in relation to the ground of being and the path we have to negotiate to discover the source of our being—by realizing the indivisibility of intrinsic awareness and the sphere of ultimate reality. As far as the ground is concerned, there is no separation between the source of our being and the realizations we attain as the fruit of our practice, for the simple reason that everything is spontaneously perfect in itself, in the ground of being. There is no division between the interior dimension of our being as dharmakaya, which fulfills our own needs, and the corporeal aspect of our being as nirmanakaya, which fulfills the needs of others. They are inextricably bound so there is no question of the interior and exterior aspects of our being coming together or separating.

The same can be said of the sphere of ultimate reality and innate wisdom. We cannot say, "They have become united" or "They have become separated." Similarly, in the true state of the ground of our being, we do not see samsaric and nirvanic existence as two, because of the unity of intrinsic awareness and the sphere of ultimate reality. In this state of the ground, everything is at peace and completely undisturbed by the proliferation of discursive mind. For this reason, the ground is called "the undifferentiated dwelling place of Kuntuzangpo."

There is no activity in this ground, only quietude, but we do not remain in this state of passivity because a refined form of the light of wisdom arises from the depths of this state of being. This light illuminates our interiority while making everything comprehensible and unobstructed. We remain in such a way that there is no division between our physical and mental dimensions. They are totally integrated. The enlightened quality of our physical nature and the quality of the mind that manifests through wisdom can neither come together nor be separated. This state is called "dwelling in the unwavering samadhi of equality."

A further development takes place when outward manifestations arise from this original state. All external phenomena and internal experiences arise from the projection of clear light in the form of Kuntuzangpo and his consort and they become material for spiritual enjoyment. The five buddha-fields arise from this, because the five wisdoms and the five Dhyani Buddhas are inherent in the mind. The five wisdoms are the wisdom of ultimate reality, mirror-like wisdom, the wisdom of equanimity, the wisdom of discrimination, and the wisdom of all-accomplishment. The energies of these five wisdoms can manifest through either the peaceful or the wrathful channels as different images, which reflect a particular buddha-family. These peaceful or wrathful energies are associated with either Vairocana, Ratnasambhava, Akshobya, Amitabha, or Amoghasiddhi.

The ability to benefit others through body and mind—by adopting different guises, disguises, or personas in correspondence with what will have a transformative effect for those in need of aid—arises from this state. You can adopt any appearance in accord with the situation. Different people and audiences will see different personas of the same realized being because that being's appearance is not fixed. The enlightened being has learned to integrate the three aspects of buddha's being—the physical and wisdom aspects of dharmakaya, sambhogakaya, and nirmanakaya.

The way the wisdom manifests and the domains of enlightenment are all interconnected and integrated like this. The powers of enlightenment will continue to operate in this way until samsara is emptied of all deluded beings. A being who reaches the end point of the journey realizes that cause and effect have no origin—the cause of enlightenment and enlightenment itself have coexisted or been spontaneously present, right from the beginning.

When we have learned to do nothing and can remain in the nature of the mind, we will see the true meaning of things. We have to remain naturally in the expanse of our original state of being, without applying unnecessary exertion, to discover our own intrinsic freedom. This freedom is not newly discovered. To acquire Dzogchen insight is to actualize what has been spontaneously perfect from the beginning.

This concludes the third chapter of the root text of *Dzogpa-chenpo mnyam-nyid rang-drol*, which was devoted to a description of how the fruits of enlightenment are spontaneously acquired.

Yidzhin Nyingpo—The Wish-fulfilling Heart Essence
Longchenpa's auto-commentary on the root text
of the Equality Cycle

Chapter Eleven
Retreat Instructions:
The Pith Instructions on Natural Freedom of Equality

1. The Preliminaries

GURU YOGA

In the space in front of you, visualize a throne supported by two decorative lions, upon which rests a sun disk, a moon disk, and a lotus flower. On top of the lotus flower, visualize Guru Padmasambhava, who is indistinguishable from your own lama, with all the signs and attributes of an enlightened being. He is sitting cross-legged, wearing a gown, and holding a bell and vajra. His complexion is white with a reddish glow. Guru Padmasambhava is surrounded by all the lineage masters who have direct links to the practice. Then, visualize a multitude of other enlightened beings—gurus, buddhas, bodhisattvas, and dakinis—forming like clouds on the outer periphery.

Imagine you are making offerings to them while you visualize your own image multiplied many times, with each one of you holding a container in their hand and making offerings to each of these enlightened beings. Then imagine that all the gurus, buddhas, bodhisattvas, and everyone who has gathered there are pleased and content. Do not think you are doing this on your own; you should visualize many other sentient beings alongside you doing the same thing. Then all of you should supplicate the refuge objects with this verse:

> Precious lama, please purify my karma, defilements, and conflicting emotions. Please grant me the ordinary and extraordinary siddhis and bless me so that I attain

enlightenment in this very life.

If you know any other supplications, you can also say them at this point. Then visualize lights radiating from Guru Padmasambhava and penetrating you and all other sentient beings that need help. Imagine that all the defilements of yourself and others have been purified and that the siddhis have all been attained. Then you and all other sentient beings gravitate toward Guru Padmasambhava and disappear into him through his heart chakra, just like the condensation that forms when you blow on a mirror and then quickly vanishes. Then even Guru Padmasambhava is no longer there as an object. Just like gazing into space without seeing anything and without thinking about anything, you should remain in that state for a short time. When you arouse yourself from that state, you should see it as if you are arising from a dream, and without abandoning that feeling, do the dedication prayers.

The point of this short Guru Yoga practice at the beginning of retreat is that, in Tantrism, we need to become a proper vessel for practice. To become a proper vessel, we need to receive the blessings of the lineage. We must also learn to humble ourselves. It is necessary to expel haughtiness and arrogance because they get in the way of being a good vessel for containing the teachings. We need to practice Guru Yoga for these reasons.

MANDALA OFFERING

This should be followed by short mandala offerings. You should wipe the mandala disk in a clockwise direction three times and imagine the whole universe in the form of the continents, subcontinents, Mount Meru, and so on. Then recite the mandala formula aloud in the following way:

> I purify this great earth with incense and scented water and scatter flowers all over it. I offer the whole universe, the sun and moon and everything contained within it. I make this offering with the intention of attaining buddhahood. May all sentient beings attain enlightenment through this offering.

If you would like to recite any other offering formulas, you should do so at this point. The mandala is then offered to the lamas, tutelary deities, other deities, their mandalas, and so on. These factors are again contingent on your own personal practices. You need to purify your mind to make progress on the path and mandala offering will have that effect.

VAJRASATTVA

The hundred-syllable mantra of Vajrasattva involves visualizing Vajrasattva who is white in color and holds a vajra in his right hand and a bell in his left. He has a lotus at his heart center, upon which rests a moon disk bearing a white vajra, marked with the syllable HUNG in the middle. Imagine the hundred-syllable mantra circling around the syllable HUNG while white light radiates from those syllables. This light pours down from Vajrasattva's body into your body through your crown center. As the light begins to fill your body, imagine it is a healing light that has dispelled all of your physical ailments, and your mental defilements and obscurations.

Then recite the hundred-syllable mantra with your mind focused on that thought. You should also imagine that the mental and physical defilements and ailments of other sentient beings are being cured simultaneously with your own. Then imagine you have become Vajrasattva and without thinking anything, rest in the nonconceptual state for a split second, before reciting the dedication prayers. Vajrasattva practice purifies defilements and ensures that realization will occur more quickly.

BODHICITTA

You conclude these preliminary practices by engaging in the yoga of bodhicitta. Think of all the sentient beings that roam the samsaric world and remind yourself that every one of these beings has been your mother at some time in the past. Since they are wandering in samsara, they are subject to all manner of intense and intolerable suffering and pain. Generate compassion as you think about the extent of their suffering and then generate the thought of doing something to alleviate that suffering. You should generate the desire to work toward buddhahood so you can liberate these sentient creatures from their present condition. Then, having generated compassion in that way, perform the following visualization.

Imagine you have invited the numberless buddhas and bodhisattvas of the ten directions and three times and they are now all present before you. Then recite the Seven-Limb Prayer, while imagining that you are performing each one of the limbs as you recite it. The seven limbs consist of the following:

1. prostrating to the buddhas and bodhisattvas to symbolize that you offer your body, speech, and mind to them,

2. offering all manner of pleasant things to them,

3. confessing all the things you are ashamed of doing or that you knew were clearly wrong, immoral, improper, or harmful,

4. rejoicing in the path and in the enlightened qualities of the buddhas and bodhisattvas so that you feel inspired by them,

5. requesting the enlightened beings to remain in the world and continue to guide sentient beings on the spiritual path through discourses on the Dharma,

6. requesting the enlightened beings to forgo entering into nirvanic quietude so they can continue to work for the benefit of others,

7. dedicating your own merit toward the enlightenment of all sentient beings.

Then recite the following formula three times:

> Buddhas and bodhisattvas, wherever you may be,
> please, Compassionate Ones, grant me your ears:
> Just as previous sons and daughters of the buddhas
> gave birth to precious bodhicitta to benefit others,
> I, too, will give birth to precious bodhicitta.
> Just as previous sons and daughters of the buddhas
> trained on the path to enlightenment,
> I, too, will engage in the training of the graduated path.
> May I be able to liberate those still in bondage,
> and give encouragement to all those who feel defeated.

Recite any other dedication prayers that you know and then dedicate the merit for the benefit of all sentient beings.

That should be followed by a feeling of real joy in the fact you have been able to generate bodhicitta and become part of the family of the buddhas. Giving rise to bodhicitta means you have become converted into an ideal being of the great vehicle. If your heart has been seized by compassion, the wisdom that does not fall into any extreme will arise naturally. We cultivate bodhicitta for these reasons.

TRALEG KYABGON COMMENTARY ON THE PRELIMINARIES

You can do these preliminaries every time you sit down to meditate. Longchenpa has presented a very shortened version of the normal preliminary practices because you are meant to incorporate them at the beginning of your other meditation practices. There is no contradiction between following Mahamudra and Dzogchen and doing the preliminary practices. We need to have the Dzogchen and Mahamudra perspectives in our practice, but we still need to use all kinds of methods and practices. We need to do a lot of purification practice, but we have to know that, ultimately, only self-liberation really counts, because then we will not become too bogged down with the idea of purification. We have to accumulate merit and wisdom and we do have to purify the defilements. We should engage in any kind of practice that helps us to achieve that. We need to rest in the natural state and remain in that state, but if our mind is incapable of doing that, we need to do other practices. The preliminaries are complementary to Dzogchen practice in that way.

Vajrasattva or Dorje Sempa means "diamond mind" or "indestructible mind" and refers to our own natural state of being. Vajrasattva practice is about forgiving yourself for anything you have ever done wrong in the past and actually feeling that you are forgiven. However, you are not forgiving yourself in a flippant manner, because you are also acknowledging to yourself that you shouldn't have done those things. You really bring that to your consciousness and become fully aware of it, then you literally lay that at the feet of Vajrasattva and say, "I am sorry I did that, but it won't happen again."

In Buddhism, we take that practice very seriously and it really is very powerful. It is also part of what we call "confession practice." You are confessing to Vajrasattva, not to a living person, but you imagine that Vajrasattva is there, and you confess all of your secrets, hurts, frustrations, and any terrible things you think you have done. Then you leave it and feel liberated. It is really a very powerful practice in that way. It is a lot harder to confess to a living person than to an idealized being such as Vajrasattva, but you are still taking the confession very seriously, as if you were addressing a real, living being. The fact that Vajrasattva is not a real being doesn't make any difference.

If you are very open and confess your resentments, frustrations, and negative states of mind, you will feel energized and liberated. A lot of things can be achieved through dialogue. If you want to be a good writer or poet, you have to be engaged in dialogue with many characters. You invent these different characters and then converse with them. You can relate that to your tantric practices to understand why they might be very powerful. We relate to what other people do by imagining things. It is no different here. The fact that we are only imagining Vajrasattva does not take anything away. Visualizing Vajrasattva, being open to Vajrasattva, and confessing to Vajrasattva can be a very therapeutic thing. This practice really is a type of psychological and spiritual healing.

2. The Main Practice

SPIRITUAL PHENOMENA

The main practice comprises a series of introductions to various spiritual phenomena. You begin by adopting the meditation posture of Vairochana, ensuring the posture is correct in every respect and paying particular attention to your eye gaze. You should be looking straight ahead and holding your gaze steady without moving your eyes.

In an encounter with your teacher, you will be instructed to think of your daily waking experiences as dream-like and to realize that everything you have experienced during the day is very much like what you experienced the previous night during sleep. In both cases, every experience is a magical display of your own mind. While maintaining that understanding, you try not to condition or contrive your present mental state.

When it remains unexamined, your present mental state may seem tangible and locatable but when you examine your mind properly, you will see that it is substanceless and nowhere to be found. This is an indication that the nature of mind is no different from dharmakaya. Although mind is found to be elusive, insubstantial, and ungraspable when you examine it, it is also innately lucid and luminous. The fact that mind has this ability to illuminate is the expression of sambhogakaya. Mind is also very creative and produces all kinds of experiences, but these experiences have no substance, which means everything that you experience has the potential to be self-liberated at the very moment of its arising. This aspect of mind is the expression of nirmanakaya. As Guru Padmasambhava says:

> This present state of mind is empty: that is dharmakaya.
> Mind is essentially luminous: that is sambhogakaya.
> How mind expresses itself is varied: that is nirmanakaya.
> Do not look for buddhahood elsewhere.
> Rest in that authentic state of neither meditation nor
> nonmeditation,
> neither view nor non-view, neither fixation nor nonfixation,
> neither thought nor non-thought, neither mental withdrawal
> nor outflow,
> neither distraction nor non-distraction.
> Let your mind rest with whatever mental state you are in,
> for the true nature of mind is immaculate, just like a clear blue
> ocean.
> In that natural state of rest, you will find that bliss, luminosity,
> and non-conceptuality are spontaneously present.

That is why, without preventing the proliferation of thoughts, you should learn to relax into the mind without contrivance, even when it is in a state of movement, where it entertains thoughts about the past or mental occurrences generally. This form of release should be practiced in the present moment. You should not think about what has gone before, run elaborate commentary on what you think is happening, or try to anticipate what may or may not come up in the future. If you think something has happened, you don't try to make sense of it by following it or tracing the movement of your thoughts. Just allow your mind to come to rest automatically, of its own accord, without trying to force it. Let it settle through its own momentum. If you practice in this way, you will find freedom while your mind is in a state of movement, because liberation will occur simultaneously with the movement of the mind. If you can achieve that, you will have fully established the view of insight meditation.

In post-meditation situations, your whole mental outlook will have changed. Instead of viewing everything from the perspective of a permanent, substantial self or with a dualistic point of view, you will have moments with clear experiences of bliss, luminosity, and nonconceptuality. These are the visible, tangible signs of wisdom. Allowing your mind to rest naturally is what allows the luminosity of the mind to become manifest. This experience may not last. You might only have episodic experiences of it during the course of your day, so that your old ways of looking and experiencing things will arise again, and your mind may become agitated. You should not view this with alarm. If you react to it in a negative way, that is an indication you are still attached to certain experiences.

If agitation returns, let that agitation be released, and the turbulence will subside. Everything will become lucid again. When that sense of clarity and lucidity return to the mind, so will the experiences of bliss, luminosity, and nonconceptuality, and various types of meditative experiences and realizations will become more regular companions.

THE INTRODUCTIONS

In brief, the introduction to various spiritual phenomena entails the following sets of sequences:

- Normal phenomenal experiences are introduced to the mind itself,
- The mind itself is introduced to ultimate reality or emptiness,
- Emptiness is introduced to liberation and phenomenal

experience.

This series of introductions leads you to arrive at a genuine and certain view.

- Ultimate reality is introduced to the original and immaculate nature,
- The original and immaculate nature is introduced to bliss and luminosity,
- Bliss and luminosity in turn are introduced to emptiness.

This series of introductions leads you to establish yourself in genuine and authentic meditation.

- Phenomenal experience and the mind are introduced as illusion-like,
- Illusion-like phenomena are introduced as insubstantial,
- Insubstantial phenomena are introduced as all-pervasive.

This series of introductions leads you to establish genuine and proper action.

- Mind is introduced as buddha,
- Buddhahood is introduced as your own natural state of being,
- Your own natural state of being is introduced as inseparable from various experiences and freedoms.

This series of introductions guarantees that you will obtain the fruition stage without going astray.

You perfect the view, meditation, action, and fruition (*lta-ba sgom-pa spyod-pa 'bras-bu*) of spiritual practice in this way. You need to bear in mind that when you encounter certain perceptual or mental objects, they present themselves in various ways, but the mind should not latch onto any of those presentations. At that very moment of any mental occurrence, you should learn to rest on that. You mind should rest on whatever mental occurrence arises at the very moment it arises, without trying to do anything with it. Don't try to transform it, don't try to get rid of it, and don't try to modify it by using certain antidotes. If you can practice in this way, nothing you experience will disrupt your meditative state. In fact, whatever you experience will be understood as a display of ultimate reality itself.

CULTIVATING POST-MEDITATION

This section deals with three major experiential situations in post-meditation: 1) waking experiences are similar to dreams, 2) dream experiences can be used to realize the luminous nature of the mind, and 3) we can remain in the state of luminosity.

Waking experiences are similar to dreams

Our senses are fully operational during waking hours, and we apprehend and contact the objective physical world through the various sensory apparatuses of sight, sound, smell, taste, and touch. In addition to these sensory operations, we are also continuously aware of varied and prolific inner states of mind. Whether our experiences are only on the sensory level or also on the cognitive level, we should not think of them as totally real, but instead regard them as not so different from last night's dreams.

If we can learn to recognize the similarity between our waking states and dreams during post-meditation, we will relinquish our hold on things and stop taking everything so seriously. If we can carry that attitude over into daily life, our minds will become less disturbed, whether we are awake, sitting, lying down, or whatever.[30] When we engage in our daily activities with the view that everything that we experience is not much different from our dreams, we will not latch onto things so quickly and our reactions will begin to slow down. This comes about because the dualistic notion of something out there to react to and someone in here to do the reacting is no longer there. We are now able to maintain the nondual luminosity of mind.

When you go about your daily life, you are in contact with the external world all the time, and your senses will be in touch with that world, but what has changed is the way your mind responds to sensory impressions. Instead of being disturbed by the sensory inputs, your mind remains lucid and unperturbed, and you are able to stop conceptualizing and elaborating on whatever is processed through them. That is what is meant by "maintaining the luminosity of the mind." This is also what is meant by "realizing the mind that recognizes itself." Maintaining this attitude will not only help you in this world, but it will also help you in your post-mortem bardo state. If you can maintain this level of mental clarity, it will guide you through the turbulence of the bardo experiences. That gives you some idea about how to carry your practice into your daily life in your post-meditation waking hours.

Using dream experiences to realize the luminous nature of mind

You can put your sleep to profitable use because you can still maintain and cultivate luminosity during sleep. In fact, when we fall sleep, we experience a border between the waking and sleeping states. The mind is lucid and less active in that interim period because the sensory apparatuses are no longer operational. When the outer workings of the sensory operations cease, the inner workings of the mind also slow down, but you have not yet fallen into a state of deep sleep. You are in a deep state of relaxation, but you have not gone into a state of deep sleep and your mind is totally relaxed. This is a perfect opportunity to come into contact with the luminous nature of the mind.

A seasoned meditator will be able to recognize that they are in that state and remain there without distraction. That is a form of meditation. If you are able to rest in that state then, even within a very short time, you will develop various abilities and capabilities. Dreams arise during this period when the sensory operations have ceased, and the internal workings of the mind have slowed down. When you can recognize that state, you will first gain the ability to transform nightmares and disturbing dreams into more exciting or pleasant dreams. Then you will learn to gain mastery over your dream experiences. Instead of being drawn into your dream experiences without any freedom, you can willfully change your dreams in various ways so that, instead of being visitations from the mind, your dream experiences can be used as the creative power of the mind itself.

How to remain in the state of luminosity

Finally, you will be able to let all your dream experiences go into the natural state of mind, where nothing remains except luminosity. Then, even when you are dreaming, you can make use of that experience to progress on the path. If you cannot do this while sleeping without the aid of formal training, you can do a very simple visualization practice. You should visualize a very small, five-colored ball of light resting in your heart center. Your mind should focus on that. Then think that multicolored lights, like the colors of a rainbow, are radiating from this ball. As you drift into sleep, focus your mind on that, and you will gradually develop the abilities to deal with dreams in the way described above.

In that way, we should not think it is only during formal meditation practice that we are able to hold that lucid, luminous state of mind. The opportunity to partake in the mandala of light is there during both waking and sleeping hours. If you can enter into that mandala of light, you can become liberated in this very life. We have the ability to liberate ourselves from the samsaric condition in this life by making use of our waking and dream experiences.

If you are unable to attain liberation in this life, there is no doubt that you will be liberated from the samsaric state in the bardo because of this practice. The experience of ösel, the luminosity of the mind, will be actualized then.

TRALEG KYABGON COMMENTARY
ON THE MAIN PRACTICE

INTRODUCTION TO SPIRITUAL PHENOMENA

In the section about *introduction*, Longchenpa says the nature of the mind should be introduced to emptiness, and emptiness should be introduced to the proliferation of thoughts and liberation, and then you establish your view from that. He is saying that the nature of the mind should be understood as the same as emptiness. The nature of mind does not have emptiness; the nature of mind is emptiness. That emptiness, or ultimate reality, is also not different from mental occurrences. It is not the case that mental events and emptiness are separate. We shouldn't think that way. Our mental occurrences—whether they are good or bad, wholesome or unwholesome—are never separate from ultimate reality. Even unwholesome states are imbued with the same reality. To understand that is to have the correct view.

Otherwise, it is very easy to think, "My proliferating thoughts, concepts, and ideas and my unwholesome thoughts are the source of my delusions. They act as blinkers or obscuring agents, and I'm unable to realize emptiness because of this." In that approach, you have the deluded state of mind, which you need to overcome, and you have emptiness, which you want to realize, and you view them in a dualistic way. To view them in a nondualistic way is to have the correct view. That is an example of how the view is introduced.

Longchenpa is talking about view, meditation, action, and fruition, which is supposed to cover the whole gamut of our spiritual practices. We have to have them all; we can't have any of them missing. Through this series of introductions, we automatically perfect all of them. We will have genuine view, authentic meditation, authentic action, and genuine fruition. This series of introductions is an attempt to break down or deconstruct our dualistic concepts. As Longchenpa says, we think of the mind and phenomena as separate—mind relates to the subject and phenomena relate to the object—but when phenomena are introduced to the mind, you see that what you know about the phenomenal world comes from the mind. There is no demarcation line that can be drawn between what is internal and what is external. Where does the internal stop, and the external begin?

When we think dualistically, we tend to overestimate and underestimate everything. We have a mistaken notion about ourselves, due to ignorance. The problem lies in our false perception of the self. Exaggeration comes from needing either to protect yourself or to consolidate and glorify the ego. We chase and hanker after things and cling onto the things we think we need, in order to have a well-defined and sufficiently strong sense of self-worth and self-identity. We feel a need to protect that and to see any sign of threat as something that might undermine us. That is why Buddhism constantly focuses on the notion of the self. Here, Longchenpa is saying that self and non-self are intimately related and intertwined. This is what we have to understand. If we can understand that interrelationship, our need to protect and to react with hostility and violence will diminish. Our need to be clingy, grasping, and greedy will hopefully decrease as well. That does not mean we will end up as zombies, stumbling along without likes or dislikes; we just won't be fixated on our likes and dislikes any more. That's what is important.

As Longchenpa says, we will continue to have varieties of experiences. This is not a bad thing. It is the expression of nirmanakaya. The point is not to get caught up in our own drama. To paraphrase one Buddhist scripture, "The world we have created is like a theatre and we are all actors in it. We've just forgotten we are acting a role and we now take that role very seriously." If you can remind yourself that you are only acting, you will still generate the appropriate emotions because an actor who doesn't project anything is a lousy actor. The same thing applies to real life. You realize what is going on and stop getting all worked up about it. You are still able to have great variety and richness in your life.

It is not the case that our options decrease as we become more and more enlightened. An enlightened being is not thinking, "Why do that? It's just another symptom of my unsettled, untamed, and deluded mind." The only option left then would be to sit at home and do nothing. Some people do think that way though. They think you have to stop this and that because it is all a product of deluded mind. Longchenpa is saying that we can more or less continue in the same way that we have been, except with a different attitude. We will relate to what we are doing differently, and see everything differently, so we will be living our lives differently too, but in some ways, there will always be continuity. It is not that everything that was familiar has now vanished. You don't have to change everything or see everything that is familiar as bad, and everything that is new as good. That is also the view of the Mahayana teachings, which have always said there is no difference between samsara and nirvana. That doesn't mean that samsara and nirvana have the same qualities, but that when understood properly, samsara becomes nirvana.

CULTIVATING POST-MEDITATION

Longchenpa talks less about self-liberation in dreams, although it can be done, because while you can change the way you think during your waking hours, it is very hard to change what you are thinking during your dreams. When you are having a nightmare, you can't just say, "I think I've had enough of that one." During waking hours, you mistakenly think you are in charge, but you're not, because your karmic traces and dispositions, habits, prejudices and biases are at work all the time. However, if you can learn to become aware of yourself when you are sleeping and dreaming, you do not need to be a victim of your dreams any more.

There are ways you can learn to change your dreams, to exercise mental control, just as you learn to do in your waking hours. For example, you might have developed a very negative way of thinking about certain things, which has become well-entrenched, but by becoming more aware of that through practice, you learn to deal with it and that tendency ceases. In fact, not only can it cease, but the opposite tendency can replace it. A negative tendency that was so much a part of your psychological make-up for so long can be transformed into something positive. The same thing can happen in the context of your dreams. That is the point.

The final point is to see our dreams as insubstantial. Longchenpa pointed out three stages. The first is the ability to change negative or unpleasant dreams into positive ones; the second is to have control over your dreams so that you can dream all kinds of things, like daydreaming at will; and the third is the ability to dissolve all dreams into the natural luminosity of the mind.

Chapter Twelve

Practice at the Time of Death

Not only can we utilize our post-meditation experiences on the path while we are alive, but we can also utilize our experiences in the bardo state after we are deceased. To explain in slightly more detail, if we want to make use of practice in our post-mortem state, the real practice centers around attaining liberation by remaining in the luminosity of the mind.

THE BARDO BETWEEN BIRTH AND DEATH

Right now, as living beings, we are in a bardo state, which is called "the bardo between birth and death" (*skye-gnas bar-do*), so we have to become familiar with that. The two most certain things in life are that we were born and that we are going to die. We have many experiences lodged between the states of birth and death, so we have to become familiar with how to deal with that. First, we need to develop the proper view so that we are not susceptible to erroneous views and don't see our lives in a distorted fashion. Having established a healthy view about our life, we have to become familiar with that and profit from it through meditation. We then put to use that maturity and what we have learned by converting our healthy attitudes and views about life into action. That then leads to the fruition of self-realization, to the recognition of our self.

This is extremely important, and we must try to get a handle on all of it while we are still alive so that we become a reasonable yogi. When death approaches, we will need to be detached so that we can let go of things. This doesn't simply mean letting go of external things like our possessions, but it also means letting go of our inner states of mind, the things we hang onto in our mental states and conditions. We must learn to stop hanging onto both internal and external things.

THE BARDO OF DYING

The time of death is called the "bardo of dying" (*'chi-kha'i bar-do*). The dying yogi should recall all the pointing-out instructions they have received during their lifetime. They should bring them into clear focus and engage in practice without distraction. As you begin to lose your grip on life, your body will dissolve in stages. First, the body will become heavy and weighed down because the earth element is dissolving into the water element. As the water element dissolves into the fire element, you will begin to suffer from extreme thirst. As the fire element dissolves into the air element, the heat of the body dissipates. The air element then dissolves into consciousness, and at that point all breathing stops—both the external breathing and the internal breathing—because there is no longer any oxygen in the body. Then consciousness dissolves into space and the mind is rendered unconscious. All forms of gross and subtle mental processes cease. This is the point at which you can experience the clear light luminosity of mind in four sequential moments:

1. This is called "the first moment of luminous experience," because the mind is not thinking, but is very clear in that instant. This is a true case of wisdom manifesting and the brilliance of that wisdom is such that it surpasses any fleeting momentary insights you may have had during practice while alive. However, this only lasts for a moment.

2. This is followed by another flash of luminosity, which is even brighter. This also lasts for a moment and is called "the second moment of luminous experience."

3. After that comes another flash of wisdom insight, which is even greater and more intense than the previous two. At "the third moment of luminous experience," we have been able to take full possession of that experience of luminosity instead of just having flickering moments of it.

4. That is then followed by the final, full manifestation of wisdom experience, which is called "approaching the wisdom of near attainment."

THE LUMINOUS BARDO OF DHARMATA

When we are in the luminous bardo of dharmata (*chos-nyid bar-do*), the various appearances we encounter are very much like our dream states while sleeping. If we don't become overly upset or provoked by these appearances by becoming fixated on them, and can realize their true nature, we will find freedom or liberation at that point. We will be able to "recognize our true face," (*rang-myur shes-pa*). If we fail to recognize ourselves during this bardo of ultimate reality, we will be roused from that state and the bardo of becoming will be put into motion.

THE BARDO OF BECOMING

In relation to the dying process, various stages of absorption are spoken of, so if we fail to recognize ourselves during the bardo of dharmata, the bardo of becoming (*srid-pa bar-do*) will begin with its stages of emergence. The bardo of becoming has many different stages, but they are normally subsumed under seven main categories, marked by the seven levels of consciousness. These stages are called "seven moments."

Realization in the seven moments

The first moment of the bardo of becoming is the separation of the mind from matter. The second moment relates to the element of earth, the third moment relates to the element of water, the fourth relates to the element of fire, the fifth to the element of air, the sixth to the element of space, and the seventh moment relates to conditioned existence, as it is brought about by our karmic traces and dispositions.

When the first moment of the separation of mind and matter occurs, the sensation is very dull, almost like a state of unconsciousness.

That is followed by the second moment, where the unborn child has become more sentient and therefore more conscious of the solidity of its body, hence the earth element is related to this moment. This unborn child also has certain quasi-apparitional experiences that are like seeing a mirage, but these are not very clear or well-defined. If that being had been a Dzogchen practitioner in their previous life, they would be able to recall certain Dzogchen practices and teachings on how to naturally free the body, even at this level, and could find liberation by recalling these practices.

The onset of the third moment is signaled by a greater clarity of mind, where consciousness has become more lucid, and the child is aware of the liquid in and around itself. The infant also has quasi-visual experiences at this stage where it sees something like smoke, but these are still ill-defined. We should realize that even this experience has its origin in the luminous nature of mind and should try to recall practices that emphasize liberating the mind by paying attention to our sensory experiences. If we can experience the indivisibility of luminosity and emptiness, we can also find liberation here.

When the fourth moment comes into effect, consciousness becomes even more lucid, as if it were being roused from sleep. The infant becomes sensitive to the heat in its surroundings, as well as to its own body, which is why this moment relates to the element of fire. This is again accompanied by apparitional experiences that are like flying sparks or fireflies buzzing about in the dark. Even here, there is the possibility to recognize that these experiences come from the luminous nature of our mind. If we can recall practices that give rise to experiences of the indivisibility of bliss and emptiness, we can find liberation here as well.

In the fifth moment we become aware of the movement of air, which in this case means breathing, and we experience seeing something like a burning flame. These experiences also have their origin in our own natural state of luminosity, so we should recall the practice of luminosity in relation to the five-colored lights that give rise to the experience of luminosity and emptiness. We can then find liberation at that point.

These are the five elements related to the formation of the fetus and they are called "the five external signs." The experiences of apparitions are called "the inner signs" and come about due to the causes and conditions that are present.

At the sixth moment the infant becomes conscious of space and the accompanying psychovisual experience is like seeing the empty space of a cloudless sky. We should therefore recall practices associated with the realization of luminosity and emptiness combined with nonconceptuality, and we can also find liberation through that.

In the seventh moment, the nature of mind is immaculate, like a mirror. Based upon this immaculate mind, the reflections of the karmic body are created, and we experience pain and pleasure, just like we do in dreams. When this occurs, we should try to recollect practice on clear light, which emphasizes the notion of the indivisibility of appearance and emptiness. We should also recall our tantric practices of the development and fulfillment stages and any experiences we may have gained from those practices. Then we should think of ourselves as the deity, hear all sounds as echoes, and see any discursive thought that arises as dream-like. If we can do this, we will realize that everything we experience is wisdom imbued with the three qualities of bliss, luminosity, and nonconceptuality. We can attain buddhahood at that point. We can attain liberation in the seventh moment in two different ways: "other-powered" (*sheng-drup*) liberation or "self-powered" (*rang-drup*) liberation.

Other-powered liberation comes about when we think of the great masters of the lineage, such Padma 'Byung-gnas or Padmasambhava and recall how powerful and necessary their blessings are for us. This process of other-powered liberation is comparable to the rays of the sun on a lotus flower, where the sun's rays have the power to open the petals. We should also remember the various lineage masters and deities and supplicate them, thinking they have heard our pleas and responded to them. We become liberated through their compassion.

Self-powered liberation comes from having a proper understanding of the view, through being familiar with meditation, and through gaining a greater understanding of action. The power to self-liberate comes from the fruition of engaging in those three types of practices.

Description of the seven moments

The first moment is about understanding the proper view. As was said in the bardo of dying, what we have to realize is that the phenomenal world that appears to our mind and the mind itself have no intrinsic essence—they are both empty by nature. Having that proper understanding can liberate us.

The second moment is about becoming familiar with meditation, which in this case means meditation on clear light, and familiarity with the experiences of bliss, luminosity, and nonconceptuality. Those three are the ingredients of wisdom so we have to become accustomed to them. When we can do that, we can mix that familiarity with self-existing awareness.

The third moment is about action, where whatever we experience should be seen as illusion-like and we act in such a way that we are not concerned about thoughts of acceptance, cultivation, or abandonment. Acting in that way is said to be "acting in the way of Samantabhadra." We need to become very dexterous at that. To become free of the dualistic notion of cultivation and abandonment is how we become a buddha.

The fourth moment is the fruition, which is about realizing that our own intrinsic awareness is already free. It has never been bound.

The fifth moment is about establishing this realization spontaneously.

The sixth moment is about gaining real certainty about that spontaneous establishment. Otherwise, we might think we have to do something to attain buddhahood, that we have to bring about some fundamental change in the structure of our being. That is not the case, because our intrinsic self-awareness is free, has never been bound. It is established spontaneously and isn't contingent on causes and conditions. It is not something we realize through relying on various antidotes or stripping away the different layers of defilements.

The seventh moment is where these thoughts are totally dismantled. They totally subside and disintegrate, and we find ourselves in the state of dzogpa chenpo or maha-ati. To realize or remember that allows our unborn being to be liberated instantly.

These seven moments actually stretch over a period of seven days and are also called "the seven facets of existence." As it is said in a sutra, "We must traverse through the seven facets of existence."

For these reasons, it is extremely important for us to practice the bardo teachings. We must become well-acquainted with them, because it is only when we have familiarity with these practices that we will be good at them when it really matters. We have to be really good at them. It will not be possible otherwise to find liberation during the bardo of dying, the bardo of dharmata, or the bardo of becoming. But if we are familiar with the bardo teachings and practices, it will be extremely easy to find liberation in the post-mortem states. For example, if we do Dream Yoga practice, our dream experiences will subside, even when we have nightmares. We will be able to suddenly realize that we are dreaming, and that our dream experiences are not real. The same thing applies to the bardo teachings and practices.

The bardo of becoming is heralded by a combination of ignorance, desire, and anger. When we are about to take on a new birth in the bardo of becoming, we should make every effort to curb our desire and aggression by realizing that the mind has no abiding root. Our mind will be set free through the power of this recognition, and we will not re-enter the samsaric condition.

It is important to remember that we can never deviate from our original authentic condition, our original ground of being. We must realize that the mind in itself is luminous, and its original condition is pure. By paying attention to the current state of our mind, we come to recognize and free ourselves into the state of Samantabhadra or Kuntuzangpo, the primordial buddha. We should also realize that the so-called "six realms" have no intrinsic reality or truth. The ability to recall the practice of deity visualization will also be helpful. We should try to think about not taking rebirth in any of the six realms, but instead think of the pure realms of the buddhas. These are the thoughts we should entertain in the bardo of becoming.

TRANSFERENCE OF CONSCIOUSNESS

You should practice phowa or the transference of consciousness (*sankranti, 'pho-ba*) while you are alive. In this practice, you can visualize yourself as the deity of your choice. You visualize a ball of multi-colored light at your heart center, as a symbol of your mind, and utter the mantra HA'I as you imagine the ball of light being ejected through the crown of your head. You should do this twenty-one times.

When you eject your consciousness, you think that it enters into one of the buddha-fields presided over by one of the five Dhyani Buddhas, such as Akanishtha (*'og min*). For example, you can eject your consciousness into the buddha-field of Vairochana (*rnam-par snang-mdzod*) and then imagine that the ball of light enters into the heart center of Vairochana. You then think that your mind and the mind of Vairochana have become completely intermingled and you have reached a point of no return. It doesn't have to be Vairochana; it could be Ratnasambhava or Amitabha or any of the other Dhyani Buddhas.

You should practice this ejection of consciousness consistently for three days. If you are successful, the crown of your head may break out in a boil or something of that nature. Then you should continue with this practice once every month.

It is important to also refresh your mind about phowa practice by recalling it every day or whenever you are able, imagining that your mind is a multi-colored ball of light that you have ejected into a certain buddha-field and that your consciousness has been absorbed into the consciousness of that respective Buddha. You do not have to utter HA'I verbally during this exercise; it is sufficient to imagine it. If you become sufficiently acquainted with phowa practice, you will enter into a pure realm of one of the buddha-families at the time of death and secure buddhahood there.

DEDICATION

May the eloquent sound of the Dharma be spread by beating
its drum.
May its sound rouse sentient beings from the sleep of ignorance.
May you perfect all the buddha-qualities,
by knowing abandonment and realization.
May you realize the three spontaneously complete kayas.

TRALEG KYABGON COMMENTARY ON THE PRACTICE AT THE TIME OF DEATH

THE BARDO OF DYING

At the beginning of those four sequential moments of death, all the gross and subtle mental processes cease, and you are rendered unconscious. After having become unconscious, the first moment of the luminosity of the mind arises. We shouldn't think of these moments as a very linear thing, with one moment coming after the other in a serial fashion. It may happen very quickly, which is why it is called "instant" or "momentary." Longchenpa is saying that if we do Dzogchen practice, then whether we are going about our business during waking hours or when we are asleep or even when we die, we can make use of what we have realized during meditation. We can also use what we have learned during our practice in the bardo. Even though these four moments of the luminosity of mind occur to all sentient beings, irrespective of their training or background, only a practitioner is going to recognize what is happening.

We are not seeing lights or anything like that. It is about an aspect of the mind that we would not have seen unless we were meditating or unless we were familiar with these mental states. For a meditator who has become deceased, it may be a case of déjà vu. For somebody else, it may not mean anything. That is what Longchenpa is saying. We all dream, but how many of us profit from our dreams? Not many at all. Similarly, when we die, even fewer people will profit from their death or post-mortem states. We can use that analogy.

What Longchenpa is saying is that our waking, dream, and post-mortem experiences are not dissimilar. We go from one experiential situation to the other. For that reason, if we can get a handle on what is really going on within our mind right now, in our practice, we will be able to understand what is happening during our waking hours, sleeping hours, and post-mortem experiences. That we think our waking experiences should be used as the yardstick for judging what is truly real or what is unreal is a misconception we have developed in the course of our lives. Our waking experiences do not correspond to actual reality.

Longchenpa is not saying that waking hours are the same thing as dreaming hours, but he is saying there are enough similarities between them to provide the basis for experience to be continuous, rather than the dramatic transition from one state to another that we assume it to be. We know that even in normal situations, our waking hour experiences impact on our sleep and vice versa. How well we sleep is often related to what we were thinking during the day, and how we wake up the next day has a lot to do with the kind of sleep we had. The content of our dreams is also largely determined by our waking experiences.

We are therefore mistaken if we think we are in control of our life while we are awake and not in control while we are dreaming. We are not in control when we are awake, and we are not out of control when we are dreaming. We don't have to be not in control when we die either. Even if we don't believe in an afterlife, we can have a good death or a bad death, just as we can have a good birth or a bad birth. When we die, even if we have dismissed the possibility of future existences or any form of disembodied state, we can still decide to have a good death or a bad death, so even then, we don't have to be not in control. That is really the gist of the teachings.

We don't have to think we are out of control when we dream or when we are dying. That is why a lot of people freak out. People are filled with trepidation, anxiety, fear, and all kinds of things because they think they are going to be invalidated, that any form of control over their life will be gone. There may be a few people who are not afraid of death, but almost everyone is afraid of dying itself. If you don't believe in an afterlife, if you don't believe in survival after death, you must think that when you exit, that is it and it doesn't matter. However, even with people like that, the thought of losing control over your physical and mental faculties is a frightening thing. What Longchenpa and the Dzogchen teachings are saying is that while outwardly this may be the case, if you have done practice, your mind will still be clear, sharp, and focused. You will still be in charge of the whole process, even though outwardly you are not able to manifest that.

THE BARDO OF BECOMING

Being in the bardo of becoming means you are going to take rebirth, but Longchenpa is basically saying that rebirth is not inevitable; we can prevent our rebirth. We have to think about that too. When we talk about the bardo of becoming, we are talking about beings with no choice but to be reborn. That is not to say that a realized being will not continue to be an embodied being or assume some kind of physical form. It just means that normally we do not have any choice about where we are born, who our parents are, our race or skin pigmentation, our genetic background, or any number of things.

If you recognize the four sequences of luminosity at death, your mind will automatically rest in that state. You would rest with that and the bardo of becoming would be preempted. There would be no bardo of becoming for you to worry about. But again, that doesn't mean that an enlightened being may not choose to assume some form or other and come back into the world. That would be of their own choosing; they wouldn't be coming back because they were compelled to by overpowering karmic forces. If you are able to rest your mind in those moments of luminosity, you will attain enlightenment in that moment. That is the bardo of dharmakaya. You will have realized buddhahood in that instant.

As Longchenpa says, even in the bardo you will have déjà vu experience: "This is the same as what I experienced when I practiced." The gist of all of our practices is to be aware, to be present, to let go and stop hanging onto things. We are trying to learn how to let go of external and internal things, to jettison all the stuff we carry around. That doesn't mean we shouldn't love the people we love, or we shouldn't cherish the things we cherish, but we should not have this overwhelming attachment to things. That attachment is like a disease. That is what we have to overcome.

"Letting go" does not mean that everything is the same and we should discard everything that is good along with everything that is bad. There are things that are worth cherishing and there are a lot of things that are not worth cherishing. Most of the things that we cherish are not worth cherishing, but we still cherish them, so we have to do a bit of sorting out. At the end of the day, there are still things worth cherishing, but even when we do cherish them, the idea of letting go should still be present.

While the luminosity of the mind appears at death during those four moments, it is not only in those times that it appears. If we have been practicing, we will experience the luminosity of the mind during meditation. So when we die, we will have glimpses of that same luminosity in those moments, and we should be able to recognize what's happening. However, if we have not been practicing, it won't mean anything to us and that will be at our own peril.

In the bardo of becoming, consciousness arrives in the fetus simultaneously with the moment of conception. It is not the case that first there is conception and then the consciousness finds lodging there. The moment of conception is the moment the consciousness enters the womb. Until the moment of conception, there is no egg or sperm. It's not very clear in the teachings, but we do talk about bardo bodies. A bardo body is a subtle body, not a gross body, but the fetus is seen as a gross body. You have consciousness and you have the physical component, so it's an embodied body.

The seven moments of the bardo of becoming don't necessarily proceed immediately after the four moments at the time of death. Normally we talk about forty-nine days in the bardo, which take place in the bardo of dharmata. The bardo of becoming comes after that. If someone is very advanced spiritually, they do not spend any time in the bardo of dharmata because they will be liberated at the time of death in one of the four moments.

It doesn't have to be forty-nine days before rebirth takes place. Longchenpa mentions the series of absorptions in the bardo of dying, those four moments where we are absorbed into our own natural state of being. Then you have a series of bardo visions and experiences. If you don't become liberated then, the bardo of becoming comes into effect. The bardo of becoming is like being roused from that state of dharmata. First there are the series of absorptions in the bardo of death and dying and then there are a series of evolutionary stages in the bardo of becoming. There is a process of devolution and evolution. The bardo of death and dying has the devolution, where consciousness is becoming less and less conscious. With the bardo of becoming, consciousness becomes more and more alert again.

We can also gain freedom through other-powered liberation during the seventh moment of the bardo of becoming. This is a particularly auspicious time to think about the blessings of the lineage. As Longchenpa says, the blessings of the lineage masters are like the rays of the sun. Sometimes it is said that we are like unripe fruit, and when the rays of the sun are cast on unripe fruit, they ripen. Similarly, we become ripe from the blessings that we receive from our lineage masters.

Even when we are infants still in the womb, if we have been practicing and our consciousness is very advanced, we have the ability to recollect our spiritual practices. That's the idea. You should not think when you are reborn that you have to start all over again. If you have reached a certain level of realization, you cannot relapse. You cannot revert to where you were before, so even an unborn infant would be able to recollect their previous life experiences, especially because, when you are in the womb, there is less of a gap between your previous life and your present situation. If you believe in a stream of consciousness, that does make sense. If we can remember what we did sixty or seventy years ago, it wouldn't be that difficult to remember when we are in the womb what we did several months ago.

Tibetan Buddhism has all kinds of practices—phowa practice, pure lands, Dream Yoga, and so on—and we should be familiar with all of them. We may become very proficient at a particular practice, but we still shouldn't ignore the others. According to tradition, Milarepa was very good with tummo practice, and he became famous for that, but that doesn't mean he didn't do Dream Yoga, Illusory Body Yoga, or phowa practices. All of these practices, as you may have noticed, are about having power over your own mind. Normally, we do not dictate what the mind should be thinking or doing because we have no power over it. These practices are all about being able to direct the mind so even though the practices themselves are very different from each other, their purpose is nonetheless the same: to gain control over our mind, to see through our mind. The mind may think that something is real or overwhelming or important, but we don't have to get duped by that. We can see through it. We should also think that the six realms are contingent on the mind and the buddha-fields are contingent on the mind. That's how we should see it.

Some people regard certain days as more auspicious for practice, so that if you do your practice on those days, your merit will be multiplied one hundred-fold. We should not really think like that because every day is a good day for practice, but nonetheless, it is good to have some special days: the tenth, the fifteenth, and so on. Even if we don't necessarily think those days are special, if we set particular days aside for group practice, it does create a certain special atmosphere. What would have been just a normal day is made into a special day. I feel the specialness comes more from the people who are participating in a communal activity, but not necessarily from the fact that the day itself is special. That is my feeling. The main point is really to get together like that. For instance, we commemorate Buddha's birthday, we commemorate Buddha's parinirvana. They are important because we are Buddhists and Buddha was and is a very important figure for us. If you loved your parents, then commemorating their passing away is an important day for you. Coming together and doing things like spiritual practice communally creates a very wholesome and spiritually charged atmosphere.

Longchenpa gives us a general description of phowa practice here but there are phowa manuals that we can use that include all the details of the practice. You need to have an initiation before you can do phowa practice and the manual that you use will depend upon the yidam or deity you are using. Your practice manual will be determined by that and the empowerment that you need to receive will also be related to that deity.

PART FOUR

Supplement
The Precious Boat of Bodhicitta, the Creator of All Things

Chapter Thirteen

Root Text: Interpretive and Definitive Teachings

TEACHINGS THAT NEED TO BE INTERPRETED

The Buddha was a very skilled and compassionate teacher and because of that, he did not teach just one thing; he gave many kinds of teachings. For this reason, there are numerous divisions within the body of Buddha's teachings. They are grouped together differently and are referred to as "yanas" (*vehicles, theg-pa*). We can find many kinds of yanas in the body of Buddha's teachings. When we study and practice these teachings, we realize that because Buddha taught in many different ways in order to suit the needs of different people, most of the Buddha's teachings fall into the category of teachings that need to be interpreted (*neyartha, drang-don*). They are not to be taken literally. You cannot find teachings with a definitive (*nitartha, nges-don*) meaning in any one particular set of teachings. As one tantric text says:

Buddha taught according to the needs of varied individuals.

The Sixty-four *Slokas* says:

To please and attract people with different interests, the Buddha presented many different paths to enlightenment. Many spiritual aspirants who have embarked on the path have very small hearts. To put them on the path, Buddha gave many teachings with contents that need to be interpreted. Their meanings need to be unpacked.

Unconditioned Existence says:

People with an interest in realizing the ultimate truth should know:

The Buddha revealed the truth in different ways,
but most of these teachings are not to be taken literally.
They should be taken as needing interpretation.

For instance, the Dzogchen system has nine yanas, beginning with the shravaka-yana, going up to anu-yoga in the tantric system, and culminating in ati-yoga or Dzogchen. The teachings of the first six vehicles—from the shravaka-yana level to the maha-yoga level—can only lead the interested practitioner as far as entering the path; they cannot lead to the realization of ultimate truth. Even if you practice these teachings and become proficient in the practices, they will not allow you to realize the all-creating (*kun-byed*) mind itself. You will not see that. As one of the Dzogchen tantras says:

> If you do not realize me, the All-creating Mind, you will never understand me, even if you engage in all the tantric practices.

DEFINITIVE TEACHINGS

For these reasons, when you are following the Dzogchen teachings, you should always try to cultivate and understand teachings with a definitive meaning (*nitartha, nges-don*). These teachings have never been spoken by the buddhas of the three times. They have been spoken by the All-Creating Revealer of all things. In the tantra known as *Eighty Slokas*, it says:

> My name is the All-Creating Revealer.
>
> The real essence of the spiritual vehicles has never been revealed by other buddhas. This mind has never been born, but the continuum of the mind itself is pregnant with revelations. This has never been revealed by the Victorious Ones of the three times in the past; nor will they speak about it or reveal its true essence in the future.
>
> However, I, the All-Creating King, the creator of all things, do not suffer fluctuations. I have spoken about this in the past, I will speak about it in the future, and I speak about it now, in the present, to those who are fortunate enough to hear.
>
> What I reveal and speak are the definitive teachings. I reveal the essence of the teachings as preserved in the oral tradition. What

has been spoken about and revealed does not increase or decrease. One has to grasp the essence. I, the Creator of All, reveal that essence to others. Thus, it has been said.

What is revealed by the creator of all things is the essence of all the vehicles. Another Nyingma tantra says:

The king, the creator of all things, reveals that condition which is unconditioned. The unconditioned state is the essence of all things. Whatever arises, whatever is perceived, can only be understood if we understand the essence. The essence is the same, although the manifestation of things is varied. Everything that exists is inseparable from the Creator of All. Hence, the importance of realizing this creator of all things. You should aspire to become more intimate with that and to understand its true essence.

In that way, you should understand that knowing the creator of all things is the same as being able to extract the essence of the teachings in the multi-layered system of vehicles. What is this creator of all things? It is nothing other than bodhicitta. Even though nine yanas are spoken of, in truth there is only one yana and that is bodhicitta. Bodhicitta is the essence of all the yanas.[31]

THE MAHA-ATI TEACHINGS

The system of Maha-ati or dzogpa chenpo—Dzogchen for short transcends the previous eight spiritual yanas that are expounded in Buddhist thought. The ati-yoga yana is the ninth yana. It is also called the "Maha-ati yana" because it embodies the essence of all the teachings contained in the other yana systems.

The teacher-student relationship

To understand this properly, you have to fully appreciate the significance of the teacher-student relationship. First, you need to understand what kind of teacher you should rely on, and second, the teacher needs to examine and understand the character of the student. Finally, you have to pay attention to the teachings transmitted from the teacher to the student.

The teacher should be learned and well-informed about the various Buddhist and non-Buddhist systems of thought. The teacher has to be especially well-versed in the teachings of Maha-ati. The teacher must also be skilled in the process of conveying and instilling the essential points of the Maha-ati teachings in the mindstream of the student. Furthermore, the teacher should not be tainted or corrupted by worldly distractions. They should not be distracted by or caught up in and fixated on worldly affairs. That is the kind of teacher you should seek.

The opposite of that kind of teacher would be someone who has no knowledge of the Buddhist or non-Buddhist systems of thought, someone who is generally ignorant about spiritual matters. Such a teacher would also only be concerned with worldly riches and the distractions the world offers. They would be completely careless with and inattentive to their own actions and the preservation of their precepts. Such a teacher may still attract well-meaning students, but instead of showing them the way to liberation, they will put their students on the wrong path. Even if they have the ability to teach, they will only do so with the intention of receiving material offerings. This kind of behavior is the complete opposite of all that is held in high regard in the ati teachings. Such a teacher may have done a certain amount of study and be able to articulate the ati teachings because they know the words, terms, and definitions of those teachings, and they may teach others in that way, but since they have never had the opportunity to practice, it is really only a kind of act or theatrical performance. A sensible student must reject teachers of this kind.

The student must generally have a very open mind and a great inclination to learn. They should be attentive, not careless, and pay attention to their behavior. They should also not be temperamental or fickle but be stable and of a compassionate and caring disposition. They should be generous and not miserly. It is very important for the student not to be haughty or arrogant, but to be humble and display humility. A student should also be able to correctly follow the spiritual instructions that are given. They must have a certain degree of courage and bravery so that they are not easily defeated and can commit themselves to something and stick to it once they have made a commitment. The student should make material offerings of all kinds to their teacher and the teacher in turn should make use of those offerings to propagate the teachings.

When a compatible teacher and student meet under these circumstances, the student must think about the practice of Maha-ati. In this case, you first have to establish your practice of Maha-ati, in terms of the lineage, and then you must learn the actual practice of mind-to-mind transmission.

The Maha-ati lineage

To establish yourself in the lineage, you have to appreciate that the lineage of Maha-ati is traced to the Adi-Buddha, the primordial Buddha, the creator of all things, known as Kunjed Gyalpo or Samantabhadra. Samantabhadra, the primordial Buddha, was residing in the infinite state of ultimate reality in Akanishtha. Then Samantabhadra became roused from this state of eternal equilibrium. Having been roused from this state, Samantabhadra transmitted what was to be transmitted to the five buddha-families. Then, from the heart of Samantabhadra, (the primordial Buddha), Vajrasattva (the indestructible mind), manifested with the force of self-arising wisdom. From that, arose the sambhogakaya manifestation of the enlightened beings.

In this sambhogakaya form, the essential teachings of Maha-ati were transmitted to a nirmanakaya manifestation. In this case, the nirmanakaya form was assumed by Garab Dorje. Garab Dorje then transmitted the teachings to Manjushrimitra. Manjushrimitra, in turn, transmitted the teachings to Sri Singha, who transmitted them to the great translator, known as Vairochana. Vairochana transmitted the teachings to Yudra Nyingpo, who transmitted them to Gyalwa Gesung, and so on. The Maha-ati teachings were received through these great lineage masters.

TRALEG KYABGON COMMENTARY ON THE ROOT TEXT—INTERPRETIVE AND DEFINITIVE TEACHINGS

When the text says, "I, the Creator of All," it is referring to the mind itself, which Longchenpa is calling "bodhicitta." In Dzogchen, bodhicitta means the "mind itself"or the "nature of the mind." The mind itself is also called Kunjed Gyalpo, the All-Creating King. *Kun* means "everything," *byed* means "create," and *gyal-po* means "king." As we say, "The mind itself is the creator of samsara and nirvana." There is nothing that exists outside of that because samsara and nirvana include everything.

When Longchenpa says the buddhas in the past haven't spoken about this and the buddhas in the future will not speak about it, he is saying that buddhas cannot reveal bodhicitta. Bodhicitta has to reveal itself to us. It is a direct transmission, in that sense. Our own spiritual essence, for want of a better word, has to reveal itself to us and that is direct transmission, that is true revelation. The buddhas can only allude to it. When buddhas are teaching or doing other things to convey what they want to convey, it is still not direct. Longchenpa is saying that it is not being revealed and it will never be revealed by anybody else. It can only be revealed by Kunjed Gyalpo. Kunjed Gyalpo is our own true condition, our authentic state of being.

Even though the word "creator" is used in this context, Samantabhadra does not create anything; everything emanates from the primordial state. The analogy that comes to mind is that of a field. Grass may grow in the field, but the earth does not create the grass. However, without the earth, there would be no grass. Similarly, Samantabhadra does not create anything, but everything arises from the state of Samantabhadra. There is no chasm or gap between the created world and the creator, because Samantabhadra is present in everything. The true nature of everything is Samantabhadra. Our true nature is Samantabhadra, and the true nature of the external, conditioned world is also Samantabhadra. That doesn't mean everything that exists is Samantabhadra; it means that the *nature* of everything that exists is Samantabhadra. There is separation, in that sense. If everything were Samantabhadra, we should be able to recognize it without too much effort, but that is not true. The true nature of things remains occult, hidden from us.

The difference between definitive (*nitartha, nges-don*) and interpretive (*neyartha, drang-don*) teachings is that *nges-don* literally means "teachings that reveal the definitive meaning," while *drang-don* means "teachings that are given in order to liberate sentient creatures, and which need to be interpreted." For example, Mahayana sutras say things like, "If you recite a specific number of dharanis (dharanis are like mantras) for a certain period of time, you will definitely attain this or that spiritual realization." That would be an interpretive teaching. There are dharanis that are written on pieces of paper and stuck above doors so that if you walk under them certain things will be prevented from happening. For instance, you will never be reborn as a pig, or whatever. There are teachings like that, but they are not to be taken literally.

The point here is that different kinds of things are said to bring people onto the spiritual path. For example, even if people are doing something without a completely pure motivation or understanding, thinking, "If I do this, I'm going to get something in return," they are still doing something spiritual. They are still doing something wholesome, and for that period of time, their minds will be focused. Their minds are not being dominated by confusion, mental agitation, and emotional upheaval, even if only for a short time. Their mind will be focused on lofty or spiritual matters. Not everyone who is brought up in a religious or spiritual environment will end up being practitioners, but people who are not practitioners still need some kind of spiritual focus, to be involved with teachings and practices on some level.

The intentionality of the primordial Buddha is difficult to understand because a buddha's intentionality (sangs-rgyas dgongs-pa) is not the same as our normal concept of intentionality. In a sense it is the same as thugs-rje in the Dzogchen teachings, which means something like "responsiveness." As it is said, buddhas do not have intentions. A buddha's mind is not intent upon anything, because a buddha's mind does not distinguish between subject and object. A buddha's mind does respond to things, nonetheless. In other words, while a buddha's mind is free of deliberation and not consciously intent on anything, a buddha's mind responds to things and that is intentionality. For example, it is said a buddha doesn't deliberately try to liberate sentient creatures, but sentient beings are liberated because a buddha responds to the need of sentient creatures. In that sense, it happens spontaneously. A buddha does not have to sit down and think, "What would be the best strategy to liberate sentient creatures? I have so many options: A, B, C. Which one should I choose?" A buddha, with their infinite wisdom, would be able to respond spontaneously, in an appropriate fashion, to whatever it is that needs to be done. That is buddha-intentionality. I translate it as "intentionality" because *dgongs-pa* means that, but we have to understand the context of *dgongs-pa* to grasp its full meaning.

Chapter Fourteen

Retreat Instructions—Preliminary Practice

1. GURU YOGA

Firstly, to realize the nature of the mind, you need to have wisdom, the wisdom that allows you to recognize your own true nature. To do that, you need a lama who can instruct you in the practice. Since the lama is important for you to make progress on the path, you need to practice Guru Yoga. This must precede your main practices.

To practice Guru Yoga, you sit comfortably on a meditation cushion and then recite the refuge formula. That should be followed by the contemplation of loving-kindness and compassion. Then, while you are in that meditative state, you remind yourself that your own true nature is uncreated and unoriginated. Then visualize a dark blue HUNG. This HUNG should be viewed as the representation of the true nature of your body-mind complex in indivisible union.

Light radiates outward from this dark blue HUNG illuminating the external world, as well as your own inner body cavities. You should view this light as having purificatory and healing powers so that everything outside you and everything within you is washed clean. You should also imagine that this light has touched on all living creatures, particularly human beings, and transformed them into gods and goddesses.

You then imagine that you have been transformed into Vajrasattva. In this case, Vajrasattva is not white, but dark blue in color, with one face and two hands. Vajrasattva is sitting cross-legged and is adorned with silk garments, anklets, bracelets, and so on. His right hand holds a vajra at his heart, and his left hand holds a bell raised against his hip.

Multi-colored rainbow lights emanate from Vajrasattva's heart chakra and spread out in the ten directions. Visualize a lotus on a stem above your crown, supported on a throne flanked by lions. Upon the lotus sits your own guru, inseparable from Kunjed Gyalpo, the All-Creating King (Samantabhadra), who is also dark blue in color. He has one face and sits cross-legged with his two hands in meditation posture, the right hand resting on the left. The primordial Buddha, Samantabhadra, is visualized in his naked form and without jewelry of any kind to signify that he is devoid of all characteristics and attributes.

You should think that this Adi-Buddha, who is inseparable from your own guru, is surrounded by all the lineage masters, the buddhas of the five buddha-families, and all the other buddhas. You shouldn't visualize them as flesh and blood beings, but as illuminating beings of light that are visible but insubstantial. You visualize them in their traditional form, in terms of their gestures, implements, and so on, and imagine that they are radiating light that spreads in the ten directions. Various expressions of enlightenment arise from that light, expressions such as buddhas in sambhogakaya form and buddhas in nirmanakaya form. You should recite the mantra OM AH HUNG as many times as you can while creating these visualizations.

When you want to conclude the practice, imagine that all these beings of light are attracted to the Adi-Buddha sitting above the crown of your head and that they are all absorbed into that Adi-Buddha, Samantabhadra. At this point, rest your mind, without thinking anything. Then simply utter the syllable AH and repeat it as many times as possible. At the conclusion of this recitation, you should say, "May all the conditioned phenomena of samsara and nirvana find liberation in the primordial state," and rise from your cushion.

This form of Guru Yoga is of a more secret nature. If you perform this practice for two weeks, you will have various experiences. Even when you are asleep and dreaming, you will be able to recognize your dreams. You will also be moved to compassion spontaneously, without having to deliberately cultivate loving-kindness. You will gain insight into the nature of things by seeing that they have no intrinsic reality or substance. You will be less given to distractions and will be able to resist the attractions of worldly things, as well as the temptation to be overcome by spiritual sadness. You will also be able to see through the duplicity of the nature of samsara.

This preliminary practice of Guru Yoga is important if you hope to understand the intentionality of Samantabhadra. The practice of Guru Yoga should always precede the actual practice of Maha-ati.

TRALEG KYABGON COMMENTARY ON GURU YOGA

We have gone through the entire ngondro in the course of this trilogy. What we find in this, and many Dzogchen texts, is that the practices are very simple. The visualizations are very simple and informal. It is not so important in Maha-ati to think about how things are structured. You just need to have that sense of connection to the lineage, that connection to the guru, and be in touch with your own primordial state. That's the main thing.

The Guru Yoga presented here is not very structured. When you do Dzogchen practice it's important to focus on the main practice, not the preliminary practices. The preliminary practices are simply joined to the main practice. We have to pay attention to the context. Is your main practice the preliminaries or is it something else, where you are doing the preliminaries to supplement your main practice? If you were doing preliminary practices separately, that would be your main focus, but here, you are being asked to get the gist of the preliminary practices and to add that onto your main practice.

If you are doing the main practice in retreat situations, you have to make use of these preliminary practices, but you shouldn't get fixated on them. You are trying to go beyond all these images, so you just use them as convenient devices to support your main practice. You are not counting here. If you do Vajrasattva practice, you don't count Vajrasattva mantras; you just do as many as you can and that's it. When we start out, we have to begin with the preliminaries, but even after you get into more advanced practices, you don't leave the preliminary practices behind altogether. You still need to make use of them as part of your daily practice.

Even in the ngondro preliminary texts, it is said that we should see every sound as the guru's voice, every object as the guru's body, and so on. In this context, Longchenpa is saying we should see everything as a manifestation of Samantabhadra. Samantabhadra is present in everything. Samantabhadra is everywhere. Samantabhadra is within us and Samantabhadra is without us. Samantabhadra is in the mountains, the rivers, the trees. Samantabhadra is in our blood, bones, and minds. Samantabhadra is inseparable from your own guru. Samantabhadra is the primordial state, where everything rests. There is no outer and inner. Samantabhadra is present in everything and everyone.

Longchenpa mentions "spiritual sadness," which should be distinguished from normal kinds of sadness. It's not a sadness that comes from loss or from not having achieved something in life, and so on. Spiritual sadness is about realizing how one has been fooled by the seductions of the samsaric condition. When we are able to distance ourselves from those seductions, we are filled with spiritual sadness. Our familiar world has suddenly crumbled, and we feel a sense of sadness because the old security is not there; all the props are gone. This is a different kind of sadness to what we feel when we are still housed in the samsaric condition.

2. MAIN PRACTICE

The main practice will be discussed in relation to three aspects: 1) establishing the proper view with a degree of certainty, 2) establishing the proper practice of meditation, and 3) clearing away the debris in the narrow gorges of the spiritual path through action.

ESTABLISHING THE PROPER VIEW

The establishment of the proper view has two stages: recognizing that everything we experience as sentient creatures is a reflection of the mind itself and realizing that the mind itself is inherently empty by nature.

Everything we experience is a reflection of the mind itself

To grasp this point, the Dzogchen meditator has to understand that everything we experience in relation to the phenomenal world is like last night's dream. Just as you can't have a dream without a dreamer, you can't have an experience of the phenomenal world without a mind. Your perception of the phenomenal world is therefore viewed as a reflection of the mind itself. A Dzogchen root tantra says:

> The principal creator of all things is bodhicitta. Whatever presents itself has the same nature as I, the All-Creating King, Kunjed Gyalpo. Everything that occurs is my doing. Whatever sounds are produced, and whatever words are uttered, they are all verbal expressions of my meaning. The positive qualities of the buddhas, in relation to their physical manifestations and to their wisdom—along with the ordinary bodies and karmic traces and dispositions of sentient beings—are all expressions of me. Furthermore, the phenomenal world itself, in terms of its physical aspects and the sentient beings who inhabit it, are simply manifestations of bodhicitta itself. They do not deviate from the true nature of bodhicitta. Thus, it has been said.

The meditator has to realize that everything we experience are the workings of the mind itself. Our failure to realize that is the main cause of our entrapment in cyclic existence. The same root tantra says:

> Not realizing the true nature of the all-creating principle, not realizing that everything that appears to your mind is your creation, you become attached to phenomenal appearances, but what you are attached to is impermanent, illusory, and subject to dissolution. Without this understanding, we remain lost. Thus, it has been said.

In order to establish conviction that the mind and the phenomenal world are inseparable and that your experience of the phenomenal world is a reflection of the mind itself, you have to concentrate on your dream experiences. Just as you would never think what we experience while dreaming could occur without a dreamer, you should not think that the phenomenal world has some kind of objective existence, independent of the mind. Another Dzogchen root tantra says:

> The phenomenal world and your mind are the same. The causes

and effects that you perceive are not independent of the mind, and furthermore, the mind is no different from the nature of things. So constantly examine your mind. By so doing, you will realize bodhicitta. Thus, it has been said.

This is what you should be doing to establish the proper view. Even in terms of the five elements of earth, water, fire, air, and space, you should come to the realization that they do not exist independently of the mind. You should meditate on this point for up to ten days. When you familiarize yourself with this and really come to understand that everything you experience is simply a reflection of the mind itself, you will see that the mind does not encounter certain material things that exist independent of it. You will realize that outside bodhicitta, you cannot find an item even the size of an atom that exists. This kind of meditation will help free you from your attachment to the idea that things out there exist independently of mind.

However, you need to be very careful, in this context, about how you realize the phenomenal world to be a reflection of the mind. You should not conclude from this that everything is *created* by the mind, as the Chittamatra system of thought maintains. We have to understand that, in terms of its nature, bodhicitta is emptiness, and in terms of the appearances of the phenomenal world, they are the unceasing play of bodhicitta.

To see everything in the phenomenal world as the *play* of the mind is not the *same* as seeing the phenomenal world as the same as the mind. In other words, the phenomenal world cannot be reduced to consciousness. Even though the phenomenal world is seen as the play of bodhicitta, that doesn't mean the phenomenal world is created by specific mental events of the mind, as it is explained in Chittamatra thought. We have to distinguish the Dzogchen view about the relationship between mind and the phenomenal world, from the Chittamatra view. A failure to understand this difference would mean conflating two distinct notions about the conscious mind.

In the Dzogchen teachings, deluded mind and non-deluded mind have two completely separate functions. Deluded mind is called *sems* (*citta*) and the non-deluded mind is called *byang-chub kyi sems* (*bodhicitta*). So *citta* and *bodhicitta* have separate functions, and they appear differently. Bodhicitta refers to "the non-conceptual wisdom mind which is self-luminous and untainted." Citta, on the other hand, is the "mind that produces all kinds of concepts, ideas, and general discursive thoughts, the principal cause of the samsaric condition." A Mahayana text called *Two Truths* says:

> Mind (*citta, sems*) and mental events (*caitta, sems-byud*) are the cause of the triple-world system. All forms of conceptual categories are produced by this mind.

When we talk about bodhicitta, we are talking about a mind where mental events have ceased to operate. Citta, on the other hand, thrives on the continuation of mental events. Citta also has specific intentional objects, whereas bodhicitta doesn't know of any specific intentional object. This relates to the separation of citta and bodhicitta. It must also be said that the grasping mind that hangs onto citta as our true consciousness, also has its origin in bodhicitta.

The mind itself is inherently empty by nature

You also need to realize that mind itself is devoid of any substance. Another Dzogchen root tantra says:

> When we search inwardly for mind, there is nothing to be found. When we search outwardly for phenomena, there is nothing to be grasped.

The mind has never come into being and has not entered into any state, so it has no definable identity. To realize this when meditating, you should observe the current state of your mind that is conscious and aware. You should search for it, asking, "Where is it?" "Where is this thought?" "Is it inside my body or outside my body or is it somewhere in between?" Whenever a discursive thought arises, you should try to trace where it came from. Whenever you have a thought, try to find its location. "Where exactly is my thought?" When that thought has dissipated, try to see where it has gone.

You can also try to picture your thoughts. "Do my thoughts have color?" "Do my thoughts have shape?" When a thought arises about an external object, you should examine the connection between the thought and the object that gave rise to it. Look for that thought and try to locate it. The more you search for the contents of your mind, the more elusive they will become, precisely because the nature of the mind is emptiness. By looking for it and searching, you will discover there is nothing tangible to find.

You should also examine the mind in relation to your practice. We may talk about establishing the proper view, but you have to examine how that view is confirmed by using the mind. Then you examine the mind in relation to your meditation practices, and to the precepts and vows you have taken. You should examine the mind in relation to your spiritual activities and to the visualization of mandalas and the receiving of empowerments. "What does that mean?" "How is my mind being affected or transformed?" "How is my mind changed or transformed through embarking on the spiritual journey and traversing the paths and stages?"

You should also examine the mind in relation to practices that are supposed to purify the mind, and you should think about the mind in relation to the wisdom that is free from delusions. In all these cases you should ask, "Is there mind?" "Is there someone who has a mind?" "Is there an agent who actually makes the mind engage in all these activities?"

If you pursue this kind of analysis, you will not find a mind that can be owned or put to use by an agent. You will not find anything tangible and will come to understand that the nature of a mind is empty. Nothing solid or real can be found, precisely because the mind's nature is emptiness. As another Dzogchen root tantra says:

> Since I, bodhicitta, possess the transcendental nature of all things,
> there is no great spiritual transmission to be obtained outside of me.
> Since there is no view and no meditation outside of me,
> there are no precepts or vows to be observed outside of me.
> Since there is no spiritual activity outside of me,

I have transcended the mistaken notion of deliberately engaging in spiritual activities.

Since no one can rest outside of my domain,
I have transcended the notions of paths and stages.

Since there is no delusion and confusion outside of me,
I have transcended the spontaneously arisen wisdom.

Since there is no dharmakaya outside of me,
the subtlest and most profound nature of ultimate reality is transcended within me.

Since no one can travel anywhere outside of me,
the spiritual journey is transcended within me.

Since I embody the true essence of enlightenment,
I have transcended the notion of nondual wisdom.

Since I possess the spontaneously arisen wisdom within me,
I have transcended the notion of spiritual transmission.

Since there are no entities that exist outside of me,
I am the creator of all things and have transcended all things.

Thus, it has been said.

Dzogchen practitioners should try to establish the correct view. Firstly, by seeing that the phenomenal world is the play of bodhicitta; and secondly, by realizing that the nature of the mind itself is emptiness. You should see that the nature of the mind is the same as bodhicitta: the All-Creating King, Kunjed Gyalpo.

ESTABLISHING THE PROPER MEDITATION

You need to practice meditation by keeping the view in mind—the view based on arriving at a sense of certainty that ultimate reality, when apprehended, is free from all extremes, such as the concepts of existence and non-existence. You should find an isolated place while maintaining this view and learn to relax the mind in the meditation posture of Vairochana, the Buddha of Infinite Light. Then you should think of the meditation instructions you have received from your teacher on understanding that the appearance of the phenomenal world and the mind itself are pure, right from the beginning, and that everything exists in their primordiality in a state of equality.

You shouldn't try to create a specific state of mind during meditation. Your mental state can become contrived if you entertain thoughts of hope and fear, so you should allow your mind to rest naturally. Allowing the mind to rest in its own natural state is to rest in dharmakaya. The *Nyi pa'i tshig shes* says:

> The mind apprehends varied things, and while what we experience about the phenomenal world is direct and multiple, in their essence, they are the same. If we can rest in the essence, we don't need to do anything about the myriad appearances of phenomena. To remain with the essential unity of all things in this way, is to dwell in the state of dharmakaya, which is beyond all conceptual categories.

When we are meditating, we are not trying to attain a meditative state; we are instead trying to access our current mental state of being, which in itself is as expansive and unobstructed as space. You should therefore not think of meditation as a form of "doing" that involves physical, verbal, or mental effort. It has to be free of any traces of exertion. You just remain effortlessly in that state of equality. While you are meditating, do not block anything out, either externally or internally; just leave the sensory impressions and internal movements of the mind alone.

Whatever you encounter amongst the myriad presentations of phenomena should not be blocked out. At the same time, you should not consciously grasp after what you experience on the sensory level. You shouldn't form judgments about your experiences, but just gaze at whatever you experience with naked awareness. Whatever you are experiencing at any given moment should be experienced vividly, but without identifying or labelling them through your various cognitive processes. You simply apprehend them vividly. If you are able to do that, the natural state of mind will become manifest even during the apprehension of sensory phenomena. Another Dzogchen text says:

> When a true practitioner is training in the art of Dzogchen,
> they are meditating on the unoriginated state. When their mind

is focused on that state of unoriginatedness, they are meditating on the meaning of unoriginated primordial purity, so that even when they encounter various things through their senses, their sensory impressions will not lead to distraction.

If you can remain in that state of unoriginatedness, you will not grasp at whatever you are experiencing, and you will not label your experiences. The sensory impressions will reveal the unoriginated state and everything you experience will become self-liberated. From the Dzogchen point of view, everything becomes dismantled automatically without your having to meditate on emptiness—everything will become self-liberated in the state of pure understanding. As another Dzogchen text says:

The primordial, authentic, original state
is non-fabricated and blissful.
We don't need to search for it,
by putting body, speech, and mind to use.
We don't need to create a special state of mind,
to have this illumination.
We don't need to direct our minds toward anything to realize it.
We simply let ourselves be in meditation,
without entertaining thoughts or following symbols.

If you can learn to relax in this way, you will automatically relax into the state of blissful, spontaneously arisen, wisdom. This is what you have to realize. The spontaneously present, luminous, blissful, primordial state of being is none other than the buddha-intentionality of Samantabhadra, the primordial Buddha. In meditation, you do not try to block out your sensory impressions or suppress the internal workings of the mind, you don't follow or label signs and symbols, you don't use your body, speech, and mind to create special states of being or to induce spiritual illumination. You simply let yourself be and try to remain in that space as much as you are able.

Discursive thoughts will arise while you are meditating in this way. When they do, do not try to suppress them. Discursive thoughts should just be looked at nakedly, while you remain in that state of contemplation. When you do not make any effort to overcome them, discursive thoughts will be liberated by themselves, and you can go back to the state of contemplation as before. When discursive thoughts arise during the state of contemplation, they should leave no trace. If you simply look at them nakedly without doing anything with them, they will be just like drawings on the surface of water and will disappear without a trace. As another Dzogchen text says:

> All kinds of discursive thoughts arise from the primary mind and mental events when you meditate, but you should not be alarmed by them—just remind yourself that the nature of these discursive thoughts is unoriginated, because discursive thoughts have themselves arisen from the state of unoriginatedness. The discursive thoughts will be self-liberated in that way, and you will become free of any thoughts of doing or exertion.

You cannot be in a state of non-distraction if you focus on remembering things from the past or get preoccupied with what is going on in the present and the various other fluctuations of the mind. We are in a state of non-distraction when we realize that all the modulations in the mind have their origin in that state of unoriginatedness. That is contemplation.

In any case, Dzogchen meditators must realize that whatever arises in the mind is or can be meditation. If you recognize that, you will be in a state of meditation without meditating, because you will be able to relax with anything and everything that has arisen in your mind.

You should then contemplate successively on the five external elements of earth, fire, water, air, and space, so that you realize that even the five elements have their origin in that state of unoriginatedness. As mentioned in the context of the view, even the manifestations of the external world have to be seen as the play of the nature of the mind, or bodhicitta. Everything that is there in the external world is a reflection of bodhicitta.

You need to realize that whatever you perceive in the external world is inseparable from ultimate reality. When you perceive a particular phenomenon—if you do not get fixated on it and just allow whatever arises to be there—you will recognize it for what it is. In that way, you can even use the five elements to recognize yourself, because everything that you perceive in the external world is itself the play of the bodhicitta. You should meditate on that and think, "These five elements are the play of bodhicitta." The meditation on the five elements can then become meditation on bodhicitta.

Right now, even though we may not recognize it as such, from our deluded point of view, everything that exists is perfect in its own natural state of being. They have never had defects or deformities in their primordial originality. Everything that is good is present and spontaneously accomplished. Even though we ourselves may appear as ordinary human beings, we are enlightened in terms of our own true state of being. Another Dzogchen text says:

If we realize it, nothing is lacking; everything is already present.

When the view is fully established, it establishes everything else, so that even our spiritual activities are accomplished. How does that come about? It comes about by being accomplished in one, accomplished in two, and accomplished in all. Everything is accomplished in one, through bodhicitta, the enlightened mind. Bodhicitta, here, doesn't mean "the compassionate mind," but refers to the natural state of being, so the natural state of being is where it is accomplished in one. To be accomplished in two means it is accomplished in the activities of the mind. To be accomplished in three means that everything is accomplished automatically without effort. Everything is accomplished and completed in one, because this is the buddha-intention, this is where a buddha's intentionality rests. That is the meaning of true accomplishment.

That state has brought auspicious circumstances together, so that without trying to do anything and without any activity, you are simply being. The very body you have may be the body of a human being or the body of a god, so an accomplished person could be either of those two, but that accomplished person should know their very form embodies buddhahood, because it is imbued with buddha-intentionality. That is what we have to realize. While remaining in this state, we try to benefit other sentient creatures, but we do not have to exert ourselves to transport them to the state of bliss.

ESTABLISHING THE PROPER ACTION

Proper action is about action in relation to your conflicting emotions so that they can be liberated by themselves. As one tantric text says:

> There is no such thing as acceptance and rejection. All the desires that come from the six sense consciousnesses—the things we want to look at, the things we want to hear, the things we want to smell, the things we want to taste, the things we want to touch, and the things we want to think—are understood as the workings of the mind.

Another text known as *The Victorious Banner that Illuminates the Darkness of the Ages* says:

> Even our three conflicting emotions—desire, especially sexual desire, anger, and ignorance—arise from our enlightened state of mind. Our emotional responses to things and the sensory enjoyment of what we grasp at through our senses—beautiful objects, melodious sounds, enticing smells, and so on—should all be seen as ornaments of ultimate truth. The authentic state of being is adorned with the five conflicting emotions and the five sensory objects.

The text known as *Nothing to Do* says:

> Meditation is not about going forward or backward.
> It is about not doing anything.[32]

A true practitioner of Dzogchen has to go against common sense and disagree with the ideas promoted by everybody else in the world. You should reject whatever worldly people say. You should foster that attitude and work with that. Worldly people might say that desire, anger, jealousy, and pride are no good, but we should say they are good. You do not have to abandon or renounce desire, anger, jealousy, and pride, and so on.

How do we get emotionally charged? We get emotionally charged because of what we see, hear, smell, taste, and touch, and by thinking that we want to have more or less of something, in relation to those sensory experiences. That is how emotions come into being, but those emotions can be self-liberated. For example, if we really pay attention to what we see, hear, smell, taste, and touch, we will see them as manifestations of ultimate truth.

All the sensory impressions hold this compulsion for us, even when something is not so attractive, but they are simply a manifestation of the true nature of things. You need to realize that what you see is combined with emptiness, what you hear is combined with emptiness, what you smell is combined with emptiness, what you taste is combined with emptiness, and what you touch is combined with emptiness. You do not have to avoid experiencing these things. You simply need to recognize that all these sensory impressions have their origin in emptiness. This is what you should realize.

This is how we practice in daily life in terms of view, meditation, and action. You view everything that you experience in the external world through your sensory impressions as adornments of the natural state of being. You should also be doing the same thing in relation to your emotional conflicts. You should not repress the excessive desire, anger, ignorance, pride, jealousy, and whatever else arises in your mind, but instead, allow their power to take hold of you completely. You should completely allow the true potential and true expression of those conflicting emotions to happen.

How can we do that? Firstly, you have to learn to identify the conflicting emotion that is ruining your life, because if you can't identify it, then you obviously cannot do anything about it. Secondly, having identified that conflicting emotion, you don't judge it, but instead take it on board without rejection. If you can do that, whatever emotional poison arises, it will dissipate by itself. All the so-called "five poisons" will manifest as forms of nonconceptual wisdom (*mi-rtog-pa'i y- shes*): excessive desire will manifest as discriminating wisdom, anger will manifest as mirror-like wisdom, ignorance will manifest as the wisdom of ultimate reality, pride will manifest as the wisdom of equanimity, and jealousy will arise as the wisdom of intrinsic awareness and emptiness (this is called "all-accomplishing wisdom" in tantric texts).

What does this mean? Having identified whatever conflicting emotion you are experiencing at any given moment for what it is, you realize that each of those deluded emotions can find some kind of fulfillment in wisdom. This understanding is not found in the Hinayana systems of the shravaka and pratyekabuddha. In the Hinayana systems, we are encouraged to renounce conflicting emotions and defilements. However, in Dzogchen, we are counseled not to renounce the conflicting emotions. In the Mahayana system of the bodhisattva, we are encouraged to purify our defilements and conflicting emotions with the notion of emptiness. However, in Dzogchen, we do not do that. The secret mantra teachings encourage us to transform the mind by transmuting the five poisons into five wisdoms, but in Dzogchen, we do not even follow that system. In Dzogchen, the conceptual component of the conflicting emotions is liberated naturally. This is what is meant by "the supreme path of the all-accomplishing, self-arising, king of awareness." It is called that, precisely because it does not make use of those methods.

A Dzogchen practitioner comes to deal with their emotional states by practicing that way. We can use the same approach in relation to our experiences of phenomena itself. As *The Sphere of Primordial Purity* says:

> Primordial wisdom resides in that place that has no center or periphery—a place where there is nothing to be rejected because nothing exists. Everything is understood to exist in a state of equanimity, because there is no separation between mind and our mental events, or between mind and our karmic dispositions. Even though we see and identify things as this or that because of our compulsive tendency to name them, when we recognize primordial wisdom, that behavior will be seen as our own adornment. We should therefore not denounce or renounce that tendency.

TRALEG KYABGON FINAL
COMMENTARY ON PRACTICE

These verses are loaded with many layers of Dzogchen meaning, which really require us to unpack every word. One can devote hours of discussion for every line of this section. Here I can do my best to summarize them. We need to cultivate the proper view when we start out with our spiritual practice, but when we become enlightened, we will have the proper view. It is not a matter of establishing the correct view once and for all; it is an ongoing process, it has to be. Otherwise, the view would just become some kind of dogma, where we say, "This is the right view and that is the wrong view." Cultivating the view does not come just from reading about the view. As Longchenpa says, you have to do these meditative exercises and then you need to gain some kind of experience of them for yourself. It is not a matter of you believing that everything is the play of bodhicitta; you have to see how that is created and actually experience it.

We need to be constantly observing how we experience the world. However, as Longchenpa says, to see the phenomenal world as the play of the mind does not mean that there is no difference between the phenomenal world and the mind. We can say that citta is part of the play of the mind. In this context, bodhicitta means "the enlightened mind." We could say it means something like "buddha nature," but there is a difference between the concepts of buddha nature and bodhicitta. In the sutric teachings, "buddha nature" means we have the potential to become enlightened, but here "bodhicitta" does not mean potential; it refers to enlightenment that is present in all its fullness. That is the difference. *Tathagatagarbha* (or buddha nature) means that we have the seed of enlightenment, but that seed has to be nurtured for the seedling to blossom. In Dzogchen, "bodhicitta" doesn't imply the notion of a spark you have to fan into a raging fire. All the qualities of enlightenment are present already.

As Longchenpa says, bodhicitta is the ground of all things, it is an all-creating principle. Buddha nature has never been presented in that way in the Mahayana teachings—it is not the ground of all being. For example, the *Mahayana-uttara Tantra* does not say the delusions of the mind arise from buddha nature. On the contrary, it says that delusions act as some kind of encasement that obscures our buddha nature. It is like the husk of a grain, and you have to peel away the husk to reveal that grain. The husk and the grain are totally separate and our job as practitioners is to get the husk off the grain. The Mahamudra and Dzogchen teachings, on the other hand, say the delusory states of mind have their origin in our authentic state of being. We call this bodhicitta, Kunjed Gyalpo, the all-creating principle. It's called "all-creating" because everything is the play of bodhicitta, as Longchenpa keeps reminding us. That is a big difference in view.

The shentong view says that buddha nature, in itself, is not empty. Buddha nature is only empty of the defilements that have obscured our original state. Emptiness, in this context, means "empty of defilements." For shentong, buddha nature is not emptiness; it becomes empty of defilements because defilements have no intrinsic reality. The defilements are referred to as "adventitious" because they are temporary. So there is quite a difference between the sutric understanding of buddha nature and the non-sutric understanding, as propounded in the Mahamudra and Maha-ati teachings. Even in the Mahamudra teachings, as the Karmapa says in his *Song of Karmapa*, "Not understanding the nature of mind, you wander around in samsara. When you do realize it, buddhahood is not to be found elsewhere."

From the Mahamudra and Maha-ati point of view, the sutric understanding of buddha nature still has traces of some kind of dualism. The delusions need to be peeled away so that the ultimate reality of our original state can be revealed. But, as Longchenpa himself says, "Even the mind that grasps onto citta originates in the unconditioned nature of bodhicitta." Even that grasping onto conceptual mind is grounded in the unoriginated, unconditioned state of being. What does that mean? Even though the Dzogchen teachings distinguish between bodhicitta and citta as having separate functions, they are nonetheless related. The functions of citta are dependent upon bodhicitta.

When Longchenpa says we should not pursue symbols, he is referring to everything from written words to concepts and ideas. His basic point is that, when you see a table, you do not immediately think, "That's a table." You simply look at the object with naked awareness, without forming any judgments at all. Normally we think things like, "That's a wooden table," "that's an antique table," or "that's a Tibetan-style table." The point is to simply look and observe. We can't do that all the time when we are just going about our normal business, but we can do it during the practice of meditation. We can use sensory objects as part of our meditation if we are just seeing, just hearing, just smelling, just tasting. This is what we should be doing in meditation. Not to do that is to follow symbols. If we learn to simply observe and suspend our judgments, whatever we are experiencing at that moment can reveal itself to us as having arisen from that state of unoriginatedness. The state of completeness. That is what Longchenpa is saying.

Normally we are relating with citta, the primary mind and its mental events. That consists of what we call "the six sense consciousnesses," which comprise the visual consciousness, audial consciousness, nasal consciousness, tactile consciousness, gustatory consciousness, and the thinking mind. The thinking mind gives rise to the primary and secondary conflicting emotions and the mental events associated with wholesome, unwholesome, and neutral dispositions, predilections, and tendencies. They are usually translated as "mind and mental events." The mind is the one that thinks, and the mental events are the states that have arisen from the mind. The point is that mental events are more transitory, and the mind is more stable in terms of your self-consciousness and identity; basically, in terms of your ego-consciousness. We tend to see ourselves as the same person.

Mental events are meant to explain how change and transformation can occur in a person. In the traditional Buddhist psychology of the Abhidharma literature, all of this is explained in great detail. When we practice, we are working with the mental events, and by doing so, we become transformed. Mental events are supposed to explain our personalities, character traits, dispositions, habits, and things of that kind. Why are we predisposed to acting in a certain way? Why do we have certain tendencies? It is because of mental events. The Abhidharma teachings are supposed to help us work with that differently.

There are many different ways to do vipashyana practice. In this context, you are not saying, "Where did this thought come from?" "Where was it when I was thinking that other thought, and where has it disappeared to now?" You are just looking at things with naked awareness in order to realize the unoriginated state. This is actually how we should be doing vipashyana practice. However, to get to this level, we first have to do the analytical type of vipashyana. The Dzogchen approach is more difficult. You begin with the analytical approach, which tells you that mind cannot be found anywhere. You have to be convinced of that. You become convinced of that by doing those analytical exercises about your thoughts: where it has come from, where it is dwelling, where it has gone. In the end, you will realize that a particular thought has not come from anywhere, does not dwell anywhere, does not go anywhere.

The correct way to practice vipashyana from the Dzogchen perspective is to do it as Longchenpa has described here. Whatever comes up in the mind, you look at it and just let it be. You do not think, "This thought is good," "That thought is bad," "Why am I thinking this?" "I should not have thoughts, I should be in a contemplative state, thoughts are distractions," "If I have thoughts, I am not in meditation." As Longchenpa says, the state of contemplation (*mnyam bzhag*) and discursive thoughts (*rnam rtog*) can coexist. If you look at your discursive thoughts nakedly, you are in a state of contemplation. That is said in Mahamudra teachings also. The Mahamudra Lineage Prayer says, "The nature of discursive thoughts is dharmakaya." The Dzogchen teachings may not say that, but instead they say, "The discursive thoughts have their origin in the unoriginated primordial state, which is Kuntuzangpo or dharmakaya."

In other words, wanting to get rid of discursive thoughts is another dualistic thought that we need to overcome. We are thinking, "Bodhicitta is something that's very good, and discursive thoughts are bad, because the discursive thoughts obscure the bodhicitta that I have to realize." Instead, we need to realize that if the discursive thoughts are let be, the bodhicitta is realized simultaneously. It's not the case that first the discursive thoughts have to subside and then you realize bodhicitta. Being able to pay attention to the discursive thoughts and let them be, occurs simultaneously with the realization of bodhicitta. Our dualistic samsaric mind prevents us realizing bodhicitta because we cannot be convinced that discursive thoughts are unable to prevent its realization.

That is why Longchenpa tells us we should not even think, "To realize bodhicitta, I have to be in a mental state more favorable to realization." All mental states are equally favorable to the realization of bodhicitta. We should not be thinking, "If I cultivate this or that mental state, I will have a better chance of realizing my authentic state. What I have now is complete anathema to what I want to realize." That is totally mistaken. Any mental state has the potential to occasion a spiritually illuminating experience. That is what we should be thinking in the Dzogchen context. When we are learning the Buddhist teachings, we have to put everything in context. This is the Dzogchen context. Longchenpa says we have to be convinced that everything is spontaneously established as perfect. This means that any mental state we are in is a spontaneously perfected state (*lhun grub*), if we can only see it. We have to keep reminding ourselves of that.

The things we think are constricting us, the things we think are responsible for imprisoning us in our samsaric state, just fall away naturally. We are not set free by anything or anyone. We become free naturally because those imprisoning factors are no longer seen as imprisoning. What is self-liberated? The delusions, obscurations, and defilements of the mind, the conflicting emotions, negative states of mind, ignorance, and confusion—all of those things are self-liberated. Normally, if we have a problem or something needs to be fixed, we think that we need something else to deal with it. We carry the same attitude over into our spiritual practices. If we have defilements, if we have karmic debt or karmic inheritance, if we have delusion and confusion, then we must find ways and means to overcome them or deal with them. The Dzogchen teachings say that we don't have to rely too much on the techniques. It is not about doing.

Whenever we perceive there is a certain problem that we need to deal with, we think we have to do something. We assume that if we aren't doing something about the problem, we won't be able to solve it. Longchenpa specifically says we should not apply ourselves diligently in an effort to do something. He is talking about learning *to be* in a different way. It is not about doing things differently, or doing something we have done before, to remedy the situation. It is about learning to be in a different way so that what used to be a problem ceases to be a problem.

In terms of phenomena, a multitude of things appear, but in terms of the essential nature, there is no multiplicity to be found because everything dwells in that state of unoriginatedness. In that way, on the phenomenal level, everything is different, but on the ultimate level, there is no difference. He is not talking about oneness either, because to say, "everything is one" is to say, "everything is not multiple," and here we are going beyond all concepts that say that things are one or not one. This is why the view that we are trying to maintain should be free of all extremes. To say "things exist" is one extreme. To say "things do not exist" is another extreme, et cetera. It is like the relationship between relative truth and ultimate truth. We cannot deny the reality of either of the two truths. To do so would be to fall into one or the other extreme. For example, if we say, "The five elements do not exist at all, in reality," that would be one extreme. The other extreme would be to say, "There is no such thing as the unoriginated or authentic state." We cannot fall into the extreme of ultimate truth and we cannot fall into the extreme of relative truth.

The Mahayana teachings even explain buddhahood in terms of the two levels of truth. If the phenomenal world were non-existent, then buddhas would not appear in the world and if the phenomenal world were all there was to it, if there were no transcendental dimension, there would be no buddhas. As well, there is the relative aspect of a buddha's being, in terms of their physical presence, activities, and interactions with other members of the community, and then the transcendental aspect of a buddha's being in terms of their infinite wisdom. So a buddha embodies the two truths as well.

The ultimate truth is not shunyata, but the inseparability of relative and absolute truth. That is why so many Mahayana teachers have tried to avoid positing shunyata as the antithesis of the empirical world. They make all kinds of maneuvers to avoid that claim, to avoid falling into one or the other extreme. In the teachings, the nature of relative truth is ultimate truth, although ultimate truth is not contained in relative truth. In other words, the relative truth is not the same as ultimate truth, but the nature of relative truth is ultimate truth, because the nature of relative truth is emptiness. Relative truth is finite, but we cannot say that the ultimate truth is either finite or infinite, which is why it is called "emptiness." There are many different interpretations about the relationship between the two truths. However, practically all Mahayana schools would agree on this point: the two truths cannot cancel each other out.

Longchenpa also compares the Dzogchen approach to the sutric and tantric systems, pointing out that we need to go beyond those methods. We have to go beyond the renunciation of the shravaka-yana and pratyekabuddha-yana, beyond the purification practices of the bodhisattva-yana, and beyond the transformation practices of the tantra-yana. We need to come to the practice of Dzogchen, which is the approach of self-liberation. We do not try to renounce or to purify our conflicting emotions. First, you do not try to renounce your anger, jealousy, pride, and so on. Secondly, you do not try to purify them by thinking, "Oh, the nature of my anger is emptiness, the nature of my jealousy is emptiness." On the secret mantra path, we do not try to control or transform our conflicting emotions through secret incantations. Longchenpa says not to do that, but that if you can nakedly observe whatever conflicting emotion is there in your meditation without judgment then, at that very point, it will become purified by itself. That is the Dzogchen meditation method.

The Mahamudra approach is the same as this. The Dzogchen teachings include trekcho and thogal practices. Trekcho is exactly the same as Mahamudra; there is no difference whatsoever. It is only in the thogal practice that there are some differences. Thogal practice talks about visions. The Mahamudra teachings talk less and less about visions as you go along the path, whereas the Dzogchen teachings are almost the reverse. At the beginning, you do the trekcho practices and then, as you go on, you have all these spontaneous visions.

In trekcho practice, we just allow our emotions to arise without trying to analyze or resolve anything. We do the same with our sensory impressions. You look at something and just be with it. If you don't like what you are looking at, you don't have to convince yourself that you do, saying, "I must like it; if I don't, I'm judging it. I have to learn to like it." You don't have to do any of that. Longchenpa is saying that we can get to a state where we can judge without getting all worked up. We do this all the time, even when we are practicing and progressing on the path. We have to make judgments, we have to make choices, and we have to make decisions in life. We can't simply say, "Anything will do; whatever." We would be a very ineffectual person if we did that. It is not about what we do in our meditation. In this particular context, Longchenpa means that whatever we do, it has to come from a place where we are not being so judgmental. That is where liberation lies.

Otherwise, as he says, we are constantly bombarded by all kinds of things and compelled to think in ways that may not be very relevant, in terms of our conflicting emotions. Even to think, "I should not have anger, jealousy, or a judgmental mind," is not, in itself, something that is going to help us. We should not be thinking, "I have a judgmental mind, I can't progress on the path when I'm like this." Longchenpa is saying that this is okay, that is just how it is, but we need to know that this judgmental mind comes from that state of being where you are not concerned about it. In the end, it is all about nonfixation. That is really what is being emphasized: not getting too fixated on things. It's not about the sort of mental states we are in. That is important, but how much fixation do we have about what has brought those mental states about in the first place? That's what we should be concerned about.

How are our negative emotions perpetuated? Fundamentally speaking, it happens in two ways. First, we perpetuate them by dwelling on them. We think things like, "Oh, he behaved in such an atrocious fashion. I can't forgive him! He has really hurt me so much." We might also think, "I have to do something about this anger. I must come up with a solution, because if I don't, I'm going to get out of hand." I'm not saying that those methods will not work; according to the Buddhist teachings, they will work. However, here, we are talking about it in the context of the Dzogchen teachings. Dzogchen teachings say we should not be too fixated on that way of thinking. If you have this anger and you recognize it, that anger will naturally be transformed into mirror-like wisdom. In Tantrism, we deliberately try to transform anger into mirror-like wisdom through visualization practice, by visualizing a certain deity that embodies that wisdom.

In the Mahayana practices, the difference in approach comes from the use of analysis. To realize the emptiness in relation to the bodhisattva-yana you have to analyze it, in terms of causes and conditions. You have to look at your anger and say, "Well, the anger that I'm experiencing is a product of causes and conditions. That is why it is empty." When you are doing Dzogchen meditation practice, you are not analyzing. You simply experience what you experience and try to get the idea that everything you experience is imbued with emptiness. You can still analyze your experiences as the product of causes and conditions and therefore emptiness, but that's not strictly Dzogchen practice. Mahamudra and Dzogchen encourage that analytic approach because you can get the idea that everything is emptiness, but to fully understand emptiness, you have to realize that everything you are experiencing is imbued with emptiness.

This doesn't necessarily imply that a Dzogchen practitioner has a stable realization of emptiness. That would depend on the practitioner. Someone could be following the Mahayana or Theravada path and get ahead of a so-called "Dzogchen practitioner." That really depends on the person and the practice. You always have to practice. Whether one has a Mahayana or a Theravada approach, whatever Buddhist tradition one follows, the quality of the outcome is always dependent on the practitioner.

When you see the five senses and the five conflicting emotions as adornments of the natural state of mind, you are going beyond the sacred outlook of the tantric path. You are not thinking in terms of sacred or not sacred. These are advanced teachings. Even when you look at things with this sacred outlook, you are still trying to see something as sacred. If you are really there in an unvitiated authentic state, you don't have to see your outlook as sacred, you just are. Then everything is as it should be, and everything is where it should be, it is perfect. That is the true Dzogchen view, to see everything as true completion. Everything being complete in itself is not the same as having a sacred outlook.

Our human understanding, "our conditioned minds," means we have some inbuilt limitations that can be liberated. We cannot normally comprehend all there is in life. If there is any meaning in life, it has to do with trying to see more of what is out there, than we normally comprehend. There is so much in this world that we miss. Dzogchen is all about addressing our immediate life experiences. In relation to our transcendental aspect, there is no separation, in other words and we have to take life seriously. As Longchen Rabjam said, we can find our liberation in this very world. Many other Buddhist traditions say the same thing, including the beautiful Theravadin teachings.

We need to understand that being a Buddhist practitioner is about working with our day-to-day life experience to find self-transcendence. To find self-transcendence in a state of immanence, we do not have to denigrate, despise, or denounce the world. We can embrace the world, we can be in it and work with it—we can struggle with it, as we always do—and in the end we will come out so much stronger and better for it. If we try to escape from it, we will be worse off. There will be less compassion in us, but more and more selfishness, neediness, and anger. It is very important for all of us to take everything we experience in life seriously, and not ignore our everyday life experiences, saying, "This is just a samsaric matter." What is samsaric and what's not samsaric can overlap. We can go to one extreme or the other, but that which is samsaric can also be non-samsaric. Not everything that's related to our self-interest has to be selfishly or egocentrically motivated. Our lives are important and what we think about regarding our religious traditions and the things we believe, have a big impact on how we conduct our lives.

NOTES

Part One
Mind Cycle—Lamrim Nyingpo (*lam-rim-snying-po*):
The essential stages of the path

1. The six realms of existence are the god realm, the demigod realm, the human realm, the animal realm, the hungry ghost realm, and the hell realm.

2. The "sensory world" refers to the six realms of existence.

3. Often dharmakaya is translated as "dharma body" or "ultimate body," but "body" is the translation of *lu* not *sku*. *Chos sku*, *long sku*, and *sprul sku* are the Tibetan terms for the three kayas. *Chos sku* refers to the authentic aspect of buddha's being, the dharmakaya. It does not refer to any kind of physical body, which is *lu* in Tibetan.

4. The five kayas are the manifest aspect of buddha's being (*nirmanakaya, sprul-sku*), the communicative aspect of buddha's being (*sambhogakaya, longs-sku*), the authentic aspect of buddha's being (*dharmakaya, chos-sku*), the essential aspect of buddha's being (*svabhavikakaya, ngo-bo-nyid-sku*), and the perfect body of complete awakening. The fifth kaya is just meant to signify that the three kayas are embedded within the fourth, svabhavikakaya. It signifies the inseparability of those four kayas. All four kayas have their grounding in rigpa. Rigpa is the pre-condition for the existence of the other kayas. The five wisdoms comprise the wisdom of equanimity (*samata-jnana*), the wisdom of accomplishment (*krtyanusthana jnana, bya-ba grub-pa'i ye-shes*), mirror-like wisdom (*adarsa-jnana, me-long gi ye-shes*), the wisdom of discrimination (*pratyavekasana jnana, so-sor rtog-pa'i ye-shes*), and the wisdom of the dharmadhatu (*dharmadhatu-jnana, chos-kyi dbying ye-shes*). These five wisdoms are associated with the five buddha-families.

5. "Fulfillment stage" and "completion stage" are terms that have the

same meaning. Rinpoche used both terms throughout the teachings.

6. Longchenpa doesn't use the term "real world." This is a Western invention. He says *natsok*, which means "the myriad forms."

7. It is worth noting that there are many kinds of Yogacarans. The founders of the Yogacara system didn't say that everything is mind only and nothing exists externally. They didn't say there is no such thing as a material world. It was later commentators who became more and more idealistic and started describing everything as "mental." The basic point of Yogacara philosophy is the world we perceive is dependent on our karma. The world we perceive is conditioned by the mind, but that doesn't mean there is no difference at all between the mind and physical things.

8. The three baskets refer to the three sections of the Buddhist teachings: Vinaya, Sutra, and Abhidharma.

9. The four tantras of the new schools (*Sarma*) are kriya-yoga, charya yoga, upaya-yoga, and anuttara-yoga tantras. The nine yana system of the old school (*Nyingma*) comprises the shravaka-yana, pratyekabuddha-yana, bodhisattva-yana, kriya-yoga, upa-yoga, yoga, maha-yoga, anu-yoga, and ati-yoga yanas. Longchenpa is saying all these vehicles are embodied in the Dzogchen teachings.

10. The five buddha-families are the Buddha family (*tathagatakula, de bzhin gshegs-pa'i rigs*), the Indestructible family (*vajrakula, rdo-rje'i rigs*), the Jewel family, (*ratnakula, rin-chen rigs*), the Lotus family (*padmakula, pa-ma rigs*), and the Action family (*karmakula, las-kyi igs*). The Buddhas who represent these families are Vairocana, Akshobya, Ratnasambhava, Amitabha, and Amoghasiddhi respectively.

11. *Dus* means "time," *gsum* is "three," *dus ma'i* means "not time," Kuntuzangpo is "Samantabhadra" and *dus* again means "time." There are not three times; there is only one time, the time of Samantabhadra.

12. Some Dzogchen lineages start with Garab Dorje, but most

Nyingmapas would go back to Guru Padmasambhava. They even call him "the second Buddha."

13. The Triple Gem refers to the "Buddha, Dharma, and Sangha."

14. Mitrupa is mi 'khrugs pa in Tibetan, where *mi 'khrugs* means "non wavering." Mitrupa is called "the Immovable" or "Unshakable Buddha." He is sometimes also called "Acala," although not necessarily in the context of the five buddha-families.

15. Nampar Nangdze (*rnam-par snang-mdzad*) means "the Supreme and Eternal Buddha" or "the Radiant One."

16. Rinchen Jungnay (*rinchen 'byung-gnas*) translates as "the Source of Precious Things" or "the Jewel-Born One."

17. Nawithaya (*'od-dpag med mtha'-yas*) means "the Buddha of Infinite Light."

18. Donyo Drubpa (*don-yod grub-pa*) is "the Almighty Conqueror" or "Lord of Karma."

19. Enlightened work is a synonym for "great compassion," which is *maha-karuna* in Sanskrit and *thugs-rje chen-po* in Tibetan. In Dzogchen, compassion is related to the characteristic of mind, (*thugs rje*) not the usual notion of compassion (*snying rje*). Great compassion is superior to our everyday experiences of compassion.

Part Two
Ultimate Reality Cycle—Rinchen Nyingpo (*rin-chen snying-po*):
The precious heart essence

20. The analogy used by Longchenpa has a number of possible comparisons. It may be suggesting that you can be looking at yourself as you were in the past, while simultaneously seeing what you are like now.

21. These lists reflect the primary thoughts and attitudes associated with a particular conflicting emotion. They are designed to help us understand something. As human beings, we always relate to labels,

and we relate to our emotions in that way, whether we like it or not. When we label our emotions, we have a better grip on them, because something that is very amorphous, ambiguous, and elusive, cannot even be articulated properly.

22. Longchenpa is not himself saying that this is so; he is quoting what has been presented in the Buddhist teachings.

Part Three
Equality Cycle—Yidzhin Nyingpo (*yid-bzhin snying-po*):
The wish-fulfilling heart essence

23. The five female consorts are White Tara, Buddhalochana, Mamaki, Pandaravasini, and Green Tara.

24. It is not the mind (*sems*) that we are normally familiar with but the nature of the mind (*sems-nyid*) that is rootless.

25. This is a very technical Dzogchen term.

26. The point Longchenpa is making here is that when our delusions arise, they arise very quickly and spontaneously, and we don't recognize them.

27. The five devices that bring about awakening are the moon disk, the sun disk, the implements held by deities, the seed syllable, and the complete visualization of the deity.

28. The four spiritual powers are the charismatic powers of blessing, meditative concentration, empowerment, and offerings

29. Sometimes abhisheka is translated as "initiation." Abhisheka is *dbang*, (pronounced wang) in Tibetan. In Tibetan, the four abhishekas are vase empowerment (*dbang bum*), secret empowerment (*gsang dbang*), wisdom empowerment (*she- rab ye shes kyi dbang*), and empowerment of logos (*tshig dbang*).

30. Longchenpa doesn't say so, but he means we will have fewer hang ups. That's a very good expression because it suggests we have fewer things to hang anything onto.

Part Four
Supplement
The Precious Boat of Bodhicitta, the Creator of All Things

31. Bodhicitta does not mean "compassion" in Dzogchen. It means "the mind itself" or "the nature of the mind."

32. To learn about Tibetan mystical teachings, texts similar to the text quoted may be helpful. *Bjar med* means "nothing to do" or "not doing."

GLOSSARY
Tibetan words

Part One
Root Text—Semnyi Rangdrol—Natural Freedom of the Mind
Mind Cycle—Lamrim Nyingpo (lam-rim-snying-po):
The essential stages of the path

accustomed (*bhavana, bsgom-pa*)

agitation (*nyam-pa*)

all-pervasive wisdom (*kun-khyab ye-shes*)

appearances (*aloka, snang-ba*)

aspiration (*pranidhana, smon-lam*)

authentic state of being (*dharmakaya, chos-sku*)

authenticity (*ngo-bo*)

awareness (*jneya, shes-bzhin*)

bare awareness (*shes-rkyang*)

blessings (*adhisthana, byin-brlabs*)

bliss (*sukha, bde-ba*), mental clarity/luminosity (*abhinvesa, gsal-ba*), and nonconceptuality (*nirvikalpa, mi rtog-pa*)

bodhisattva stages: second stage "immaculateness" (*vimala-bhumi, dri-ma med-pa sa*)

buddha's being (*kayas, sku*)

clarity (*gsal-ba*)

clear light (*prabhasvara, 'od-gsal*)

compassion (*thugs-rje*)

complete (*rdzogs*)

conceptual proliferation (*vikalpa, rnam-rtog*)

conflicting emotions (*klesha, nyong-mongs*)

conscious mind (*citta, sems*)

creative energy (*kun-khyab*)

definitive meaning (*nitartha, nges-don*)

desire realm (*kama-dhatu*)

development (*utpattikrama, bskyed-rim*)

discriminating awareness (*pratya-veksana-prajna, so-sor rtog-pa'i shes-rab*)

discriminating wisdom (*prajna, shes-rab*)

discursive thought (*prapanca, spros-pa*)

dualistic notions (*dvayastha, gnyis-'dzin*)

eight functions of consciousness (*asta-vijnana, rnam-shes tshogs-brgyad*), the six sense consciousnesses (*sad-vijnana, rnam-shes tshogs-drug*) and the ego-mind (*mano-vijnana, yid kyi rnam-shes*), the mental reservoir (*alayavijnana, kun-gzhi rnam-shes*)

empirical determinants (*dharmas*)

empty yet luminous (*stong-gsal*)

essence (*rang-bzhin*)

essence is luminous (*rang-bzhin gsal-ba*)

ethical conduct (*sila, tshul-khrims*)

equality (*mnyam-nyid*)

equanimity (*upeksha, btang-snyoms*)

ever-present (*lhan-skyes*)

fearlessness (*abhaya, mi-'jigs-pa*)

First stage "pure joy" (*pramudita-bhumi, ra-tu dga-ba sa*)

fixation (*graha, 'dzin-pa*)

four Brahmaviharas: (Rinpoche calls them four Infinities in the Mind Cycle): love (*maitri, byams-pa*), compassion (*karuna, snying-rje*), joy (*mudita, dga'-ba*), equanimity (*upeksha, btang-snyoms*)

freed (*shar-grol*)

fruition (*phala, 'bras-bu*)

fulfillment (*sampannakrama, rdzogs-rim*)

getting lost (*khor-ba*)

great bliss (*mahasukha, bde-chen*)

heart of our own being (*snying-po dang shar-wa*)

how things appear to us (*snang-lugs*) and how things are (*gnas-lugs*)

ignorance (*avidya, ma-rig-pa*)

illusion (*maya, sgyu-ma*)

insight (*vipashyana, lhag-mthong*)

interpretive meaning (*neyartha, drang-don*)

intrinsic awareness (*vidya, rig-pa*)

kingly state of dharmakaya (*chos-sku rgyal-po*)

liberation through recognition (*stong-grol*)

liberation through understanding (*shes-grol*)

luminosity (*prabhasvara, 'od-gsal*)

means (*upaya, thabs*)

meditation (*bhavana, bsgom-pa*) and post-meditation (*prsthalabdha, rjes-thob*)

meditative equipoise (*samadhi, bsam-gtan*)

meditative equipoise (*samadhi, ting nge 'dzin*)

Meditative experience: experience of bliss (*bde-ba nyams*), experience of clarity (*gsal ba'i nyams*) experience of nonconceptuality (*mi rtog pa'i nyams*)

mental clarity (*gsal-ba*)

method (*upaya, thabs*) and insight (*prajna, shes-rab*)

mindfulness (*smriti, dran-pa*)

mirror-like wisdom (*adarsa-jnana, me-long gi ye-shes*)

natural condition (*gnas-lugs*)

natural freedom (*rang-grol*)

natural state (*rang-bzhin*)

natural wisdom (*rang-byung ye-shes*)

nature (*ngo-bo*)

nature (*ngo-bo*), essence (*rang-bzhin*), and responsiveness (*thugs-rje*)

nature is empty (*ngo-bo stong-pa*)

nature of the mind (*sems-nyid*)

nature of mind (*sems-nyid*)

nonduality (*advaya, gnyis-med*)

one-taste (*ekarasa, ro-gcig*)

original dwelling place (*gdod ma'i gnas-pa*)

original sphere (*dharmadhatu, chos-kyi dbying*)

original state (*ye-yin gyi ngang*)

original wisdom (*gdod-ma'i ye-shes*)

ornament (*rgyan*)

overactive mentation (*manasikara, yid-la byed-pa*)

paths (*marga, lam*) and stages (*bhumi, sa*)

physically transformed state of being (*rupakaya, gzugs-sku*)

post-meditation (*prsthalabdha, rjes-thob*)

post-mortem state (*antarabhava, bar-do*)

power (*bala, stobs*)

preliminary practice (*sngon 'gro*); actual practice (*nyuge*)

primordial freedom (*ye-grol*)

primordially pure (*ka-dag*)

primordial wisdom (*jnana, ye-shes*)

psychophysical constituents (*skandhas, phung-po*)

pure from its own side (*rang-bzhin dag-pa'i*)

pure presence (*thag-nang*)

pure presence of awareness (*rig-pa'i rang-rdzogs*)

pure view (*lta-ba rnam-dag*)

responsiveness (*thugs-rje*)

responsiveness is creative energy (*thugs-rje kun-khyab*)

self as a deity (*samayasattva, dam-tshig sems-dpa*) and wisdom deity (*jnanasattva, ye-shes sems-dpa*)

self-cognizing awareness (*samma-svasamvitti, so-sor rang-rig*)

self-liberate the moment they arise (*shar-grol*)

self-liberation (*rang-grol*)

self-luminous (*rang-gsal*)

self-manifesting (*rang-mdangs*)

self-presencing (*rang-shar*)

self-presencing awareness (*rang-shar ye-shes*)

self-recognition (*rang-shar shes-pa*)

spiritual boons (*siddhis, dngos-grub*)

spiritual indulgence (*rol-ba*)

spontaneously arisen intrinsic awareness (*lhun-grub rig-pa*)

spontaneously present (*anabhaga, lhun-grub*)

Tantric stages: development (*utpattikrama, bskyed-rim*) and fulfillment (*sampannakrama, rdzogs-rim*) three aspects of mind: nature (*ngo-bo*), essence (*rang-bzhin*), and three aspects of rigpa: emptiness (*shunyata, stong-pa nyid*), luminosity (*prabhasvara, 'od-gsal*), and the myriad manifestations of phenomena (*niruddha, ma 'gags-pa*)

three kayas (*sku*): dharmakaya (*chos-sku*), sambhogakaya (*longs-sku*), nirmanakaya (*sprul-sku*)

three qualities of the three aspects of mind: empty nature (*ngo-bo stong-pa*), luminous essence (*rang-bzhin gsal-ba*), and creative responsiveness (*thugs-rje kun-khyab*)

three times (*kalatraya, dus-gsum*)

traces and dispositions (*vasanas, bag-chags*)

tranquility meditation (*shamatha, gzhi-gnas*)

true condition (*gnas-lugs*)

ultimate reality (*dharmadhatu, gnas-lugs*)

unconditioned (*asamskrta, rang-bzhin gyi gnas*)

unfabricated (*bcos-med*)

upliftedness (*Dang-ba*)

vehicles (*yana, theg-pa*)

view (*lta-ba*)

vipashyana meditation (*vipashyana, lhag-tong*)

wisdom (*jnana, ye-shes*)

wisdom of discrimination (*pratyavekasana-jnana, so-sor rtog-pa'i ye-shes*)

Part Two
Root Text— Chonyi Rangdrol—Natural Freedom of Ultimate Reality
Ultimate Reality Cycle—Rinchen Nyingpo (*rin-chen snying-po*): The precious heart essence.

agitation (*nyam-pa*)

already a buddha (*sangs rgyas*): *sangs* means "to be purified," *rgyas* means "someone who has flowered or grown"

bardo: bardo of this life (*rang-bzhin bar-do*); bardo of dreams (*rmi-lam gyi bar-do*); bardo of the moment of death (*chi-kha bar-do*); bardo intermediate state (*antarabhava, bar-do*); bardo of dharmata (*chos-nyid bar-do*); bardo of becoming (*srid-pa bar-do*)

compassion (*karuna, snying-rje*)

completely immersed in overactive mentation (*manasikara, yid-la byed-pa*)

conceptual activities (*vikalpa, rnam-thog*)

conceptual activity that has the potential to liberate you (*shes-grol*)

conceptual proliferation (*vikalpa, rnam-rtog*); a denser or demonic form of conceptual proliferation is collectively referred to as (*dun*)

cultivate love (*maitri, byams-pa*)

delusion that has arisen from ignorance (*avidya, ma-rig-pa*)

fear that includes doubt, indecision, and so on (*dog-pa*)

four Brahmaviharas—cultivate love (*maitri, byams-pa*); contemplation on compassion (*karuna, snying-rje*), joy (*mudita, dga'-ba*), and equanimity (*upeksha, btang-snyoms*)

fundamental ground (*gzhi*)

getting lost, wandering mind (*khor-ba*)

great bliss (*mahasukha, bde-ba chen-po*)

hope (*re-ba*)

intrinsic awareness (*vidya, rig-pa*)

kingly state of dharmakaya (*chos-sku rgyal-po*)

nonfixation ('*dzin-med*)

notion of presence of mind in meditation (*aloka, snang-ba*); *snang-ba* is also commonly translated as "appearances" and "phenomenal experiences"

preliminary practices (*sngon 'gro*); actual practice (*nyuge*)

radiance (*dang*)

radiancy, intense ('*od-gsal*)

responsiveness (*thugs-rje*)

Rigpa can be seen from three perspectives: emptiness (*shunyata, stong-pa nyid*), luminosity (*prabhasvara, 'od-gsal*), and the myriad manifestations of phenomena (*niruddha, ma 'gags-pa*); empty (*stong-pa*). Within emptiness there is clarity (*gsal-ba*), our cognitive capabilities, and that arises from sambhogakaya, responsiveness (*thugs-rje*) arises from nirmanakaya

self-liberated (*rang-grol*)

self liberation of thoughts, the experience: bliss (*bde-ba nyams*), clarity (*gsal ba'i nyams*), and nonconceptuality (*mi rtog pa'i nyams*)

son and mother luminosity meeting (*ma-bu 'phrad-pa*)

spaciousness, or like an expansive field (*yangs-pa che*)

teachings with a definitive meaning (*nitartha, nges-don*)

teachings with an interpretive meaning (*neyartha, drang-don*)

three modes of existence (*trikaya or sku gsum*)

three qualities of enlightenment: emptiness (*stong*), luminosity (*gsal*), and awareness (*rig-pa*)

transference of consciousness practice (*sankranti, 'pho-ba*)

three kayas (*trikaya, sku-gsum*); dharmakaya (*chos-sku*), sambhogakaya (*longs-sku*), and nirmanakaya (*sprul-sku*)

triple world (*tri-loka, khams-gsum*): the realm of sensuality (*kama-dhatu, 'dod khams*), the realm of form (*rupa-dhatu, gzugs kyi khams*), and the realm of formlessness (*arupa-dhatu, gzugs med pa'i khams*)

true spiritual boon (*siddhi, dngos-grub*)

ultimate reality (*dharmata, chos-nyid*)

union, when external Vajrasattva appears in front of you and is absorbed into you *dam-tshig sems-dpa'* (*samayasattva*) and *ye-shes sems-dpa'* (*jnanasattva*)

uplifting ourselves in meditation helps us to recognize how the mind gets lost: upliftedness (*dang-ba, khor-ba,* and *byams-pa. Dang-ba*), getting lost (*khor-ba*), love (*byams-pa*)

wisdom (*ye-shes*)

wonderful meditation experiences (*vetana, nyams*)

yoga of insight (*vipashyana, lhag-mthong*)

Part Three
Root text— Nyamnyi Rangdrol— Natural Freedom of Equality
Equality Cycle—Yidzhin Nyingpo (*yid-bzhin snying-po*):
The wish-fulfilling heart essence

aboriginal state of thatness—nondeviation (*tattva, de-nyid*)

Akanishtha all-encompassing (*og min*)

bardo—luminous bardo of dharmata (*chos-nyid bar-do*); recognize our true face (*rang-myur shes-pa*); bardo of becoming (*srid-pa bar-do*); seventh moment in two different ways: "other-powered" (*sheng-drup*) liberation or "self-powered" (*rang-drup*) liberation

characteristics (*dharmata*)

dharmata state (*chos-nyid*) arise experiences; dharmas, mental and physical phenomina (*chos-kun*)

divine pride (*lha'i nga rgyal*)

great wisdom (*maha-jnana, ye-shes chen-po*)

king of the mind (*kun-byed gyal-po*)

mind: nature is openness (*ngo-bo*); essence is gentleness (*rang-bzhin*); responsiveness is unceasing (*thugs-rje*)

spiritual vehicles: causal vehicle (*hetu-yana, rgyu theg-pa*), and the fruition vehicle (*phala-yana, 'bras-bu'i theg-pa*)—

> causal sutric yana comprises five paths (*panca-marga, lam lnga*) and ten stages (*dasa-bhumi, sa bcu*) of bodhisattva accomplishment:
>
> first bodhisattva stage, "pure joy" (*pramudita-bhumi, rab-tu dga'-ba sa*); second bodhisattva stage is "the state of being unsullied" (*vimala-bhumi, dri-ma med-pa sa*); third bodhisattva stage is "greater illumination" (*prabhakari-bhumi, 'od-byed-pa sa*); fourth bodhisattva stage is "brilliant shining" (*arcismati-bhumi, 'od-phro-ba sa*); fifth bodhisattva stage is "difficult to attain" (*sudurjaya-bhumi, shin-tu-sbyangs dka'-ba sa*); sixth bodhisattva stage is "directly facing" (*abhimukhi-bhumi, mngon du-gyur sa*); seventh bodhisattva stage is "gone far" (*durangama-bhumi, ring du song sa*); eighth bodhisattva stage is "non-waveringness" (*acala-bhumi, mi-gyo sa*); ninth bodhisattva stage is "supreme intellect" (*sadhumati-bhumi, legs-pa'i blo-gros sa*); ultimate and tenth bodhisattva stage is "the cloud of Dharma" (*dharmamegha-bhumi, chos-kyi sprin sa*)
>
> five paths that are outlined in the sutric teachings: the path of accumulation (*sanbhara-marga, tshog lam*), the path of application (*prayoga-marga, sbyor lam*), the path of seeing (*darsana-marga, mthong lam*), the path of meditation (*bhavana-marga, sgom lam*), and the path of no more learning (*ashaiksha-marga, mi-slob lam*)
>
> fruition vehicle : tantric development stage (*utpattikrama, bskyed rim*) and the fulfillment stage (*sampannakrama, rdzogs rim*)

spontaneously arisen wisdom (*lhun-grub ye-shes*)

things (*dharma*)

three times are undifferentiated, terms used in Mahamudra and Dzogchen (*dus gsum byer med*): time (*dus*), three (*gsum*), undifferentiated (*byer med*)

ultimate reality (*dharmadhatu, gnas-lugs*)

Vairochana Buddha field (*rnam-par snang-mdzod*)

Yana system of Dzogchen—nine vehicle (*yana, theg-pa*); three yanas comprise the hearers (*sravaka-yana*), the solitary realizers (*pratyekabuddha-yana*), and the enlightened warriors (*bodhisattva-yana*)

Part Four
Supplement
The Precious Boat of Bodhicitta, the Creator of All Things

All-Creating King (*Kunjed Gyalpo*): everything (*kun*), create (*byed*), king (*gyal-po*), all-creating (*kun-byed*)

buddha nature (*tathagatagarbha*)

intentionality, Buddha intentionality (*dgongs-pa*)

mental events (*caitta, sems-byud*)

mind: deluded mind (*sems, citta*), non-deluded mind (*byang-chub kyi sems, bodhicitta*)

responsiveness (*thugs-rje*)

spontaneously perfected state (*lhun grub*)

teachings that need to be interpreted (*neyartha, drang-don*); teachings that are given in order to liberate sentient creatures (*drang-don*)

teachings with a definitive meaning (*nitartha, nges-don*); teachings that reveal the definitive meaning (*nges-don*)

yanas (*vehicles, theg-pa*)

INDEX